CHARMAINE SOLOMON'S
ORIENTAL
COLLECTION

CHARMAINE SOLOMON'S

ORIENTAL COLLECTION

MORE THAN 700
OF HER BEST RECIPES

CHANCELLOR
PRESS

First published in England in 1995 by
The Chancellor Press
a division of Reed Consumer Books
Michelin House, 81 Fullham Rd, London SW3 6RB

Produced by Lansdowne Publishing Pty Ltd
Level 5, 70 George Street, Sydney 2000, Australia

Managing Director: Jane Curry
Production Manager: Sally Stokes
Publishing Manager: Cheryl Hingley

Photography by Ray Joyce, Reg Morrison, Rodney Weidland, Geoff Lung.
Cover photographs by Geoff Lung.

Designed by Avenir Design
Printed in Singapore by Kyodo Printing Co Ltd

ISBN 1 85152 908 x

Photographs:
Opening page, red curry of beef (recipe page 208);
opposite contents page, pork and shrimp balls (recipe page 204).

Contents

Asian Tastes & Accompaniments

• STOCKS •

BASIC BEEF STOCK
China

2 lb (1 kg) soup bones
1 lb (500 g) gravy beef
8 cups (64 fl oz, 2 L) cold water
1 onion
1 stalk celery with leaves
1 star anise
4 cilantro (fresh coriander) or parsley stalks
3 teaspoons salt

Put bones and beef into a large pan with water to cover. Add all other ingredients. Bring to a boil, then cover and simmer for 2 hours. Strain and allow to cool, then chill. Remove fat from surface. Use as a base for soup or as part of the liquid in sauces for beef, chicken, or pork dishes.

BASIC CHICKEN STOCK
China

Chicken bones and trimmings (giblets, neck, feet, etc)
6 cups (2½ pts, 1.5 L) cold water
10 peppercorns
2 small stalks celery with leaves
1 onion
4 cilantro (fresh coriander) or parsley stalks
2 slices fresh root ginger
salt to taste

Put bones and trimmings in a saucepan, add water and other ingredients, bring to a boil. Cover and simmer 45 minutes to 1 hour. Strain. Skim if necessary. The stock is now ready for use in soups and sauces.

BASIC FISH STOCK
China

Fish heads and trimmings or shrimp (prawn) heads and shells as available
8 cups (64 fl oz, 2 L) cold water
10 peppercorns
3 slices fresh root ginger

1 carrot
2 stalks celery
1 large onion
2 stalks cilantro (fresh coriander)

Wash fish trimmings, shrimp heads, and shells thoroughly. Put into a large pan with cold water to cover, add remaining ingredients and bring to a boil. Cover and simmer 1 hour or longer. Strain stock and use in soups or as part of the liquid in seafood dishes.

BASIC SEAFOOD STOCK
Dashi • Japan

6 cups (48 fl oz, 1.5 L) water
2 in (5 cm) square kombu (dried kelp)
3 tablespoons katsuobushi (dried flaked bonito)

Wash dried kelp under cold tap and add to the water as it comes to a boil. Stir and let boil for 3 minutes, then remove from water and add flaked bonito. Return to a boil and remove from heat immediately. Leave for a few minutes until flakes settle, then strain and use as required. It will keep in the refrigerator for 2 days. Instant dashi can be bought from Japanese produce stores.

CHICKEN STOCK
Japan

½ chicken and bones from other ½ chicken
3 or 4 large slices of fresh ginger
1½ teaspoons salt
8 cups (64 fl oz, 2 L) water
2 scallions (spring onions)

Put chicken and bones into a large saucepan with all the other ingredients and bring to a boil. Reduce heat, cover and simmer for about 1 hour, skimming surface as necessary.

Cool to lukewarm, strain through cheesecloth (muslin) and then chill so that any fat solidifies on the surface and can be removed. The stock should be very clear. This is a good substitute for the more traditional dashi.

Ingredients for garam masala (page 9).

◆ CURRY PASTES, POWDERS & SPICE MIXES ◆

CEYLON CURRY PASTE
Sri Lanka

1 cup (3 oz, 90 g) coriander seeds
¼ cup (¾ oz, 21 g) cumin seeds
2 teaspoons fennel seeds
2 teaspoons fenugreek seeds
2 tablespoons ground rice
2 tablespoons unsweetened, desiccated coconut
12 dried red chilies
2 cinnamon sticks, broken
2 teaspoons cardamom seeds
2 teaspoons whole cloves
2 tablespoons chopped garlic
1 tablespoon chopped fresh ginger
vinegar and water for blending
16 dried curry leaves
3 rampé (pandanus leaves), cut into 2 in (5 cm) lengths

Over medium low heat, dry-roast separately the coriander, cumin, fennel and fenugreek, stirring constantly until each one smells fragrant and turns fairly dark brown. Set aside to cool. Roast ground rice and coconut until light brown and set aside to cool.

Place all roasted ingredients into blender, add chilies, cinnamon, cardamom, cloves, garlic, and ginger. Blend to a smooth paste, adding a little liquid to assist movement of blades. Remove paste from container and combine with curry leaves and rampé. Store in a screw-top glass jar in refrigerator.

Use 2 tablespoons paste to every 1 lb (500 g) of meat or poultry. Proceed as for Curry Paste for Poultry (see opposite).

CEYLON CURRY POWDER
Sri Lanka

1 cup (3 oz, 90 g) coriander seeds
½ cup (1½ oz, 45 g) cumin seeds
1 tablespoon fennel seeds
1 teaspoon fenugreek seeds
1 cinnamon stick, about 2 in (5 cm)
1 teaspoon whole cloves
1 teaspoon cardamom seeds
2 tablespoons dried curry leaves
2 teaspoons chili powder, optional
2 tablespoons ground rice, optional

In a dry pan over low heat roast separately the coriander, cumin, fennel and fenugreek, stirring constantly until each one becomes a fairly dark brown. Do not let them burn.

Put this mixture into blender together with cinnamon stick broken in pieces, the cloves, cardamom, and curry leaves. Blend on high speed until finely powdered. Combine with chili powder and ground rice if used. Store in an airtight jar.

CURRY PASTE FOR BEEF OR PORK
Malaysia

¾ cup (2¼ oz, 65 g) coriander seeds
2 tablespoons cumin seeds
¼ cup (⅓ oz, 10 g) dried red chilies, broken
2 teaspoons ground turmeric
5 candlenuts or 4 Brazil kernels, chopped
1 teaspoon laos powder
6 teaspoons chopped garlic
3 teaspoons chopped fresh ginger
4 stems fresh lemon grass, chopped, or rind of one lemon
1 tablespoon black peppercorns
3 teaspoons salt
vinegar and water for blending

Place all ingredients in blender. Add a little liquid to facilitate movement of the blades and blend to a smooth paste. Allow to cool and store in a screw-top glass jar in refrigerator. Allow 2 tablespoons of paste to every 1 lb (500 g) meat. Proceed as for Curry Paste for Poultry (see opposite).

CURRY PASTE FOR FISH & SHELLFISH
Malaysia

½ cup (1½ oz, 45 g) coriander seeds
1 tablespoon cumin seeds
2 teaspoons fennel seeds
¼ cup (⅓ oz, 10 g) dried chilies, broken
6 teaspoons chopped garlic
4 teaspoons chopped fresh ginger
5 candlenuts or 4 Brazil kernels, chopped
1 teaspoon kencur (galangal, lesser)

2 tablespoons unsweetened desiccated coconut
3 teaspoons trasi (dried shrimp paste)
2 teaspoons tamarind paste
1 teaspoon laos powder
3 teaspoons salt
2 teaspoons ground turmeric
4 stems fresh lemon grass, chopped or rind of 1 lemon
water for blending

Place all ingredients in blender. Add a little water to facilitate movement of the blades, and blend to a smooth paste. Allow to cool and store in a screw-top glass jar in refrigerator.

Allow 2 tablespoons of paste to every 1 lb (500 g) seafood. Proceed as for Curry Paste for Poultry (see recipe below).

CURRY PASTE FOR POULTRY
Malaysia

½ cup (1½ oz, 45 g) coriander seeds
1 tablespoon cumin seeds
2 teaspoons sweet cumin seeds
¼ cup (⅓ oz, 10 g) dried red chilies, broken
5 candlenuts or 4 Brazil kernels, chopped
3 stems fresh lemon grass, finely sliced or rind of 1 lemon
4 teaspoons chopped garlic
4 teaspoons chopped fresh ginger
2 teaspoons laos powder
3 teaspoons salt

Place all ingredients in blender. Add a little water to facilitate movement of the blades, and blend to a smooth paste. Allow to cool and store in a screw-top glass jar in refrigerator.

Allow 1–2 tablespoons paste to every 1 lb (500 g) poultry. Slice one onion and fry till soft and brown, then add paste. Fry till mixture smells fragrant and oil comes to the surface. Stir in 1/2 cup (4 fl oz, 125 ml) hot water, cover and simmer for 10 minutes. Add poultry pieces, stir in well and simmer covered till meat is tender. Serve with boiled rice.

FRAGRANT SPICE POWDER
Sri Lanka

2 teaspoons whole cloves
1 tablespoon cardamom seeds
1 tablespoon whole black peppercorns
2 tablespoons broken cinnamon stick
4 tablespoons cumin seeds

Roast these spices for 5 minutes in a dry pan over medium heat. Cool slightly and grind to a very fine consistency in a blender on high speed. Sprinkle a teaspoon of this powder over game or meat curries just before serving. Bottle and store away from heat and sunlight.

GARAM MASALA
India
Basic Garam Masala

4 tablespoons coriander seeds
2 tablespoons cumin seeds
1 tablespoon whole black peppercorns
2 teaspoons cardamom seeds (measure after roasting and removing pods)
4 x 3 in (7.5 cm) cinnamon sticks
1 teaspoon whole cloves
1 whole nutmeg

In a small pan roast separately the coriander, cumin, peppercorns, cardamom pods, cinnamon, and cloves. As each one starts to smell fragrant turn on to plate to cool. After roasting, peel the cardamoms, discard pods and use only the seeds. Put all into blender and blend to a fine powder. Finely grate nutmeg and mix in. Store in glass jar with airtight lid.

Fragrant Spice Garam Masala

3 x 3 in (7.5 cm) cinnamon sticks
2 teaspoons cardamom seeds (measure after removing pods)
1 teaspoon whole cloves
1 teaspoon blades of mace, or ½ nutmeg, grated

Roast spices separately and grind in a blender or with mortar and pestle; add grated nutmeg, if used.

Kashmiri Garam Masala

2 teaspoons cardamom seeds (measure after removing pods)
1 teaspoon black cumin seeds
1 teaspoon whole black peppercorns
2 x 2 in (5 cm) cinnamon sticks
½ teaspoon whole cloves
quarter of a nutmeg, grated

Roast spices separately and grind to a fine powder. Add nutmeg. Store in an airtight container.

GREEN CURRY PASTE
Thailand

4 large fresh green chilies
1 teaspoon black peppercorns
1 small brown onion, chopped
1 tablespoon chopped garlic
2 tablespoons chopped fresh coriander plant, root and leaves
1 stem fresh lemon grass, sliced or 2 teaspoons chopped
   lemon rind
1 teaspoon salt
2 teaspoons ground coriander
1 teaspoon ground cumin
1 teaspoon serai (lemon grass) powder
1 teaspoon laos powder
2 teaspoons trasi (dried shrimp paste)
1 teaspoon ground turmeric
1 tablespoon oil

Remove stems of chilies, leaving in the seeds if you want the curry paste to be hot. Roughly chop the chilies and put into blender together with all other ingredients. Blend to a smooth paste and scrape down sides of blender with a spatula. Add a little extra oil or a tablespoon of water if necessary.

GREEN MASALA PASTE
India

1 teaspoon fenugreek seeds
5 large cloves garlic
2 tablespoons finely chopped fresh ginger
1 cup (1½ oz, 45g) firmly packed fresh mint leaves
1 cup (1½ oz, 45g) firmly packed cilantro (fresh coriander
   leaves)
½ cup (4 fl oz, 125 ml) vinegar
3 teaspoons salt
2 teaspoons ground turmeric
½ teaspoon ground cloves
1 teaspoon ground cardamom
½ cup (4 fl oz, 125ml) vegetable oil
¼ cup (2 fl oz, 60 ml) sesame oil

Put fenugreek seeds in water to soak overnight. They will swell and develop a jelly-like coating. Measure 1 teaspoon of soaked seeds and put into blender with garlic, ginger, mint, coriander, and vinegar. Blend on high speed until very smooth. Mix in salt and ground spices.

Heat oils until very hot, add blended mixture, bring to a boil, turn off heat. Cool and bottle. Oil should cover the top of the herbs. If there is not quite enough oil, heat a little more and add it to the bottle.

Added to any curry or special preparation, it will give extra flavor. It does not take the place of curry paste or individual spices.

MADRAS CURRY PASTE
India

1 cup (2⅔ oz, 80 g) ground coriander
½ cup (1⅓ oz) ground cumin
1 tablespoon each ground black pepper, turmeric, black
   mustard, chili powder, and salt
2 tablespoons each crushed garlic and finely grated fresh
   ginger
vinegar for mixing
¾ cup (6 fl oz, 180 ml) oil

Combine ground spices and salt in a bowl. Add garlic and ginger and sufficient vinegar to mix to a smooth, thick purée. Heat oil in saucepan and when very hot turn in the spice mixture and reduce heat. Stir constantly until spices are cooked and oil separates from spices. Cool and bottle.

Use about a tablespoon of this paste for each 1 lb (500 g) of meat, fish, or poultry, substituting it for the garlic, ginger, and spices in a recipe.

MADRAS CURRY POWDER
India

1 cup (3 oz, 90 g) coriander seeds
½ cup (1½ oz, 45 g) cumin seeds
¼ cup (¾ oz, 21 g) fennel seeds
¼ cup (⅔ oz, 20 g) black mustard seeds
¼ cup (⅓ oz, 10 g) dried red chilies (broken)
2 tablespoons whole black peppercorns
2 teaspoons fenugreek seeds
1 tablespoon ground turmeric
20 dried curry leaves

In a dry pan roast separately all ingredients, except the turmeric and curry leaves, until they smell fragrant. Grind all ingredients to a fine powder in a blender. Mix in ground turmeric, bottle and store in freezer or other cool, dry place.

Note: Use 1–2 tablespoons of powder to each 1 lb (500 g) of main ingredient.

Ingredients for green masala paste (page 10).

MOSLEM CURRY PASTE
Thailand

7–10 dried chilies or 2 teaspoons chili powder
2 tablespoons coriander seeds or ground coriander
1 teaspoon cumin or fennel seeds or ground fennel
2 teaspoons laos powder, optional
1 teaspoon shredded lemon grass or finely peeled lemon rind
5 whole cloves or ¼ teaspoon ground cloves
1 stick cinnamon or 1 teaspoon ground cinnamon
5 cardamom pods or ½ teaspoon ground cardamom
1 blade mace or ½ teaspoon ground mace
2 tablespoons oil
2 medium size onions, finely sliced
2½ teaspoons finely chopped garlic
½ teaspoon kapi (dried shrimp paste)

You can make this curry paste two ways — either using the whole spices, roasting and grinding them (you will need a stout mortar and pestle for this) or by using the ground spices. Since in some areas it is easier to buy whole spices than in others where one can only obtain ground spices, I have tested this recipe using both forms. One is just as successful as the other, and the ground spices certainly require less effort.

Break the chilies, shake out the seeds, and roast them lightly in a dry pan. Pound in a mortar and pestle. Roast the coriander seeds until aromatic and dark brown, shaking pan frequently or stirring. Pound in a mortar until seeds are reduced to fine powder (if spices are pounded while hot, they are easily pulverized). Roast cumin seeds until they crackle and start to pop, then grind to a powder. I have not suggested grinding them in a blender because the quantities are so small there is not enough for the blades to work on.

If using ground spices, dry-roast the ground coriander and fennel over low heat, stirring constantly and taking care they do not burn. Roast until they turn a rich brown and have an aromatic smell. It is not necessary to roast the chili powder or spices.

Add laos and lemon rind to the ground spices. Parch the cloves, cinnamon stick, cardamom pods, and mace in a dry pan over low heat, shaking the pan. Separate the cinnamon into layers, it will roast more quickly. Grind all the spices in mortar and pestle to a fine powder and combine with the previously roasted and ground ingredients. Set aside.

Heat oil in a frying pan and on low heat fry sliced onions and garlic until soft and golden brown, stirring occasionally. Add dried shrimp paste and fry for a minute longer, crushing it in the oil with back of spoon. Put this fried mixture, when it has cooled slightly, into blender with lemon rind and blend to a paste. If necessary, add a little coconut cream (milk) or water to assist action of blender. Turn into a bowl and combine with dry ground spices. The curry paste is now ready to use.

If a blender is not available, crush the onions and garlic as much as posslble after they are cooked, combine with the spices and use in the same way.

⊰≫⊶⊱

PANCH PHORA
India

2 tablespoons black mustard seed
2 tablespoons cumin seed
2 tablespoons black cumin seed
1 tablespoon fenugreek seed
1 tablespoon fennel seed

"Panch" means five in Hindi, and panch phora is a combination of five different aromatic seeds. These are used whole and, when added to the cooking oil impart a flavor typical of certain Indian dishes. Put all ingredients into a glass jar with a tight-fitting lid. Shake before using to ensure an even distribution.

⊰≫⊶⊱

RED CURRY PASTE
Thailand

4–6 dried red chilies
2 small brown onions, chopped
1 teaspoon black peppercorns
2 teaspoons ground cumin
1 tablespoon ground coriander
2 tablespoons chopped fresh coriander plant, root and leaves
1 teaspoon salt
2 teaspoons chopped lemon rind
1 teaspoon serai (lemon grass) powder
1 teaspoon laos powder
1 tablespoon chopped garlic
2 teaspoons kapi (dried shrimp paste)
1 tablespoon oil
1 teaspoon turmeric
2 teaspoons paprika

Remove stems from chilies, but keep the seeds in if you want the curry paste to be as hot as it is in Thailand. Break the chilies into pieces and put into blender together with all the other ingredients. Blend to a smooth paste, stopping frequently and pushing ingredients onto blades. It may be necessary to add a tablespoon of water or extra oil.

TANDOORI MIX
India

2 teaspoons turmeric
1 teaspoon paprika
½ teaspoon chili powder, optional
1 teaspoon garam masala

½ teaspoon ground cardamom
⅛ teaspoon powdered saffron, optional
½ teaspoon garlic powder

Thoroughly mix the ingredients. A blend of hot and fragrant spices; you can buy it ready made from specialist stores.

Ingredients for panch phora (page 12).

◆ SAUCES & SEASONINGS ◆

BLACK BEAN GARLIC SAUCE FOR DIPPING
China

Rinse and mash 2 tablespoons canned salted black beans, crush 1 small clove garlic, mix beans and garlic with 2 tablespoons each of light soy sauce and Chinese wine or dry sherry. Good with pork or duck.

BLACK BEAN SHERRY SAUCE FOR DIPPING
China

Rinse and mash 1 tablespoon canned salted black beans, then combine with 3 tablespoons Chinese wine or dry sherry, 1 teaspoon sugar, a few drops of sesame oil. Subtle enough for delicate seafood like crabs and scallops.

CHILI-SOY SAUCE FOR DIPPING
China

Combine 2 tablespoons Chinese chili sauce and 1/2 cup (4 fl oz, 125 ml) soy sauce. For fried shrimp, dim sum, hot or cold hors d'oeuvre.

GARLIC, CHILI & FISH SAUCE
Nuoc Cham ◆ Vietnam

2 ripe red chilies
1 clove garlic
1 teaspoon sugar
1 lemon
1 tablespoon vinegar
1 tablespoon water
4 tablespoons fish sauce

Wearing gloves, cut off stalks from chilies, split down the middle and remove seeds and middle membrane. Cut into pieces, and pound in mortar and pestle together with peeled clove of garlic.

Add sugar. Peel lemon, removing all the white pith. Slice and remove seeds. Add a small piece at a time to the chilies and pound to a pulp. Stir in the vinegar, water, and fish sauce. Serve in a small bowl and use in small quantities.

Note: A blender may be used instead of mortar and pestle, but this makes a frothy sauce. However, it will taste the same.

GINGER-SOY SAUCE FOR DIPPING
China

Combine 1 teaspoon very finely grated fresh root ginger with 1/2 cup (4 fl oz, 125 ml) light soy sauce. Can be used with any kind of fried seafood or steamed dumplings.

GLUTINOUS RICE & SOYBEAN SAUCE
Nuoc Leo ◆ Vietnam

½ cup (4 fl oz, 125 ml) glutinous rice
4 cups (32 fl oz, 1 L) water
4 or 5 cloves garlic
1 tablespoon oil
8 oz (250 g) ground (minced) pork
½ teaspoon ground black pepper
3 tablespoons Chinese bean sauce
2 cups (16 fl oz, 500 ml) chicken or pork stock
2 tablespoons sugar
1 tablespoon fish sauce
2 teaspoons Chinese chili sauce
1 cup (4 oz, 125 g) roasted peanuts, pounded

Put rice and water in a heavy-based saucepan and bring to a boil. Cover, reduce heat and cook for 20 minutes, then uncover and allow to cook, stirring occasionally, until all the water has been absorbed.

Crush garlic with a little of the measured sugar. Heat oil in a wok, fry garlic on low heat until it starts to turn golden. Add pork and stir fry on medium heat until very light brown. Add pepper and bean sauce, stir well. Simmer for a minute, then add stock, sugar, and fish sauce, stir well and simmer a further minute or two. Add cooked rice, continue simmering for 5 minutes, stirring frequently. Remove from heat. Stir in chili sauce and peanuts ground in a blender or pounded with mortar and pestle. Serve warm or at room temperature.

Chilies, the essential ingredient for many Asian dishes.

HOT PEANUT SAUCE (QUICK METHOD)

Saus Kacang Pedis ◆ Indonesia

¼ cup (2 fl oz, 30 ml) peanut oil
1 tablespoon dried onion flakes
1 clove garlic, crushed
¼ teaspoon trasi (dried shrimp paste)
4 fresh red chilies, seeded and chopped, or 2 teaspoons
  sambal ulek (hot chili paste, page 23)
4 tablespoons peanut butter
¾ cup (6 fl oz, 180 ml) water
½ teaspoon salt
1 tablespoon dark soy sauce
2 teaspoons jaggery (palm sugar) or brown sugar
1 tablespoon tamarind liquid or lemon juice

Heat oil in a wok or small frying pan and fry onion flakes briefly until they turn golden, remove from oil and drain on absorbent paper. Leave about 2 tablespoons oil in pan, fry the garlic, trasi, and chilies for a minute on low heat, crushing the trasi with back of spoon. Add peanut butter and water and stir until blended. Remove from heat and add salt, soy sauce, sugar, and tamarind. If necessary add more water to make it a thick pouring consistency. When cool stir in crumbled onion flakes. Serve at room temperature.

MILD PEANUT SAUCE

Saus Kacang ◆ Indonesia

6 tablespoons peanut butter (smooth or crunchy)
1 cup water
¾ teaspoon garlic salt
2 teaspoons jaggery (palm sugar) or brown sugar
2 tablespoons dark soy sauce
lemon juice to taste
½ teaspoon shrimp paste or anchovy essence, optional
coconut milk or water for thinning

Put peanut butter and water in a saucepan and stir over gentle heat until mixed. Remove from heat and add all other ingredients. It will be necessary to add some coconut milk or water to make the paste a thick, pouring consistency. After doing so, check seasonings and add more salt and lemon juice if needed.

PLUM & BARBECUE SAUCE FOR DIPPING

China

Combine 6 tablespoons each plum sauce and red barbecue sauce. Stir in 1/2 teaspoon ginger juice, 2 tablespoons light soy sauce and, if a hotter dip is preferred, 1 teaspoon chili sauce or to taste. Serve with roast duck, barbecued pork, mandarin pancakes.

ROASTED PEPPER & SALT MIX

China

Roast 2 tablespoons black peppercorns in a dry pan over medium heat, shaking pan or stirring, until pepper gives off a pleasant smell. This takes 4 or 5 minutes. Allow pepper to cool slightly, then pound with a mortar and pestle and mix with 3 tablespoons salt. If this is more than you need for one time, store mixture in an airtight jar.

SALT & FIVE-SPICE MIX

China

Mix 2 tablespoons salt with 1 teaspoon five-spice powder. Serve with crisp fried chicken, roasted duck or pork.

SPICY SATAY SAUCE

Saus Bumbu ◆ Indonesia

2 tablespoons dark soy sauce
2 tablespoons tamarind liquid
1 medium onion, roughly chopped
2 cloves garlic
½ teaspoon laos powder
½ teaspoon hot chili paste (page 23)
½ teaspoon ground black pepper
½ teaspoon trasi (dried shrimp paste)
2 tablespoons peanut oil
½ cup coconut milk
1 daun salam (Indonesion curry leaf) or 3 curry leaves
1 stalk lemon grass or 2 strips lemon rind
2 teaspoons jaggery (palm sugar) or brown sugar

Put soy sauce, tamarind liquid, onion and garlic into blender and blend to a smooth paste. (If blender is not available, finely grate onion and garlic, then mix with the liquid.) Mix in laos, hot chili paste, pepper, and crushed shrimp paste. Heat peanut oil in a wok or frying pan and fry the blended mixture, stirring constantly until it turns brown and comes away from sides of pan. Add coconut milk, curry leaves, lemon grass, and sugar. Stir, reduce heat and simmer uncovered until sauce is very thick and almost dry.

❮❃❯

SWEET–SOUR SAUCE FOR DIPPING
China

1 tablespoon light soy sauce
1 tablespoon Chinese wine or dry sherry, optional
3 tablespoons tomato sauce
2 tablespoons white vinegar
2 tablespoons sugar
¾ cup (6 fl oz, 180 ml) water
1 tablespoon cornstarch (cornflour)

2 tablespoons peanut oil
1 clove garlic, crushed
¼ teaspoon finely grated fresh ginger root
2 tablespoons preserved melon shreds, optional

Combine soy sauce, wine, tomato sauce, vinegar, sugar, and water in a bowl and stir until sugar dissolves. Mix cornstarch smoothly with about 1 tablespoon of cold water. Heat oil, add garlic, ginger, and fry for 2 minutes. Add combined sauce mixture, bring to a boil, then stir in cornstarch and cook, stirring constantly until thickened. Remove from heat and stir in melon shreds.

Serve with hot hors d'oeuvre or fried won ton. If liked, stir in a teaspoonful of chili sauce at the end.

❮❃❯

In an Indian market.

◆ SALADS & ACCOMPANIMENTS ◆

BANANA RAITA
India

3 large ripe bananas
lemon juice
1 cup (8 fl oz, 250 ml) natural yogurt
3 tablespoons freshly grated or unsweetened desiccated
    coconut
½ teaspoon salt
2 teaspoons sugar
½ teaspoon ground toasted cumin seeds

Slice the bananas and sprinkle with lemon juice. Combine the yogurt with the other ingredients. If unsweetened desiccated coconut is used, moisten it first by sprinkling with about 2 tablespoons water and tossing it with the fingers until it is no longer dry. Chill and serve.
Serves 6

BEEF SAMBAL
Malaysia

8 oz (250 g) Scotch filet, sliced thin
2 tablespoons peanut oil
5 candlenuts or 4 Brazil kernels, chopped
1 teaspoon dried shrimp paste
2 medium onions, roughly chopped
5 dried red chilies
½ teaspoon ground turmeric
1 teaspoon ground laos
1 teaspoon chopped garlic
1 teaspoon tamarind paste
1 teaspoon salt
2 teaspoons sugar

Slice beef into thin shreds. Blend all ingredients except oil to a fine paste in blender, adding a little hot water to facilitate blending. Heat oil in saucepan or wok. Add mixture to hot oil and stir-fry till mixture smells cooked and oil surfaces. Add sliced beef and stir till well coated with the mixture. Cover and simmer till gravy thickens (about 5 minutes). Serve with boiled rice and curry.
Serves 4

BEETROOT RAITA
India

1 cup (5 oz, 155 g) canned beetroot
1 cup (8 fl oz, 250 ml) natural yogurt
salt to taste

Chop the beetroot roughly and mix into the yogurt, adding a little of the juice from the can to give color and flavor. Taste and add more salt if desired. Chill and serve cold as a cooling accompaniment to a curry meal.
Serves 4

BOMBAY DUCK
India

A pungent dried fish which is served as an accompaniment to rice and curry meals. Sold in packets, they should be cut into pieces about 2 in (5 cm) in length and deep fried in hot oil until light golden brown. Drain and serve as a crisp nibble between mouthfuls of rice.

An alternative method is to fry finely sliced onions in the same oil after the Bombay ducks are fried, and if liked, some broken dried chilies may be fried along with the onions. Fry slowly, stirring, until onions are golden brown. Add a little salt and sugar, stir well, combine with the fried Bombay duck and serve as a sambal.

BRAISED BITTER MELON SALAD
Thailand

2 x 3 in (7.5 cm) tender bitter melons
1 tablespoon peanut oil
2 teaspoons grated garlic
4 fresh red chilies, chopped
1 tablespoon shrimp (prawn) powder
1–2 tablespoons fish sauce
½ teaspoon ground black pepper

Cut bitter melon lengthwise in half. Slice thinly across and set aside. Heat wok, add oil and when hot, stir-fry the bitter melon for 1 minute, then stir in the garlic and red chilies for another minute. Add the rest of the ingredients. Stir and cover for 1 more minute, then remove to a dish. Serve with curry and boiled rice.

Cilantro (fresh coriander) and coconut chutney (recipe below).

CHILI SALAD
Thailand

10 fresh green chilies, chopped
1 tablespoon shrimp powder
2 teaspoons grated garlic
1–2 tablespoons fish sauce
3 teaspoons finely chopped lemon rind
juice of half a lemon

Mix all ingredients together and serve with curry and boiled rice.

CILANTRO (FRESH CORIANDER) & COCONUT CHUTNEY
India

1 cup (8 oz, 250 g) cilantro (fresh coriander leaves)
2 tablespoons unsweetened desiccated coconut
3 tablespoons water
1 teaspoon chopped garlic

1 green chili, seeded
1 teaspoon garam masala (page 9)
1 teaspoon salt
2 tablespoons lemon juice

Put the well-washed cilantro into blender with all other ingredients and blend on high speed until smooth. If necessary, add a little water to facilitate blending, but do not make the mixture too wet.
Serves 6

CILANTRO (FRESH CORIANDER) CHUTNEY
Dhania Chatni ◆ India & Pakistan

Proceed as for fresh mint chutney (see page 20), but replace mint with an equal quantity of cilantro (fresh coriander). A teaspoonful of chopped fresh ginger may also be added if desired.

COCONUT CHUTNEY
Nariyal Chatni ◆ India

½ a coconut, freshly grated or 1 cup (3 oz, 90 g)
*   unsweetened desiccated coconut*
1 lemon or lime
2 or 3 fresh green chilies
½ cup (¾ oz, 21 g) chopped fresh mint
1 teaspoon salt
2 teaspoons ghee or oil
⅛ teaspoon ground asafoetida, optional
1 teaspoon black mustard seeds
1 teaspoon black cumin seeds
10 curry leaves
½ teaspoon urad dhal (black gram)

If using desiccated coconut, sprinkle with about 1/4 (2 fl oz, 60 ml) water and toss to moisten evenly. Peel the lemon or lime so that no white pith remains. Cut in pieces and remove the seeds. Put lemon into blender with the seeded and roughly chopped chilies
and mint and blend until smooth. Add the coconut and continue blending to a smooth paste, scraping down sides of blender and adding a little more liquid if necessary. Add the salt and mix.

Heat ghee or oil in a small pan and fry the remaining ingredients, stirring frequently, until mustard seeds pop and dhal is golden. Mix with the coconut, pat into a flat cake and serve as an accompaniment to a curry meal.
Serves 6–8

❖

CRISP SPICED COCONUT WITH PEANUTS (1)
Serundeng ◆ Indonesia

1 cup (3 oz, 90 g) unsweetened desiccated coconut
1 small onion, very finely chopped
1 clove garlic, crushed
1 teaspoon finely grated fresh ginger
½ teaspoon trasi (dried shrimp paste)
2 tablespoons peanut oil
1 teaspoon ground coriander
1 teaspoon ground cumin
1 teaspoon salt
1 tablespoon tamarind liquid or lemon juice
1 cup (4 oz, 125 g) roasted unsalted peanuts

In a bowl mix the coconut, onion, garlic, and ginger. Heat peanut oil in a wok or frying pan and fry the trasi, crushing it with the frying spoon, for a minute or two on low heat. Add coconut mixture and fry on medium low heat, stirring constantly, until coconut is golden brown. Add coriander, cumin, salt, tamarind liquid or lemon juice and continue stirring and frying on very low heat until coconut is dry and crisp. This takes quite a while and cannot be hurried by raising the heat. Allow to cool, then mix in peanuts. Serve as an accompaniment to a rice meal, or use as a garnish to sprinkle over dishes.

❖

CRISP SPICED COCONUT WITH PEANUTS (2)
Serundeng ◆ Indonesia

½ cup (1½ oz, 45 g) unsweetened desiccated coconut
½ teaspoon instant minced garlic
2 tablespoons dried onion flakes
½ teaspoon ground coriander
½ teaspoon ground cumin
½ teaspoon salt
½ cup (2 oz, 60 g) roasted unsalted peanuts

Quick method: In a dry frying pan stir the coconut over medium low heat until golden. Add dried garlic and onion flakes, crushing the onion flakes into small pieces first. Continue stirring the mixture over heat until the coconut is deep golden and the garlic and onion flakes are toasted too. Add coriander, cumin, and salt, stir well, then remove from heat. Allow to cool and mix in the peanuts. This can be stored in an airtight container for weeks.

❖

CUCUMBER SAMBOL
Pipinja Sambola ◆ Sri Lanka

1 large or 2 small green cucumbers
2 teaspoons salt
½ cup (4 fl oz) thick coconut cream
1 fresh red chili, seeded and sliced
1 fresh green chili, seeded and sliced
1 small onion, cut in paper-thin slices
2 tablespoons lemon juice

Peel cucumber and slice very thinly. Put in a bowl, sprinkle with salt and let stand for at least 30 minutes. Press out all liquid and if too salty, rinse with cold water. Drain well. Mix with remaining ingredients and serve as an accompaniment to a curry meal.

DRY BALACHAUNG
Burma

20 cloves garlic
4 medium onions, finely sliced
2 cups (16 fl oz, 500 ml) peanut oil
1 x 8 oz (250 g) packet of shrimp (prawn) powder
2 teaspoons chili powder, optional
2 teaspoons salt
1 teaspoon trasi (dried shrimp paste)
½ cup (4 fl oz, 125 ml) vinegar

Peel garlic, cut into thin slices. Cut onions into thin slices. Heat oil and fry onion and garlic separately on low heat until golden. Lift out immediately and set aside. They will become crisp and darken as they cool.

Pour off all but 1 cup (8 fl oz, 250 ml) oil and in this, fry shrimp powder for 5 minutes. Add chili powder, salt, and shrimp paste mixed with vinegar, stir well and fry until crisp. Allow to cool completely. Mix in fried onion and garlic, stirring to distribute evenly. Store in an airtight jar. Serve with rice or noodles, and Burmese curries.

FRESH LEMON GRASS SALAD
Thailand

4 stems lemon grass
5 fresh red chilies, chopped
1–2 tablespoons fish sauce

Use only the pale, tender base of the lemon grass. Wash well and chop finely. Place in a bowl, add chilies and fish sauce. Mix well and serve with curry and boiled rice.

Top, fried bananas (page 22) and green bean sambal, (page 22); bottom, crisp spiced coconut with peanuts (recipe opposite).

FRESH MINT CHUTNEY
Podina Chatni ◆ India

1 cup (4 oz) firmly packed mint leaves
6 scallions (spring onions), including green leaves
2 fresh green chilies, roughly chopped
½ teaspoon chopped garlic, optional
1 teaspoon salt
2 teaspoons sugar
1 teaspoon garam masala (see page 9)
⅓ cup lemon juice
2 tablespoons water

Put mint into blender together with scallions cut into short lengths and all other ingredients. Blend on high speed to a smooth purée. If blender is not available finely chop mint, onions and chilies and pound a little at a time in mortar and pestle, then mix in remaining ingredients. Pack the chutney into a small dish, smooth the surface, cover and chill.

FRIED BANANAS

Pisang Goreng ◆ Indonesia

6 medium or 3 large bananas, ripe but quite firm
oil for frying

Peel bananas. If large, cut in half crosswise. Smaller bananas need only to be cut down the centre lengthwise. Heat a little oil in a frying pan, put in the bananas and fry over medium high heat until brown all over. Turn bananas carefully, for they break easily when hot. Lift on to a small plate to serve, and sprinkle lightly with salt. Serve as an accompaniment to rice and curries.
Serves 6

FRIED EGGPLANT SAMBOL

Badhapu Vambotu Sambola ◆ Sri Lanka

2 eggplants (aubergines)
2 teaspoons salt
2 teaspoons ground turmeric
oil for frying
3 fresh red or green chilies
2 small onions
lemon juice
3 tablespoons thick coconut cream

Slice eggplants thinly, rub with salt and turmeric, put in a bowl and leave at least 1 hour. Drain off liquid and dry eggplant on paper towels.

Fry in hot oil and drain on absorbent paper. Mix with seeded and chopped chilies, finely sliced onion, lemon juice to taste, and thick coconut cream.

FRIED ONION FLAKES

Bawang Goreng ◆ Indonesia

An important garnish and flavoring for many Indonesian dishes, the easiest way to make these is to use the dried onion flakes readily available. These cook in seconds, so put them on a wire strainer and lower them into deep oil that is hot but not too hot. They will take a few seconds to turn golden brown. Lift them out immediately and drain on absorbent paper. When cool, store in an airtight jar.

Using fresh onions takes much longer. Slice the onions very thinly, making sure not only that the slices are paper-thin, but also that they are all the same thinness, otherwise some will burn while others are uncooked. Fry in deep hot oil until dark brown, but not black. Lift out, drain and bottle when cool. They must be cooked slowly so that all the moisture is cooked out.

GREEN BEAN SAMBAL

Sambal Buncis ◆ Indonesia

8 oz (250 g) fresh green beans
1 tablespoon peanut oil
½ teaspoon instant minced garlic
½ teaspoon sambal ulek (hot chili paste, opposite)
½ teaspoon salt to taste
1 small onion, finely diced

String beans and cut in very fine diagonal slices. Heat oil in a wok or frying pan and toss beans on high heat 2 minutes, add garlic and fry 1 minute more. Add sambal and salt and fry 1 minute longer. Beans should be tender but still crunchy crisp. Remove from heat, mix in the onion slices and serve as an accompaniment or side dish to a rice and curry meal.

GREEN MANGO CHUTNEY

Am Chatni ◆ India

1 large green mango
½ teaspoon salt
½ teaspoon chili powder or to taste

Peel and slice the mango thinly and cut it into fine slivers. Toss with the salt and chili powder and serve as an accompaniment to a curry meal, or as an appetizer at the start of a meal.

Note: Tart green cooking apples may be used instead of mango.

GROUND ONION & CHILI SAMBOL
Lunu Miris Sambola • Sri Lanka

10 dried chilies
1 tablespoon pounded maldive fish or dried shrimp
  (prawns)
1 small onion, chopped
lemon juice and salt to taste

Remove stalks from chilies. If a less hot result is preferred, shake out the seeds. Pound all the ingredients together in a mortar and pestle. In Sri Lanka this would be either pounded or ground on the grinding stone. (It can be done in a blender, but a wet result is not desirable, since the end result should be a paste.)

This simple sambol is as basic to the food of Sri Lanka as salt and pepper are to Western food. Very hot, very acid and distinctly salty, it is often the only accompaniment to serve with rice, or any of the starches that are the staple of the native diet.

⋈

HOT CHILI PASTE
Sambal Ulek • Indonesia

25 fresh red chilies
vinegar or tamarind liquid
2 teaspoons salt

Put the chilies, seeds and all, into blender. Add enough vinegar or tamarind liquid to keep the mass moving and blend to a paste. Add salt. Put into a sterilized bottle and store in the refrigerator.

⋈

MALAY VEGETABLE PICKLES
Acar Kuning • Malaysia

1 cup (2½ oz, 75 g) carrot sticks
1 cup (2½ oz, 75 g) green (string) beans
10 fresh red and green chilies
1 green cucumber
½ a small cauliflower
2 tablespoons peanut oil
1 teaspoon finely chopped garlic
2 teaspoons finely grated fresh ginger
3 candlenuts or Brazil kernels, grated
1 teaspoon ground turmeric
½ cup (4 fl oz, 125 ml) white vinegar

½ cup (4 fl oz, 125 ml) water
2 teaspoons sugar
1 teaspoon salt

Cut carrots into julienne strips. Cut beans into pieces of the same length, then slice each piece in two lengthwise. If beans are very young and slender it will not be necessary to slice them. Leave the chilies whole, but remove stems. Peel cucumber and cut in half lengthwise, remove seeds and slice into pieces the same size as the carrots and beans. Cut cauliflowers into sprigs leaving a bit of stem on each piece.

Heat oil in a saucepan and fry garlic and ginger on low heat for 1 minute, stirring. Add grated nuts and turmeric and stir for a few seconds longer. Add vinegar, water, sugar, and salt and bring to a boil. Add carrots, beans, chilies, and cauliflower sprigs, return to a boil and boil for 3 minutes. Add cucumber and boil for 1 minute longer.

Remove immediately to an earthenware or glass bowl and allow to cool. Use at once or bottle and store in refrigerator for a week or two.

⋈

ONION & TOMATO SAMBAL
India

2 medium onions
salt
1 tablespoon tamarind pulp or 1 teaspoon instant tamarind
¼ cup (2 fl oz, 60 ml) hot water
2 tablespoons jaggery (palm sugar) or brown sugar
2 firm ripe tomatoes
1 tablespoon finely shredded fresh ginger
2 or 3 fresh red or green chilies, seeded and sliced
2 tablespoons chopped cilantro (fresh coriander leaves)

Peel the onions, cut them in halves lengthwise and then cut across into fine slices. Sprinkle generously with salt and leave for an hour. Press out all the liquid and rinse once in cold water. Drain well.

Soak tamarind pulp in hot water for a few minutes, then squeeze to dissolve pulp and strain, discarding the seeds. If using instant tamarind, dissolve in the hot water. Dissolve jaggery in the tamarind liquid.

Scald tomatoes, peel and dice. Combine all the ingredients, add salt to taste, chill and serve. Salads of this type are served as accompaniments to rice and curries.
Serves 6

⋈

PAPPADAMS
India

pappadams
peanut oil for deep frying

These spicy lentil wafers are sold dried in packets. Heat the oil and test with a small piece of pappadam: if the oil is not hot enough the piece will sink to the bottom and stay there. The oil should be hot enough for the pappadam to double its size within the first two or three seconds.

Deep fry one pappadam at a time for three or four seconds in the oil. They will swell and turn pale golden. Drain well on absorbent paper. Pappadams are best fried just before serving, but they may be cooled and stored in an airtight container if prepared a few hours beforehand.
Allow 2 per person

PIQUANT FRIED SHRIMP SAMBAL
Indonesia

1 lb (500 g) shelled raw shrimp (prawns)
2 tablespoons peanut oil
1 onion, finely chopped
1½ teaspoons finely chopped garlic
½ teaspoon finely grated fresh ginger
2 teaspoons sambal ulek (hot chili paste) or 4 fresh red chilies
½ teaspoon laos powder
2 strips thinly peeled lemon rind, chopped
⅓ cup tamarind liquid
1 teaspoon salt
1 teaspoon jaggery (palm sugar) or brown sugar

If shrimp are large, chop into pieces the size of a peanut. Small shrimp may be used whole. Heat oil in a frying pan and fry onion, garlic, and ginger until onion is soft and starts to turn golden. Add sambal ulek (hot chili paste), laos powder, and lemon rind, then add chopped shrimp and fry, stirring constantly, until shrimp turn pink.

Add tamarind liquid and simmer on low heat until gravy is thick and oil starts to separate. Stir in salt and sugar. Taste and correct seasoning if necessary. Serve as a side dish with rice and curries.
Serves 6

POUNDED SHRIMP PASTE
Burma

2 tablespoons shrimp (prawn) powder
2 tablespoons ngapi (dried shrimp paste)
2 medium onions
4 cloves garlic
2 teaspoons chili powder, optional
1 teaspoon salt
juice of half a lemon

Press the dried shrimp paste into a flat cake, wrap in foil and put under a hot broiler (grill) for 15 minutes, turning to cook both sides. Wrap onions and garlic in foil and put under broiler with the dried shrimp paste. Pound together these ingredients in a mortar and pestle. Then mix in remaining ingredients.

Alternatively, the crumbled dried shrimp paste, peeled onions, and garlic can be blended with lemon juice and combined with other ingredients. To be eaten in very small quantities with rice.

RED COCONUT SAMBOL
Sri Lanka

1 cup (3 oz, 90 g) unsweetened desiccated coconut
1 teaspoon salt
1–2 teaspoons chili powder, to taste
2 teaspoons paprika (for color)
2 teaspoons maldive fish or shrimp (prawn) powder, optional
3 tablespoons lemon juice
1 small onion, finely chopped
2 fresh red or green chilies, seeded and chopped

Combine all the ingredients in a bowl and mix with your hands, so that the coconut is moistened by the onion and lemon juice. If necessary sprinkle a couple of tablespoons of hot water over so that the coconut is thoroughly moistened.
Serves 6–8

ROASTED COCONUT SAMBOL
Sri Lanka

1 cup (3 oz, 90 g) unsweetened desiccated coconut
2 medium onions, finely chopped
1 teaspoon salt
2 teaspoons maldive fish or dried shrimp (prawn) powder
4 tablespoons lemon juice or to taste

Left, piquant fried shrimp sambal (page 24); right, shrimp wafers (page 26).

In a heavy-based frying pan heat the coconut, stirring constantly so it will brown evenly. It should be a deep brown, not merely golden, so that it gives this sambol its distinctive taste. Remove from pan immediately and spread on a plate to cool. Combine all ingredients in blender, cover and blend until a smooth paste is formed. if liquid is insufficient it may be necessary to add a little more lemon juice or finely grated onion. Shape the paste into a flat cake on a small plate. Mark the top in a criss-cross pattern with the back of a knife.

⋗⋈⋖

SAMBAL UDANG
Malaysia

1½ lb (750 g) medium-sized shrimp (prawns), shelled and
   deveined
2 tablespoons peanut oil
6 dried red chilies
1 medium onion, roughly chopped
6 candlenuts, or 4 Brazil kernels, chopped

1 teaspoon trasi (dried shrimp paste)
2 teaspoons chopped garlic
1 teaspoon chopped fresh ginger
2 teaspoons tamarind paste
1 teaspoon salt
2 teaspoons sugar

Place chilies, onion, nuts, dried shrimp paste, garlic, ginger, and tamarind paste in blender. Add a little water to assist movement of the blades, and blend to a smooth paste.

Heat wok or saucepan, add oil and when hot add blended mixture. Stir-fry for a few minutes till mixture smells cooked and oil comes to the surface. Add shrimp and stir-fry till well coated with the mixture then add salt and sugar. Continue to stir-fry till shrimp are cooked and gravy thickens. Serve with rice and curry.
Serves 6

⋗⋈⋖

SHRIMP BLACHAN
Sri Lanka

1 cup (4 oz, 125 g) dried shrimp (prawn) powder
½ cup (1½ oz, 45 g) unsweetened desiccated coconut
2 teaspoons chili powder or to taste
2 medium onions, chopped
5 cloves garlic, sliced

1 tablespoon finely chopped fresh ginger
⅔ cup lemon juice
1 teaspoon salt, or to taste

Put shrimp powder in a dry frying pan and heat for a few minutes, stirring. Turn on to a large plate. Put unsweetened desiccated coconut in the same pan and heat, stirring, until a rich brown. Turn onto a plate to cool.

Put other ingredients except shrimp powder into blender, cover and blend until smooth. Add shrimp powder and unsweetened desiccated coconut, cover and blend again, adding a little water if necessary to bind ingredients. Scrape down sides of container occasionally with a spatula. Turn onto a plate and shape into a round, flat cake. Serve with rice and curries.

SHRIMP (PRAWN) PASTE
Tom Bam ✦ Vietnam

1 lb (500 g) raw shrimp or prawns
1 egg white
2 oz (60 g) pork fat, finely chopped
1 tablespoon oil
1 tablespoon fish sauce
½ teaspoon salt
¼ teaspoon sugar
⅛ teaspoon ground black pepper

Shell and devein the shrimp, wash well and drain thoroughly. Mince or chop very finely, then blend or pound in mortar and pestle to a soft paste. If using blender add oil and fish sauce to facilitate blending. Add all other ingredients and mix thoroughly. Use in shrimp soup, fried shrimp cakes or shrimp toast.

SHRIMP PASTE SAUTÉ
Burma

½ cup (4 fl oz, 125 ml) vegetable oil
1 onion, chopped
3 teaspoons finely chopped garlic
¼ teaspoon turmeric
1 tablespoon ngapi (dried shrimp paste)
3–4 tomatoes, quartered
1 cup (3 oz, 90 g) dried shrimp (prawn) powder
2 green chilies, sliced
1 tablespoon tamarind liquid
½ teaspoon salt or to taste

Heat oil until very hot, reduce heat to medium and fry onion, garlic, and turmeric till dark golden and nearly catching to pan. Add dried shrimp paste, tomatoes, shrimp powder, green chilies, and tamarind liquid. Stir and cook until all the liquid has evaporated and oil separates from the mass. Add salt to taste.

SHRIMP WAFERS (PRAWN CRISPS)
Krupuk Udang ✦ Indonesia

These come in a variety of shapes and sizes, but the tastiest are the large, salmon-pink variety roughly as long as an average hand and half as wide.

Should they become damp due to climatic conditions, and do not puff as they should, you can dry them out in a low oven for 10 to 15 minutes, spread out in a single layer on a baking sheet. Let them cool, then store in a really airtight container. Or dry them out in the oven as required just before cooking.

Heat oil in a wok or deep frying pan and fry the larger wafers one at a time, spooning oil over them as they cook. The oil should be hot enough to make them swell within 2 or 3 seconds of being dropped in. Test with a small piece first. If oil is not the right temperature they will be tough and leathery, not crisp and melting. On the other hand if the oil is too hot they will brown too fast. A little practice will tell how hot the oil should be. Lift out with tongs or a slotted spoon and drain on absorbent paper. Cool thoroughly before storing in an airtight container. The smaller wafers can be fried a few at a time, in the same way as the large ones.

SPICED SPINACH
India

1 lb (500 g) spinach
2 teaspoons toasted cumin seeds, crushed
1 clove garlic crushed with ½ teaspoon salt
1 teaspoon finely chopped fresh ginger
1 green chili, finely chopped
salt to taste
½ teaspoon garam masala
1 cup (12 fl oz, 250 ml) natural yogurt

Wash spinach well, place in a saucepan with 1/2 cup water, cover and cook for 10 minutes. Drain and place spinach in blender and purée at high speed. Remove, drain and set aside. Toast cumin seeds in a dry pan till brown and fragrant, set aside.

Add garlic, ginger, chili, salt, and garam masala to yogurt and mix well. Place spinach on serving dish, spread over with yogurt mixture and sprinkle with crushed cumin. Serve with boiled rice and curry.

Serves 4

⋘≫

SPICY FRUIT SALAD
Rujak Buah–Buah Pedis ✦ Indonesia

1 grapefruit or pomelo
1 orange or mandarin
2 tart green apples
1 cucumber
1 small pineapple
½ teaspoon trasi (dried shrimp paste)
½ teaspoon sambal ulek (hot chili paste)
1 tablespoon jaggery (palm sugar) or brown sugar
1 tablespoon dark soy sauce
2 tablespoons lemon juice

Peel grapefruit and orange with a sharp knife, removing peel and white pith. Cut in between membranes to release segments. Do this over a bowl, saving juices from fruit. Remove seeds. Peel and slice apples thinly. Peel and dice cucumber. Peel pineapple, remove core and dice flesh. Wrap the trasi in a piece of foil and roast for 5 minutes under broiler (grill), turning once. Dissolve trasi, sambal ulek (hot chili paste), and sugar in soy sauce and lemon juice, pour over fruit and mix well. Allow to stand for a few minutes before serving.

Serves 6–8

TAMARIND CHUTNEY
Imli Chatni ✦ India

3 tablespoons dried tamarind pulp
1 cup (8 fl oz, 250 ml) hot water
1 teaspoon salt
2 teaspoons jaggery (palm sugar) or brown sugar
1 teaspoon ground cumin
½ teaspoon ground fennel
2 teaspoons finely grated fresh ginger
lemon juice to taste
pinch chili powder, optional

Put tamarind pulp in a bowl with hot water and allow to soak until water is cool. Knead and squeeze pulp away from the seeds until it is dissolved in the water, then strain through a fine nylon sieve, pushing all the pulp through. If necessary, add a little more water to assist in getting all the pulp from the seeds. Add salt, sugar, and other ingredients to the tamarind and stir to mix well. Taste and add more salt if necessary, lemon juice to sharpen the taste and if liked, a small pinch of chili powder.

⋘≫

TOMATO &
SCALLION SAMBAL
India

2 large firm red tomatoes
½ cup (2 oz, 60 g) finely chopped scallions (spring onions),
    green leaves and all
½ teaspoon chili powder
½ teaspoons salt or to taste
2–3 tablespoons lemon juice

Cut the tomatoes in small dice and sprinkle with all the other ingredients, tossing gently until well mixed. Cover and chill until required and serve as an accompaniment to rice and curry.

Serves: 4

⋘≫

Soups, Appetizers & Snacks

BEAN PASTE SOUP
Miso Shiru ◆ Japan

5 cups (2 pts, 1200 ml) dashi (see page 6)
2 tablespoons aka miso (red bean paste)
4 cubes of tofu (bean curd)
2 scallions (spring onions), sliced diagonally
2 sliced mushrooms

Bring dashi to a boil. Then in a small bowl mix some of the hot liquid with the bean paste, stirring until smooth. Pour mixture back into saucepan, stir well, add tofu and scallions and return to a boil. Simmer for a few seconds only.

Ladle into bowls, garnish each with a slice or two of mushroom, and serve hot.
Serves 4

BEAN SPROUT FRITTERS
Pe Thee Pin Pauk Ngabaung Kway ◆ Burma

8 oz (250 g) fresh bean sprouts
1 cup (4 oz, 125 g) all-purpose (plain) flour
1 cup (8 fl oz, 250 ml) lukewarm water
1 tablespoon peanut oil
salt and pepper to taste
1 egg white
oil for deep frying

Dipping Sauce:
1 tablespoon fish sauce
2 tablespoons water
2 teaspoons chili sauce
¼ teaspoon garlic powder, optional

Wash bean sprouts, drain and dry on absorbent paper. Sift flour into a bowl, add warm water, salt, and pepper and beat with a wooden spoon until smooth. Stir in oil and allow to stand for 30 minutes. Just before using, stiffly beat egg white and fold into batter. Mix the bean sprouts through the batter.

Heat oil in wok and deep fry mixture by tablespoons over medium high heat until golden brown. Do not fry too many fritters at a time or temperature of oil will be reduced. Drain on absorbent paper. Serve warm with dipping sauce.

Dipping Sauce: Mix together the ingredients and serve in a small bowl alongside the fritters.

BEEF SOUP WITH SALAD
Pho ◆ Vietnam

6 lb (3 kg) beef rib bones
1 lb (500 g) stewing steak (gravy beef)
2 onions, sliced
thumb-size piece of fresh ginger
stick of cinnamon
1 teaspoon whole black peppercorns
salt to taste
1 lb (500 g) fresh rice noodles or 8 oz (250 g) dried rice noodles
1 lb (500 g) fresh bean sprouts
6 scallions (spring onions)
4 firm ripe tomatoes
2 white onions
1 lb (500 g) rump steak
fish sauce
lemon wedges
fresh red or green chilies, chopped
chopped cilantro (fresh coriander leaves)

You may well think a soup and a salad are an odd combination when served together, but don't miss out on this national dish by being too cautious. The strong stock is combined with other ingredients to make a meal in a bowl. Serve it right at the table, keeping the stock hot in an electric utensil and adding other components to each bowl.

Put bones and stewing steak in a very large pan, add cold water to cover, sliced onions, scraped and sliced ginger, cinnamon stick, whole peppercorns. Bring to a boil, turn heat very low, cover and simmer for at least 6 hours. Add salt to taste.

If using fresh rice noodles (look fun, chee chong fun), slice them into 1/2 in (1 cm) strips and pour boiling water over, then drain, or steam in a colander for 5 minutes. If using dried rice noodles, they must be soaked in warm water for at least 2 hours, then drained and cooked in boiling water until just tender. Drain well.

Prepare salad ingredients. Scald bean sprouts by pouring boiling water over them in a colander. Run cold water over. If necessary pinch off any straggly brown tails. Slice scallions thinly. Cut tomatoes in half lengthwise, then slice each half. Peel and slice onions thinly. Slice steak paper thin in bite-size pieces. Arrange all on a serving plate.

To serve: Put a ladle of noodles and a ladle of bean sprouts in each large soup bowl. Put a few slices of rump steak, tomato, and onion in a large ladle, immerse in the boiling stock until

Top, savory farina (semolina) (page 58); right, lentil & vegetable soup (page 44); bottom right, coconut chutney (page 20); bottom left, spicy fried potatoes (page 279).

steak begins to lose its redness; it should be pale pink. Pour contents of the ladle over the noodles and bean sprouts. Guests add fish sauce, lemon juice, chilies, and cilantro to taste.
Serves 6–8

CAULIFLOWER SOUP
Sup Kembang Kol ◆ Indonesia

8 cups (64 fl oz, 2 L) strong beef stock
¼ teaspoon ground black pepper
¼ teaspoon ground mace
2 teaspoons ground coriander
1 teaspoon ground cumin
1 onion, finely copped
1 clove garlic, crushed
1 lb (500 g) cauliflower, coarsely chopped
2 small bundles fine egg noodles

If making the beef stock for the soup, add 3 or 4 whole cloves, 10 peppercorns, a few blades of mace, a tablespoon of coriander seeds, and half that amount of cumin seeds. This will eliminate the need for the ground spices. If, however, the stock is a by-product of something else and has not been cooked with whole spices, add all the ground spices listed, the onion and garlic, and simmer for 10 minutes. Add the cauliflower and bring to a boil again. Simmer for 4 minutes. In the meantime soak the noodles in hot water for a few minutes, until the strands separate. Drain and add to the boiling soup. Return to boil and cook for 3 minutes. Serve at once so that cauliflower and noodles do not overcook. Garnish with fried onion flakes if desired.
Serves 6

CHICKEN & ASPARAGUS SOUP
China

8 cups (64 fl oz, 2 L) chicken stock
1 chicken breast
7 oz (220 g) asparagus pieces
3 teaspoons cornstarch (cornflour)
2 tablespoons cold water
1 tablespoon Chinese wine or sherry
2 eggs, beaten

Make stock according to recipe on page 6 or use chicken stock cubes. Cut flesh from chicken breast into small dice. Set aside. Drain asparagus pieces, reserving liquid. Combine stock and liquid from asparagus, add diced chicken and bring to a boil.

Lower heat, simmer 5 minutes, then add cornstarch mixed with cold water and return to a boil, stirring until soup thickens slightly.

Add wine or sherry, slowly dribble in the beaten eggs, stirring. Add asparagus pieces, heat through and serve.
Serves 4–5

CHICKEN & VEGETABLE SOUP (1)
Kenchin-Jiru ◆ Japan

4 dried mushrooms
7 cups (56 fl oz, 1.75 L) dashi (see page 6) or chicken stock
1 small carrot
1 stalk celery
half a daikon (giant white radish)
½ cup chicken meat, diced small
salt to taste

Soak mushrooms in very hot water for 30 minutes, then discard stems and cut mushrooms into thin slices. Put into pan with stock, cover and cook for 10 minutes.

Cut carrot, celery, and radish into fine matchstick strips and add to pan with chicken. Cook for 5 minutes, taste and correct seasoning. Serve hot.
Serves 6

CHICKEN & VEGETABLE SOUP (2)
Kenchin-Jiru ◆ Japan

4 oz (125 g) button mushrooms (champignons)
1 small chicken breast
3 scallions (spring onions)
few sprigs watercress
6 cups (2½ pts, 1.5 L) chicken stock

Wipe mushrooms clean with damp kitchen paper, slice or, if very small, leave whole. Remove skin and bone from chicken breast, cut into dice with a sharp knife. Wash and trim scallions and cut into bite-size lengths, using part of the green portion as well as the white. Wash watercress and break small leafy sprigs for garnish. The thick stalks may be simmered in the stock and strained out.

Heat chicken stock which has been previously strained and cleared of all fat. Add chicken and simmer for 3 minutes, then add mushrooms and scallions and return to a boil.

Divide among soup bowls and garnish each with a sprig of watercress.
Serves 6

CHICKEN & WINTER MELON SOUP

Canh Ga Bi Dao ◆ Vietnam

1 lb (500 g) chicken wings or half a chicken
2 lb (1 kg) Chinese winter melon
6 scallions (spring onions)
5 cups (2 pts, 1.25 L) water
1 teaspoon salt
1 tablespoon fish sauce
black pepper to taste

Cut chicken wings or half chicken into joints. Peel melon, discard skin and spongy middle with seeds. Cut melon into bite-sized pieces. Slice scallions. Put chicken into saucepan with scallions, water, and salt. Bring to a boil, then cover and simmer for 1 hour or until liquid is reduced and well flavored. Add winter melon, bring to a boil for one minute only. Add fish sauce and pepper to taste. Serve immediately, with rice if desired.

Note: Peeled, sliced and seeded cucumber can be used as a substitute for winter melon.

Serves 6

CHICKEN VELVET & SWEET CORN SOUP

Gay Lim Sook Mi Gai Tong ◆ China

1 large chicken breast
½ teaspoon salt
2 tablespoons cold water
5 cups (2 pts, 1.25 L) chicken stock
7 oz (220 g) can creamed corn
1½ tablespoons cornstarch (cornflour)
1 teaspoon sesame oil
2 tablespoons Chinese wine or sherry
2 thin slices smoked ham or bacon

Bone the chicken breast. Use the bone, a stalk of celery, an onion, and a slice of ginger to make the stock. Or use chicken stock cubes. Remove skin from chicken and very finely chop the flesh until it is almost a paste. Add the salt and water to it, mixing well. Mix corn and chicken together. Strain chicken stock into a saucepan, bring to a boil, add the chicken mixture.

Return slowly to a boil, then stir in cornstarch mixed with a little cold water. Return to a boil, stirring, and cook until thickened, about 1 minute. Stir in sesame oil and wine or sherry.

Serve at once, sprinkled with the finely chopped ham.

Serves 4–5

CHINESE OMELETS

Egg Fu Yung ◆ China

4 eggs
½ teaspoon salt
1 cup fresh bean sprouts
3 scallions (spring onions), finely chopped
peanut oil for frying

Beat eggs with salt. Wash and drain sprouts well, removing any brown tails or loose skins. Add sprouts and scallions to beaten egg. Lightly grease a heavy frying pan or wok with peanut oil. Pour in 1/4 cup (2 fl oz, 60 ml) of the egg mixture. Cook until brown on underside, turn and cook other side. Repeat with remaining mixture. Stack 2 or 3 fu yung for each serving.

Serves 2

COCONUT AND BEEF CROQUETTES

Indonesia

8 oz (250 g) unsweetened desiccated coconut
about ½ cup (4 fl oz, 125 ml) hot water
1 lb (500 g) hamburger (minced beef)
½ teaspoon dried shrimp paste
2 cloves garlic
1½ teaspoons salt
½ teaspoon ground black pepper
1½ teaspoons ground coriander
1 teaspoon ground cumin
½ teaspoon ground kencur (aromatic ginger)
2 eggs, beaten
peanut oil for deep frying

Put coconut into a bowl and sprinkle with the hot water. Mix until all the coconut is moistened. Combine coconut and hamburger.

In a small bowl crush shrimp paste with back of spoon and dissolve in a tablespoon of hot water. Crush garlic with salt. Add to shrimp paste together with black pepper and all the spices, add beaten eggs and mix well. Pour over the meat and coconut, mix and knead well with the hands so that spices are evenly distributed and mixture is smooth. Shape into small balls. Deep fry in hot oil until they are crisp and golden brown all over. Drain on absorbent paper and serve warm or cold.

These meatballs may be served as appetizers or as an accompaniment to a meal of rice and curry.

Makes 50–60 cocktail-size meatballs

COLD HORS D'OEUVRE
Lahng Poon ◆ China

1 x 1 lb (500 g) can abalone
braised mushrooms (recipe page 264), ½ quantity
8 oz (250 g) barbecued pork
1 cooked chicken breast
2 pairs lap cheong (dried red Chinese sausages)
6 tea eggs (page 76), quartered
1 large cucumber, thinly sliced
1 large radish, thinly sliced

Marinade:
4 tablespoons light soy sauce
1 tablespoon sugar
1 tablespoon Chinese wine or dry sherry
1 tablespoon sesame oil
½ teaspoon finely grated fresh ginger

Drain abalone and discard liquid from can. Cut abalone into very thin slices and put in marinade. Cook mushrooms according to recipe on page 264, without the bean curd. Thinly slice braised mushrooms. Cut barbecued pork and chicken breast in thin slices. Steam sausages for 10 minutes or until plump, cool and cut in paper-thin diagonal slices. Drain abalone slices and reserve the marinade. Arrange ingredients attractively on a large serving plate and serve marinade in a small bowl as a dip

Marinade: Mix all ingredients together.
Serves 6–8

❧⊷⊷❧

COMBINATION LONG SOUP
China

6 Chinese mushrooms, soaked and cut in strips
2 eggs, beaten
salt
pepper
a few drops of sesame oil
8 oz (250 g) fine egg noodles
8 cups (64 fl oz, 2 L) chicken stock (or water and stock cubes)
8 oz (250 g) lean pork or chicken
2 tablespoons peanut oil
1 clove garlic, bruised
2 slices fresh ginger root
3 cups (24 oz, 750 g) Chinese (Napa) cabbage, cut in strips
1 canned bamboo shoot, diced
2 tablespoons soy sauce

2 tablespoons Chinese wine or sherry
salt to taste
1 teaspoon sesame oil

Soak dry mushrooms in hot water for 30 minutes, discard stems and slice mushrooms finely.

Season eggs with a little salt and pepper. Heat an omelet pan, grease lightly with a few drops of sesame oil, and pour in half the beaten egg to make a thin omelet. Repeat with remaining egg. Slice finely and set aside.

Cook noodles for 2 minutes in plenty of lightly salted boiling water. Drain in colander and run cold water through to separate. Drain again. Heat chicken stock.

Shred pork or chicken very finely. Heat peanut oil in a wok, fry garlic and ginger and discard when they are brown. Add pork or chicken to the flavored oil, fry quickly, stirring, until golden. Add vegetables, fry 2 minutes longer.

Add fried mixture and noodles to chicken stock, return to a boil. Add soy sauce, sherry, and salt to taste. Stir in sesame oil. Serve immediately, garnished with omelet strips.
Serves 6

❧⊷⊷❧

COMBINATION SOUP
China

8 oz (250 g) chicken, lean pork, or beef
6 cups (2½ pts, 1.5 L) water
1 clove garlic
2 slices fresh ginger root
1 stalk celery
2 teaspoons salt
4 oz (125 g) cooked shrimp (prawns)
3 cups (24 oz, 750 g) Chinese (Napa) cabbage, sliced
3 scallions (spring onions), cut in 2 in (5 cm) lengths
a few drops of sesame oil

Cut pork or beef into thin slices. If using chicken, use wings or thighs for preference.

Place meat in a saucepan, add water, garlic, celery, and salt and bring to a boil. Cover and simmer for 30 minutes. Remove ginger and garlic and discard.

If chicken thighs or other large joints are used, remove flesh from bones, cut and dice. Discard bones.

Add shrimp and vegetables, return to a boil for 1 minute, stir in sesame oil and serve.

You can use any combination of meat and vegetables in this soup.
Serves 4–6

Crab and corn soup from China (page 34).

CORN FRITTERS
Pergedel Jagung ♦ **Indonesia**

12 oz (375 g) whole kernel corn (fresh, frozen, or canned)
½ cup (2 oz, 60 g) all-purpose (plain) flour
½ cup ground rice
⅛ teaspoon double-acting baking powder (¼ teaspoon baking powder)
½ teaspoon salt
1 teaspoon ground coriander
½ teaspoon ground cumin
¼ teaspoon laos powder, optional
½ teaspoon chili powder, optional
1 medium onion
1 clove garlic
pinch salt
1 stalk celery
½ cup (4 fl oz, 125 ml) water
1 egg, beaten
½ teaspoon trasi (dried shrimp paste), optional
squeeze of lemon juice
oil for frying

Cut corn from cobs with a sharp knife, drain canned corn or thaw frozen corn.

Sift into a bowl the flour, ground rice, baking powder, salt, coriander, cumin, laos, and chili powder.

Quarter the onion and cut into very thin slices. Crush the garlic to a smooth paste with a little salt. Chop celery into fine dice.

Mix together the water, beaten egg, trasi, and lemon juice and add to the flour mixture, beating until smooth. Stir in the corn, onion, garlic, and celery. Heat vegetable oil in a frying pan to a depth of 1/2 in (12 mm). When oil is hot drop mixture by large tablespoons into the oil, spreading it with the back of the spoon to make a circle about 3 in (7.5 cm) across. Fry until underside of fritter is golden brown, then turn with tongs and fry other side. Lift out and drain on absorbent paper placed on a wire rack. This keeps the fritters crisp.

Note: Without the chili powder and shrimp paste the fritters are milder in taste. If ground rice is difficult to obtain use all-purpose flour, but ground rice adds crispness.
Makes 12–14

CRAB AND CORN SOUP
China

8 oz (250 g) crabmeat, fresh or frozen
1¾ pints (1 L) chicken stock
2 tablespoons cornstarch (cornflour)
10 oz (315 g) can creamed sweet corn
1 tablespoon light soy sauce
2 tablespoons Chinese wine or dry sherry
salt and white pepper to taste
2 teaspoons sesame oil
2 tablespoons finely chopped scallions (spring onion)
2 tablespoons chopped cilantro (fresh coriander leaves)

Pick the crabmeat out of its shell if using fresh cooked crab, or thaw if using frozen crab. Flake the crabmeat and discard any bony pieces.

Bring the stock to a boil. Mix the cornstarch smoothly with 3 tablespoons of cold water and stir this into the stock until it boils and thickens. Add the corn, soy sauce, wine, salt, and pepper to taste. Add the flaked crabmeat and heat through.

Turn off the heat and stir in the sesame oil. Sprinkle with chopped herbs, cover the pan with a lid for 1 minute, then serve.

Note: You can use canned abalone instead of crab. Slice the abalone thinly, then shred it finely. Add it at the last minute, only heating through, because cooking can toughen it.
Serves 6

CRAB & EGG SOUP
Hai Yook Dahn Gung ◆ China

1 large crab
6 cups (2½ pts, 1.5 L) fish or chicken stock
4 eggs, slightly beaten
2 tablespoons cornstarch (cornflour)
4 tablespoons cold water
6 scallions (spring onions), finely sliced

Cook crab in water with seasoning as for fish stock for 10 minutes, cool, then pick out flesh and reserve. Discard shell and fibrous tissue from stomach. Flake crab meat, discarding any bony tissue.

Bring stock to a boil. Slowly dribble in the beaten eggs. Stir gently. After 2 minutes stir in the cornstarch mixed smoothly with the cold water, return soup to a boil and stir constantly until it is clear and slightly thickened. Add crab meat and heat through. Serve immediately, sprinkled with scallions. Canned or frozen crab meat may be substituted if fresh crab is difficult to obtain.
Serves 5–6

CRISP FRIED SPLIT PEAS
Channa Dhal ◆ India

1 cup channa dhal (Bengal gram) or yellow split peas
2 teaspoons baking (bicarbonate of) soda
oil for deep frying
½ teaspoon chili powder or to taste
½ teaspoon garam masala
1 teaspoon salt

Wash the peas in cold water, then soak overnight in water to cover with the baking soda. Drain in a colander, rinse in fresh water and drain once more. After the peas have drained for at least 30 minutes, turn them onto absorbent paper, spread them out and leave to dry.

Heat oil in a deep frying pan and fry about 1/2 cup of split peas at a time on medium heat until they are golden. Lift out on slotted spoon and drain on absorbent paper. Repeat until all the peas are fried, then toss them in a mixture of the chili powder, garam masala, and salt. Leave to get quite cold before storing in an airtight container.
Makes approximately 2 cups

CURRY PUFFS
Sri Lanka

2 tablespoons oil or ghee
1 teaspoon finely chopped garlic
2 teaspoons finely grated fresh ginger
2 large onions, finely chopped
1 tablespoon Ceylon curry powder (page 8)
2 lb (1 kg) ground (minced) meat
2 teaspoons salt
2 tablespoons lemon juice
½ cup (4 fl oz, 125 ml) hot water
2 potatoes, diced small
6 hard-cooked (boiled) eggs
oil for deep frying

Pastry:
2 cups (8 oz, 250 g) all-purpose (plain) flour
pinch baking powder
½ teaspoon salt
1 teaspoon superfine (caster) sugar
4 oz (125 g) butter or margarine
2 tablespoons lemon juice
4–5 tablespoons iced water
1 egg white

Heat oil or ghee in a large, heavy saucepan and fry the garlic, ginger, and onions, stirring frequently, until soft and golden. Add the curry powder and fry for a minute longer. Add the meat and fry, stirring constantly, until it has lost its pinkness and no lumps remain. Add the salt, lemon juice, and water, cover and cook on low heat for 15 minutes. Add the potatoes and continue cooking for a further 15 minutes or until potatoes are tender and almost all the liquid is absorbed. Allow to cool, then mix in the chopped hard-cooked eggs.

Pastry: Sift flour, baking powder, salt, and sugar into a bowl and rub in the butter. Mix lemon juice and iced water and add to flour, mixing to a smooth dough. Add a little more water if necessary. Wrap in waxed (greaseproof) paper and chill for 30 minutes before rolling out.

Roll out a quarter of the pastry at a time on a lightly floured board. It should be very thin, about 1/8 in (3 mm). Cut into circles using a large biscuit (scone) cutter 3 1/4 in (8 cm) in diameter. Put a teaspoon of the filling on each pastry round. Wet the edges of the pastry with slightly beaten egg white, fold over to make a half circle and press edges firmly together to seal. Press with a fork or pastry cutter to make a decorative edge.

When all the curry puffs are made, fry a few at a time in deep, hot vegetable oil. Drain on absorbent paper and serve warm, or prepare ahead and heat in a moderately hot oven before serving.

Makes about 75 small puffs

Duck and lettuce soup (page 36).

DEEP-FRIED LENTIL SAVORY
Sev or Murukku ◆ India & Pakistan

1½ cups (7½ oz, 130 g) besan (chickpea flour)
¾ cup (5½ oz, 170 g) ground rice
1½ teaspoons garam masala (page 9)
½ teaspoon chili powder, optional
½ teaspoon ajowan seeds, optional
½ teaspoon cumin seeds
1½ teaspoons salt, or to taste
3 tablespoons ghee, melted
about ⅔ cup (5 fl oz, 170 ml) water
oil for deep frying

Sift chickpea flour into a large bowl, stir through the ground rice, ground spices, aromatic seeds, and salt. Rub in ghee until evenly distributed. Add water and knead to a stiff dough, about the consistency of a piped cookie (biscuit) dough. Heat oil in a deep pan until smoking hot, then put some dough into a potato slicer or mouli shredder and push through into the hot oil. Fry on medium heat until golden brown. Lift out with slotted spoon and drain on absorbent paper. Repeat until all the dough is used up. Cool, then store in an airtight container. If liked, more spice and salt can be sprinkled on the servings after cooking.

❖

DEVILED SHRIMP CANAPES
Sri Lanka

6 slices day-old white bread
oil for deep frying
1 large onion, finely chopped
1 clove garlic, finely shopped
½ teaspoon chili powder
1 teaspoon paprika
2 tablespoons tomato sauce
1 teaspoon salt
1 lb (500 g) small raw shrimp (prawns), shelled and
    deveined

With a small circular cutter, cut 4 rounds from each slice of bread. Heat oil in wok and deep fry the bread rounds, a few at a time, until golden brown. Drain on absorbent paper. Pour off oil from wok, leaving about 2 tablespoons.

Add the onions and garlic to the oil and fry on low heat, stirring frequently, until they are soft and golden. Add the chili powder, paprika, tomato sauce, salt and cook, stirring, until the mixture is a thick paste. Add the shrimp and cook, stirring, until they are done. Cool, then top each piece of bread with a shrimp.

Serve as a pre-dinner savory.
Makes about 24

DUCK AND LETTUCE SOUP
China

1¾ pints (1 L) duck stock
4 oz (125 g) diced cooked duck
salt to taste
2 tablespoons cornstarch (cornflour)
half a small lettuce
1 scallion (spring onion)
2 teaspoons white vinegar
dash of chili oil, optional
1 teaspoon sesame oil
1 teaspoon Chinese wine or dry sherry

A well-flavored stock is essential for Chinese soups. Duck stock has a distinct flavor and is made by simmering the neck and carcass of duck in water with 2 or 3 slices of fresh ginger and a scallion. This is simmered for about 2 hours to extract as much flavor as possible. Even the bones of cooked ducks can be used to make stock, which is then strained and can be frozen for future use.

Bring the stock to a boil, add the cooked duck meat and salt to taste. Mix the cornstarch smoothly with 1 tablespoon of cold water and stir this into the stock until it thickens slightly and becomes clear.

Shred the lettuce, first cutting it in two lengthwise so that the shreds will not be too long. Slice the scallion in fine diagonal slices.

Remove the soup from heat and add the lettuce, scallion, vinegar, and (optional) chili oil. Taste for seasoning, and add salt if necessary. Cover the pan and leave for 2 minutes. Then stir in sesame oil and wine, and serve the soup at once.
Serves 4

❖

DUMPLING SOUP
Mandoo ◆ Korea

9 cups (3½ pts, 2.25 L) beef stock
2 tablespoons light soy sauce
salt to taste
omelet strips to garnish
toasted, crumbled nori (dried seaweed) to garnish

Dumplings:
2 tablespoons oil
4 oz (125 g) ground (minced) pork
4 oz (125 g) lean ground (minced) beef
½ cup (4 fl oz, 125 ml) water
8 oz (250 g) fresh bean sprouts

half a small white Chinese (Napa) cabbage
1 square fresh tofu (bean curd)
3 scallions (spring onions), finely chopped
1 tablespoon toasted, crushed sesame seeds
1 clove garlic, finely chopped
½ teaspoon salt
¼ teaspoon ground black pepper
4 oz (125 g) wonton pastry

Prepare and clear beef stock. Add soy sauce and salt, have garnishes ready. Prepare dumplings, cover with plastic wrap (film) and have ready (they may be made 2 or 3 hours before required). Bring stock to a boil, drop in the dumplings one at a time, taking care they do not stick together. Depending on size of the pot, it may be necessary to cook them in two or three batches. Simmer for 10 minutes or until dumplings come to the surface and are cooked. Serve immediately in small bowls.

Dumplings: Heat oil in saucepan and fry pork and beef until turning brown. Add half cup (4 fl oz, 125 ml) water and simmer gently until liquid evaporates. Set aside. Boil bean sprouts in lightly salted water for 3 minutes, drain and chop. Boil cabbage for 5 minutes, drain well and chop finely. Mash the tofu. Mix all these ingredients with the scallions, sesame seeds, garlic, salt, and pepper. Taste for seasoning. Put a teaspoonful of the filling in the middle of each wonton pastry square, dampen edges with water and press together to form a triangle. Cover so they do not dry out before cooking.
Serves 6

EGG FLOWER SOUP
Dahn Far Tong ◆ China

4 cups (1¾ pts, 1 L) chicken stock
2 tablespoons Chinese wine or dry sherry
1 teaspoon sesame oil
salt to taste
3 eggs, beaten slightly
3 tablespoons scallions (spring onions), chopped

Bring stock to a boil, add sherry, and sesame oil. Taste and add more salt if necessary.

Season beaten eggs with 1/2 teaspoon salt, pour slowly into the boiling soup. Stir once or twice. The beaten egg will set when poured into the boiling soup and look like chrysanthemum petals. Serve at once, sprinkled with chopped scallions.
Serves 4–5

EGG ROLLS (SPRING ROLLS)
China

8 oz (225 g) pork filet
1 lb (500 g) raw shrimp (prawns)
12 water chestnuts
6 scallions (spring onions)
4 oz (125 g) bean sprouts
1 small Chinese (Napa) cabbage
3 tablespoons peanut oil
½ teaspoon crushed garlic
½ teaspoon grated fresh ginger
1 tablespoon light soy sauce
1 tablespoon oyster sauce
1 teaspoon salt
1 tablespoon cornstarch (cornflour)
1 teaspoon sesame oil
1 packet frozen egg (spring) roll pastry, thawed in wrapping
peanut oil for deep frying

Traditionally eaten on New Year's Day and again in the spring, these can be easily made at home using the frozen wrappers which are available from Chinese stores and delicatessens.

Slice the pork thinly and then cut into fine shreds. Shell, devein and finely chop the shrimp. Chop the water chestnuts and scallions. Pinch the tails from the bean sprouts. Shred crisp leaf ribs of the cabbage to give 8 oz (250 g).

Heat a wok, add half the peanut oil and fry the garlic and ginger over low heat until fragrant (do not brown). Add the pork, increase the heat and stir-fry until it loses all the pinkness. Add shrimp and continue stirring until they are cooked. Remove from the wok to a large mixing bowl.

Heat the remaining peanut oil in the wok and fry the vegetables for 2 minutes. Add the sauces and salt. Make a space in the middle and stir in cornstarch mixed with 1-2 tablespoons of cold water. Stir until the sauce boils and thickens. Remove from the wok to the pork-shrimp mixture. Add the sesame oil and mix well. Allow to cool.

Put 2–3 tablespoons of the filling in the center of each egg roll wrapper and roll it up, turning in the ends so that the filling is completely enclosed. Dampen the edges with water and press to seal.

Heat plenty of oil in a wok and fry the rolls a few at a time until golden. Drain on absorbent paper, and serve immediately with chili sauce.
Makes 20

EGG ROLLS, SINGAPORE-STYLE

6 dried Chinese mushrooms
3 tablespoons peanut oil
1 tablespoon sesame oil
½ teaspoon finely chopped garlic
½ teaspoon finely chopped fresh ginger
8 oz (250 g) finely ground (minced) pork
8 oz (250 g) raw shrimp (prawns), deveined and chopped
2 cups shredded Chinese cabbage
12 water chestnuts, chopped or 1 cup canned bamboo shoot, chopped
4 oz (125 g) bean sprouts
6 scallions (spring onions), finely chopped
1 tablespoon dark soy sauce
1 tablespoon oyster sauce
1 teaspoon salt
3 teaspoons cornstarch (cornflour)
1 packet frozen egg (spring) roll pastry
oil for deep frying

Cover mushrooms with hot water and soak for 20 minutes. Discard stems and chop mushrooms. Heat peanut and sesame oil in a wok and slowly fry garlic and ginger for a few seconds. Add pork and fry until it browns. Add shrimp and continue stir-frying until they are cooked. Add vegetables, soy sauce, oyster sauce, and salt, combine thoroughly. Push mixture to one side and tilt wok so liquid gathers. Stir in cornstarch which has been mixed with a little cold water until smooth. Cook, stirring continuously, until thick.

Remove wok from heat and mix thickened liquid through the filling. Allow to cool completely. Place 2 tablespoons of the mixture at one end of each egg roll wrapper and roll up, turning in the sides so that filling is completely enclosed. Dampen edges with water or a mixture of cornstarch and water and press to seal. Fry one or two at a time in deep hot oil until golden brown. Drain on kitchen paper and serve immediately, with chili sauce if desired.
Makes 20–24

⋖≫⋗

FARINA WAFERS
Pani Puri ◆ India & Pakistan

½ cup (3 oz, 90 g) medium fine farina (semolina)
½ cup (2 oz, 60 g) roti flour or all-purpose (plain) flour
2 teaspoons besan (chickpea flour), optional
½ teaspoon salt
½ cup (4 fl oz, 125 ml) lukewarm water
oil and ghee for deep frying

Put dry ingredients into a bowl, add all the water at once and mix to a dough. Knead hard for 10 minutes, adding very little more flour if mixture is too soft, or a few drops of water if it is too stiff. (Flours vary in absorbency and it is difficult to give an exact measure of water, but the dough should be the consistency of bread dough.) Cover dough with a small bowl or with plastic food wrap (film) and let it rest for 30 minutes at least.

Pinch off small pieces of dough and roll into balls the size of a filbert (hazelnut) without its shell. On a floured board, using a floured rolling pin, roll each one to a thin circle no more than 2 in (5 cm) in diameter. Put on a tray and cover with a damp kitchen towel to prevent drying out. Let the pastry rest for 10 to 15 minutes before starting to fry.

When all the circles are rolled out, heat the oil and ghee in a karahi or wok or frying pan to a depth of at least 2 in (5 cm). Use at least 3 tablespoons ghee to flavor the oil and wait until it is smoking hot before adding 2 or 3 pastry circles at a time. As soon as they are put into the oil, splash the hot oil over them with a frying spoon to make them puff up. Do not add too many at a time, for this brings down the temperature of the oil and results in greasy wafers. Also, it is difficult to splash oil on too many at once, and the splashing with oil is important.

As they turn golden lift them out on a slotted spoon and drain on absorbent paper laid over a cake cooler or wire rack. This helps to keep them crisp when they cool. If not serving at once, cool completely and store in an airtight tin.

To eat, push a finger through one side and drop in 2 or 3 savory chickpeas (page 247), a couple of cubes of potato and some piquant tamarind sauce. Other accompaniments are shown in the picture on page opposite.
Makes about 80

⋖≫⋗

FISH & CELLOPHANE NOODLE SOUP
Canh Bun Tau ◆ Vietnam

1 lb (500 g) white deboned fish
1 teaspoon finely grated fresh ginger
3 tablespoons fish sauce
1 teaspoon salt
½ teaspoon ground black pepper
2 oz (60 g) cellophane noodles
1½ tablespoons peanut oil
1 medium onion, thinly sliced
2 cloves garlic, crushed
2 daun salam (Indonesian curry leaf) or few curry leaves
1 teaspoon turmeric

1 teaspoon dried shrimp paste
1 teaspoon finely grated lemon rind
6 cups hot water
3 tablespoons finely sliced scallions (spring onions)

Remove skin from fish and chop flesh coarsely. Mix fish with ginger, 1 tablespoon of fish sauce, and half the salt and pepper. Set aside. Soak noodles in warm water for 15 minutes. In a large saucepan heat oil and fry onion, garlic, daun salam, until onion is soft. Stir frequently while frying. Add turmeric and dried shrimp paste and fry for another minute, crushing paste against side of pan. Add lemon rind, water, and cellophane noodles and remaining fish sauce, salt, and pepper. Boil 5 minutes, then add fish and simmer for 5 minutes longer. Remove from heat, pour into soup tureen or serving bowl, sprinkle with scallions and serve hot.

Serves 6–8

Egg rolls, Singapore-style (recipe opposite).

Farina wafers (pani puri), with some of the ingredients that may be used to stuff these delicious Indian snacks (page 38).

FISH BALLS WITH SESAME
Machchi Kofta ◆ Bengal

2 cups flaked cooked fish
1 teaspoon finely grated fresh ginger
½ teaspoon crushed garlic or garlic powder
¼ teaspoon ground cumin
⅛ teaspoon chili powder or to taste
¾ teaspoon salt
¼ teaspoon ground black pepper
1 small onion, finely chopped
2 tablespoons chopped cilantro (fresh coriander leaves),
  optional
1 egg, separated
1 tablespoon yogurt
2 tablespoons sesame seeds
4 tablespoons dry breadcrumbs
oil for deep frying

Leftover curried fish is ideal for this, or any cooked fish will do. Carefully remove all skin and bones and mix the flaked fish with the ginger, garlic, cumin, chili, salt, pepper, onion, cilantro (if used), egg yolk, and yogurt. If the fish is very moist, the yogurt may not be necessary, and in fact it may be replaced with a tablespoon or two of soft breadcrumbs. Use your discretion about this, the mixture should be of a good molding consistency.

Form into small balls and roll these first in the slightly beaten egg white, then in the sesame seeds and breadcrumbs mixed together. Deep fry in hot oil until golden brown. Drain on absorbent paper and serve warm.
Makes about 24

FISH BROTH
Sakana Ushiojiru ◆ Japan

1 lb (500 g) bones, head and trimmings of any delicate fish
6 cups (2½ pts, 1.5 L) water
2 slices fresh ginger
1 scallion (spring onion) cut into 4 pieces
1 tablespoon Japanese soy sauce
1 tablespoon sake
salt to taste
3 tablespoons finely sliced scallions (spring onions)
4 slices raw fish, optional

Put fish into saucepan with water, ginger, and cut scallion. Bring to a boil, reduce heat and simmer, skimming surface as necessary.

Cook for 10 to 15 minutes, then cool slightly and strain into a clean pan and stir in soy sauce, sake, and salt. To serve, heat soup to boiling and stir in sliced scallions. Remove from heat immediately and serve. If desired, a thin slice of raw fish can be put in each bowl and the boiling broth ladled over.
Serves 4

FISH COOKED IN COCONUT
Machchi Molee ◆ India

1 lb (500 g) firm fish filets or steaks
½ teaspoon ground turmeric
1 teaspoon salt
1 tablespoon ghee or oil
1 medium onion, finely sliced
2 cloves garlic, finely chopped
1 teaspoon finely grated fresh ginger
8 curry leaves
2 or 3 fresh red or green chilies, slit and seeded
2 cups thin coconut cream
1 cup thick coconut cream
lime or lemon juice to taste

Wash the fish, rub with turmeric and salt, and set aside. In a saucepan heat the oil and fry the onions, garlic, ginger, curry leaves, and chilies until onions are soft. Keep stirring and do not let them brown. Add the thin coconut cream and stir while it comes to simmering point. Add the fish and bring slowly to simmer, cook uncovered for 10 minutes. Add thick coconut milk, heat through and remove from heat before adding lemon juice and salt to taste. Serve with white rice.
Serves 4

FISH SOUP WITH NOODLES
Yue Tong Min ◆ China

1 tablespoon peanut oil
1 clove garlic, crushed
1 teaspoon finely chopped fresh ginger root
6 cups (2½ pts, 1.5 L) fish stock (page 6)
1 lb (500 g) deboned white fish
2–3 bundles egg noodles, boiled
few drops sesame oil
2 tablespoons chopped cilantro (fresh coriander leaves)

Heat oil in a saucepan and fry garlic and ginger over low heat for a few seconds. Add fish stock and bring slowly to a boil. Add fish cut into bite-size pieces, cook 5 minutes, then add noodles and return to a boil. Stir in sesame oil and garnish with cilantro. Serve at once.
Serves 5–6

FRIED PASTRY TIDBITS
Nimki ◆ India

2 cups (8 oz, 250 g) all-purpose (plain) flour
1 teaspoon salt
½ teaspoon chili powder
½ teaspoon ground cumin
½ teaspoon ajowan seeds
1 teaspoon black cumin seeds
1 teaspoon garam masala
3 tablespoons melted ghee
approximately ¼ cup (2 fl oz, 60 ml) cold water
oil for deep frying

Sift flour and salt, chili powder and ground cumin, into a bowl. Stir through the ajowan seeds, black cumin seeds, and garam masala. Rub the melted ghee into the flour, then add enough cold water to mix to a firm dough and knead for 10 minutes until smooth and elastic. Cover and leave aside for 30 minutes.

Roll out small portions of the dough on a lightly floured board until very thin. Cut into finger-size strips and fry a few at a time in hot oil until golden. Drain on absorbent paper. Serve warm, or allow to get quite cold and store in an airtight container. If desired, more salt and garam masala may be sprinkled over the strips before serving.
Serves 6–8

FRIED PORK & CRAB ROLLS
Cha Gio ◆ Vietnam

½ cup soaked cellophane noodles
1 small onion, finely chopped
6 scallions (spring onions), finely chopped
8 oz (250 g) ground (minced) pork
6 oz (185 g) crab meat, frozen or canned
½ teaspoon salt
1 tablespoon fish sauce
¼ teaspoon ground black pepper
half packet Chinese egg (spring) roll wrappers
oil for deep frying
lettuce leaves
fresh mint, parsley or cilantro (fresh coriander leaves)
strips of cucumber
garlic, chili, and fish sauce or nuoc cham (page 14)

Soak a small amount of cellophane noodles in hot water for 10 minutes, then drain and measure 1/2 cup. Cut into 1 in (2.5 cm) lengths with a sharp knife. Put into a bowl with the onion, scallions, pork, flaked crab meat (pick out any bits of bony tissue), salt, fish sauce, and pepper. Mix well.

Cut each egg roll wrapper in half and put 2 teaspoons of filling on one end, shaping it into a neat roll. Roll up, turning in the sides so that the filling is completely enclosed. Moisten edge of wrapper with a little water or egg white to stick. When all the rolls are made, heat oil in a wok and fry a few at a time on medium heat until they are crisp and golden. Do not have oil too hot or the filling will not cook through. Drain on absorbent paper.

To serve: Wrap each roll in a lettuce leaf including a small sprig of mint, parsley or cilantro and a strip of cucumber. Dip in nuoc cham and eat right away.

Vietnamese rice papers are very difficult to buy, but it is worth trying the recipe using Chinese egg roll wrappers which are sold in many Oriental stores.
Makes about 24

FRIED SCALLOP ROLLS
China

6 oz (185 g) scallops
3 dried Chinese mushrooms
6 water chestnuts, canned or fresh
2 French shallots
½ teaspoon finely grated fresh ginger root
½ teaspoon salt
1 teaspoon light soy sauce
1 teaspoon sesame oil
5 or 6 egg (spring) roll wrappers
1 egg
1½ tablespoons all-purpose (plain) flour
peanut oil for deep frying

Beard scallops, rinse and drain on kitchen paper, then cut into small pieces. Soak mushrooms in hot water 30 minutes, cut off and discard stems, chop mushrooms finely. Chop water chestnuts roughly, leaving pieces large enough to provide a crunchy texture in the filling. Chop shallots finely. Mix these ingredients with the ginger, salt, soy sauce, and sesame oil.

Cut each egg roll wrapper into quarters. On each quarter place a teaspoonful of the filling, near one end. Fold pastry over filling, then fold sides in to enclose filling, and roll over again as for the first fold. Beat egg until frothy, add flour and beat again to a smooth, thick paste. Smear end of egg roll pastry with this paste and press gently to seal.

When all are made, fry in deep oil over medium heat until golden brown all over, about 1 1/2 minutes. Drain on absorbent paper and serve hot.
Makes approximately 20–24

FRIED SHRIMP BALLS
Burma

1 lb (500 g) raw shelled deveined shrimp (prawns)
2 medium onions
2 fresh green or pickled chilies
3 tablespoons chopped cilantro (fresh coriander leaves)
¼ teaspoon ground turmeric
½ teaspoon garlic, crushed
1 teaspoon salt, or to taste
¼ teaspoon ground black pepper
all-purpose (plain) flour
oil for frying

Chop very finely the shrimp, onions, chilies and cilantro and mix well with the turmeric, garlic, salt, and black pepper. Shape into 1 in (2.5 cm) balls and roll in flour to coat.

Heat 2 cups oil in a wok and fry balls for 2 minutes. Drain and serve immediately.
Serves 4

❖

GANGHWE
Korea

2 eggs, separated
sesame oil
12 oz (375 g) filet of beef
½ teaspoon finely grated fresh ginger
1 teaspoon finely chopped or crushed garlic
1 teaspoon finely chopped spring onion
1 teaspoon sesame oil
1–2 teaspoons toasted, crushed sesame seed
4 teaspoons light soy sauce
2 teaspoons honey or sugar
¼ teaspoon ground black pepper
thin strips of silgochu (dry red chili)
very fine young scallions (spring onions) or large chives

Beat egg yolks and whites separately with a fork. Lightly grease a heavy frying pan with oil and pour in the beaten yolks. Swirl frying pan to make a paper-thin omelet; when set, turn and lightly cook other side. Turn onto a plate. Repeat with white of eggs. Cut yellow and white omelets into fine strips. Slice beef into very fine shreds, marinate in seasonings for 20 minutes, then stir-fry in heated wok without any oil or cook on an ungreased pre-heated griddle for just a few minutes.

Cut off white portion of scallions and save for salads, etc. Pour boiling water over scallion leaves to make them pliable. Drain off water after 1 minute, then make little bundles of egg strips, beef strips, and strips of chili. Bind them tightly with the scallion leaves, leaving strips of egg and beef showing at either end. Dip in sesame seed sauce which is made by mixing 1/2 cup toasted, crushed sesame seeds with 1 tablespoon sugar, 3 tablespoons vinegar and 4 tablespoons light soy sauce.

❖

GLAZED CHICKEN WINGS
China

1½ lb (750 g) chicken wings
3 scallions (spring onions), cut into 2 in (5 cm) lengths
1 teaspoon grated fresh ginger
4 tablespoons Chinese wine or dry sherry
5 tablespoons dark soy sauce
2 teaspoons lump sugar, crushed
¼ teaspoon ground Sichuan pepper
1 tablespoon sesame oil

Remove the tips from the chicken wings and divide the wings at the joint. Put the wings into a saucepan of water to cover, and bring to a boil.

Drain, return the wings to the saucepan and add all other ingredients except sesame oil. Bring to a boil, then reduce the heat and simmer covered for 20 minutes, or until the chicken meat is tender. Turn the wings occasionally so that they are evenly coated with the sauce.

Remove the chicken wings to a plate. Reduce the sauce by cooking uncovered until thick. Turn off the heat, return the wings to the saucepan, sprinkle with the sesame oil and leave to cool. Serve at room temperature.
Serves 4–6

❖

GOLDEN CUTTLEFISH BALLS
China

3 oz (75 g) very tiny bread cubes
1 lb (500 g) cleaned cuttlefish (or squid)
1 teaspoon salt
1 teaspoon sugar
1 teaspoon sesame oil
4 cups (1¾ pts, 1 L) oil for deep frying

Dipping Sauce:
½ cup (4 fl oz, 125 ml) white vinegar
½ cup (4 fl oz, 125 ml) water or pineapple juice
2 tablespoons sugar
1 tablespoon tomato purée

½ teaspoon salt
1 teaspoon cornstarch (cornflour)

To prepare the bread cubes, trim the crusts off several thin slices of day-old bread and cut into thin strips, then into tiny dice no more than 1/8 in (4 mm) each way.

Wash the cuttlefish well and remove any of the fine membrane that may be clinging to the flesh. Chop the cuttlefish finely or grind (mince) in food processor using steel chopping blade. Transfer to a bowl and mix in the salt, sugar, and sesame oil. Take teaspoons of the mixture and roll into small balls about 3/4 in (2 cm) in diameter.

Spread the bread cubes on a sheet of paper and roll the cuttlefish balls in them until they are covered.

Heat the oil and deep fry the balls, a few at a time, until golden; do not overcook. Drain on absorbent paper and serve warm, with sauce for dipping if desired.

Dipping Sauce: Heat vinegar, water (or pineapple juice), sugar, tomato purée, and salt in a small saucepan. When boiling, stir in the cornstarch mixed smoothly with 1 tablespoon of cold water. Cook, stirring, until it boils and becomes thick and clear.

Note: Squid may be substituted for cuttlefish. And if a hot sauce is preferred, serve a dip of bottled chili sauce.
Serves 6

HEARTY NOODLE SOUP
Nabeyaki Udon ◆ Japan

6 shiitake (dried mushrooms)
1 lb (500 g) udon (thick wheat noodles)
1 can kamaboko (fish cakes)
1 large chicken breast
2 scallions (spring onions)
6 cups soup for noodles (page 66)
fried shrimp (prawns) to garnish

Soak the mushrooms in very hot water for 30 minutes. Remove stems and slice caps thinly. Bring a large saucepan of water to a boil and add the noodles. Return water to a boil, add 1 cup (8 fl oz, 250 ml) cold water. Bring to a boil again and cook until noodles are just tender, being careful not to overcook. Drain in colander and run cold water over the noodles to cool. Drain well.

Slice the fish cakes. Bone chicken breast and cut into thin bite-size slices. Cut scallions into thin diagonal slices. Bring the soup for noodles to a boil, add mushrooms and chicken and simmer for 3 minutes. Add noodles and heat through, then garnish top with fish cake, fried shrimp and scallions, cover and allow a further minute or so for the shrimp to heat through. Serve immediately.
Serves 6

LAOTIAN FISH SOUP
Kang Som Pa ◆ Cambodia & Laos

1 lb (500 g) freshwater fish
4 cups (1¾ pts, 1 L) water
1 stalk lemon grass, bruised, or 2 strips lemon rind
½ teaspoon salt
2 tablespoons fish sauce
2 medium tomatoes, quartered
4 scallions (spring onions), finely sliced
1 tablespoon chopped cilantro (fresh coriander leaves)
lemon juice to taste

Buy the fish cleaned and scaled, then cut it into slices. Bring water to a boil with lemon grass and salt and let it simmer for 10 minutes. Then add the fish and the fish sauce and return to a boil. Add tomatoes and simmer gently, uncovered, for 10 minutes. Remove from heat, discard lemon grass or lemon rind and add the scallions and cilantro. Add lemon juice. Taste and add more fish sauce or salt if necessary. Serve hot.
Serves 4–6

LENTIL & RICE PANCAKES
Thosai ◆ South India

1½ cups (10½ oz, 333 g) uncooked rice
¾ cup urad dhal (black gram dhal)
2 teaspoons salt
1½ teaspoons sugar
2 teaspoons ghee or oil
½ teaspoon black mustard seeds
1 small onion, finely chopped
1 fresh green chili, seeded and chopped

Wash rice and urad dhal separately and soak each in cold water to cover for 8 hours. Drain and grind rice in electric blender, adding just enough water to facilitate blending. Strain through a fine sieve and discard rough residue, if any.

Rinse blender and grind the urad dhal, adding a little cold water as necessary. This should not need straining, as urad dhal blends more easily than rice. Combine urad dhal and rice and mix well, adding salt and sugar. Cover and leave to ferment in a warm place for 2 or 3 hours.

Heat ghee or oil in small saucepan and fry the mustard seeds until they pop. Add onion and chili and fry, stirring now and then, until the onions start to color. Remove from heat and when cool stir into the batter. The batter should be of a thick pouring consistency. Thin it down if necessary with a little cold water.

Heat a tawa, heavy frying pan or pancake pan and grease

with very little ghee or oil. Pour in about 1/3 cup of batter, or just enough to cover base of pan thinly. The trick is to spread the batter very quickly with the back of the ladle or metal cup used for pouring. Allow to cook on low heat until the bottom is well browned. Turn over and cook other side. Serve with coconut chatni (see page 20) and a vegetable preparation such as spicy fried potatoes (page 279).

Makes about 18

⋙⋘

LENTIL & VEGETABLE SOUP
Sambar ◆ South India

1 cup (6 oz, 185 g) mattar ki dhal (split peas), masoor dhal (red lentils) or toor dhal (red gram lentils)
6 cups (2½ pts, 1.5 L) water
1 tablespoon tamarind pulp or 1 teaspoon instant tamarind
1 cup (8 fl oz, 250 ml) hot water
2 tablespoons oil
1 tablespoon ground coriander
2 teaspoons ground cumin
½ teaspoon ground black pepper
½ teaspoon chili powder
½ teaspoon ground turmeric
⅛ teaspoon asafoetida
3 cups mixed vegetables; eggplants, marrow, beans, pumpkin, cubed
2 fresh green chilies, seeded and sliced
2½ teaspoons salt
½ teaspoon black mustard seeds
1 small onion, finely sliced

Wash the dhal well and soak overnight, or for 2 hours. Drain and put in a saucepan with the water and simmer until soft. Soak tamarind pulp in hot water and squeeze to dissolve the pulp. Strain, discarding seeds and fibers. Alternatively, dissolve instant tamarind in hot water. Add tamarind liquid to lentils.

In another pan heat 1 tablespoon oil and fry the ground spices and asafoetida on low heat, stirring, for a minute or two. Pour the dhal mixture into this pan, add the vegetables and chilies and simmer until vegetables are cooked.

Heat remaining tablespoon oil in small saucepan and fry the mustard seeds and sliced onion until seeds pop and onion is brown. Add to the soup, simmer a few minutes longer and serve. Sambar should be fairly thick, with a pronounced sour and hot flavor. Serve with rice.

Serves 6

LENTIL SOUP WITH COCONUT
Amti ◆ India (Maharashtra)

¾ cup toor dhal (red gram lentils) or mattar ki dhal (split peas)
½ teaspoon ground turmeric
8 cups (64 fl oz, 2 L) water
1½ teaspoons salt
1 cup (8 fl oz, 250 ml) hot water
1 tablespoon tamarind pulp or 1 teaspoon instant tamarind
2 teaspoons brown sugar or jaggery (palm sugar)
1 tablespoon ghee or oil
½ teaspoon black mustard seeds
8 curry leaves
3 fresh green chilies, seeded and chopped
1 teaspoon crushed garlic
2 tablespoons unsweetened desiccated coconut

Garnish:
1 tablespoon chopped cilantro (fresh coriander leaves), optional

Wash dhal well and put into a saucepan with the turmeric and 8 cups water. Bring to a boil, cover and cook until dhal is very soft, about 1 hour. If water reduces to less than 5 cups (2 pts, 1.25 L), add more. Add salt. Pour 1 cup hot water over tamarind pulp, leave to soak for 5 minutes, then squeeze to dissolve the pulp or stir instant tamarind into water until dissolved. Strain liquid into the boiling dhal mixture and discard seeds and fibers. Add sugar or jaggery.

In another saucepan heat ghee or oil and fry the mustard seeds, curry leaves, and chilies until the mustard seeds pop. Add the garlic and stir for 1 minute or until garlic is golden. Add the coconut and the dhal mixture and simmer another 5 minutes. Sprinkle with cilantro (if used) and serve hot as a soup or as an accompaniment to rice and curry.

Serves 6

⋙⋘

Ingredients for the popular Chinese appetizer of lettuce rolls with pork and shrimp (sang choy bao) (page 46). On the right, a small bowl of shark fin soup (page 60).

LETTUCE ROLLS WITH PORK AND SHRIMPS
Sang Choy Bao ◆ China

2 tablespoons peanut oil
2 tablespoons pine nuts
1 teaspoon crushed garlic
1 teaspoon finely grated fresh ginger
8 oz (250 g) ground (minced) pork
2 tablespoons hot water
4 oz (125 g) raw shrimp (prawns), finely chopped
2 teaspoons bean sauce (mor sze jeung)
2 teaspoons oyster sauce
1 teaspoon hoi sin sauce
1 teaspoon red bean curd
1 teaspoon white sugar
¼ cup (1 oz, 30 g) chopped bamboo shoot
1 scallion (spring onion), finely chopped
1 teaspoon cornstarch (cornflour)
1 tablespoon cold water
12 lettuce cups

Heat peanut oil in a wok and on gentle heat fry the pine nuts until golden. Lift out on slotted spoon and drain on absorbent paper. Raise heat and when wok and oil are very hot add the garlic and ginger, stir quickly and almost immediately add the pork. Stir-fry until the pork has lost every trace of pinkness. Add the hot water, cover and cook for a few minutes so that pork is well done.

When liquid has evaporated add the shrimp and stir-fry for 1 minute, mix together all the sauces, bean curd, and sugar then add to wok. Stir and cook for 1 minute, mixing the seasonings well through the pork and shrimp. Add bamboo shoot and scallion and stir until heated through. Push ingredients to side of wok and thicken any remaining liquid with the cornstarch mixed smoothly with cold water, allowing it to boil for 1 minute. Remove from heat and mix the pine nuts through. Serve the savory mixture in a bowl, accompanied by crisp lettuce cups on a separate platter.

The rolls are meant to be assembled and eaten using the fingers. Put a spoonful of filling in one of the lettuce cups, roll up and eat it rather like a spring roll without pastry.
Serves 4–6

LONG RICE SOUP
Khao Poun ◆ Cambodia & Laos

¾ cup (4 oz, 125 g) soaked cellophane noodles
½ teaspoon salt
5 cups (2 pts, 1.25 L) boiling water or chicken stock
4 oz (125 g) finely ground (minced) pork
⅓ cup finely chopped smoked ham
1 tablespoon chopped water chestnuts
½ teaspoon cornstarch (cornflour)
2 teaspoons light soy sauce
1 teaspoon finely chopped scallions (spring onions)

Soak noodles in cold water for 30 minutes. Drain and cut into 6 in (15 cm) lengths. Add to boiling water with salt and boil for 20 minutes. Mix pork, ham, water chestnuts, cornstarch, and soy sauce, shape into small balls and drop into the soup. Return to a boil for 10 minutes. Do not stir. Add scallions and serve immediately.
Serves 4–6

LONG SOUP WITH LARGE SHRIMP (KING PRAWNS)
China

1 lb (500 g) large raw shrimp (prawns)
8 Chinese dried mushrooms
8 oz (250 g) fine egg noodles
6 cups (2½ pts, 1.5 L) fish or shrimp (prawn) stock (page 6)
salt to taste
3 cups (24 oz, 750 g) Chinese (Napa) cabbage, shredded
1 teaspoon sesame oil
2 tablespoons peanut oil
1 clove garlic, crushed
½ teaspoon fresh ginger root, finely grated
2 tablespoons soy sauce
1 teaspoon cornstarch (cornflour)
4 tablespoons cold water

Shell and devein shrimp, leaving tails on. Soak mushrooms 30 minutes in hot water, discard stems and slice mushrooms finely. Cook noodles in lightly salted boiling water. Rinse in cold water and drain. Bring stock to a boil, add cabbage and noodles and stir in sesame oil. Turn off heat and leave while cooking shrimp.

Heat peanut oil in a wok, gently fry garlic and ginger for a few seconds, add shrimp and toss on high heat, stirring constantly for 2 to 3 minutes or until they turn pink. Add mushrooms and toss.

Long soup with large shrimp (king prawns) (page 46).

Combine soy, cornstarch, and water until a smooth liquid and add to pan. Stir until it boils and thickens, about 1 minute. Ladle the hot soup into bowls, put a portion of shrimp on top of each soup and serve immediately.

Serves 5–6

⬦⬥⬦

MEAT-FILLED PASTRIES
Empanadas ◆ The Philippines

Pastry:
2 cups (8 oz, 250 g) all-purpose (plain) flour
½ teaspoon salt
½ cup (4 fl oz, 125 ml) water
1 tablespoon sugar
1 egg yolk, beaten
¼ cup (2 oz, 60 g) melted butter or margarine
1 egg white, lightly beaten
lard or oil for deep frying

Filling:
3 rashers bacon
1 tablespoon shortening (lard) or oil
2 cloves garlic, finely chopped
1 medium onion, finely chopped
8 oz (250 g) ground (minced) pork and veal, or Spanish sausage, finely chopped
4 oz (125 g) finely chopped raw chicken
¾ teaspoon salt
¼ teaspoon ground black pepper
2 tablespoons tomato sauce
3 hard-cooked (boiled) eggs, chopped
2 tablespoons chopped pickled gherkins

Pastry: Sift flour and salt into a bowl. Mix together water, sugar, and egg yolk. Make a well in the middle of the flour and pour in the mixture, then blend and knead until smooth. Leave to rest for 15 minutes. Roll out half the pastry very thinly on a lightly floured board and brush with half the melted butter. Roll up pastry to a long, thin roll, making sure it is rolled tightly and firmly. Cut into slices about 1 in (2.5 cm) thick and roll each slice out again to a circle about the size of a small saucer.

Put a spoonful of filling on each, brush edges of pastry with lightly beaten egg white, fold to a half circle shape and press edges firmly together to seal. Decorate with tines of a fork. Repeat with remaining pastry and filling.

Heat shortening or oil in a deep frying pan and when moderately hot fry the empanadas, a few at a time, until golden brown. Drain well on absorbent paper and serve warm.

Filling: Remove rind, chop bacon into small pieces and fry until fat runs. Remove bacon from pan, add shortening or oil and fry garlic and onion over low heat until soft and golden. Increase heat, add meats and fry, stirring, until browned. Add salt, pepper, and tomato sauce, stir well. Lower heat, cover and cook for 15 minutes. Stir in hard-cooked eggs and pickled gherkins and allow to cool before filling pastry. Taste, and add more seasoning if necessary.

Makes about 2 dozen

⋘⋙

MELON & DRIED SHRIMP SOUP
Kang Kung ◆ Cambodia & Laos

½ cup dried shrimp (prawns)
6 dried Chinese mushrooms
1 lb (500 g) soup melon (any variety) or cucumbers
8 cups (64 fl oz, 2 L) chicken stock
1–2 tablespoons fish sauce
6 thin slices fresh ginger
2 tablespoons Chinese wine or dry sherry

Soak dried shrimp in water overnight. Soak mushrooms in hot water for 30 minutes, cut off and discard stems, slice mushroom caps finely. Peel melon and discard middle spongy portion with seeds. Cut melon flesh into bite-size pieces. Put stock, fish sauce, ginger, mushrooms, and dried shrimp into a saucepan, bring to a boil and simmer for at least 30 minutes. Discard ginger slices. Add melon or cucumber and simmer for 5 minutes longer. Serve hot.

Serves 6

⋘⋙

MILD SOUP
Hin Cho ◆ Burma

You can use any of the following vegetables: marrow, peeled and cut in thin strips; zucchini (aubergine), cut thinly in discs; pumpkin, diced; okra (ladies fingers), topped and tailed and sliced diagonally; cauliflower, each floweret sliced lengthwise; cabbage, shredded finely; Chinese (Napa) cabbage or other leaves, shredded crossways.

4–6 cups (1¾– 2½ pts, 1–1.5 L) stock or water
2 medium onions, peeled and sliced finely
1 tablespoon powdered dried shrimp (prawns) or 3 whole fresh shrimp
3 peppercorns
¼ teaspoon ngapi (dried shrimp paste), optional
2 to 3 cups prepared vegetables

Bring stock or water to a boil. Add onions, shrimp powder, peppercorns, and ngapi paste and boil for a further 5 minutes. Last of all add half cup of the vegetable chosen to each cup (8 fl oz, 250 ml) of water or stock. Pumpkin and cauliflower may take about 5 minutes to cook sufficiently, but other vegetables should be done in about 3 minutes. Add salt if necessary.

Serves 4–6

⋘⋙

MOCK BIRD'S NEST SOUP
China

1 oz (30 g) dried fish maw
1 chicken breast
2 egg whites
2½ pints (1.5 L) chicken stock
salt to taste
4 tablespoons cornstarch (cornflour)
4 tablespoons finely chopped canned water chestnuts
3 tablespoons finely chopped ham

Soak the fish maw in very hot water and put a weight on top to hold it down. When cool, squeeze out all the water and cut into fine shreds.

Remove skin and bones from the chicken breast, scrape to a fine paste, as in the recipe for Chicken Velvet Fu Yung (page 143), adding 4 teaspoons (20 ml) of cold water to lighten, then folding in the stiffly beaten egg whites.

Bring the chicken stock to a boil, add salt to taste. Add the shredded fish maw and simmer for 5 minutes. Mix the cornstarch with 1 tablespoon (15 ml) of cold water to a smooth consistency and stir it into the stock until it thickens slightly

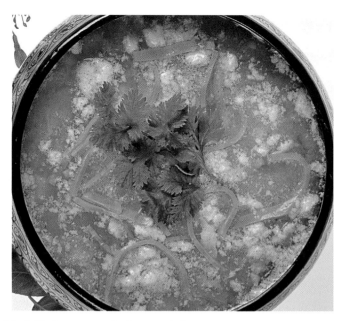

Mock bird's nest soup (recipe opposite).

and becomes clear. Add the water chestnuts. Stir in the chicken velvet then remove from the heat. Ladle into a tureen, sprinkle the ham over, and serve.

Note: Fish maw (stomach lining), available from Chinese produce stores, is a texture ingredient so use strongly flavored ham to add interest.

Serves 6

MULLIGATAWNY
India & Pakistan

2 lb (1 kg) stewing steak (gravy beef)
2 lb (1 kg) soup bones
6 cardamom pods
1 tablespoon curry leaves
2 tablespoons coriander seeds
1 tablespoon cumin seeds
3 cloves garlic
12 black peppercorns
2 teaspoons salt
1 tablespoon tamarind pulp or 2 tablespoons lemon juice
1 onion
3 whole cloves

For finishing:
1 tablespoon ghee
2 onions, finely sliced
½ teaspoon black mustard seed
8 curry leaves
3 cups thin coconut cream
salt to taste

Put beef and bones in a large saucepan with sufficient water to cover. Add cardamom pods, curry leaves, coriander, and cumin seeds, garlic, peppercorns, salt, tamarind pulp, and whole onion studded with cloves.

Bring to a boil, reduce heat and simmer gently for 1 1/2 to 2 hours or until beef is tender and stock is reduced. Cool slightly. Remove beef and bones from stock, discard bones. Cut beef into small dice and reserve. Pour stock through a fine strainer; there should be approximately 6 cups of stock.

To finish: Heat ghee and fry onion until dark brown. Add mustard seed and curry leaves and stir a minute or two. Pour hot stock into pan. (It will hiss and spit, so be careful.)

Simmer for 5 minutes. Just before serving, add coconut cream. Season to taste with salt. If tamarind pulp is not used, add lemon juice. Return diced beef to pan. Heat but do not boil. Serve hot.
Serves 8–10

MUSHROOM, PORK & CHICKEN SAUSAGE
Doong Gwoo Lap Cheong Jing Ju Yook ◆ China

8 dried Chinese mushrooms
1 lb (500 g) chicken breast
4 oz (125 g) barbecued pork
1 canned bamboo shoot or small can water chestnuts
1 large clove garlic, crushed
1 teaspoon salt
½ teaspoon finely grated fresh ginger
2 tablespoons light soy sauce
1 tablespoon Chinese wine or dry sherry
¼ teaspoon pepper
1 teaspoon sugar
3 teaspoons cornstarch (cornflour)
1 tablespoon sesame oil
1 tablespoon barbecue sauce
length of sausage skin, large size

Soak mushrooms in hot water for 30 minutes. Cut off stems with sharp knife and keep for adding to stock, or discard. Chop mushroom caps finely. Bone and skin the breast of chicken and cut flesh into small dice. Dice barbecued pork. Drain bamboo shoot or water chestnuts and chop finely. Crush garlic with the salt, mix ginger and garlic together, and add to all the chopped ingredients. Add soy sauce, wine, pepper, sugar, cornstarch, sesame oil, and barbecue sauce, and combine ingredients and seasonings thoroughly.

Using a funnel, push filling into the sausage skin. Tie a knot in the skin about 3 ft (1 m) from where you start. When you have filled the skin you will have a handsome sausage, which you coil around and put on a wire rack. Prick the sausage with a very fine sharp skewer to prevent bursting. Put the rack over a roasting tray with an inch (2.5 cm) of hot water in it. Roast in a moderate oven for 25 minutes, turn over and roast until brown on the other side too. Cut into short lengths to serve. If desired, you can twist the sausage skin at intervals, while filling, to form small sausages.

Note: Try to buy barbecued pork with a fair amount of fat on it. When buying the sausage skin from your butcher, emphasize that you need the large one. (My butcher once gave me the small size by mistake, and you should have seen the fun I had getting the filling in.) The skin should be thoroughly cleaned and ready for use, but you can soak it in salted water at home while preparing the filling, then fit one end of it on the cold water tap and run water through it.

Serves 8–10

⋘⋙

MUSHROOM SOUP WITH CILANTRO
Kang Hed Say Hom Pom ◆ **Cambodia & Laos**

1 lb (500 g) fresh mushrooms
1 small white onion, finely chopped
1 tablespoon butter or ghee
1 tablespoon vegetable oil
1 teaspoon ground coriander
½ teaspoon ground cumin
1 teaspoon salt
¼ teaspoon ground black pepper
2½ cups (20 fl oz, 600 ml) hot water
3 chicken stock cubes, optional
3½ cups (28 fl oz, 875 ml) milk or thin coconut cream
3 teaspoons cornstarch (cornflour)
1 tablespoon cold water
2 tablespoons chopped cilantro (fresh coriander leaves)

Chop mushroom stems finely. Cut caps into thin slices, then cut across two or three times, depending on size of mushrooms. Chop onion finely. Melt butter or ghee and oil in saucepan large enough to hold the amount of liquid. Add onion and fry gently for 5 minutes, stirring frequently. Add mushrooms, coriander, and cumin and continue to stir for a few minutes. Add salt and pepper, then cover saucepan, turn heat very low and allow to cook for 10 minutes, lifting lid and stirring two or three times. Add hot water and stock cubes and bring to a boil. Simmer 10 minutes. Add coconut cream and return to boil, stirring occasionally. Mix cornstarch with cold water and add to soup off the heat, then return to heat and stir constantly until it boils and thickens. Serve immediately, sprinkled with cilantro.

Serves 8

NINE SNACKS
Guchulpan ◆ **Korea**

Pancakes:
1½ cups (6 oz, 185 g) all-purpose (plain) flour
¼ teaspoon salt
2 eggs, beaten
1 cup (8 fl oz, 250 ml) milk
1 cup (8 fl oz, 250 ml) water
vegetable oil for frying
few pine nuts and parsley sprigs, optional

Fillings:
10 dried Chinese mushrooms
3 eggs, separated
8 oz (250 g) filet of beef
vegetable or sesame oil for frying
soy sauce to taste
ground black pepper to taste
3 tender carrots
salt to taste
12 scallions (spring onions)
1 daikon (giant white radish)
8 oz (250 g) zucchini (courgettes)
sprinkle of sugar

Dipping Sauce:
¾ cup (6 fl oz, 180 ml) soy sauce
3 tablespoons mild vinegar
3 tablespoons crushed, toasted sesame seeds
2 tablespoons finely chopped scallions (spring onions)

Pancakes: Sift flour and salt into a bowl. Mix beaten eggs with milk and water. Make a well in the middle of the flour and add liquid, stirring rapidly with a wooden spoon. Beat until smooth and let the batter stand while preparing fillings.

Heat a large frying pan and grease very lightly with oil. Pour in a ladle of the batter, sufficient to make a fairly thin pancake. Cook on medium-low heat so pancake does not brown. Turn and cook other side, then turn onto a large board. When all the pancakes have been made, cut into small circles with a 3 in (7.5 cm) round pastry or cookie (biscuit) cutter and pile pancakes on a tray or dish. Decorate with a few pine nuts and a sprig of parsley if desired.

Fillings: Soak dried mushrooms in hot water for 30 minutes.

Beat egg yolks and egg whites separately and cook separately in a lightly greased frying pan to make large, flat omelets. Do not allow to brown. Turn out on plate or board and allow to cool, then shred into very fine strips.

Shred the beef very finely. It is easier to do this if the beef is partially frozen first. Heat about a tablespoon of oil in a pan and stir-

Nine snacks (guchulpan) from Korea (recipe opposite).

fry the beef, adding soy sauce and ground black pepper to taste. Beef should be well done and any liquid should be evaporated.

Scrape the carrots, cut into very thin slices, then cut slices into thin shreds, finer than matchsticks. Stir-fry in very little oil, adding salt and pepper to taste. Cut scallions into similar size lengths and stir-fry briefly. Peel and shred radish and stir-fry until wilted. Season with salt. The aim is to keep the natural color of the vegetables so cook for only a short time and do not allow anything to brown. Do not peel zucchini — the green skin adds to the appearance of the dish. Slice finely, then cut into fine strips and stir-fry for a few minutes, season with salt.

Squeeze out water from the mushrooms, cut off and discard tough stalks, then shred the caps into thin slices. Heat very little oil and stir-fry, then add soy sauce and pepper and a sprinkling of sugar and half cup (4 fl oz, 125 ml) of the water the mushrooms soaked in. Cover and cook 15 to 20 minutes or until mushrooms are tender and liquid absorbed.

Arrange all the filling ingredients in separate piles around the edge of a plate or in a compartmented tray, leaving the middle for the pancakes.

Dipping Sauce: Blend together ingredients and divide between individual sauce bowls.

Serves 6 as a main dish, 12 as an appetizer

⊰≫⋈≪⊱

OXTAIL SOUP
Gorigomtang ◆ Korea

3 lb (1.5 kg) oxtail, jointed
8 cups (64 fl oz, 2 L) water
2 slices fresh ginger
1 teaspoon salt

Sauce:
3 tablespoons light soy sauce
1 tablespoon sesame oil
1 tablespoon toasted, crushed sesame seeds
¼ teaspoon ground black pepper
3 tablespoons finely chopped scallions (spring onions)
3 teaspoons finely chopped garlic
1 teaspoon finely chopped ginger

Put oxtail into a large pan with water, ginger, and salt. Bring to a boil, then reduce heat and simmer until meat is tender; this may take about 2 hours. Skim off any froth and scum that forms on the surface. If a pressure cooker is used, it should take about 45 minutes. Liquid should be reduced to about 6 cups (2 1/2 pts, 1.5 L). Combine remaining ingredients and serve with soup as a dipping sauce for the pieces of oxtail.

Serves 6–8

PEPPER WATER
Rasam ◆ South India

1 tablespoon tamarind pulp or 1 teaspoon instant tamarind
1 cup (8 fl oz, 250 ml) hot water
1 teaspoon sliced garlic
½ teaspoon ground black pepper
1 teaspoon ground cumin
4 cups (32 fl oz, 1 L) cold water
2 teaspoons salt
2 tablespoons chopped cilantro (fresh coriander leaves)
2 teaspoons oil
1 teaspoon black mustard seeds
8 curry leaves

Soak tamarind pulp in hot water for 10 minutes, then squeeze to dissolve pulp in the water. Strain, discarding seeds and fibers. Alternatively dissolve instant tamarind in hot water. Put tamarind liquid, garlic, pepper, cumin, cold water, salt, and cilantro into a saucepan and bring to a boil. Turn heat down immediately and simmer for 10 minutes. In a small saucepan heat the oil and fry mustard seeds and curry leaves until leaves are brown. Add to the simmering soup and serve.

Serves 6

⊰≫⋈≪⊱

PORK & CABBAGE SOUP
China

2 lb (1 kg) pork bones
½ teaspoon five-spice powder
½ teaspoon fresh root ginger, finely grated
1 clove garlic, crushed
1 teaspoon salt
3 teaspoons cornstarch (cornflour)
2 tablespoons cold water
1 tablespoon Chinese wine or dry sherry
8 oz (250 g) barbecued pork filet
3 cups (24 oz, 750 g) Chinese cabbage (celery cabbage), finely sliced

Put bones with five-spice powder, ginger, and garlic into a saucepan, add 8 cups (64 fl oz, 2 L) water and bring to a boil. Cover and simmer for 1 1/2 to 2 hours.

Strain stock, return to a boil, add cornstarch mixed with water. Boil for 3 minutes, then add sherry, barbecued pork cut in thin slices, and the cabbage. Return to boil and boil for 1 minute. Stir well and serve.

Serves 6

PORK & CHICKEN SOUP
Kaeng Chud Mu Kai ◆ **Thailand**

1 lb (500 g) pork loin
6 cups (2½ pts, 1.5 L) water
½ cup (4 fl oz, 125 ml) fish sauce
½ cup (3 oz, 90 g) jaggery (palm sugar) or brown sugar
½ small chicken or 2 chicken legs
1 teaspoon peppercorns
1 whole coriander plant, including root
½ teaspoon salt
5 dried Chinese mushrooms
3 oz (90 g) cellophane noodles
3 tablespoons chopped scallions (spring onions) including
*   green leaves*
3 tablespoons chopped cilantro (fresh coriander leaves)
1 red chili, seeded and sliced, optional

Remove rind and cut pork into thin slices. Put pork and rind into a saucepan with about 3 cups water, the sugar and fish sauce. Bring to the boil, skim top, reduce heat and cook for 30–40 minutes. Uncover and cook until pork is tender and fat transparent. The skin too should be very soft. Allow to cool in the sauce.

Remove fat from surface of stock.

Put chicken into a saucepan with 3 cups water, peppercorns, well-washed coriander plant, and salt. Bring to a boil then cover and simmer until chicken is tender. Soak mushrooms in hot water for 20 minutes, cut off stems and add stems to simmering chicken for extra flavor. Slice the caps finely and set aside. Soak cellophane noodles in hot water for 15 minutes, drain and cut into short 2 in (5 cm) lengths.

When chicken is ready, remove from heat and allow to cool in the stock, then lift out, remove skin and bones and cut chicken into small dice. Strain the stock. There should be about 4 cups (1 3/4 pts, 1 L). Cut half the pork into dice, reserving remaining pork for use in another dish, or simply serve as sweet pork. Measure pork stock and use 2 cups (16 fl oz, 500 ml) to combine with chicken stock. Bring to a boil, add cellophane noodles and mushrooms and simmer for 10 minutes. Add diced chicken and pork, chopped scallions, and coriander and turn off heat immediately. Serve at once, and if desired garnish with the chili slices.
Serves 6

⟨⟩⟩∞⟨⟨⟩

PORK & LOTUS ROOT SOUP
Canh Cu Sen ◆ **Vietnam**

1 lb (500 g) lean pork ribs
1 lb (500 g) fresh lotus root or 8 slices canned lotus root
3 scallions (spring onions)
½ teaspoon salt
6 cups (2½ pts, 1.5 L) water
1–2 tablespoons fish sauce

Ask your butcher to cut the pork ribs into short lengths. Peel lotus root thinly and cut into slices. Slice scallions, using both green and white parts. Put these ingredients into a saucepan with the salt and water, bring to a boil, then cover and simmer for 1 1/2 hours or until well cooked and the liquid reduced to 4 cups (1 3/4 pts, 1 L). Add fish sauce to taste. Serve with white rice.
Serves 4

⟨⟩⟩∞⟨⟨⟩

PORK & SHRIMP BALL SOUP
China

Pork balls:
8 oz (250 g) ground (minced) pork
¼ teaspoon finely grated fresh ginger root
¼ teaspoon crushed garlic
½ teaspoon salt
1 tablespoon finely chopped scallion (spring onion)

Shrimp balls:
8 oz (250 g) raw shrimp (prawns)
¼ teaspoon finely grated fresh ginger root
¼ teaspoon salt
1 slice soft white bread, crumbed
1 teaspoon cornstarch (cornflour)

Soup:
2½ pints (1.5 L) pork or chicken stock
1 tablespoon Chinese wine or dry sherry
1 tablespoon cornstarch (cornflour)
½ teaspoon sesame oil
2 tablespoons finely chopped scallion (spring onion)

Pork balls: Combine all ingredients, and form into balls the size of a large marble. Bring the stock to a boil, drop in the pork balls and return to a boil. Simmer for 15 minutes. Meanwhile make the shrimp balls.

Shrimp balls: Shell and devein the shrimp and chop very finely. Combine with all other ingredients, and form into balls the same size as the pork balls. Drop the shrimp balls into the simmering stock after the pork balls have cooked for 15 minutes. Return to simmering point, cook for a further 3 minutes.

Stir in the wine, then the cornstarch mixed with 1 tablespoon of cold water. Boil, stirring, until the soup is clear and slightly thickened (about 1 minute). Stir in the sesame oil and serve, garnished with the scallion.

Serves 6

PORK SOUP
Samlor Chhrook ◆ Cambodia & Laos

1 lb (500 g) pork chops
1 tablespoon shortening (lard) or oil
5 cloves garlic, finely chopped
5 cups (2 pts, 1.25 L) stock or water
1 tablespoon fish sauce
1 tablespoon lemon juice
2 teaspoons sugar
1 tablespoon finely shredded tender ginger
2 tablespoons chopped cilantro (fresh coriander leaves)

Cut pork from the bones and chop into small pieces. Use the bones to make stock. Heat the shortening or oil and gently fry garlic until soft, add pork pieces and fry for 1 minute, then add stock and all other ingredients except cilantro. Cover and simmer for 30 minutes. Serve, sprinkled with cilantro.

Serves 4

POTATO & PEA PASTRIES
Alu Mattar Samosa ◆ India

1 lb (500 g) potatoes
¾ cup fresh or frozen peas
1 teaspoon salt
1 teaspoon ground cumin
½ teaspoon chili powder, optional
½ teaspoon panch phora (see page 12)
2 tablespoons lemon juice
1 quantity pastry as for samosas (see page 56)
oil for deep frying

Prepare pastry and set aside while preparing filling. Boil the potatoes, peel and dice. If using fresh peas, cook them until tender. Frozen peas need only to be thawed. Combine potatoes and peas with the salt, cumin, chili powder (if used), panch phora, and lemon juice and make up samosas using method

described for samosas on page 56. Deep fry in hot oil. Drain on absorbent paper and serve warm or cold.

Makes about 36

RADISH & CABBAGE SALAD
Namasu ◆ Japan

1 daikon (giant white radish)
¼ firm white cabbage
1 tender carrot

Kimizu dressing:
3 egg yolks
¼ teaspoon salt
1 tablespoon sugar
3 tablespoons white vinegar
¾ cup (6 fl oz, 18 ml) water
1 tablespoon cornstarch (cornflour)
1 teaspoon prepared wasabi (Japanese horseradish) or mustard

Peel radish and cut into very fine strips. Shred cabbage finely, discarding leaf ribs and tough stalks. Scrape carrot and cut into very fine strips. Chill in iced water for 1 hour or until crisp. Drain well.

To make dressing, put all ingredients into container of electric blender and blend until smooth, about half a minute. Pour into a small saucepan and cook over very low heat, stirring constantly with a wooden spoon, until mixture thickens and coats back of spoon. Do not allow it to approach simmering point or it will curdle. Take off heat and keep stirring until it is half cool. Makes about 1 1/4 cups. Chill and serve with salad.

Serves 6

RAW FISH SALAD
Koy Pa ◆ Cambodia & Laos

1 lb (500 g) white fish filets
½ cup lemon juice
6 tender raw green (string) beans, thinly sliced
4 scallions (spring onions), thinly sliced
2 cloves garlic, crushed
1 fresh red chili, seeded and sliced
1 tablespoon fish sauce

For serving:
lettuce leaves
mint leaves
cilantro (fresh coriander leaves)

Pork and shrimp ball soup (page 53).

Remove all skin and bones from the fish and chop flesh rather fine. Put into a glass or earthenware bowl and pour the lemon juice over. Mix and leave for 3 hours, or overnight in the refrigerator, then combine with the other ingredients.

To serve: Put some of the fish mixture in the middle of a lettuce leaf, add a sprig of mint or a few leaves of cilantro. Fold over and eat.

Serves 4–6

<><><>

RICE FLOUR CRISPS
Murukku ◆ South India

1½ cups (9 oz, 270 g) rice flour
4 tablespoons besan (chickpea flour)
2½ teaspoons salt
2 teaspoons cumin seeds
1 teaspoon chili powder or to taste
½ teaspoon ajowan seeds, optional
2 tablespoons ghee
approximately ½ cup (3½ oz, 100 ml) thick coconut cream
oil for deep frying

Combine rice flour and besan with all the dry ingredients. Rub the ghee into the flour until evenly distributed, then add enough coconut cream to form a soft dough. Heat oil and force dough into oil in circles through a forcing bag using a star icing nozzle. Fry a few at a time on medium heat until golden brown and crisp, lift out and drain on absorbent paper. Serve warm or cool completely and store in an airtight container. Serve as a snack or cocktail savory.

Serves 6–8

RICE WITH RAW FISH
Nigiri Zushi ◆ Japan

3 cups sushi rice (page 255)
2 tablespoons sushi dressing (page 255)
1 lb (500 g) very fresh deboned tuna, snapper (sea bass),
 porgy (bream), or other suitable fish
2 teaspoons wasabi powder or dry mustard
2 teaspoons cold water
pickled ginger, in strips

Prepare rice according to recipe on page 255 and reserve 2 tablespoons of dressing from the quantity made for flavoring the rice.

Skin the fish and cut into very thin slices with a sharp knife, angling the knife so that the slices are larger than they would be if cut straight. Cover with plastic wrap (film) and refrigerate until just before required.

Mix reserved sushi dressing with 2 tablespoons cold water and use it to moisten your hands before starting to shape the rice. Take a rounded tablespoon of sushi rice at a time and form each into a neat oval shape. They should be a little smaller than the slices of fish, so that the fish completely covers one side of the rice. Spread each slice of fish with a little wasabi dressing (made by mixing the powder with the cold water) and put it, dressing downwards, on the rice. Mold to a neat shape. Arrange on tray, garnish and serve with a few strips of pickled ginger.

Note: Similar open sandwiches can be made with cooked shrimp, shelled, deveined and opened out butterfly fashion by slitting through the inside curve.

If squid is used, remove and discard everything in the body cavity and wash well under running water, rubbing off the skin. Slit squid down one side and lay it flat, then cut into pieces just large enough to cover the mounds of rice. Blanch in boiling water for 1 minute. Drain, cool and place over the rice. Decorate with a strip of nori (dried laver seaweed).
Makes about 24

❖❖❖

RICE WITH SEAFOOD & VEGETABLES
Chirashi–Zushi ◆ Japan

1 quantity sushi rice (page 255)
4 dried mushrooms
1 tablespoon Japanese soy sauce
1 teaspoon sugar
½ cup cooked crab or shrimp (prawns)
½ cup finely sliced raw fish, optional

2 eggs
pinch salt
vegetable oil
½ cup finely shredded bamboo shoot
½ cup cooked green peas
1 piece canned lotus root, sliced
1 tablespoon pickled kombu (kelp), thinly sliced
1 tablespoon takuan (pickled radish), thinly sliced
few shreds beni shoga (pickled ginger root) for garnish

Prepare sushi rice and cool. Soak mushrooms in boiling water for 30 minutes, remove and discard stems, slice caps thinly and simmer 10 minutes in 1/2 cup (4 fl oz, 125 ml) of the soaking water with soy sauce and sugar. Flake crab or slice shrimp. Remove any bones from fish.

Beat eggs slightly, season with salt and cook in a lightly oiled pan to make a thin omelet, taking care not to let it brown. Cool, then cut in thin shreds.

Toss rice gently with all the ingredients, reserving a few of the most colorful for garnish. Serve cold.
Serves 6

❖❖❖

SAMOSAS
Keema Samosa ◆ North India

Pastry:
1½ cups (15 oz, 185 g) all-purpose (plain) flour
¾ teaspoon salt
1 tablespoon ghee or oil
½ cup (4 fl oz, 125 ml) warm water

Filling:
1 tablespoon oil or ghee
2 medium onions, finely chopped
1 fresh red or green chili, seeded and chopped
½ teaspoon crushed garlic
2 teaspoons finely chopped fresh ginger
1 teaspoon ground coriander
1 teaspoon ground cumin
½ teaspoon ground turmeric
½ teaspoon chili powder, optional
½ teaspoon salt or to taste
1 tablespoon lemon juice
8 oz (250 g) ground (minced) lamb
½ cup (4 fl oz, 125 ml) hot water
½ teaspoon garam masala
2 tablespoons chopped fresh mint or cilantro (fresh
 coriander leaves)
oil for deep frying

Pastry: Sift flour and salt into a bowl, lightly rub in ghee or oil, add warm water and mix until ingredients are combined and the dough comes away from side of bowl. Add a little more water if necessary. Knead firmly for 10 minutes or until dough is smooth and elastic. Cover with plastic wrap (film) and set aside for at least 30 minutes, while preparing filling.

Filling: Heat oil or ghee in a saucepan and fry half the chopped onion and fresh chili until soft, then add garlic and half the ginger and continue to fry, stirring, until it starts to brown. Add coriander, cumin, turmeric, and chili powder (if used) and fry for a few seconds longer. Add salt and lemon juice. Add meat and fry over high heat, stirring constantly, until meat browns. Lower heat and add hot water, cover pan and cook until meat is tender and all the liquid has been absorbed, about 25 minutes. Stir frequently towards end of cooking, when mixture is dry. Stir in the garam masala and allow mixture to cool. Mix in the chopped herbs and remaining chopped onion and ginger, which get half cooked during frying, giving good texture and extra flavor to the filling.

Make small balls of dough and roll out each one on a lightly floured board to the size of a saucer. Dough should be fairly thin. Cut each circle of dough in half. Put a teaspoon of filling on one side of each half circle, brush edges with water, fold dough over and press edges together firmly to seal. The samosas should be triangular.

When all the samosas are made, heat oil in a deep pan and fry a few at a time on medium high heat, spooning the oil over the tops. Fry until golden brown on both sides. Drain on absorbent paper and serve hot. These samosas are sometimes accompanied by fresh mint chatni (see page 21) or tamarind chatni (see page 27), for dipping.

Note: A quick and easy method is to use frozen egg (spring) roll pastry. Buy the large size pastry squares, thaw the packet and carefully peel away 12 sheets. Wrap the remainder and return to freezer. This pastry keeps well. Cut each sheet into three equal strips and keep them covered while working or they will dry out. Put 1 teaspoon of filling at one end and fold the strip of pastry over diagonally, then fold again and again, making sure there is a perfect triangle every time. Moisten end of strip with water or a mixture of beaten egg and flour to seal. Fry as above.

Makes about 36

SAVORY CHICKPEA SNACK
Channa ◆ India & Pakistan

8 oz (250 g) dried chickpeas
salt
1 teaspoon ground turmeric
1 teaspoon ground cumin
½ teaspoon chili powder
lemon juice to taste

Soak chickpeas overnight in plenty of water. Next day cover with fresh water, add 2 teaspoons salt and the turmeric, bring to a boil, cover and simmer until peas are tender, 35 to 45 minutes, or cook in a pressure cooker if preferred. Drain while hot. Sprinkle with cumin, chili powder and lemon juice to taste. Salt if needed. Toss well to distribute seasonings. Serve the peas as a snack by themselves, or as part of the accompaniment to farina wafers (see page 38).

SAVORY BATTER DROPS
Namkin Boondi ◆ India (Punjab)

1 cup (6 oz, 185 g) besan (chickpea flour)
1 cup (4 oz, 125 g) self-raising flour
½ teaspoon cumin seeds
1 teaspoon chili powder or to taste
1 teaspoon garam masala
½ teaspoon ground turmeric
½ teaspoon crushed garlic or garlic powder
½ teaspoon ajowan seeds
1½ teaspoons salt
approximately 1½ cups (12 fl oz, 375 ml) tepid water
oil for deep frying
2 tablespoons ghee, optional

Sift the besan and self-raising flours into a bowl. Roast cumin seeds in a dry pan, shaking or stirring constantly until brown, then crush. Stir the cumin seeds, chili powder, garam masala, turmeric, garlic, ajowan seeds, salt, and water into the flour mixture and mix to a smooth, rather thin batter. Heat oil in a karahi or frying pan and if liked add the ghee. When oil is smoking hot, hold a perforated spoon over it and pour a spoon of the batter onto the spoon. Tap the handle against the side of the pan so that drops of the batter fall into the oil. Cook only one spoon at a time. As the drops swell and turn golden brown, lift them out with another frying spoon and drain on absorbent paper. Repeat in the same way until all the batter is used up. The namkin boondi may be stored, when cool, in an airtight container. Serve as a savory with drinks, or as a tea-time nibble.

Note: The perforations in the spoon should be round and about the size of a pea. The batter should be of a medium pouring consistency. A thick batter will result in more even shapes, but the drops will not be as delightfully crisp as with a thin batter.

Serves 6

SAVORY FARINA
Uppuma ◆ South India

4½ tablespoons vegetable oil
2 cups (11 oz, 340 g) farina (semolina)
1 teaspoon black mustard seeds
8–10 curry leaves
1 tablespoon urad dhal (husked black lentils)
1 tablespoon channa dhal (Bengal lentils)
4 dried red chilies
1½ cups finely chopped onion
1 tablespoon sliced fresh red or green chilies
1 tablespoon grated fresh ginger
1½ cups diced vegetables; bell peppers (capsicums), peas,
  carrots, cauliflower
2 cups (16 fl oz, 500 ml) hot water
1½ teaspoons salt
2 teaspoons ghee
squeeze of lemon juice

In a saucepan heat 1 1/2 tablespoons oil and fry the farina, stirring constantly, until golden. Remove from pan, wipe out pan with absorbent paper. Heat remaining 3 tablespoons oil in pan and fry the mustard seeds, curry leaves, urad and channa dhals, and the dried chilies, broken into pieces. (If a hot result is not desired, shake out and discard the seeds and only use one or two chilies.)

When dhals are golden add onions and fry, stirring, until they are soft and pale golden. Add fresh chilies, ginger, and vegetables, stir and cook for about 8 minutes. Add water and salt, bring to a boil, add farina and stir constantly until it boils. Keep stirring until quite dry. Cover pan tightly and allow to cook on very low heat until farina is cooked through. Add the ghee and stir it through. Add a squeeze of lemon juice and serve warm or cold. Serve uppuma in small bowls with a spoon for eating.

Serves 4

SAVORY RICE FLAKES
Chiura ◆ India (Uttar Pradesh)

½ cup (4 fl oz, 125 ml) oil
1 cup raw peanuts
1 cup roasted chickpeas
3 dried red chilies, broken into pieces and seeded
1 teaspoon black mustard seeds
1 teaspoon garam masala
1 teaspoon salt
½ teaspoon chili powder
2 teaspoons ground cumin
1 teaspoon amchur (dried green mango powder), optional
4 cups rice flakes (powva) or rice bubbles
1 cup potato crisps, optional

In a large karahi, wok or saucepan heat the oil and fry the peanuts until golden brown, stirring constantly. Do not let them darken too much as they will continue to cook in their own heat for a while even when out of the pan. Remove with slotted spoon and drain on absorbent paper. In the oil left in pan toss the roasted chickpeas briefly and remove from pan. If necessary add a tablespoon or two of oil to the pan and fry the chilies and mustard seeds until the seeds start to pop. Turn off heat, add the garam masala, salt, chili powder, cumin, amchur, if used, and mix well. Add the rice flakes or rice bubbles and toss well to distribute salt and spices. Taste for seasoning and add extra salt and chili powder if necessary. Stir in potato crisps, peanuts and chickpeas. Cool and store in an airtight container.

Makes about 6 cups

SAVORY VEGETABLE FRITTERS
Pakorhas ◆ India & Pakistan

1½ cups (6 oz, 180 g) besan (chickpea flour)
1 teaspoon garam masala
2 teaspoons salt
½ teaspoon ground turmeric
½ teaspoon chili powder, optional
1 cup (8 fl oz, 250 ml) water
1 clove garlic, crushed
4 cups (14 oz, 400 g) mixed chopped vegetables
oil for deep frying

Sieve besan, garam masala, salt, turmeric, chili powder (if used) into a bowl. Add water gradually, mixing to a thick batter. Stir in garlic and beat well. Allow batter to stand for 30 minutes, then beat again.

Add vegetables to batter and mix thoroughly.

Shanghai dumplings (page 60).

Heat oil in a deep pan. Drop teaspoons of mixture into oil and fry over moderate heat until pale golden on both sides. Lift out with a slotted spoon and drain on absorbent paper.

Just before serving, heat oil again. When almost smoking hot, return pakorhas to pan, a few at a time, for about 30 seconds or until golden brown on both sides. (The second frying makes them very crisp.) Drain on paper and serve immediately.

Note: If you prefer to lighten the batter and lessen the strong chickpea taste, use half besan and half self-raising flour — a little liberty that results in puffier pakorhas, and won't topple the Taj Mahal!

Makes 24–36

SESAME SHRIMP TOAST
China

8 oz (250 g) raw shrimp (prawns), in shells
1 tablespoon beaten egg
½ teaspoon finely grated fresh ginger
½ teaspoon salt
1 tablespoon oyster sauce
2 teaspoons cornstarch (cornflour)
6 slices white bread
¾ cup sesame seeds
oil for deep frying

Shell and devein shrimp. If using frozen peeled raw shrimp, thaw completely and drain off liquid, then weigh 4 oz (125 g). Chop shrimp very finely and mix with the beaten egg, ginger, salt, oyster sauce, and cornstarch. Trim crusts off bread and spread the slices with the shrimp mixture. Toast the sesame seeds in a wok over low heat, stirring constantly and taking care that seeds do not burn. As soon as they are golden, turn onto a plate.

Wipe out wok with paper and heat oil for deep frying. Dip slices of bread in the sesame seeds, pressing the shrimp mixture firmly on the seeds. Put the bread on a wooden board and use a sharp knife or chopper to cut each slice into 4 narrow strips. Fry the strips, not too many at once, in hot oil until the bread is golden brown. Drain on absorbent paper and serve hot, as an appetizer or cocktail savory.

Makes about 24 pieces

SHANGHAI DUMPLINGS
China

11 oz (350 g) ground (minced) pork
½ teaspoon salt
1 teaspoon light soy sauce
1 teaspoon Chinese wine or dry sherry
2 scallions (spring onions)
½ teaspoon grated fresh ginger root
6 oz (185 g) all–purpose (plain) flour
Chinese red vinegar for dipping
light soy sauce for dipping

Mix together the pork, salt, soy sauce, wine, finely chopped scallions, and grated ginger. Slowly beat in 4 tablespoons of water. This makes the filling juicy.

Measure flour into a bowl, make a well in the middle and pour in 4 fl oz (125 ml) cold water. Using the handle of a wooden spoon or chopsticks, mix to a dough, working from the middle and gradually incorporating the flour. Turn onto a lightly floured surface and knead for 5 to 6 minutes. The dough will become very smooth.

On the floured surface, roll the dough thinly and cut about 24 rounds 2 1/2 in (6 cm) in diameter. Place a small teaspoonful of the meat mixture in the middle of each round. Make two 'box pleats' on one side of the circle. Dampen the edges with water and seal them together to make dumplings.

Bring a large saucepan of water to a boil, add the dumplings and when they rise to the top and the water bubbles furiously, add 8 fl oz (250 ml) of cold water. Once more let the water bubble up, then add another 8 fl oz (250 ml) of cold water. This keeps the dough firm and prevents bursting. Serve hot, with Chinese red vinegar and light soy sauce for dipping.

Makes about 24

SHANGHAI EGG POUCH SOUP
China

4 oz (125 g) bean starch (transparent) noodles
6 dried Chinese mushrooms
half a Chinese cabbage (wongah bak)
3½ pints (2 L) chicken stock

Egg Pouches:
4 oz (125 g) ground (minced) pork
1 scallion (spring onion), finely chopped
¼ teaspoon finely grated fresh ginger root
½ teaspoon salt
1 teaspoon cornstarch (cornflour)
3 eggs

Soak the noodles in hot water for 20 minutes; then drain. Soak the mushrooms in hot water for 30 minutes; then drain, discard the stems and cut the caps into quarters. Wash the cabbage and cut into thick slices.

To make the pouches: Combine the pork with the scallion, ginger, salt, and cornstarch; mix well. In a separate bowl, beat the eggs with 1 tablespoon of cold water and a pinch of salt.

Lightly oil a ladle and hold it over low flame. Pour in about 3 tablespoons of the beaten egg and swirl to given an even, thick coating of egg; pour excess egg back into the bowl. Put 1 teaspoon of the pork mixture on one side of the egg and fold the other side over, sealing the edge if necessary with a little of the uncooked egg. Continue making pouches until all the egg is used up. The pouches can be made in a heavy frying pan but the shape will not be as good. Place on a plate when made.

Cooking the soup: Heat the stock in a flameproof cooking pot, season with salt if necessary. Add noodles, return to a boil and simmer for 5 minutes. Arrange the egg pouches in the pot and simmer for a further 5 minutes. Put the sliced cabbage and the mushrooms in the middle, and give the soup a final 5 minutes simmering

Note: This dish can be prepared beforehand, to the stage where the noodles have been cooked in the soup. Have the egg pouches, cabbage, and mushrooms ready in the refrigerator. About 20 minutes before serving, reheat the soup and continue with the recipe.

You can add slices of egg roll (page 38) or barbecued pork (page 174) to this dish for a more elaborate meal.

Serves 6–8

SHARK FIN SOUP
Yue Chi Tong ✦ China

1 can shark fin
6 cups (2½ pts, 1.5 L) chicken stock (see page 6), chilled and defatted
1 cup chopped cooked chicken
2 tablespoons light soy sauce
salt to taste, optional
2 tablespoons Chinese wine or dry sherry
1 tablespoon cornstarch (cornflour)
2 tablespoons cold water
2 egg whites, slightly beaten
6 scallions (spring onions), finely chopped

Combine shark fin and chicken stock and bring to a boil. Add chopped chicken meat, soy, wine, and if necessary add salt to taste. Mix cornstarch smoothly with cold water and stir into simmering soup until it boils and thickens very slightly. Add egg white to the soup, stirring with chopsticks so that it sets in small shreds. Remove soup from heat, pour into tureen, sprinkle scallions over and serve.

Serves 6

✧✦✧

SHORT SOUP WITH VEGETABLES
China

6 cups (2½ pts, 1.5 L) chicken stock
short soup dumplings (see Wonton soup page 76)
1 oz (30 g) snow peas (mangetout)
1 cup (1 oz, 30 g) broccoli sprigs
2 tablespoons cilantro (fresh coriander leaves), finely
  chopped
a few drops of sesame oil

Bring chicken stock (made with cubes) to a boil and drop the dumplings in. Cook for 8 minutes. Add the peas and broccoli and cook for 2 to 3 minutes longer. Remove from heat, stir in cilantro and sesame oil and serve at once.

Serves 5–6

SHRIMP & BEAN CURD SOUP
Sumashi Wan ◆ Japan

1 small carrot
6 cups (2½ pts, 1.5 L) dashi (see page 6)
6 medium-sized shrimp (prawns)
6 cubes tofu (bean curd)
sprigs of watercress for garnish

Peel carrot and cut off both ends so you are left with a straight cross-section. With a sharp cleaver remove narrow V-shaped strips the length of the carrot at regular intervals, then slice across very thinly to make flower shapes. Drop into boiling water for 1 minute, then drain and refresh in iced water. Set aside for garnish.

Bring dashi to a boil, drop in shelled and deveined shrimp and simmer for 1 minute. Add tofu and let stock once more return to boil. Remove from heat and ladle carefully into soup bowls, putting a shrimp and a cube of tofu in each bowl. Fill bowls with stock, then garnish each with a sprig of watercress and one or two carrot slices. Serve immediately.

Serves 6

✧✦✧

Left, shark fin soup (recipe opposite); right, Shanghai egg pouch soup (recipe opposite).

SHRIMP & MUSHROOM SOUP
China

1 lb (500 g) raw shrimp (prawns)
1 tablespoon sesame oil
½ cup (3½ oz, 100 g) rice
1 cup (2 oz, 60 g) chinese soup greens (Gai choy) chopped
Braised mushrooms (see page 264)
Salt to taste

Shell shrimp, reserving heads and shells. Devein shrimp and cut into halves or, if large, into quarters. Wash the heads and shells thoroughly, drain in a colander. Heat oil in a saucepan, throw in the shrimp heads and shells and fry over high heat, stirring until they turn pink. Then add boiling water to cover, approximately 8 cups (64 fl oz, 2 L), cover pan with lid and simmer for 30 minutes. Strain, discard heads and shells.

Make up shrimp stock to 6 cups (2 1/2 pints, 1.5 L) with water, return to saucepan. Add rice and 2 teaspoons salt, cover and simmer 1 hour or longer, until rice is very soft.

Chop cabbage into bite-sized pieces. Cut braised mushrooms into thin slices. Add mushrooms to soup together with shrimp. Simmer for 5 minutes, add more salt if necessary, then add cabbage. Simmer 1 minute longer. Serve at once.

Note: This recipe may be made with mushrooms which have not been braised. In this case soak them in hot water for 30 minutes, remove and discard stems and slice mushroom caps finely. Add to soup at the same time as rice, and finish the soup with a few drops of sesame oil and a teaspoon of soy sauce.

You can use any variety of Chinese soup vegetables but Gai choy is available in most Chinese stores. It looks like a small variety of Chinese mustard cabbage and has the same slightly pungent taste.
Serves 4–5

❧❦❧

SHRIMP & SPINACH SOUP
Sayur Udang Bayam ◆ Malaysia

8 oz (250 g) raw shrimp (prawns)
3 tablespoons peanut oil
1 small bunch English spinach or Swiss chard (silverbeet)
1 onion, finely sliced
1 or 2 fresh red chilies, seeded and sliced
1 clove garlic, crushed
½ teaspoon ground turmeric
1 teaspoon salt
2 cups (16 fl oz, 500 ml) shrimp (prawn) stock
2 cups (16 fl oz, 500 ml) thin coconut cream
½ cup (3 1/2 fl oz, 100 ml) thick coconut cream

Wash, shell and devein the shrimp. Drain the heads and shells and use for making stock.

Wash spinach or silverbeet thoroughly. Separate leaves from stems and chop both roughly. Heat remaining 2 tablespoons oil in a large saucepan and fry onion and chilies until onion is soft and golden. Add the garlic and turmeric and fry for 1 minute longer. Add spinach stems and fry, stirring, for a few minutes then add salt, strained shrimp stock, and thin coconut cream. Bring to a boil, lower heat and simmer 5 minutes. Add spinach leaves and simmer for 3 minutes, then add the shrimp, finely chopped, and thick coconut cream. Let mixture return slowly to boil and simmer for no more than 2 or 3 minutes longer or shrimp will toughen. Serve immediately.

Shrimp stock: Heat 1 tablespoon of the oil in a saucepan and when very hot throw in the heads and shells. Fry, stirring, until they turn pink. Add 4 cups (1 3/4 pts, 1 L) hot water and 1 teaspoon salt, bring to a boil and simmer for 20 to 30 minutes or until liquid is reduced by half. Set aside.
Serves 6

❧❦❧

SHRIMP & SWEET POTATO FRITTERS
Ukoy ◆ Philippines

8 oz (250 g) small red shrimp (prawns)
1 cup (8 fl oz, 250 ml) water
1½ teaspoons salt
1 cup (4 oz, 125 g) all-purpose (plain) flour
½ cup (4 oz, 125 g) ground rice
¼ cup (1 oz, 30 g) cornstarch (cornflour)
2 eggs
¼ teaspoon ground black pepper
1 medium-size sweet potato
1 cup fresh bean sprouts
4 scallions (spring onions), finely sliced
oil for deep frying

Wash shrimp well, bring water and salt to a boil and drop in the shrimp. When water returns to boil, cover and cook for 3 to 4 minutes or until shrimp are pink. Drain shrimp, reserving the liquid they cooked in. Remove heads of shrimp. In the Philippines they are left in their shells and this may be done if they are very tiny shrimp. If they are not very small the shells are somewhat tough and I prefer to shell them, leaving only the tails on.

Put flour, ground rice, and cornstarch into a large bowl. Beat eggs and stir in 1 cup (8 fl oz, 250 ml) of the liquid the shrimp were cooked in, making up the amount with water if necessary. Add pepper.

Pour the liquid into the dry ingredients and beat well with a rotary beater for a minute or two, until batter is smooth.

Peel the sweet potato and grate coarsely. Measure 1 cup. Wash bean sprouts, pinch off straggly brown tails and pour boiling water over the sprouts in a colander, then run cold water over. Drain well. Stir grated sweet potato, bean sprouts and half the scallions into the batter.

Heat oil in a deep frying pan or wok and when a haze starts to form slip in about a tablespoon of the batter at a time, placing 2 or 3 shrimp and a sprinkling of scallions on top of the spoonful before sliding it into the oil. Do not fry too many fritters at a time. Spoon the oil over them as they cook and when underside is golden brown turn and fry other side. The oil should not be too hot or they will darken before they are cooked and crisp. Drain on absorbent paper and serve hot accompanied by garlic and vinegar dipping sauce. To make the sauce crush a clove of garlic with 1 teaspoon salt and stir into 1/4 cup (2 fl oz, 60 ml) mild vinegar.

Makes about 20

SHRIMP CUTLETS
China

12 raw large shrimp (king prawns)
2 tablespoons soy sauce
1 small clove garlic, crushed
¼ teaspoon salt
½ teaspoon finely grated fresh ginger
½ cup (2 oz, 60 g) cornstarch (cornflour)
1 large egg, beaten
dry breadcrumbs or cornflake crumbs
peanut oil for deep frying
lemon wedges for serving
chili sauce for dipping, optional

Shell and devein shrimp, leaving last segment of shell and the tail on. With a sharp knife slit shrimp along curve of back but do not cut right through. Combine soy sauce, garlic, salt, and ginger together and marinate shrimp in this mixture for 15 minutes or longer.

Dip shrimp into cornstarch, shake off excess, then dip in beaten egg and finally into crumbs, pressing gently to flatten shrimp and firm the coating.

Heat oil in wok until almost smoking. Fry a few shrimp at a time until golden brown, about 2 or 3 minutes. Drain on absorbent paper and serve hot with lemon wedges. Serve chili sauce for dipping if desired.

Serves 4–6

SHRIMP DROP SOUP
Canh Tom Vo Vien ◆ Vietnam

4 cups (1¾ pts, 1 L) fish or chicken stock
1 tablespoon fish sauce
½ quantity fresh shrimp paste (page 26)
2 cups finely shredded white Chinese (Napa) cabbage
salt to taste
3 scallions (spring onions), finely sliced

Bring the stock to a boil and add fish sauce. Take half teaspoons of the shrimp paste, using an oiled teaspoon, and drop them into simmering stock. When cooked they will turn opaque and rise to the top. Add cabbage, bring back to boil, cover and leave for a minute, or until cabbage is tender. Sprinkle scallions on top and remove from heat at once. Cover and leave for 1 minute, then serve.

Serves 4

SHRIMP FRITTERS
Indonesia

8 oz (250 g) shelled raw shrimp (prawns)
2 eggs, beaten
1 tablespoon water
1 tablespoon rice flour
2 tablespoons ground rice
½ teaspoon crushed garlic
¾ teaspoon salt
¼ teaspoon ground black pepper
¼ teaspoon ground kencur (aromatic ginger), optional
¼ teaspoon sereh (lemon grass) powder, optional
1 fresh red chili, seeded and sliced
1 small onion, quartered and sliced
peanut oil for deep frying

Devein shrimp and chop. Mix together the eggs, water, rice flour, ground rice, garlic, salt, pepper, and other spices. Fold in the chili, onion and shrimp.

Heat oil in wok and when very hot drop batter by scant tablespoons into the oil, 3 or 4 at a time. Fry over medium heat until golden brown on both sides, drain on absorbent paper and serve hot.

Makes approx. 18

SHRIMP PASTRIES
Jhinga Samosa ◆ India (Bengal)

1 lb (500 g) raw shrimp (prawns) shelled and deveined
8 oz (250 g) potatoes
2 tablespoons ghee or oil
2 medium onions, finely chopped
1 teaspoon chopped garlic
1 teaspoon finely grated fresh ginger
½ teaspoon ground turmeric
½ teaspoon chili powder
1 teaspoon salt or to taste
¼ cup (2 fl oz, 60 ml) hot water
lemon juice to taste
1 quantity pastry as for samosas (see page 56), or frozen egg
   (spring) roll wrappers
oil for deep frying

Chop shrimp into large pieces. Peel and cut the potatoes into pieces the same size as the shrimp. Heat the ghee or oil and fry the onions, garlic, and ginger until onions are soft and golden. Add turmeric and chili powder, the shrimp and potatoes.

Stir well, add salt and hot water, cover and cook until potatoes are tender. Remove from heat, add lemon juice to taste and allow to cool before enclosing in pastry or strips of egg roll wrappers as described for samosas.

Heat oil for deep frying and fry until crisp and golden. Drain on absorbent paper.
Makes about 30

SHRIMP SOUP
Kung Tom Yam ◆ Thailand

2 lb (1 kg) raw shrimp (prawns)
1 tablespoon oil
8 cups (64 fl oz, 2 L) hot water
1½ teaspoons salt
2 stalks lemon grass or 4 strips lemon rind, thinly peeled
4 lemon or other citrus leaves
2 or 3 fresh whole chilies
1 tablespoon fish sauce
2 tablespoons lemon juice, or to taste
1 fresh red chili, seeded and sliced
2 tablespoons chopped cilantro (fresh coriander leaves)
4 scallions (spring onions) with green tops, chopped

Shell and devein shrimp. Wash shrimp heads well, drain thoroughly. Heat oil in saucepan and fry heads and shells of

shrimp until they turn pink, add hot water, salt, lemon grass or lemon rind, citrus leaves, and whole chilies. Bring to a boil, cover and simmer for 20 minutes. Strain stock, return to a boil, add shrimp and simmer for 3–4 minutes or until shrimp are cooked. Add fish sauce and lemon juice to taste. This soup should have a pronounced acid flavor, so add sufficient lemon juice to achieve this. Serve in a large tureen or in soup plates, sprinkled with sliced chili, cilantro and scallions.
Serves 6

SHRIMP TOAST, CHINESE-STYLE
China

6 square slices white bread
8 oz (250 g) raw shrimp (prawns)
1 egg, beaten
½ teaspoon finely grated ginger root
½ teaspoon salt
1 tablespoon oyster sauce
2 teaspoons cornstarch (cornflour)
sprigs of cilantro (fresh coriander leaves)
2–3 tablespoons sesame seeds
peanut oil for deep frying

Trim the crusts off the bread, cut each slice in half diagonally or into three strips, and leave on a tray for an hour or two to dry out a little.

Shell and devein shrimp. If using frozen shrimp, thaw completely and drain off any liquid, chop the shrimp very finely and put in a bowl. Add 1 tablespoon of the beaten egg, ginger, salt, oyster sauce, and cornstarch; mix well to blend to a smooth paste.

Spread the bread with shrimp mixture. Press a sprig of cilantro on some of the pieces. Brush other pieces lightly with the remaining beaten egg, and dip in sesame seeds to coat.

Heat the oil for deep frying and when hot, put in a few pieces of bread at a time, shrimp side down. Fry until the bread is golden, lift out on wire spoon and drain on absorbent paper. Serve hot.

Serve as a tasty appetizer with drinks, as part of a meal, between courses, or as a snack.
Serves 6

SHRIMP TOAST VIETNAMESE-STYLE
Banh Mi Chien Tom ◆ Vietnam

12 slices stale bread
1 quantity fresh shrimp (prawn) paste (page 26)

Shrimp toast, Chinese-style (recipe opposite).

oil for deep frying
lettuce leaves
cilantro (fresh coriander leaves) or mint
cucumber slices
nuoc cham (page 14)

Bread that is two days old is better than fresh bread for this recipe. Trim off crusts and cut each slice into halves lengthwise. Spread shrimp paste on the bread. Heat oil for deep frying and put in a few pieces of bread at a time, shrimp side down. Fry until golden, drain on absorbent paper. Serve hot, with lettuce leaves for wrapping, nuoc cham for dipping and cilantro or mint sprigs and cucumber slices as accompaniments.

Serve as hors d'oeuvre or a snack.
Makes 24 pieces

SHRIMP VELVET & MUSHROOM SOUP
China

1 lb (500 g) raw shrimp (prawns)
1 tablespoon cornstarch (cornflour)
1 teaspoon salt
3 egg whites
2 pints (40 ml) stock
1 small can straw or button mushrooms (champignons)
additional 2 tablespoons cornstarch (cornflour)
2 tablespoons Chinese wine or dry sherry
1 tablespoon light soy sauce
2 teaspoons sesame oil, optional
1 oz (30 g) frozen peas

Wash and drain the shrimp. Remove shells and heads, but simmer these in the stock for extra flavor, strain.

Devein and chop shrimp very finely until almost a purée, gradually adding 1 tablespoon of cold water while chopping. Blend 1 tablespoon of cornstarch with 1 tablespoon of cold water and the salt, then combine this with prawn purée. Beat the egg whites until stiff and fold in. This may be done beforehand and the shrimp velvet refrigerated.

Drain and slice the mushrooms. Combine 2 tablespoons of cornstarch with the wine, soy sauce, and sesame oil.

Bring the stock to a boil, add the sliced mushrooms and the cornstarch mixture, and stir until the soup boils and thickens. Add the shrimp velvet and the frozen peas, and allow the soup to reach a gentle simmer once more. Taste and adjust seasoning if necessary; serve at once.

Serves 6

⊰≈⊱

SICHUAN SOUP
China

8 dried Chinese mushrooms
1 tablespoon dried wood fungus (cloud ears)
2 oz (60 g) bean starch (transparent) noodles
1 tablespoon oil
4 oz (125 g) finely chopped cooked pork
1 tablespoon dark soy sauce
2 teaspoons sugar
4 oz (125 g) chopped shrimp (prawns)
1 square fresh bean curd, diced
2½ pints (1.5 L) chicken or pork stock
1 tablespoon light soy sauce
1 tablespoon Chinese sweet vinegar
1 tablespoon Chinese wine or dry sherry
1 teaspoon chili oil
2 tablespoons cornstarch (cornflour)
2 eggs, beaten
salt and pepper to taste

This is a rich, robustly flavored soup which is served in smaller-than-usual bowls.

Soak the mushrooms in hot water for 30 minutes; then drain (reserve the liquid), discard the mushroom stems, and slice the mushroom caps finely. Soak the wood fungus in water for 10 minutes; then trim off any gritty portions and cut the fungus into small pieces. Soak noodles in hot water for 15 minutes, drain and cut into short lengths.

Heat oil in a wok and fry the mushrooms and pork, stirring constantly, until they start to brown. Add the dark soy sauce, sugar, and 4 fl oz (125 ml) of the mushroom water. Simmer,

covered, until the mushrooms have absorbed almost all the liquid. Add shrimp and bean curd, and stir-fry for 1 minute.

Bring stock to a boil, add the noodles and return to a boil; simmer for 5 minutes. Add the light soy sauce, vinegar, wine, chili oil, and the fried mixture. Mix the cornstarch smoothly with 3 tablespoons of cold water, and stir into the soup until it boils and thickens.

Dribble the beaten eggs into the simmering soup, stirring constantly so the egg separates into fine shreds. Season to taste with pepper and salt. Put a spoonful of wood fungus in each soup bowl and pour a ladle of the boiling soup over. Serve immediately.

Serves 6–8

⊰≈⊱

SOUP FOR NOODLES
Kakejiru ◆ Japan

6 cups (2½ pts, 1.5 L) dashi (see page 6)
½ cup (4 fl oz, 125 ml) mirin or dry sherry
½ cup (4 fl oz, 125 ml) Japanese soy sauce

Put the prepared dashi, mirin, and soy sauce in a saucepan and bring to a boil. Reduce heat, cover and simmer for 10 minutes. Taste and add extra salt if necessary.

You can serve noodles of all kinds in this basic stock. Chicken stock may be substituted for dashi.

⊰≈⊱

SOUP NOODLES
Mah Mee ◆ Singapore

1 lb (500 g) raw shrimp (prawns)
1 tablespoon peanut oil
4 cups (1 ¾ pts, 1 L) water
1½ teaspoons salt
2 cups (16 fl oz, 500 ml) chicken stock
8 oz (250 g) barbecued pork (page 174)
8 oz (250 g) bean sprouts
1 tablespoon sesame oil
3 cloves garlic, finely grated
½ teaspoon finely grated fresh ginger root
4 oz (125 g) fine egg noodles
1 teaspoon five-spice powder
3 oz (90 g) canned crab meat
½ cup finely chopped scallions (spring onions)
1 small cucumber, peeled and diced

Shrimp velvet & mushroom soup (page 65).

Shell and devein shrimp. Wash shrimp shells and heads thoroughly, drain. Heat peanut oil in a saucepan and fry heads and shells over a high heat until they turn pink. Add water and salt, cover and cook for 20 minutes. Strain. (If liked, the shrimp heads and a little of the stock can be blended for a few seconds in an electric blender, then passed through a fine strainer and the liquid added to the shrimp stock. This produces a tastier soup.) Combine shrimp and chicken stocks.

Cut barbecued pork into thin slices. Wash and drain bean sprouts. Heat sesame oil and gently fry garlic and ginger. When starting to brown add stock and shrimp. Bring to a boil and cook for 5 minutes. Add noodles and cook for a further 5 minutes. Add pork, bean sprouts, and five-spice powder, simmer for 2 minutes and serve in a large bowl, garnished with crab meat, scallions, and cucumber.

Serves 5–6

SOUP OF SOYBEAN SPROUTS

Kong Namul Kuk ◆ Korea

1 lb (500 g) soybean sprouts
12 oz (375 g) lean steak
1 tablespoon soy sauce
1 tablespoon sesame oil
¼ teaspoon ground black pepper
2 cloves garlic, crushed
8 cups (64 fl oz, 2 L) water
finely chopped green leaves of 2 scallions (spring onions)

Wash and drain bean sprouts, pinch off straggly tails. Roughly chop the sprouts if they are very long. Shred meat into fine strips and marinate in soy sauce, sesame oil, pepper, and garlic. Heat a wok, put in beef and stir-fry until it browns. Add water and bean sprouts, bring to a boil, cover and simmer for 30 minutes. Remove from heat, add scallion leaves and cover for 5 minutes. Add more soy sauce or salt if necessary and serve hot.
Serves 6

⟨≈⟩

SOUP WITH BEAN CURD

Canh Dau Hu ◆ Vietnam

2 cups (16 fl oz, 500 ml) strong chicken stock
2 squares fresh tofu (bean curd)
½ cup chopped cooked chicken
1 tablespoon chopped cilantro (fresh coriander leaves)

Chill stock and remove all fat from surface. Bring stock to a boil, add tofu and chicken and heat through. Sprinkle with cilantro and serve immediately.
Serves 2

⟨≈⟩

SOUR SOUP

Chin Hin ◆ Burma

2 teaspoons sesame oil or corn oil
1 onion, finely sliced lengthwise
2 cloves garlic, crushed
¼ teaspoon ground turmeric
2 or 3 green tomatoes, chopped
1 cup torn English spinach or other greens
4–6 cups (1¾–2½ pts, 1–1.5 L) rhubarb stock, fish stock
*   or boiling water*
¼ teaspoon ngapi (dried shrimp paste)
salt to taste

Heat oil in a saucepan and when very hot fry the onion, garlic, and turmeric, stirring for 30 seconds. Add the tomatoes and spinach, stir well, then add the stock or water and bring to a boil. Add ngapi, cover and simmer until vegetables are tender. Taste and add salt as necessary. Serve with rice.

Sour greens such as tender young tamarind leaves are used to make the stock for this soup (or substitute green tomatoes or rhubarb stalks). If rhubarb stalks are used, cut them into short lengths and boil, then strain and use the liquid combined with spinach or other green leaves.
Serves 4–6

⟨≈⟩

SPICY CHICKEN SOUP

Soto Ayam ◆ Malaysia

3 lb (1.5 kg) chicken
8 cups (64 fl oz, 2 L) cold water
3 teaspoons salt
½ teaspoon whole black peppercorns
few celery tops
1 large brown onion, sliced
2 tablespoons peanut oil
2 daun salam (Indonesian curry leaves) or 6 curry leaves
2 cloves garlic, finely grated
½ teaspoon finely grated fresh ginger
½ teaspoon blachan (dried shrimp paste)
½ teaspoon ground turmeric
2 teaspoons ground coriander
1 teaspoon ground cumin
4 buah keras (candlenuts), finely grated
4 oz (125 g) rice vermicelli
2 large potatoes, cooked and diced
lemon juice to taste

Garnish:
8 scallions (spring onions), finely sliced
2 hard-cooked (boiled) eggs, finely chopped
crumbled potato crisps

Cut chicken into joints and put into a large saucepan with cold water. Water should cover the chicken. Add salt, peppercorns, celery tops, and half the onion. Bring quickly to a boil, then lower heat, cover and simmer for 30 minutes or until chicken is tender. Allow to cool to lukewarm (if chicken is taken out while it is hot, the flesh will be dry) then strain stock into a bowl.

Remove skin and bones from chicken. With a sharp knife cut flesh into dice or strips. Set aside. Heat peanut oil in the saucepan and when very hot fry the daun salam and onion until onion is golden brown. Add the garlic, ginger, blacan, and stir

over medium heat, crushing the blacan with back of spoon. Add the turmeric, coriander, cumin, and buah keras and fry, stirring, for a few seconds longer. Add the strained stock and bring to a boil, then reduce heat, cover and simmer for 10 minutes. Meanwhile, soak the rice vermicelli in hot water for 10 minutes, drain and cut into short lengths. Add it to the simmering soup, return to boil and cook for 1 minute. Add chicken meat, potatoes, and lemon juice and heat through. Pour into a large soup tureen and garnish with the scallions and egg. Serve the potato crisps in a separate bowl for sprinkling on individual servings.
Serves 6

SPICY FRIED NUTS
Masala Kaju Badam ◆ India & Pakistan

8 oz (250 g) raw cashews
8 oz (250 g) blanched almonds
1 lb (500 g) raw peanuts
oil for frying
1 tablespoon salt
2 teaspoons garam masala (page 9)
2 teaspoons chili powder, or to taste
1 teaspoon amchur (dried green mango), optional

Heat oil in a deep frying pan and fry the nuts on medium heat, a handful at a time, keeping each variety separate. As they are fried to a pale gold, remove them from the oil with a slotted spoon and drain on absorbent paper. Do not leave them in the oil until they darken because they go on cooking in their own heat. When all have been fried and drained sprinkle with combined spices and salt. If an acid taste is liked, add amchur to the mix. Cool completely and store in an airtight container.

SPLIT PEA & ONION FRITTERS
Beya Kway ◆ Burma

1 cup split peas
2 medium onions, finely chopped
2 fresh red chilies, finely chopped or ¼ teaspoon chili powder
½ teaspoon ground turmeric
½ teaspoon salt
oil for deep frying

Garnish: sliced onion and lemon wedges

Soak split peas overnight, or for at least 6 hours, in water to cover. Drain, grind to a paste in blender or put twice through fine screen of a meat grinder (mincer). Mix in the onions, chilies, turmeric, and salt. Make small balls and flatten to 1/2 in (12 mm) thick.

Heat oil in a wok and put fritters one at a time into the oil. Fry only 6 or 7 at a time. Spoon hot oil over the fritters until they are golden brown. Drain on absorbent paper. Serve garnished with sliced raw onion and lemon wedges.
Serves 6–8

Sichuan soup (page 66).

STEAMED EGG ROLL
China

Filling:
6 oz (185 g) chicken, raw shrimp (prawns) or lean pork
½ teaspoon salt
2 teaspoons light soy sauce
½ teaspoon sesame oil
1 teaspoon cornstarch (cornflour)
1 tablespoon finely chopped cilantro (fresh coriander leaves)
1 tablespoon finely chopped scallions (spring onion)

Wrappers:
5 eggs
½ teaspoon salt
1 tablespoon peanut oil
1 teaspoon sesame oil

Filling: Put the chicken, shrimp, or pork into an electric blender with salt, soy sauce, and sesame oil and blend until smooth. Because the mixture is thick, it will be necessary to switch the blender on and off frequently and move the mixture onto the blades with a spatula. Then scrape it into a bowl and mix in the other ingredients, combining well. Alternatively, chop everything very, very finely with a sharp chopper until it has the consistency of a paste, or use a food processor.

Wrappers: Beat the eggs well with salt. Reserve about 1 tablespoon of beaten egg for sealing the egg rolls.

Heat a small omelet pan. Measure the peanut and sesame oils into a saucer. Dip a piece of absorbent kitchen paper in the oil and grease the pan. Pour 3–4 tablespoons of egg mixture into the pan and make a thin omelet, cooking it on one side only; turn it onto a plate. Repeat with remaining egg mixture, greasing the pan each time. There will be 4 or 5 omelets, depending on the size of your pan.

Divide the filling into the same number of portions as there are omelets. Place each omelet on a board, cooked side up, and spread the filling almost to the edges using an oiled spatula or back of a spoon. Roll up like a Swiss roll and seal the edges with reserved beaten egg.

Lightly oil a plate with the mixed oils and place the rolls on it. Set the plate in a steamer (or on a rack in a saucepan of boiling water), cover and steam for 15 minutes. (The plate needs to be smaller than the steamer to allow steam to circulate.)

Remove from the steamer, allow to cool a little, then cut into diagonal slices. Serve hot or cold.
Serves 8

STEAMED MUSHROOMS WITH SHRIMPS
Korea

8 oz (250 g) fresh mushrooms
8 oz (250 g) peeled raw deveined shrimp (prawns)
6 canned water chestnuts, finely chopped
2 tablespoons finely chopped scallions (spring onions)
1 tablespoon cornstarch (cornflour)
1 tablespoon light soy sauce
1 teaspoon oyster sauce
½ teaspoon salt
½ teaspoon finely grated fresh ginger
cilantro (fresh coriander leaves) for garnish, optional

Choose small mushrooms at the cup stage. Wipe clean with absorbent paper and remove stems, leaving caps intact. Chop shrimps finely. Combine with all other ingredients in a bowl, mixing thoroughly. Fill mushroom caps, mounding filling slightly. Put mushrooms on a heatproof plate which has been lightly oiled, place on steamer rack in wok, cover and steam for 20 minutes. Serve warm or at room temperature, garnished with cilantro.
Serves 4–6

STEAMED SAUSAGE BUNS
China

6 oz (185 g) lap cheong (Chinese pork sausages)
4 dried Chinese mushrooms
2 teaspoons peanut oil
½ teaspoon finely chopped garlic
¼ teaspoon salt
½ cup hot water
1 canned bamboo shoot, finely chopped
1 tablespoon dark soy sauce
1 teaspoon sesame oil
2 teaspoons oyster sauce
1 tablespoon cornstarch (cornflour)
2 teaspoons hoi sin sauce
2 teaspoons sugar
1 quantity bun dough (see page 291)

Steam sausages for 15 minutes, cool and thinly slice diagonally. Soak Chinese mushrooms in hot water for 30 minutes, squeeze out excess water, discard stems and slice caps finely. Heat oil in a wok, add garlic and cook very slowly, not allowing garlic to brown. Add salt, hot water, mushrooms, bamboo shoot, soy sauce, sesame oil, and oyster sauce. Mix cornstarch with a

Sung Dynasty fish soup (page 72).

STEAMED SHRIMP DUMPLINGS
Siew Mai ◆ **China**

1 lb (500 g) small raw shrimp (prawns)
6 dried Chinese mushrooms
6 canned water chestnuts, chopped finely
3 tablespoons finely chopped bamboo shoot
3 scallions (spring onions), chopped
8 oz (250 g) ground (minced) pork
1½ teaspoons salt
1 tablespoon light soy sauce
1 tablespoon Chinese wine or dry sherry
1 teaspoon sesame oil
1 egg white
4 oz (125 g) wonton wrappers

Peel shrimp, reserve about 24 for garnish and chop the remainder. Soak mushrooms in hot water 30 minutes, then slice off and discard stems. Chop mushroom caps. Combine all chopped ingredients with pork, salt, soy sauce, wine, sesame oil, and egg white. Mix well together and put 1 heaped teaspoon of mixture in the middle of each wonton wrapper. Gather the wrapper around filling and press it close to give the shape of a little money bag, open at the top. Press a shrimp on top of each for garnish.

Lightly oil a steamer tray and put siew mai in a single layer on the tray. Pour enough water into a wok to come just below the level of the steaming basket. Cover with lid and steam over boiling water for 20 minutes. Serve hot or cold.
Makes about 24

⟨⟩∞⟨⟩

STRONG SOUP
Hin Gha ◆ **Burma**

Follow recipe for Mild Soup (see page 48), but add 4 cloves garlic, sliced, and 1/4 teaspoon ground black pepper together with onions and other ingredients.

⟨⟩∞⟨⟩

tablespoon of cold water and stir in, then cook, stirring, until thick and clear. Remove from heat, stir in hoi sin sauce and sugar. Cool, then stir in sliced sausages. Shape and steam buns as described below.

Bun dough: To make buns, divide dough into 12 portions and shape each into a smooth ball. Roll out on a very lightly floured board to a circle about 4 in (10 cm) across. Put a tablespoon of filling in middle and gather sides together, folding and pleating to make a neat join. Twist dough to seal. Put each bun, join downwards, on a square of waxed (greaseproof) paper lightly brushed with sesame oil. Put in bamboo steamer, cover and steam for 20 minutes. Serve warm. The cooked buns can be refrigerated overnight and reheated by steaming for 3 minutes before serving.

Note: If using a metal steamer, put a clean kitchen (tea) towel across steaming tray before covering with lid to prevent condensation dropping on top of buns.
Makes 12 buns

⟨⟩∞⟨⟩

SUNG DYNASTY FISH SOUP
China

3 dried Chinese mushrooms
4 oz (125 g) snapper (sea bass) filet
2 stems Chinese broccoli (Gai larn)
2 oz (60 g) barbecued pork (page 174)
oil for deep frying
1¾ pints (1 L) stock
1 tablespoon Chinese wine or dry sherry
salt to taste
2 tablespoons cornstarch (cornflour) mixed with a little cold
*   water*
1 egg white, slightly beaten

Soak the mushrooms in hot water for 20 minutes. Discard the mushroom stems, and steam the mushroom caps for 15 minutes. Slice finely.

Cut the fish into paper-thin slices. Cut the stems of broccoli diagonally into very thin slices. Cut the barbecued pork into thin slices, then into small squares.

Heat the oil in a wok for deep frying and when very hot, immerse the fish and broccoli on a wire frying spoon for about 10 seconds only. This is long enough to cook both fish and broccoli if they are sliced thinly, and the quick heat turns the broccoli a vivid emerald green. Drain.

Heat the stock in a saucepan and when boiling, add wine, fish, broccoli, mushrooms, and pork. Taste, and add salt if necessary. Add the cornstarch mixture a little at a time, stirring constantly, until the soup is thick and clear.

Finally, dribble in the egg white which will set into shreds. The entire cooking process should take only a few minutes. Serve immediately.
Serves 4

⟨≋⟩

SUSHI ROLLED IN SEAWEED
Norimaki Zushi ◆ Japan

1 quantity sushi rice (page 255)
4 dried mushrooms
2 tablespoons Japanese soy sauce
1 tablespoon sugar
2 eggs
¼ teaspoon salt
few drops vegetable oil
1 green cucumber
1 small piece takuan (pickled radish)
4 oz (125 g) raw tuna, bonito or kingfish (halibut)
1 teaspoon prepared wasabi (Japanese horseradish)
6 sheets nori (dried laver seaweed)

Prepare sushi rice. While it cools, soak mushrooms in hot water for 20 minutes. Cut off and discard stems, shred the caps into very thin slices and simmer in half cup (4 fl oz, 125 ml) of the soaking liquid mixed with soy and sugar until liquid is almost all evaporated.

Beat eggs with salt and cook in lightly oiled pan like a flat omelet. Cool, then cut in thin strips. Peel cucumber thinly, leaving a trace of green. Cut lengthwise in strips the size of a pencil. Drain the takuan and cut in similar sized strips.

Remove skin and bones from fish, cut in strips and smear with wasabi.

Toast sheets of nori by passing them back and forth over a gas flame or electric hotplate a few times.

Put a sheet of nori on a bamboo placemat, or on a clean linen napkin. Divide the rice into six equal portions and spread one portion evenly over two-thirds of the sheet of nori, starting at the end nearest you. In a row down the middle of the rice put one of the ingredients or a combination of ingredients.

Roll up sushi in the mat, keeping firm pressure on the rice so that a neatly packed cylinder results. Let the rolls rest for 10 minutes before cutting into about six pieces. Arrange on a tray, decorate with tiny leaves or green paper cut in fancy shapes. Serve cold.
Makes about 36

⟨≋⟩

SUSHI WRAPPED IN OMELET
Fukusa Zushi ◆ Japan

half quantity chirashi-zushi (page 56)
4 eggs
2 tablespoons cold water
½ teaspoon salt
few drops vegetable oil
thin strips of nori (dried laver seaweed)

Press chirashi-zushi firmly into a square or rectangular cooking pot or cake pan to a depth of 1 in (2.5 cm). Weight down and leave while cooking omelet wrappers.

Beat eggs lightly, add water and salt and cook in small, lightly oiled pan to make 8 or 9 very thin omelets. Cook on low heat and do not allow omelets to brown.

Cut pressed chriashi-zushi into 8 or 9 pieces about 2 in (5 cm) square. Put a square of chirashi-zushi in the middle of an omelet and roll up or fold, envelope fashion, to enclose the rice. Wrap a thin strip of nori around the parcel and put on serving plate with joins underneath. Repeat with remaining mixture and omelets. Serve cold.
Makes 8 or 9

Opposite, sushi rolled in seaweed, norimaki zushi (recipe this page).

TEA EGGS
China

Place 6 eggs in a saucepan, cover with cold water and bring slowly to a boil, stirring gently. (This helps to center the yolks.) Simmer gently for 7 minutes. Cool eggs thoroughly under running cold water for 5 minutes. Lightly crack each egg shell by rolling on a hard surface. Shell should be cracked all over, but do not remove.

Bring 4 cups (1 3/4 pts, 1 L) water to a boil, add 3 tablespoons tea leaves, 1 tablespoon salt, and 1 teaspoon five-spice powder. Add cracked eggs. Simmer, covered, for approximately 30 minutes or until shells turn brown. Let eggs stand in covered pan for 30 minutes (or longer, overnight if possible). Drain, cool and shell. The whites of eggs will have a marbled pattern on them.

THICK NOODLE SOUP
Hokkien Mee Soup ◆ Singapore

1 lb (500 g) small cooked shrimp (prawns)
1 lb (500 g) hokkien mee (thick yellow noodles)
4 oz (125 g) rice vermicelli
1 lb (500 g) fresh bean sprouts
12 English spinach leaves

Garnishes:
4 oz (125 g) pork fat, cut into diny dice
4 tablespoons dried onion flakes
4 dried chilies, optional
soy sauce
oil for frying

Soup:
8 cups (64 fl oz, 2 L) pork or chicken stock
2 dried chilies, seeded
1 tablespoon oil
sugar, soy sauce, and salt to taste
½ cup cooked pork cut into small strips, optional

Peel the shrimp. Bring a large amount of lightly salted water to a boil in a saucepan or wok, drop in the fresh noodles and parboil. Drain in colander, run cold water over to stop cooking process. Put rice vermicelli in a bowl, cover with hot water, leave to soak for 10 minutes, drain. Scald the bean sprouts by pouring boiling water over them in a colander, then run cold water over to cool. Remove stems of spinach, cook in a little boiling water until half done, drain and cut into short strips. Have all these ingredients ready in separate bowls.

Garnishes: Put about 1 tablespoon oil in a wok, heat and add pork fat. Stir-fry until crisp. Remove from pan and drain on absorbent paper. Add about 3 or 4 tablespoons oil to the wok and fry the dried onion flakes over low heat, watching very carefully for they can burn and taste bitter in a few seconds. Do not have the oil too hot. A good way to fry dried onion or garlic is to put the flakes in a fine strainer and lower them gently into the oil, let them fry in the strainer and lift them all out together. Drain on absorbent paper. Cut tops off the chilies and shake out seeds, then fry them until they turn dark. Drain. When cool, crumble them into small pieces. Put each of these garnishes into a small bowl, and have a bowl of soy sauce for seasoning individual portions.

Soup: Bring the stock to a boil. In another pan heat the tablespoon of oil (oil left over from frying the garnishes can be used) and fry the chilies. When they turn dark, add the hot stock, sugar, soy and salt, and simmer for 5 minutes.

To serve the soup, put a serving of noodles, rice vermicelli, bean sprouts, shrimp, and spinach leaves into each large soup bowl. Pour the boiling soup over, then serve with the garnishes already on the table so each person can add according to taste.
Serves 6 as a main dish, 8–10 as an accompaniment

VEGETABLE FRITTERS
Pakorhas ◆ India

1½ cups besan (chickpea flour)
1 teaspoon garam masala
2 teaspoons salt
½ teaspoon ground turmeric
½ teaspoon chili powder, optional
1 cup (8 fl oz, 250 ml) water
1 clove garlic, crushed
4 cups mixed chopped potato, onion, eggplant (aubergine),
*   cauliflower or other raw vegetables*
oil for deep frying

Sift into a bowl the flour with the garam masala, salt, turmeric, and chili powder. Add water gradually, mixing to a thick batter. Stir in garlic and beat well, allow batter to stand for 30 minutes and beat again.

Add vegetables to batter and mix thoroughly. Heat oil to a depth 4 in (10 cm) in a wok and test with a drop of batter. When batter rises immediately to the surface, oil is hot enough. Drop teaspoons of mixture into oil and fry over medium heat until fritters are pale golden on both sides. Do not fry too many at once or the temperature of the oil will be lowered too much and the fritters will be greasy and heavy. Lift out with a slotted spoon and drain on absorbent paper.

Just before serving, reheat oil and when almost smoking hot

Wonton soup (page 76).

return fritters to wok, a few at a time, for about 30 seconds or until golden brown all over. The second frying makes them very crisp. Drain on absorbent paper and serve immediately.
Makes about 30 fritters

⊰⊱〰⊰⊱

VEGETARIAN DIM SUM
Chai Dim Sum ◆ China

4 cups cooked and minced gluten
6 dried Chinese mushrooms
3 tablespoons peanut oil
¼ cup finely chopped scallions (spring onions)
1 clove garlic, crushed
1 teaspoon finely grated fresh ginger

2 cups finely sliced cabbage
½ cup finely chopped bamboo shoot and/or water chestnuts
2 tablespoons light soy sauce
2 teaspoons sesame oil
3 teaspoons salt
2 tablespoons cornstarch (cornflour)
2 eggs, beaten
8 oz (250 g) wonton wrappers

To make gluten: Measure 2 cups (16 fl oz, 500 ml) water into a large mixing bowl. Sprinkle in 2 cups (16 fl oz, 500 ml) gluten flour, mix well and knead until smooth, then leave for an hour or more. Bring water to a boil in saucepan, cut pieces of gluten dough off and drop into the water. Return to boil, then simmer for 30 minutes or until they rise to the surface. Drain and cool, then chop or mince finely.

Stuffing mixture: While making gluten, soak mushrooms in hot water for 30 minutes. Then remove and discard stems, chop caps very finely. Heat peanut oil in a wok or large frying pan and fry scallions, garlic, and ginger on low heat for a minute or two. Add cabbage and continue to fry, stirring, until cabbage is soft. Add bamboo shoot, water chestnuts, mushrooms, gluten and cook for a minute or two longer. Remove from heat, put into a large bowl and add seasonings, cornstarch, and enough beaten egg to bind the mixture together.

Take a wonton wrapper in the palm of your hand. Put a tablespoon of mixture in the middle and gather up the pastry to enclose filling. With the back of a teaspoon, press points of the dough down to cover. Squeeze dumpling firmly to make dough adhere to filling. Put in an oiled steamer and steam for 10 minutes.

These may be served at once, or refrigerated for a day or two and deep fried, or reheated by further steaming before serving.
Makes about 36

⋖⋗⋉⋊⋗⋖

WHOLE CHICKEN SOUP
China

2 lb (1 kg) chicken
cold water
1 cup (8 oz, 250 g) rice
2 teaspoons salt
½ teaspoon five-spice powder
1 stalk celery, sliced
1 onion, sliced

Put whole chicken into a large saucepan with sufficient cold water to completely cover it. Wash rice in 3 or 4 changes of water, drain, add to pan. Add salt, five–spice, celery, and onion, bring to a boil, then simmer, covered, for 1 1/2 hours or until rice is very soft. If necessary, add more boiling water during cooking time.

Serve soup first, then serve chicken, which should be tender enough to break with chopsticks. Serve dipping sauces with the chicken.
Serves 4–5

⋖⋗⋉⋊⋗⋖

WONTON SOUP
China

4 oz (125 g) raw shrimp (prawns)
4 oz (125 g) ground (minced) pork
2 scallions (spring onions), finely chopped
½ teaspoon salt
1 tablespoon light soy sauce
¼ teaspoon crushed garlic
¼ teaspoon finely grated fresh ginger root
4 oz (125 g) wonton wrappers
2½ pints (1.5 L) stock
4 tablespoons finely chopped cilantro (fresh coriander leaves)
   or scallions (spring onions)

In some restaurants this is known as 'Short Soup', the name referring to the dumplings as opposed to the long strands of noodles in 'Long Soup'.

Shell and devein the shrimp and chop them finely. Mix with the pork, scallions, salt, soy sauce, garlic and ginger.

Place about a teaspoon of the mixture on each square of wonton pastry. Moisten the edges, fold diagonally over the filling to make a triangle and press the edges together to seal. Moisten the two corners at the base of the triangle and join them together.

In a saucepan, bring a large amount of lightly salted water to a rolling boil and add a dash of oil. Drop in the dumplings, a few at a time, and after the water has returned to a boil, cook them for 5 minutes; add a small glass of cold water and bring to a boil again. Drain in a colander. Repeat until all dumplings are cooked.

Bring the stock to a boil, add the dumplings and return to a boil once more. Sprinkle with chopped cilantro or scallions, and serve hot.
Serves 6

⋖⋗⋉⋊⋗⋖

YUNNAN POT CHICKEN SOUP
WITH WINTER MELON
China

6 large dried mushrooms
3 lb (1.5 kg) roasting chicken
2 teaspoons shredded fresh ginger root
2 scallions (spring onions)
8 oz (250 g) peeled winter melon, chopped in chunky pieces
2 tablespoons Chinese wine or sherry
1 tablespoon light soy sauce
½ teaspoon sesame oil
½ teaspoon salt

Soak the mushrooms in hot water for 30 minutes. Then squeeze out excess water, discard the stems, and cut the caps into halves or quarters. Rinse the chicken, cut off and discard the tail and excess fat. Cut the bird in half down the middle.

Remove thighs and drumsticks and pull off the skin. Chop the legs into 5 or 6 pieces, but do not cut through the joint. Remove the skin from the breast and cut each half of the breast into 4 pieces. Chop off wing tips (keep wing tips, neck, and back for stock) and cut each wing into 3 pieces, again leaving the joint intact.

Put the chicken pieces into the pot and add ginger and scallions. No water is needed in a Yunnan pot, but add a small amount (about 8 fl oz (250 ml)) to a pot that does not have a funnel.

Choose a saucepan just large enough to hold the Yunnan pot above water level when it has 2–3 ins (5–7.5 cm) of water in it. Bring to a boil and place the Yunnan pot on it. (If using a chicken pot or ordinary covered cooking pot, place in a large pan with hot water to come half-way up the pot. Cover the pan with lid.)

Cook on medium high heat, keeping the water boiling briskly and adding more water as required, for 1 1/2 to 2 hours.

Add melon and cook for a further 10 minutes or until the melon is transparent. At the end of cooking, discard the scallions and any large pieces of ginger. Stir in the wine, soy sauce, sesame oil, and salt.

Serve the soup in the pot and accompany with steamed rice. Provide small individual sauce bowls for dipping the pieces of chicken in a dipping sauce before eating.

Dipping Sauce: Mix equal parts of light soy sauce and Chinese wine or dry sherry with a few drops of sesame oil or a little finely grated fresh ginger, or toasted and crushed sesame seeds. For those who prefer a hot flavor, offer chili sauce.

A Yunnan pot is made from clay and features a narrow funnel which conducts steam up into the pot.

Serves 6

Yunnan pot chicken soup with winter melon (recipe opposite).

Seafood

ABALONE IN OYSTER SAUCE
Singapore

16 oz (500 g) canned abalone
4 dried Chinese mushrooms
12 snow peas (mangetout) or 4 leaves gai choy (Chinese mustard cabbage)
4 scallions (spring onions)

Sauce:
1 tablespoon oyster sauce
1 teaspoon soy sauce
1 tablespoon Chinese wine or brandy
¾ cup (6 fl oz, 180 ml) liquid from abalone
2 teaspoons cornstarch (cornflour)

Drain abalone, reserving liquid. Cut abalone into paper-thin slices. Soak mushrooms in hot water for 30 minutes, then cut off and discard stalks and slice each mushroom into 4. String snow peas (or cut gai choy leaves into bite-sized pieces). Cut scallions into similar lengths.

Sauce: Combine all liquid ingredients, add a little to the cornstarch and mix until smooth, then combine with remaining liquid. In a small pan bring to a boil, stirring constantly. Add mushrooms, snow peas (or gai choy) and scallions. Cook, stirring, until the vegetables are tender but still crisp, about 2 or 3 minutes. Add abalone and just heat through. Do not cook abalone on high heat or for longer than is necessary to just heat it or it will toughen.

Serve with small portions of rice or noodles.
Serves 4–5

ABALONE WITH CHINESE CABBAGE
China

8 oz (250 g) canned abalone
1 Chinese (Napa) cabbage
1 tablespoon dry sherry
1 tablespoon oyster sauce
1 tablespoon light soy sauce
½ teaspoon sugar, optional
½ teaspoon sesame oil
1 tablespoon peanut oil
½ teaspoon finely grated fresh ginger
2 scallions (spring onions), cut into bite-size pieces

Slice the abalone paper-thin and set aside. Wash the Chinese cabbage well and cut into bite-size lengths, using all the stems and all but the tough portions of the leaves.

Combine the sherry, oyster sauce, soy sauce, sugar, and sesame oil and have ready in a small bowl.

Heat a wok, add the peanut oil and swirl to coat. Add ginger and cabbage and stir-fry over high heat for 1 minute. Add all the seasonings and the scallions. Lower heat, cover and simmer for 2 minutes, then stir in the abalone slices and heat gently only until abalone is hot. Do not over-cook or it will become tough. Serve immediately.
Serves 2 as a main meal, 4 with other dishes

BAKED FISH
Ikan Bandeng ◆ Indonesia

1 medium snapper (seabass) or halibut (jewfish)
1 medium onion, chopped
2 cloves garlic
1 teaspoon finely chopped fresh root ginger
2 tablespoons tamarind liquid
1 tablespoon soy sauce
1 tablespoon oil
1 teaspoon sambal ulek (optional) (page 23)
1 teaspoon salt
1 teaspoon ground turmeric
3 tablespoons finely chopped cilantro (fresh coriander leaves)

Wash fish and dry well with kitchen paper. Score the flesh diagonally on each side.

Place onion, garlic, ginger, tamarind liquid, soy sauce, oil, sambal ulek if used, salt, and turmeric into blender container, cover and blend until smooth. Rub ground mixture well into the fish on both sides. Place fish on 2 or 3 large pieces of banana leaf (or foil) in a baking dish, sprinkle with cilantro and fold leaves over to enclose fish. Secure with bamboo skewers.

Bake in a moderate oven for 35 to 40 minutes or until fish is cooked. When ready to serve, the flesh will look milky white and flake easily when tested with a fork. Replace banana leaves, lift fish onto a serving plate and open banana leaves at the table.

Note: Banana leaves give a subtle and appetizing fragrance.
Serves 4

Balinese-style fish (page 80).

BAKED SNAPPER STUFFED WITH PORK
China

1 medium size snapper (sea bass)
1 teaspoon salt
1 teaspoon finely grated fresh ginger
4 oz (125 g) ground (minced) pork
1 clove garlic, crushed
1 tablespoon finely chopped scallion (spring onion)
¼ teaspoon salt
⅛ teaspoon pepper
¼ cup (2 fl oz, 60 ml) dark soy sauce
2 tablespoons dry sherry
1 cup (8 fl oz, 250 ml) water
2 teaspoons sesame oil
2 teaspoons sugar
6 thin slices fresh ginger
2 cloves garlic, bruised
1 whole star anise
1 scallion (spring onion), cut into pieces

Wash and clean fish thoroughly, leaving head on. Cut slashes on either side of fish and rub over with 1 teaspoon salt and half the grated ginger.

Combine pork with remaining ginger, the crushed garlic, chopped scallion, salt, and pepper. Fill the cavity of the fish with the pork mixture and place it in an oiled baking dish. Combine all the other ingredients and pour over the fish. Bake in a moderate oven 30 to 35 minutes or until fish is cooked, basting frequently with the sauce.

Lift fish onto serving dish and spoon some of the sauce over. Garnish with sprigs of cilantro (fresh coriander leaves) or scallion flowers and serve hot.

Note: If preferred the fish may be braised instead of baked. First fry for 2 minutes on each side in 6 tablespoons of peanut oil. Pour off oil and add sauce. Cover and simmer for 7 minutes on one side, then turn fish carefully and simmer for 15 minutes on the other side. Make sure liquid is sufficient to half cover the fish so that pork filling in cavity is submerged. If necessary add more water.

Serves 2 as a main dish, 4 with other courses

⋈

BALINESE-STYLE FISH
Ikan Bali ◆ **Indonesia**

2 lb (1kg) fish steaks
2 tablespoons peanut oil
2 medium onions, finely chopped
1 teaspoon finely chopped garlic
1½ teaspoons finely grated fresh ginger
1½ teaspoons sambal ulek or fresh chili paste
1 teaspoon finely grated lemon rind
1 teaspoon laos powder
2 tablespoons lemon juice
2 tablespoons palm sugar or substitute
2 tablespoons dark soy sauce
½ teaspoon salt
peanut oil for frying

Wash fish, dry on absorbent paper towels and cut into serving portions. Heat about 2 tablespoons oil in a small saucepan and fry the onions until soft. Add garlic and ginger and stir over medium heat until golden brown. Add sambal ulek, lemon rind, laos powder, lemon juice, sugar, soy sauce, and salt and simmer for 2 or 3 minutes. Set aside.

Heat peanut oil for deep frying and fry the fish until golden brown on both sides. Drain, put on serving plate and spoon the sauce over. Serve with rice.

Serves 6

⋈

BARBECUED FISH
Tandoori Machchi ◆ **North India**

1 whole fish, mullet, halibut (jewfish) or other firm fish
  about 2 lb (1 kg)
coarse salt
2 teaspoons crushed garlic
2 teaspoons finely grated fresh ginger
1½ teaspoons salt
1 teaspoon ground cumin
1 teaspoon chili powder
1 teaspoon ground turmeric
pinch red food coloring powder or 2 teaspoons paprika
approximately 2 tablespoons lemon juice
3 tablespoons melted ghee
2 teaspoons garam masala (page 9)

Asian cuisine offers boundless ways to make use of fresh, tangy seafood.

Buy fish cleaned and scaled with head removed. Clean the cavity of the fish with several pieces of kitchen paper dampened and dipped in coarse salt. Wash the fish well under cold running water, then blot dry with kitchen paper. With a sharp knife cut slashes on each side of the fish, almost to the bone. Combine the garlic, ginger, salt, cumin, chili powder, turmeric, and coloring powder or paprika. This is what gives tandoori fish its distinctive color. Add enough lemon juice to form a thick paste.

Rub the marinade all over the fish, inside and out, and leave for 1 hour or longer in the refrigerator.

Pass a long metal skewer through the fish from head to tail and cook over glowing coals, or under preheated broiler (grill), brushing with the melted ghee. It should take 6 or 7 minutes cooking on each side. When fish is almost cooked, sprinkle with garam masala. Serve with naan, parathas or puris.
Serves 4

BOILED FISH, SICHUAN-STYLE
China

1 whole fish, snapper (sea bass), redfish (ocean perch) or
* similar, about 2 lb (1 kg)*
4 dried Chinese mushrooms
2 scallions (spring onions)
1 tablespoon sherry
2 teaspoons bean sauce
2 teaspoons vinegar
1 tablespoon peanut oil
1 teaspoon finely grated fresh ginger
½ teaspoon crushed garlic

Clean and scale fish, but leave head on. Trim fins and tail with kitchen scissors, make 3 or 4 diagonal slashes on each side of fish half-way to the bone. Soak the dried mushrooms in hot water for 20 minutes, discard stems and cut caps into fine slices. Cut scallions in thin diagonal slices. Combine the sherry, bean sauce, and vinegar in a small bowl with 2 tablespoons of the mushroom water and set aside.

Heat enough water in a wok to cover the fish and when it is boiling lower the fish in, cover with lid and allow to just simmer for 4 to 5 minutes. Turn off heat and leave covered in the water for 15 minutes. Drain and remove to a serving dish.

While fish is cooking in the stored heat, prepare the sauce. Heat peanut oil and on fairly low heat fry the ginger and garlic until just turning golden. Add the mushrooms and scallions and fry for another minute, stirring. Add all the mixed seasonings, bring to a boil and pour over the fish. Garnish with scallion curls and serve at once.
Serves 2–4

BOILED WHOLE FISH, HONAN-STYLE
China

1 whole 1 lb (500 g) fresh snapper (sea bass), redfish (ocean
* perch) or other whole white fish*
1 teaspoon salt
1 tablespoon peanut oil
1 teaspoon finely grated fresh ginger
8 scallions (spring onions), finely chopped
1 teaspoon sesame oil
2 tablespoons light soy sauce

Scale, clean, and wash fish and trim spines and fins but leave head and tail on. Put enough water into a wok or frying pan to cover the fish (but do not add fish yet), add salt, bring to a boil and lower the fish into it, cover and return to a boil. Reduce heat and cook 5 to 7 minutes. Remove from liquid and drain well.

Heat peanut oil in a small saucepan and fry ginger and scallions very gently until soft but not brown. Remove from heat. Add sesame oil and soy sauce. Put fish on a serving dish, on a bed of lettuce if desired. Spoon the sauce over and serve at once.

Note: To serve 4, use a larger fish and increase seasonings and cooking time accordingly.
Serves 2

BRAISED FISH & SHRIMP ROLLS
China

1 lb (500 g) firm white boned fish
12 raw shrimp (prawns), shelled, deveined and chopped
2 tablespoons peanut oil
3 thin slices fresh ginger
¼ cup (2 fl oz, 60 ml) hot water
1 tablespoon light soy sauce
1 tablespoon dry sherry
3 scallions (spring onions), sliced finely

Remove skin from fish and cut into 12 strips, each large enough to roll round a portion of shrimp. Fasten with wooden toothpicks.

Heat peanut oil in wok or frying pan, add slices of ginger and fry until they turn golden. Add fish rolls and fry for 2 minutes, turning them carefully with chopsticks or tongs. Add hot water, soy sauce, and sherry. Cover and simmer for 5 minutes. Remove fish rolls to serving dish, add scallions and stir. Remove and discard slices of ginger and pour sauce over fish. Garnish as desired and serve at once.
Serves 2–4

Braised ginger crab (page 84).

BRAISED FISH WITH SAFFRON & YOGURT

Machchi Korma ◆ India (Punjab)

1½ lb (750 g) boned fish
lemon juice
1 teaspoon salt
1 teaspoon ground black pepper
1 teaspoon ground turmeric
oil for frying
1 large onion, finely sliced
1 medium onion, roughly chopped
1 teaspoon chopped garlic
1 tablespoon chopped fresh ginger
2 or 3 fresh red chilies, seeded
2 tablespoons blanched almonds
1 tablespoon white poppy seeds, optional

2 teaspoons ground cumin
2 teaspoons ground coriander
¼ teaspoon ground cardamom
¼ teaspoon ground cinnamon
small pinch ground cloves
¼ cup (2 fl oz, 60 ml) cold water
¼ teaspoon saffron strands
2 tablespoons boiling water
½ cup yogurt
salt to taste
2 tablespoons chopped cilantro (fresh coriander leaves)

Wash and dry fish, cut into large serving pieces and rub with lemon juice, salt, pepper, and turmeric. Heat oil in a frying pan for shallow frying and on high heat brown the fish quickly on both sides. Lift out onto a plate. In the same oil fry finely sliced onion until golden brown, remove and set aside. Put roughly chopped onion, garlic, ginger, chilies, almonds, poppy seeds (if used) into electric blender and purée. If necessary add a little water. Add ground spices and briefly blend again.

Pour off all but about 2 tablespoons oil from pan and fry the blended mixture until color changes and it gives out a pleasing aroma. The mixture should be stirred constantly while frying and care taken that it does not catch to pan and burn. Add 1/4 cup water to blender container and swirl out any remaining spice mixture. Add to pan.

Pound saffron strands in mortar and pestle, add boiling water and stir, add to mixture in pan. Add yogurt, stir and simmer gently for a few minutes, then add fish pieces, turning them carefully in the sauce. Add salt to taste. Cover and simmer for about 10 minutes, then sprinkle with cilantro and serve hot with rice.

Serves 4–6

❖❖❖

BRAISED GINGER CRAB
China

2 king crabs (mud crabs, blue swimmer crabs or similar)
2 tablespoons peanut oil
1 clove garlic, finely chopped
1 tablespoon finely shredded fresh ginger
2 tablespoons light soy sauce
2 tablespoons dry sherry
¼ cup (2 fl oz, 60 ml) water
¼ cup finely sliced scallions (spring onions)

Wash crabs well, remove and discard hard-top shell, fibrous tissue and stomach bag. If using king crabs, separate the large claws. Divide each crab body in halves or quarters.

Heat the wok, add peanut oil and swirl, to spread the oil. On medium heat fry the garlic and ginger just until soft and starting to turn golden. Add the soy sauce, sherry, water, and the crab, cover and simmer for 5 to 8 minutes. Sprinkle in the scallions, replace cover and cook for 1 minute longer. Serve hot.

Note: If using raw crabs fry them on high heat until they change color, then add ingredients and proceed as above.

Serves 2–4

❖❖❖

BRAISED RAINBOW TROUT IN PIQUANT SAUCE
China

1 rainbow trout, about 2 lb (1 kg)
2 tablespoons cornstarch (cornflour)
1 teaspoon salt
¼ teaspoon five spice powder
1 cup (8 fl oz, 250 ml) oil
2 scallions (spring onions), coarsely chopped
2 teaspoons finely chopped fresh ginger

Sauce:
2 tablespoons Chinese wine or dry sherry
2 tablespoons light soy sauce
2 teaspoons sugar
2 teaspoons cider vinegar
1 teaspoon sesame oil

Garnish:
3 tablespoons chopped cilantro (fresh coriander leaves)

Wipe the fish and make deep diagonal cuts on both sides. Combine the cornstarch, salt, and five spice powder, mixing thoroughly. Sprinkle the trout with this mixture, rubbing it well into the slashes, then dust off the excess.

In a bowl, combine the sauce ingredients; add 1/2 cup (4 fl oz, 125 ml) water, and stir until the sugar is dissolved.

Heat a wok, add the oil and when hot, slide the fish into the oil and fry on medium heat for 2 minutes until browned on one side, then turn it over and fry the other side for 2 minutes. Remove the fish from the wok.

Pour off all but 1 tablespoon of the oil. When this is very hot, stir-fry the scallions and ginger for 1 minute; they should not brown. Add the mixed sauce ingredients to the wok and bring to a boil. Return the fish and let it simmer, covered, on low heat for 5 minutes. Carefully turn the fish over and let it simmer for a further 4 to 5 minutes.

Lift the fish onto a warmed serving dish. The cornstarch coating on the fish may have been sufficient to slightly thicken the sauce. If not, mix 1 teaspoon of cornstarch with 1 teaspoon of cold water, stir this into the sauce and allow it to boil up and thicken. Spoon the sauce over the fish, sprinkle liberally with chopped cilantro.

Serves 4–6

❖❖❖

Braised rainbow trout with piquant sauce (recipe opposite).

BROILED FISH WITH CHILI BEAN SAUCE
China

1 whole sea bass (perch, snapper) or porgy (bream) about
*   2 lb (1 kg)*
½ teaspoon salt
½ teaspoon finely grated fresh ginger
1 teaspoon sesame oil
1 tablespoon peanut oil
1 tablespoon finely shredded fresh ginger
1 clove garlic, crushed
1 tablespoon light soy sauce
2 teaspoons purchased chili bean sauce
3 scallions (spring onions), cut into bite-size lengths
3 tablespoons water

Clean and wash fish, dry with paper towels and cut two or three diagonal slashes on each side. Rub over with salt and ginger, brush with sesame oil, making sure it goes into the slashes. Place fish on foil-lined broiler (grill) pan.

Broil fish on both sides under pre-heated broiler until cooked, testing with tip of knife at thickest part. When flesh is white, it is done. Do not cook for too long or it will be dry.

While fish is cooking, heat the peanut oil in a small pan and fry the ginger and garlic on low heat until just starting to color. Add the remaining ingredients, bring to a boil and pour over the fish before serving.

Serves 2–4

BROILED MARINATED FISH
Kinome Yaki ♦ Japan

2 large fish steaks (tuna, mackerel or other oily fish)
4 tablespoons Japanese soy sauce
2 tablespoons mirin or dry sherry
2 tablespoons sake
2 teaspoons finely grated fresh ginger
1 tablespoon sugar

Garnishes:
pickled ginger or 2 scallions (spring onions), shredded or
 1 large cucumber
3 tablespoons white vinegar
3 tablespoons sugar
1 teaspoon Japanese soy sauce
1 teaspoon salt

Wash fish, dry well and cut each steak into four pieces. Combine soy sauce, mirin, and sake.

Squeeze juice from ginger into mixture and discard fibers. Add sugar and dissolve. Marinate fish in this for about 30 minutes.

Preheat broiler (grill) and cook fish about 4 in (10 cm) away from heat source for 5 to 7 minutes, brushing two or three times with the marinade. Turn fish and broil other side. The fish should have a rich glaze of marinade. Serve immediately, garnished with pickled ginger, scallion shreds or cucumber sticks marinated in mixture of vinegar, sugar, soy sauce, and salt.
Serves 4

BUTTERFLY SHRIMP
Woo Dip Har ♦ China

12 large raw shrimp (king prawns)
2 tablespoons soy sauce
1 tablespoon Chinese wine or dry sherry, optional
1 small clove garlic, crushed
¼ teaspoon salt
½ teaspoon finely grated fresh ginger root
½ cup (3 oz, 90 g) cornstarch (cornflour)
1 large beaten egg
breadcrumbs for coating
peanut oil for deep frying

Shell and devein shrimp, leaving tail on. With a sharp knife slit shrimp along curve of back but do not cut right through. Combine soy sauce, wine, garlic crushed with salt, and ginger. Marinate shrimp in this mixture for 15 minutes.

Dip shrimp into cornstarch, shake off excess, then dip into the beaten egg and finally into the breadcrumbs. Press gently to flatten shrimp and firm on the crumb coating.

Heat oil and fry shrimp, 2 or 3 at a time, until golden brown, about 2 minutes. Drain on absorbent paper and serve hot with chili sauce if desired.
Serves 4–6

CHILI SHRIMP & BAMBOO SHOOT
China

5 tablespoons dried shrimp (prawns)
2 oz (60 g) bean starch noodles
8 oz (250 g) canned winter bamboo shoot
2 tablespoons peanut oil
½ teaspoon finely chopped garlic
½ teaspoon finely chopped fresh ginger
few drops sesame oil
2 tablespoons chopped scallions (spring onions)

Sauce:
2 teaspoons dark soy sauce
½ teaspoon salt
1 teaspoon sugar
4 fl oz (125 ml) chicken stock
2 teaspoons chili oil
1 teaspoon cornstarch (cornflour)

Soak the dried shrimp in hot water for 30 minutes. Drain well and pat dry with paper towels; pulverize in an electric blender and set aside. Chop the bamboo shoot and set aside.

Separate bean starch noodles using kitchen shears, place in a pan of boiling water and boil for 15 minutes. Drain and set aside.

Heat a wok or frying pan, add the peanut oil and swirl to coat the sides of the wok. When hot add the garlic, ginger, powdered shrimp, and bamboo shoot; stir-fry for 1 minute. Add sauce ingredients mixed together, stirring until it boils and thickens. Add sesame oil, stir, and garnish with chopped scallions.

Place the drained bean starch noodles on a serving dish, and spoon the shrimp mixture over them. Serve immediately.
Serves 4

Crab curry from Sri Lanka (page 88).

CHILI-FRIED LOBSTER
Singapore

2 fresh lobster tails, medium-size
½ cup (4 fl oz, 125 ml) peanut oil
2 teaspoons finely chopped fresh ginger
2 teaspoons finely chopped garlic
1 cup finely chopped scallions (spring onions)
3 fresh red chilies, seeded and chopped
¼ cup (1½ oz, 45 g) tomato sauce
¼ cup (2 fl oz, 60 ml) chili sauce
1 tablespoon sugar
2 teaspoons cornstarch (cornflour)
2 tablespoons Chinese wine or dry sherry
1 tablespoon light soy sauce
2 tablespoons purchased fish sauce
salt

Wash lobster tails and chop into sections. Heat a wok, add oil and when oil is very hot fry the lobster pieces until they turn red, turning them frequently so they cook on all sides. Remove to a plate. Turn heat to low and fry the ginger, garlic, scallions, and chilies, stirring constantly, until they are soft but not brown. Add the tomato and chili sauces, and sugar. Stir and simmer covered for 2 minutes.

Mix cornstarch with wine, soy sauce, and fish sauce and add to the wok. Stir and bring to a boil. Return lobster pieces to the wok, stir to coat with sauce and simmer for 3 minutes on low heat. Add a very little water if sauce reduces too much. Adjust salt and serve with hot white rice.
Serves 4

CRAB CURRY
Kakuluwo Curry ◆ Sri Lanka

2 large crabs
3 medium onions, roughly chopped
6 cloves garlic
2 teaspoons finely grated fresh ginger
½ teaspoon fenugreek seeds
10 curry leaves
3 in (8 cm) stick cinnamon
1–2 teaspoons chili powder
1 teaspoon ground turmeric
3 teaspoons salt
4 cups (32 fl oz, 1 L) thin coconut cream
2 tablespoons unsweetened desiccated coconut
1 tablespoon ground rice
2 cups (16 fl oz, 500 ml) thick coconut cream
3 tablespoons lemon juice

Remove large shells of crabs and discard fibrous tissue found under the shell. Divide each crab into 4 portions, breaking each body in half and separating large claws from body. Leave legs attached to body.

Purée onion, garlic and ginger in electric blender. Heat oil in large saucepan and fry this purée, stirring for about 10 minutes. Add fenugreek, curry leaves, cinnamon, chili powder, turmeric, salt, and thin coconut cream. Cover and simmer gently 30 minutes. Add crabs and cook for 20 minutes if using raw crabs. Cook for only 5 to 7 minutes if cooked crabs are used. If pan is not large enough, simmer half the pieces of crab at a time. Crab should be submerged in sauce while cooking.

Heat desiccated coconut and ground rice separately in a dry frying pan over moderate heat, stirring constantly to prevent burning, until each is golden brown. Put in an electric blender container. Add half the thick coconut cream, cover and blend on high speed 1 minute. Add to curry with lemon juice. Wash out blender with remaining coconut cream and add. Simmer uncovered a further 10 minutes. Serve with boiled rice.
Serves 4–6

⋖⧓⋗

CRAB MEAT ROLLS
China

Filling:
6 oz (185 g) crab meat, frozen or canned
4 dried Chinese mushrooms
2 French shallots
¼ teaspoon finely grated fresh ginger root
½ teaspoon salt
1 teaspoon Chinese wine or dry sherry
5 or 6 spring roll wrappers
1 egg
1½ tablespoons all-purpose (plain) flour
peanut oil for deep frying

Filling: Flake crab meat, removing bony tissue. Drain off any liquid. Soak mushrooms in hot water for 30 minutes, remove and discard stems and chop mushroom caps finely. Slice shallots very thinly. Mix crab, mushrooms, shallots, ginger, salt, and wine together.

Cut each egg roll wrapper into quarters. On each quarter place a teaspoonful of the filling, near one end. Fold pastry over filling, then fold sides in to enclose filling, and roll over again as for the first fold. Beat egg until frothy, add flour and beat again to a smooth, thick paste. Smear end of egg roll pastry with this paste and press gently to seal.

When all are made, fry in deep oil over medium heat until golden brown all over, about 1 1/2 minutes. Drain on absorbent paper and serve hot.
Makes 20–24

⋖⧓⋗

CRISP-SKIN FISH WITH MUSHROOM SAUCE
China

1 whole fish, about 3 lb (1.5 kg), snapper (sea bass) or
other firm white fish
flour, seasoned with salt
oil for frying
1 large lemon for garnishing

Mushroom Sauce:
6 dried Chinese mushrooms
8 tablespoons vinegar
8 tablespoons sugar
2 tablespoons light soy sauce
2 tablespoons finely chopped scallions (spring onions)
1 tablespoon cornstarch (cornflour)
2 tablespoons preserved cucumber slices in syrup (optional)

Deep-fried fish, Sichuan-style (recipe below).

Buy the fish cleaned and scaled, but with the head left on. Trim the fins and tail with kitchen scissors, and wipe out the cavity with absorbent paper dipped in course salt. Wash well and dry thoroughly. With a sharp knife, slash the fish diagonally on each side almost to the bone, forming diamond shapes in the flesh. Set the fish aside while you make the sauce.

Mushroom Sauce: Soak the mushrooms in hot water for 30 minutes. Drain, discard the mushroom stems and slice the caps finely. Put the mushrooms, vinegar, sugar, and soy sauce into a small saucepan; add 6 fl oz (180 ml) water, and boil for 5 minutes. Add the scallions. Add the cornstarch blended with 1 tablespoon cold water and cook, stirring, until the sauce is clear and thickened. Remove from heat and keep warm. Stir in the preserved cucumber if used.

Dip the fish in seasoned flour, shaking off excess. Deep fry the fish in hot oil until golden brown. Drain it on a wire spoon and transfer it to a serving dish. Spoon the sauce over and garnish with lemon butterflies. This fish is good hot or cold.
Serves 4–6

DEEP-FRIED FISH, SICHUAN-STYLE
China

2 whole firm white-fleshed fish about 1½ lb (750 g) each
4 tablespoons Chinese wine or dry sherry
2 tablespoons light soy sauce
2 teaspoons cornstarch (cornflour)
1 tablespoon cold water
2 tablespoons dark soy sauce
1 teaspoon sugar
½ cup (4 fl oz, 125 ml) peanut oil for frying
1 tablespoon finely grated fresh ginger
5 cloves garlic, finely chopped or grated
2 tablespoons hot bean or chili bean sauce
1 cup (8 fl oz, 250 ml) water
4 scallions (spring onions), finely chopped

Clean the fish thoroughly, leaving head and tail on. Trim spines with kitchen scissors. Wash well and dry on paper towels. With a sharp knife or chopper score the fish length-wise, making parallel cuts about a finger's width apart and almost through to the bone to allow seasonings to penetrate. Combine 2 tablespoons wine and light soy sauce and marinate the fish in the mixture, making sure it goes in all the cuts.

Mix cornstarch with cold water, then stir in dark soy sauce, remaining wine and the sugar. Set aside.

Heat oil in a wok or large frying pan until very hot. Drain away marinade, add fish, and deep fry about 3 or 4 minutes on each side or until the fish is golden brown. Turn fish once only when cooking. Drain on slotted spoon and put fish on a heated serving dish. Pour off oil in wok, leaving about 4 tablespoons, and fry the ginger and garlic over medium heat, stirring constantly, until garlic starts to turn golden. Add the bean sauce and stir, then add water. Stir the sauce ingredients once more to distribute the cornstarch evenly, add to wok and stir constantly until mixture comes to a boil, clears and thickens slightly. Add scallions and stir well. Pour sauce over fish and serve immediately with rice.

Serves 4 as a main dish

DEEP-FRIED FISH WITH VEGETABLES
Trei Chean Noeung Spei ◆ Cambodia & Laos

1½ lb (750 g) white boned fish
1 tablespoon egg white
1 teaspoon salt
1 tablespoon cornstarch (cornflour)
6 tablespoons oil
1 clove garlic, crushed
½ teaspoon finely grated fresh ginger
2 cups sliced white Chinese (Napa) cabbage
6 scallions (spring onions), cut in 2 in (5 cm) lengths
2 tablespoons fish sauce
½ cup water
1 teaspoon extra cornstarch (cornflour)

Cut fish into finger pieces, dip in egg white and then in a mixture of salt and cornstarch. Dust off excess flour. Heat oil in a wok and fry fish on high heat, one quarter of the quantity at a time, for just long enough to cook it through (this should take from 1 to 2 minutes depending on the thickness of the fish). Drain on absorbent paper and keep warm. Pour off all but a tablespoon of the oil, add garlic, ginger, cabbage, and stir-fry for 1 minute. Add scallions and stir-fry 1 minute more. Add fish sauce, and bring liquid to a boil, then stir in extra cornstarch

mixed with very little cold water. Stir until sauce boils and thickens. Arrange on a dish with fish pieces on top and serve immediately with rice or noodles.

Serves 4–6

DEEP-FRIED HONEY SHRIMP
China

12 oz (375 g) raw, shelled and deveined large shrimp
(king prawns)
1 clove garlic
salt and pepper
½ teaspoon sesame oil
1 tablespoon cornstarch (cornflour)
3 tablespoons sesame seeds
½ cup (2 oz, 60 g) self-raising flour
water
oil for deep frying
½ cup (5½ oz, 170 g) honey
steamed broccoli

Wash shrimp, drain well, then wrap in a clean, dry cloth and firmly press out surplus water. Crush garlic with 1 teaspoon salt, place in a bowl, add pepper, sesame oil, and cornstarch and mix well. Add shrimp, mix and allow to stand while toasting sesame seeds and preparing batter.

Toast the sesame seeds in a dry wok or frying pan, stirring constantly over medium heat until the seeds are golden brown. Remove immediately on to a plate to cool. Add sufficient cold water to the flour to make a coating batter, neither too thick nor too runny.

Heat enough oil for deep frying in a wok, on moderate heat. When oil is ready, a drop of batter should rise immediately to the surface. Dip shrimp in batter and add individually to the oil in quick succession. Fry on high heat until they turn golden. Remove shrimp with slotted spoon and drain on kitchen paper. Drain oil from wok, wipe over with kitchen paper and heat till warm. Turn off heat and add honey to wok. (The wok should be warm enough to thin the honey slightly.) Add shrimp to honey, stir so they are all coated, then transfer to heated serving dish. Sprinkle with toasted sesame seeds, surround with broccoli sprigs and serve immediately with hot white rice.

Serves 3

Deep-fried honey shrimp (recipe opposite).

DEEP-FRIED LOBSTER WITH GINGER

China

1 fresh live lobster or crayfish, about 2 lb (900 g)
1 tablespoon cornstarch (cornflour)
4 cups (1¾ pts, 1 L) peanut oil
1 tablespoon fine shreds of fresh ginger
2–3 scallions (spring onions) cut into 2 in (5 cm) lengths
1 teaspoon sliced hot chili
1 teaspoon finely chopped garlic
1 cup (8 fl oz, 250 ml) chicken stock, heated
additional 2 teaspoons cornstarch (cornflour)

There are two ways to treat this recipe. For a delicate result, use only ginger and scallions. For a more robust flavor, add chilies and garlic. Choose whichever version suits your palate or your mood.

Immobilize the lobster by whichever method you choose. One method is to place it in your deep freeze for an hour or two. Chop straight through where the head joins the body. Cut in half lengthwise down both body and head. Discard the stomach (to be found in the head) and the feathery tissue. Chop each half of the tail into four or five pieces. Chop off and discard the pointed tips of the legs. Sprinkle the tablespoon of cornstarch over the lobster pieces and mix.

Heat the wok, pour in the peanut oil and allow it to get very hot. Discard any fluid that has seeped out of the lobster and drop the pieces into the boiling water. Scoop the oil over the lobster as it fries. In about 1 to 2 minutes, the shell should turn bright red and the meat loses its transparent look and turns white. It may be better to fry the lobster in two batches, allowing the oil to get very hot again after the first batch has been removed.

Pour both the lobster and the oil into a wire sieve set over a heatproof bowl.

Return the wok to the heat with the oil that clings to the sides. Add the ginger, scallions, chili, and garlic, and stir-fry on high heat for a few seconds. Put in the lobster pieces, pour in the hot chicken stock, cover the wok and cook on high heat for 2 to 3 minutes so that the lobster finishes cooking in the steam. Uncover and stir. The liquid should be reduced by half.

Blend the cornstarch with 1 tablespoon of cold water and stir it into the wok; keep stirring until the sauce boils and thickens. Turn off the heat, take 1 tablespoon of the oil the lobster was fried in and sprinkle it over the lobster. Toss quickly. This gives a nice gloss. Serve immediately.

Serves 4

DEEP-FRIED SHRIMP WITH CHILI
Singapore

1 lb (500 g) raw, shelled, and deveined shrimp (prawns)
3 fresh red chilies
1 clove garlic
2 teaspoons finely grated fresh ginger
1 tablespoon sugar
1 tablespoon light soy sauce
1 tablespoon chinese wine or dry sherry
oil for deep frying

Rinse shrimp and dry well on paper towels. Slit the chilies and remove seeds, then chop finely. Crush garlic with a little of the sugar and mix with the chilies and ginger.

Heat about 1/2 cup (4 fl oz, 125 ml) oil in a wok until very hot and deep fry the shrimp a few at a time for 2 or 3 minutes or just until they begin to turn pink. Do not fry too long. Remove from pan and drain on absorbent paper. Pour off most of oil from pan, leaving only about a tablespoon. Add the chilies, garlic, and ginger and fry on low heat, stirring. Add the remaining sugar, soy sauce, and wine, then add shrimp and stir only until reheated. Serve immediately with rice or noodles.
Serves 4

DEEP-FRIED SEAFOOD
Harusame Tempura ◆ Japan

1 lb (500 g) boned porgy (bream, sea bass) or other firm white fish pieces
12 small to medium-size raw shrimp (prawns)
1 tablespoon Japanese soy sauce
1 tablespoon mirin or dry sherry
½ teaspoon salt
½ cup (3 oz, 90 g) cornstarch (cornflour)
1 or 2 egg whites, beaten until frothy
1½ cups finely snipped harusame (Japanese translucent noodles)
vegetable oil for deep frying
tempura sauce (see recipe below) or salt for dipping

Remove skin from fish pieces and cut lengthwise into narrow strips, then into bite-size lengths.

Shell and devein shrimp, leaving tails on. Marinate fish and shrimp in soy sauce, mirin, and salt for 30 minutes.

Roll each piece of seafood first in cornstarch, dusting off excess, then in egg white, then in harusame noodles. The noodles should be cut with kitchen scissors, a few strands at a time, to pieces not more than 1/2 in (1 cm) long.

Heat oil until moderately hot, about 350°F (170°C) and fry a few pieces at a time. Harusame will puff and swell immediately on being immersed in the hot oil. If they don't, it means the oil is not hot enough and the harusame will be tough and leathery instead of crisp and crackling. Fry for half to 1 minute, and remove from oil with a slotted spoon before the color changes. Drain on absorbent paper and serve with tempura sauce or sea salt for dipping.
Serves 4

DEEP-FRIED SEAFOOD & VEGETABLES
Tempura ◆ Japan

12–16 medium-sized raw shrimp (prawns)
1 lb (500 g) boned fish pieces
1 canned lotus root
1 can baby corn cobs
3 canned winter bamboo shoots
canned gingko nuts
8 scallions (spring onions)
8 oz (250 g) fresh mushrooms
4 tablespoons grated white radish
2 tablespoons finely grated fresh ginger
3 cups (24 fl oz, 750 ml) vegetable oil
½ cup (4 fl oz, 125 ml) sesame oil

Tempura Batter:
1 egg
1 cup (8 fl oz, 250 ml) ice-cold water
pinch baking (bicarbonate) soda
¾ cup (3 oz, 90 g) unsifted all-purpose (plain) flour or tempura flour

Tempura Sauce:
3 tablespoons mirin or dry sherry
3 tablespoons Japanese soy sauce
1 cup (8 fl oz, 250 ml) dashi (page 6)
pinch salt

Shell shrimp, leaving tails on, devein, wash and dry well on kitchen paper. Slice fish into thin, bite-size pieces. Drain all the canned vegetables thoroughly and dry them on kitchen paper. Cut lotus root crosswise into thin slices, slice bamboo shoots and if large cut in halves. Winter bamboo shoots are smaller and much more tender than ordinary bamboo shoots, and if they are not available the larger shoots will have to be cut in suitably sized pieces.

Thread 2 or 3 gingko nuts on wooden cocktail picks. Wash and trim scallions and cut into bite-size lengths. Wipe mushrooms clean with damp kitchen paper and cut in halves or quarters according to size.

Arrange all ingredients attractively on a tray, cover and refrigerate until serving time.

Set before each place a plate lined with a paper napkin, a small bowl for dipping sauce and another small bowl with a tablespoon of grated white radish and 2 teaspoons of grated fresh ginger.

Mix ingredientfs for sauce together and have ready. No more than 10 minutes before serving, make batter and stand the bowl in a larger bowl containing ice. Heat both oils until moderately hot (375°F, 190°C). If sesame oil is not available it may be omitted, but it gives a delicious and distinctive taste to the food.

When guests are seated, dip pieces of food one at a time into the batter and drop into the oil. Do not fry more than about 6 pieces at a time, as the temperature of the oil must be kept moderately high for best results. As each piece turns golden (this should take only a minute) lift it from the oil with a perforated spoon, drain for a few seconds on absorbent paper, then serve immediately to guests, who dip each piece in the sauce and eat it while crisp and hot. The radish and ginger are mixed into the sauce to suit individual taste.

Tempura Batter: Break egg into bowl of iced water and beat until frothy. Add baking soda and flour and beat just until flour is mixed in. Do not overbeat. Batter should be thin. If it seems too thick, add a few drops of iced water.

Tempura Sauce: Heat mirin in a small saucepan, remove from heat and ignite with a match. Shake pan gently until flame dies, add all other ingredients, bring to a boil quickly. Cool to room temperature, taste and adjust seasoning if necessary. Tempura is best served the moment it is ready, so cooking at the table in an electric wok or deep fryer is particularly suitable.

Note: Ready-to-use tempura sauce may be purchased in bottles if preferred.

Serves 4

FILETS OF FISH IN BLACK BEAN SAUCE
China

1 lb (500 g) boned firm white fish
1 tablespoon cornstarch (cornflour)
2 tablespoons canned salted black beans
2 cloves garlic
1 teaspoon sugar
1 teaspoon finely grated fresh ginger
½ cup (4 fl oz, 125 ml) water
2 tablespoons Chinese wine or dry sherry
1 teaspoon cornstarch (cornflour)
3 tablespoons peanut oil
2 scallions (spring onions), cut in thin diagonal slices

Wash and dry fish. Cut in two lengthwise, then cut each piece across into finger-size strips. Leave the narrow tail end of the fish in bite-size pieces. Dust the pieces with the cornstarch. Rinse the black beans in a strainer under the cold tap, put on a wooden board and chop or mash with a fork. Crush garlic with the sugar and mix with the ginger and the beans. Combine water, wine, and cornstarch in a cup.

Heat wok, add peanut oil and when hot put in the pieces of fish, a few at a time, and fry for 1 minute or until color changes. Drain on slotted spoon. Cook rest of fish, adding more oil if necessary. In 1 tablespoon oil, fry the black bean mixture for 1 minute. Stir the water, wine, and cornstarch until smooth and add to pan. Stir constantly until it boils and thickens slightly. Add fish pieces and scallions, heat through and serve.

Serves 2

FIREWORKS SHRIMP
China

1 lb (500 g) raw shrimp (prawns)
6 rashers bacon
2 tablespoons oil
1 medium onion, finely chopped
3 cloves garlic, finely chopped
2 teaspoons finely grated fresh root ginger
3 fresh red chilies, seeded and finely sliced
2 tablespoons purchased chili sauce
½ cup (4 fl oz, 125 ml) tomato purée or tomato sauce
2 tablespoons Chinese wine or dry sherry
1 tablespoon oyster sauce
1 tablespoon soy sauce
1 tablespoon honey
1 tablespoon vinegar
¼ teaspoon salt
8 scallions (spring onions), cut in 2 in (5 cm) lengths
oil

Batter:
2 eggs
½ cup (2 oz, 60 g) all-purpose (plain) flour or cornstarch (cornflour)
½ teaspoon salt

Shell shrimp, leaving tails on. Devein, then split shrimp with tip of a sharp knife, about half way through, and open out flat. Press with palm of hand. Remove rind from bacon and cut each rasher into pieces approximately the same size as the shrimp. Place a piece of bacon on each shrimp.

Heat oil and gently fry onion, garlic, ginger, and chilies until onion is soft and golden. Add chili sauce, tomato purée, wine, oyster sauce, soy sauce, honey, vinegar, and salt. Stir well and remove from heat. Add scallions.

· Heat oil in a wok or frying pan. Dip each shrimp together with piece of bacon in batter, then drop immediately into hot oil and deep fry until golden and crisp. Drain on absorbent paper, arrange on a plate and spoon sauce over. Serve immediately.

Batter: Sieve flour and salt into a mixing bowl. Make a well in the middle, add eggs and beat ingredients together until batter is smooth.

Serves 6

⪪≫∞≪⪫

FISH BALL CURRY
Burma

Fish Balls:
2 lb (1kg) halibut (jewfish) or cod filets
2½ teaspoons salt
½ teaspoon pepper
1 medium onion, finely chopped
½ teaspoon finely chopped garlic
1½ teaspoons finely grated fresh ginger
2 tablespoons lemon juice, strained
1 tablespoon finely chopped cilantro (fresh coriander leaves)
  or dill
2 slices white bread, soaked in hot water and squeezed dry
1 tablespoon purchased fish sauce or 1 teaspoon anchovy
  paste or sauce, optional

Curry:
¼ cup (2 fl oz, 60 ml) light sesame oil or corn oil
3 medium onions, finely chopped
3 teaspoons finely chopped garlic
1 tablespoon finely chopped fresh ginger
1 teaspoon ground turmeric
1–2 teaspoons chili powder, optional
1 teaspoon paprika, optional
2 tomatoes, peeled and chopped
1½ teaspoons salt
1 teaspoon dried shrimp paste
1½ cups (12 fl oz, 375 ml) hot water
2 tablespoons chopped cilantro (fresh coriander leaves)
2 tablespoons lemon juice

Fish Balls: With a sharp knife remove skin from fish. Finely grind (mince) fish, taking care to remove bones. (To do this without a grinder (mincer), cut filets in thin slices lengthwise, then chop finely across.) Put ground fish in a large bowl, add remaining ingredients. Mix thoroughly with the hands. Shape the mixture

into walnut size balls (this quantity should make 24 balls).

Curry: Heat oil in large saucepan and fry onion, garlic and ginger until soft and golden. Add turmeric, remove from heat and add chili powder and paprika (if used), tomato, and salt. (In Burmese cooking the amount of chili used would be enough to turn the gravy red, but the paprika is suggested here as a substitute for a portion of it, with chili used to suit individual tastes.)

Wrap dried shrimp paste in aluminium foil and cook under hot broiler (griller) for a few minutes on each side. Unwrap, dissolve in hot water and add to the gravy. Cook gravy until tomato is soft and pulpy. If gravy seems too reduced, add a little hot water. There should be enough gravy to almost cover the fish balls.

Gently put the fish balls in the gravy and simmer over a moderate heat until they are cooked, about 20 minutes. Shake pan gently from time to time. Do not stir until fish is cooked and firm or the balls might break. Stir in the chopped cilantro and lemon juice and cook 5 minutes longer. Serve with white rice and balachaung (page 21).
Serves 6

⪪≫∞≪⪫

FISH BRAISED IN SOY SAUCE
China

1 whole snapper (sea bass), about 3 lb (1.5 kg)
1 teaspoon salt
2 tablespoons cornstarch (cornflour)
1 teaspoon five spice powder
2 scallions (spring onions)
8 tablespoons peanut oil
6 thin slices fresh ginger
2 cloves garlic, bruised
1 whole star anise

Sauce:
5 tablespoons dark soy sauce
2 tablespoons dry sherry
2 teaspoons sesame oil
1 tablespoon sugar

Wash and clean the fish, leaving the head on. Wipe dry with absorbent kitchen paper. Score the fish lightly, no more than half-way to the bone, making three or four diagonal slashes on each side. Combine salt, cornstarch, and five spice powder; rub this mixture over the fish to coat it lightly, dust off excess.

Cut the scallions into short lengths. In a bowl, combine the sauce ingredients with 4 fl oz (125 ml) water, and stir until the sugar dissolves.

Heat a wok or frying pan, add the peanut oil and when very

In the foreground is fish ball curry (page 94), with the Burmese accompaniment, dry balachaung (page 21), in a bowl. Top is chicken curry with noodles (page 140).

hot, slide the fish very carefully into the oil; fry over high heat for 2 minutes or until the underside of the fish is golden brown. Turn the fish, using a large spatula under the thickest part of the fish and helping it with a second spatula. Cook on the second side for a further 2 minutes or until golden.

Pour off the oil. Add the sauce mixture, pouring it over the fish. Add the scallions, ginger, garlic, and star anise. Reduce the heat so that the liquid simmers gently; cover the wok and cook for 10 to 12 minutes, basting two or three times with the sauce. Test at thickest part of fish with point of knife — if the flesh is milky white and flakes easily, the fish is cooked.

Carefully lift fish onto serving plate and spoon some sauce over it.
Serves 4–6

⬥⟨⟩⬥

FISH CAKES WITH CHINESE CABBAGE
Ca Vo Vien Xao Cai Be Trang ◆ **Vietnam**

3 Chinese-style fish cakes (see Note below)
1 tablespoon oil
1 clove garlic, crushed
½ teaspoon grated fresh ginger
½ medium-size white Chinese (Napa) cabbage
1 tablespoon light soy sauce
½ teaspoon salt
2 teaspoons oyster sauce
¼ cup (2 fl oz, 60 ml) stock or water
½ teaspoon cornstarch (cornflour)

Slice the fish cakes thinly. Wash Chinese cabbage, drain well and cut into slices 1 in (2.5 cm) wide. Heat oil in a wok and fry garlic and ginger on low heat for a few seconds, then add cabbage and stir-fry for 1 minute. Add soy sauce, salt, oyster sauce, and stir well. Add stock or water and bring to a boil, then turn in the sliced fish cakes and heat through. Push ingredients to side of wok, add cornstarch mixed with a little cold water to the liquid in the middle and stir constantly until it boils and thickens. Stir all the ingredients together and serve at once with white rice.

Note: These fish cakes are sold ready to use at Chinese provision stores. They can be kept for a few days under refrigeration and need no further cooking apart from heating through.
Serves 4

⬥⟨⟩⬥

FISH CURRY
Machchi Kari ◆ **India**

1 lb (500 g) fish steaks or filets or small whole fish
2 tablespoons oil
6–8 curry leaves
1 medium onion, finely sliced
1 teaspoon finely chopped garlic
1 tablespoon finely grated fresh ginger
1 tablespoon ground coriander
2 teaspoons ground cumin
½ teaspoon ground turmeric
½–1 teaspoon chili powder
½ teaspoon ground fenugreek
2 cups (16 fl oz, 500 ml) thin coconut cream
1½ teaspoons salt or to taste lemon juice to taste

Wash fish well. If small fish are used, clean and scale them. If large steaks or filets are used, cut them into serving pieces. Heat oil and fry the curry leaves until slightly brown, then add onion, garlic, and ginger and fry until onion is soft and golden. Add all the ground spices and fry, stirring, until they smell aromatic. Add coconut cream and salt and bring to a boil, stirring.

Simmer uncovered for 10 minutes, then put in the fish, ladle the liquid over it and simmer until fish is cooked, approximately 10 to 15 minutes. Remove from heat and stir in lemon juice to taste.
Serves 4

⬥⟨⟩⬥

FISH CURRY WITH COCONUT
India

1½ lb (750 g) fish steaks
lemon juice, salt and pepper
6 large dried red chilies
2 tablespoons unsweetened desiccated coconut
1 tablespoon coriander seeds
2 teaspoons cumin seeds
¼ teaspoon fenugreek seeds
4 teaspoons finely chopped garlic
1 teaspoon finely chopped fresh ginger
1 tablespoon tamarind pulp or 1 teaspoon instant tamarind
½ cup (4 fl oz, 125 ml) hot water
2 tablespoons ghee or oil
1 large onion, finely chopped
1½ cups (12 fl oz, 375 ml) coconut cream
1½ teaspoons salt

Fish grilled in banana leaves, from Indonesia (page 98).

Wash fish, rub over with lemon juice, salt, and pepper and set aside. Soak the chilies in hot water for 10 minutes.

In a dry pan roast the coconut, stirring constantly until brown. Remove coconut to a plate and dry roast the coriander, cumin, and fenugreek seeds, shaking pan or stirring, until brown. Put the chilies, coconut, spices, garlic, and ginger into a blender and blend to a smooth paste, adding a little water if necessary. Soak tamarind pulp in hot water, squeeze to dissolve, strain. Or dissolve instant tamarind in hot water. Reserve tamarind liquid.

Heat ghee in a heavy saucepan and fry the chopped onion until soft. Add the ground mixture and fry on medium heat, stirring, until it darkens and smells cooked. Add the coconut cream, salt, tamarind liquid and bring slowly to simmering point, stirring to prevent curdling. Add the fish and simmer for 10 minutes or until fish is cooked. Do not cover. Serve hot with rice.

Note: Ground coriander, cumin, and fenugreek may be used instead of whole seeds, but roast them on a low heat, stirring constantly and taking care that they do not burn.

Serves 6

FISH CURRY WITH TOMATO
Thakkali Malu ◆ **Sri Lanka**

1 lb (500 g) fish steaks, (kingfish, halibut, tuna, Spanish mackerel, mullet)
1 teaspoon ground turmeric
1 teaspoon salt oil for frying
1 large onion, roughly chopped
3 cloves garlic
2 teaspoons finely chopped fresh ginger
1 medium size ripe tomato, chopped
2 tablespoons oil
1 tablespoon Ceylon curry powder (page 8)
1 teaspoon chili powder
salt to taste
2 cups (16 fl oz, 500 ml) thin coconut cream

Wash and dry fish well and rub all over with turmeric and salt. Cut each steak into serving pieces. Heat oil in a frying pan and fry the fish until golden brown on both sides. Drain.

Put onion, garlic, ginger, and tomato in blender and blend to a smooth paste. Heat oil in a saucepan and fry the blended ingredients for a few minutes, until oil begins to separate from mixture. Add the curry and chili powders, and about a teaspoon of salt, then the coconut cream, and bring to a boil, stirring. Simmer for a few minutes, then add the fish and simmer for 10 minutes. Serve with rice and accompaniments.

Serves 4–5

⋘⋙

FISH FILETS WITH HOI SIN SAUCE
Hoi Seen Jeung Boon Yue Lau ◆ China

12 oz (375 g) white fish filets
2 tablespoons oil
1 clove garlic, bruised
1 tablespoon light soy sauce
½ teaspoon finely grated fresh ginger
1 teaspoon hoi sin sauce
scallion (spring onion) strips for garnish

Remove skins from fish, wash and dry well on paper towels. Heat oil in wok, fry garlic until golden, remove and discard. Add the fish, one piece at a time, turning after a few seconds and moving to side of wok to make room for the next. When all the fish has been added to the wok sprinkle with soy sauce, cover with lid and simmer for 1 minute. Add ginger to liquid in pan, cover and simmer 1 minute more. Remove from heat, stir hoi sin sauce into gravy. Arrange fish on serving dish, spoon gravy over, garnish with scallion strips and serve hot.

Serves 2

⋘⋙

FISH GRILLED IN BANANA LEAVES
Ikan Panggang ◆ Indonesia

4 small whole fish or 4 fish steaks
2 cloves garlic, crushed
3 teaspoons palm sugar or brown sugar
2 fresh red chilies, seeded and chopped
½ cup (4 fl oz, 125 ml) dark soy sauce
3 tablespoons lemon juice
¼ teaspoon kencur (aromatic ginger) powder
½ teaspoon sereh (lemon grass) powder
banana leaves and foil for wrapping
2 lemons, sliced thinly

Buy fish fresh cleaned and scaled with head left on. Rub body cavity with damp kitchen paper dripped in coarse salt until free of blood. Wash fish, make diagonal cuts on each side. If using fish steaks wash and dry well.

Crush garlic with some of the measured sugar. Combine garlic, sugar, chilies, soy sauce, lemon juice, kencur, and sereh, pour over fish in a shallow dish and marinate for 30 minutes. Drain from marinade and place each fish (or each fish steak) on a square of washed banana leaf backed with a large square of heavy-duty aluminium foil. Pour one spoonful of marinade inside fish and over top. Put a few lemon slices on fish, overlapping them slightly. Make a neat parcel, keeping the seam on top so you will know which side to open.

Grill fish over glowing coals or under a preheated boiler (grill) for 10 minutes on each side. Simmer marinade for 2 or 3 minutes, adding more soy sauce and water if necessary. Serve fish in its parcel and use marinade separately as a sauce. Serve with rice, vegetables, and sambals.

Serves 4

⋘⋙

FISH IN COCONUT MILK
Malaysia

2 large grouper (cod) or halibut (jewfish) steaks
2 teaspoons salt
½ teaspoon ground pepper
2 tablespoons lemon juice
1 oz (30 g) butter
1 small onion, finely sliced
¼ teaspoon ground turmeric
1 in (2.5 cm) piece cinnamon stick
6 curry leaves
¾ cup (5 oz, 155 g) thick coconut cream
2 teaspoons cornstarch (cornflour)

Wash fish, rub with salt, pepper, and lemon juice. Simmer, covered, in very little water in a frying pan for approximately 10 minutes. Lift out on to a serving dish and keep warm. Reserve 2/3 cup (5 fl oz, 170 ml) fish stock.

Heat butter and gently fry onion until soft and golden. Add reserved fish stock, turmeric, cinnamon stick, and curry leaves and simmer gently for 10 minutes. Add coconut cream mixed with cornstarch and stir over a low heat until sauce thickens. Remove cinnamon stick and curry leaves. Pour sauce over fish and serve with boiled rice.

Serves 2

Opposite, fish steamed in banana leaves (page 100).

FISH IN RED SAUCE
Pla Nam ◆ **Thailand**

1½ lb (750 g) boned fish
4 tablespoons oil
2 onions, finely chopped
4 ripe tomatoes, peeled and chopped
2 tablespoons vinegar
salt and pepper
2 or 3 fresh chilies, seeded and chopped
3–4 tablespoons chopped cilantro (fresh coriander leaves)

Heat oil and fry onions over moderate heat until soft and golden brown. Add tomatoes, vinegar, salt, and pepper to taste, and the chilies. Cover and simmer for 20 minutes or until tomatoes are pulpy and sauce thick. Add fish, cover and cook until fish is done. Serve hot, sprinkled with chopped cilantro.
Serves 4–6

FISH IN SOY SAUCE
Ikan Kecap ◆ **Indonesia**

1 lb (500 g) fish steaks
2 tablespoons peanut oil
1 medium onion, finely chopped
2 or 3 fresh hot chilies, seeded and chopped, or 1 teaspoon sambal ulek
2 cloves garlic, finely chopped
1 teaspoon finely grated fresh ginger
½ teaspoon ground black pepper
½ teaspoon kencur (aromatic ginger) powder
1 teaspoon laos powder
½ teaspoon ground nutmeg
3 tablespoons tamarind liquid
2 tablespoons dark soy sauce
2 teaspoons palm sugar or brown sugar

Wash the fish steaks and dry on kitchen paper. If large cut into halves or quarters.

Heat oil in a frying pan and fry onion, chilies, garlic, and ginger on low heat for 5 minutes or until the onion is soft and starts to turn golden, stirring occasionally. Add the pepper, kencur powder, laos powder, and nutmeg and stir, then add the fish and fry for 2 or 3 minutes on each side. Add the tamarind liquid, soy sauce, and sugar, cover and simmer gently for 6 to 10 minutes depending on thickness of fish steaks. Be careful not to overcook. Check after 5 minutes and if liquid is drying up add 2 or 3 tablespoons hot water. Liquid should thicken but it should not cook away completely. Serve fish with the remaining spicy soy sauce liquid.

Serve with white rice, vegetable dishes, a sayur, or a sambal.

Serves 4

FISH PICKLE-CURRY

Fish Balchao ◆ India (Goa)

10–12 dried red chilies, preferably Goan or Kashmiri type
1 lb (500 g) cutlets of firm fish such as halibut (jewfish) or
  similar
1 teaspoon ground turmeric
1 teaspoon salt
6 tablespoons oil
2 medium onions, roughly chopped
3 teaspoons chopped garlic
2 teaspoons chopped fresh ginger
½ cup (4 fl oz, 125 ml) white vinegar
2 teaspoons ground cumin
1 teaspoon shrimp paste

Soak chilies in hot water to cover for 10 minutes. Wash and dry fish cutlets and rub over with turmeric and salt. Heat oil in frying pan and fry the fish until golden brown on both sides. Remove from pan and set aside.

In electric blender purée the onions, garlic, ginger, the drained chilies, and vinegar until finely ground. Mix in ground cumin and shrimp paste.

In the same pan in which fish was fried (add a little more oil if necessary) fry the blended mixture until dark and oil shows around the edges. Stir constantly while frying. Add fish, cover and cook for about 8 minutes or until fish is cooked through. Serve with rice and curries.

Serves 4

FISH STEAMED IN BANANA LEAVES

Patrani Machchi ◆ India

4 whole fish or 1½ lb (750 g) boned fish pieces
salt
1 large lemon
2 medium onions
1 teaspoon finely chopped fresh ginger
2 cloves garlic
2 large fresh green chilies, seeded and chopped
½ cup chopped cilantro (fresh coriander leaves)
1 teaspoon ground cumin
½ teaspoon ground fenugreek
½ cup fresh grated or unsweetened desiccated coconut
2 tablespoons ghee or oil
2 teaspoons salt
1 teaspoon garam masala (see page 9)
banana leaves or foil

Wash the fish, dry with kitchen paper and rub over with salt.

Peel the lemon, removing all the white pith. Cut lemon in pieces and discard all seeds. Put into container of electric blender with one onion, roughly chopped, ginger, garlic, chilies, cilantro, cumin, and fenugreek. Blend on high speed until puréed, then add coconut and blend again.

Heat oil and fry remaining onions, finely chopped until soft and golden. Add blended mixture and fry, stirring, for a few minutes. Remove from heat. Add salt and garam masala. Coat each fish or filet with the mixture, wrap securely in banana leaves or foil and steam over gently simmering water for 30 minutes, turning parcels once. Serve in the leaf parcels. Have a bowl or plate to collect leaves as each person unwraps the fish.

Serves 4

FISH WITH CRAB SAUCE

Singapore

2 lb (1 kg) porgy (sea bass, bream) filets
½ teaspoon fresh ginger root, finely grated
1 teaspoon salt
2 teaspoons cornstarch (cornflour)
oil for deep frying

Sauce:
2 tablespoons peanut oil
6 scallions (spring onions), chopped
½ teaspoon fresh ginger root, finely grated

8 tablespoons chicken or fish stock
6 oz (180 g) crab meat
pinch pepper
2½ teaspoons cornstarch (cornflour)
1 tablespoon cold water

With a sharp knife, remove skin from fish. To do this sprinkle a little salt on the end of the filet near the tail so it can be grasped without slipping. Then slide a knife between the skin and flesh, working towards the head of the fish. Wash fish and pat dry. Lay filets on a chopping board and rub with the grated ginger. Cut into halves lengthwise, then into bite-sized pieces. Toss in a mixture of salt and cornstarch.

Heat peanut oil in a small deep pan or wok and quickly fry the fish, not too many pieces at a time, for 1 minute over medium heat. Drain on absorbent paper and keep warm while preparing sauce.

Sauce: Heat oil and gently fry scallions and ginger for a few seconds, stirring, then add stock, cover and simmer for 3 to 4 minutes. Add crab meat, heat through for not longer than a minute. Season with pepper. Mix cornstarch smoothly with the cold water and stir into sauce. Continue stirring over medium heat until sauce boils and thickens. Taste and add salt if necessary. Arrange fish pieces on a dish, spoon sauce over and serve at once.
Serves 5–6

FISH WITH GINGER
Pesa ✦ The Philippines

2 x 1 lb (500 g) flathead (small haddock, whiting) or other
    delicate white fish
3 tablespoons oil
3 tablespoons finely chopped fresh ginger
1 teaspoon ground black pepper
rice washings (water in which rice has been washed before
    cooking)
salt to taste
4 scallions (spring onions)
1 sprig cilantro (fresh coriander leaves)

Misu Tomato Sauce:
2 tablespoons chopped pork fat
2 cloves garlic, crushed
1 medium onion, finely chopped
2 tomatoes, peeled and chopped
2 tablespoons red misu (salted bean curd paste)
1 tablespoon vinegar
¼ teaspoon ground black pepper

Fried chili crabs (page 102).

Clean and scale fish and rub cavity with kitchen paper dipped in coarse salt. Rinse. Heat oil and fry ginger until soft and golden. Add pepper and stir, then put fish into the pan and add enough rice washings to almost cover. Add half teaspoon salt, lay a scallion on each fish, cover and simmer until fish is cooked. Transfer fish carefully to serving dish, replace cooked scallions with remaining uncooked onions and garnish with celery leaves. Pour cooking liquid around fish and serve with white rice and misu tomato sauce.

To make sauce, put all ingredients in a saucepan, stir and simmer for a few minutes.

Serves 4

⌤⌤⌤

FISH WITH PEANUT SAUCE
Ikan Kacang ◆ Indonesia

2 large fish steaks
lemon juice
salt
black pepper
oil for frying
2 tablespoons light soy sauce
2 tablespoons peanut sauce (see page 16)
½ cup (3½ oz, 100 g) thick coconut cream
1 tablespoon tamarind liquid or vinegar
1 tablespoon chopped cilantro (fresh coriander leaves)

Wash fish, rub all over with lemon juice and season generously with salt and pepper. Let stand 15 minutes. Heat oil and fry fish steaks (well dried on kitchen paper) until brown on both sides. Pour off all but a tablespoon of the oil, add remaining ingredients mixed together, except the cilantro. Spoon over the fish. Sprinkle with cilantro, cover and simmer 5 minutes. Serve with rice.

Serves 4–6

⌤⌤⌤

FRIED CHILI CRABS
Singapore

2 medium size raw crabs
½ cup (4 fl oz, 125 ml) peanut oil
2 teaspoons finely grated fresh ginger
3 cloves garlic, finely chopped
3 fresh red chilies, seeded and chopped
¼ cup (1½ oz, 45 g) tomato sauce
¼ cup (2 fl oz, 60 ml) chili sauce
1 tablespoon sugar

1 tablespoon light soy sauce
1 teaspoon salt

Wash crabs well, scrubbing away any mossy patches on the shell. Remove hard top shell, stomach bag, and fibrous tissue and with cleaver chop each crab into 4 pieces, or 6 pieces if they are large.

Heat a wok, add oil and when oil is very hot fry the crab pieces until they change color, turning them so they cook on all sides. Remove to a plate. Turn heat to low and fry the ginger, garlic, and chilies, stirring constantly, until they are cooked but not brown. Add the sauces, sugar, soy sauce, and salt, bring to a boil, then return crabs to the wok and allow to simmer in the sauce for 3 minutes, adding a very little water if sauce reduces too much. Serve with white rice.

Serves 4

⌤⌤⌤

FRIED FISH WITH FIVE SPICE
China

1½ lb (750 g) boned fish pieces
1 tablespoon wood fungus (cloud ears)
1 cup (6 oz, 185 g) cornstarch (cornflour)
1 teaspoon salt
½ cup (4 fl oz, 125 ml) oil for frying
½ teaspoon five spice powder

Sauce:
1 tablespoon oil
3 scallions (spring onions), finely chopped
½ teaspoon finely chopped garlic
1 teaspoon finely chopped ginger
2 tablespoons Chinese wine or dry sherry
2 tablespoons light soy sauce
½ teaspoon five spice powder
2 teaspoons cornstarch (cornflour)
2 tablespoons water

Garnish:
½ cup scallions (spring onions), sliced thin diagonally

Wash and soak wood fungus in 3 cups of water for 10 minutes, drain and set aside. Cut fish into finger-size pieces, and dust lightly in cornstarch, salt, and five spice mixture. Heat oil in a wok or frying pan until it just starts to smoke slightly, add half the fish fingers and fry until just cooked, about 3 minutes. Drain on kitchen paper and place on serving dish. Fry the rest of the fish by the same method, place on the serving dish and keep warm.

Clean wok with kitchen paper, heat and add 1 tablespoon oil

and stir-fry scallions, garlic, and ginger for 2 minutes. Add Chinese wine and soy sauce, lower heat and simmer for 3 minutes. Add five spice powder, stir and add cornstarch mixed with water and bring to a boil. Add wood fungus, stir and pour over fish. Garnish with scallions and serve with hot white rice.
Serves 4

⪻⪼

FRIED FISH WITH HOT BEAN SAUCE
Malaysia

1 lb (500 g) boned fish pieces or steaks
2 tablespoons Chinese wine or dry sherry
2 teaspoons finely chopped garlic
2 teaspoons finely chopped fresh ginger
2 tablespoons hot bean sauce or bean sauce with 2 teaspoons
  chili sauce
all-purpose (plain) flour
1 cup (8 fl oz, 250 ml) peanut oil for deep frying
3 tablespoons finely chopped scallions (spring onions)
  including green portion
1 teaspoon cornstarch (cornflour)
2 tablespoons cold water

Garnish:
cilantro (fresh coriander leaves), chopped (optional)

Lightly score the fish pieces on both sides. Mix together the wine, half the garlic, and ginger, and 1 tablespoon of the hot bean sauce. Rub the mixture well into the slashes and all over the fish pieces and allow to marinate for 15 minutes. Drain, reserving marinade. Dry on paper towels and dust with flour. Heat oil in a wok or frying pan. Fry one or two pieces of fish at a time until golden brown on both sides. Drain from the oil and put on a warm serving plate.

Pour off all but a tablespoon of oil from the wok. In this fry the remaining garlic and ginger and the chopped scallions, stirring, until garlic starts to turn golden. Add hot water to the reserved marinade to make up 1 cup (8 fl oz, 250 ml). Stir in the remaining bean sauce. Add this liquid to the wok and bring to a boil, then stir in the cornstarch mixed with the cold water and stir constantly until sauce boils and thickens. Pour over the fish and serve immediately with steaming hot white rice. If desired, garnish the fish with chopped cilantro.
Serves 4

⪻⪼

FRIED FISH WITH HOT SAUCE
Indonesia

2 lb (1 kg) fish steaks
1 cup (8 fl oz, 250 g) peanut oil for frying
1 large onion, finely chopped
1 teaspoon finely chopped garlic
2 teaspoons finely chopped fresh ginger
1 teaspoon trasi (dried shrimp paste)
3 teaspoons sambal ulek or chili sauce
2 teaspoons finely grated lemon rind
1 teaspoon laos powder
2 tablespoons lemon juice
2 tablespoons jaggery (palm sugar) or brown sugar
2 tablespoons dark soy sauce
salt

Wash fish steaks and dry on kitchen paper. If large, cut into serving portions. Heat oil in a wok or frying pan and when hot fry half the fish steaks until golden brown, on both sides. Drain, put on serving dish and keep warm. Follow this method with the remaining fish steaks.

Pour off all but 2 tablespoons oil from wok and on a low heat fry the onion until soft. Add garlic, ginger, and trasi, and stir over medium heat until golden brown. Add sambal ulek, lemon rind, laos powder, lemon juice, sugar, and soy sauce. Stir and simmer for 2 or 3 more minutes. Adjust salt and spoon sauce over fish. Serve immediately with hot white rice.
Serves 4–6

⪻⪼

FRIED FISH WITH MUSHROOMS
Thailand

1½ lb (750 g) boned fish pieces
6 dried Chinese mushrooms
3 tablespoons peanut oil
6 scallions (spring onions), cut into 1 in (2.5 cm) pieces
3 teaspoons finely chopped garlic
3 teaspoons finely chopped fresh ginger
1 tablespoon light soy sauce
1½ tablespoons brown sugar
1 tablespoon lemon juice
1 tablespoon fish sauce
¼ teaspoon ground black pepper
2 tablespoons chopped cilantro (fresh coriander leaves)
2 fresh red chilies, sliced

Soak dried mushrooms in hot water for 30 minutes, then remove stalks and slice caps finely. While mushrooms are soaking, wash fish pieces and dry well on paper towels. Heat oil in wok and fry half the fish on both sides until cooked, about 2 minutes. Remove to serving dish and keep warm. Fry the rest of the fish, remove and keep warm.

Let oil cool slightly, then fry the scallions until soft, add garlic, ginger, and mushrooms and cook on low heat, stirring until soft and golden. Add soy sauce, brown sugar, lemon juice, fish sauce, and pepper and simmer for 1 minute. Pour over the fish, garnish with cilantro and chilies and serve at once with white rice.
Serves 4

❖❖❖

FRIED FISH WITH TOMATOES & EGG
Cardillo ◆ The Philippines

1 lb (500 g) firm white boned fish pieces
salt
2 tablespoons shortening (lard) or olive oil
1 clove garlic, crushed
1 medium onion, sliced
2 tomatoes, sliced
½ cup (4 fl oz, 125 ml) water
2 eggs, beaten

Clean fish, removing any skin and scales. Cut into fingers. Rub a little salt onto fish. Heat shortening in frying pan and fry fish pieces until golden brown. Remove and set aside. Fry garlic in shortening remaining in pan and when golden add onion and tomatoes and salt to taste. Cook until tomato is soft and pulpy, then add water and simmer 3 to 5 minutes. Put fried fish into sauce, remove from heat and add the well-beaten eggs. Stir to heat through and serve immediately.
Serves 4

❖❖❖

FRIED FISH WITH TAMARIND
Pla Tod ◆ Thailand

1 whole fish, about 2 lb (1 kg)
shortening (lard) for frying
3 cloves garlic, crushed
3 tablespoons soy sauce
1 tablespoon jaggery (palm sugar) or brown sugar
2 tablespoons fish sauce
4 tablespoons tamarind liquid
1 tablespoon finely shredded fresh ginger
3 scallions (spring onions), cut into bite-size pieces
3 tablespoons chopped cilantro (fresh coriander leaves)
3 fresh red chilies, sliced

Buy fish cleaned and scaled, but with the head left on. Trim fins and tail, wipe out cavity with kitchen paper dipped in salt, wash and dry well. Fry the fish in hot shortening until brown on both sides, but do not overcook. Drain on absorbent paper, cover fish with foil and keep warm.

Pour off all but a tablespoon of the shortening and on low heat fry the garlic until starting to brown. Immediately add the soy sauce, sugar, fish sauce, and tamarind liquid and bring to a boil. Add ginger and scallions and cook for 1 minute. Spoon the sauce over the fish and garnish with cilantro and chilies. Serve with white rice.
Serves 4–6

❖❖❖

FRIED FISH WITH VEGETABLES
Cambodia

1½ lb (750 g) white boned fish
8 oz (250 g) cellophane noodles
1 tablespoon egg white
½ teaspoon salt
1 cup cornstarch (cornflour)
6 tablespoons oil
2 teaspoons finely chopped garlic
1 teaspoon finely chopped fresh ginger
2 cups sliced white Chinese (Napa) cabbage
6 scallions (spring onions), cut in 1 in (2.5 cm) lengths
2 tablespoons fish sauce
1 teaspoon extra cornstarch (cornflour)
¼ cup (2 fl oz, 60 ml) cold water

Wash fish, dry well on kitchen paper and cut into finger pieces. Soak noodles in hot water 15 minutes, then drop into lightly salted boiling water and cook 5 minutes. Drain and cut into short lengths and set aside.

Dip fish fingers in egg white and then in a mixture of salt and cornstarch. Dust off excess flour. Heat oil in a wok and fry fish on high heat (one-third of the quantity of fish at a time) for just long enough to cook it through. This should take from 1 to 2 minutes depending on the thickness of the fish. Drain on kitchen paper and keep warm.

Pour off all but 2 tablespoons of the oil, add garlic, ginger, cabbage, and stir-fry for 1 minute. Add scallions and fish sauce and stir-fry for 1 minute more. Add extra cornstarch mixed with the cold water. Stir until the sauce boils and thickens. Arrange cellophane noodles on a serving dish and spread with the cooked vegetables. Place fish pieces on top and serve immediately.
Serves 4–6

FRIED MOUNTAIN TROUT WITH GINGER
China

4 trout, about 6 oz (175 g) each
1 teaspoon salt
½ teaspoon five spice powder
4 tablespoons cornstarch (cornflour)
3 scallions (spring onions)
8 tablespoons peanut oil
2 tablespoons very finely shredded fresh young ginger

Sauce:
2 tablespoons Chinese red vinegar or wine vinegar
2 tablespoons Chinese wine or dry sherry
4 tablespoons light soy sauce
2 teaspoons sugar
2 teaspoons sesame oil
2 tablespoons chopped cilantro (fresh coriander leaves)

Clean the cavity of the trout with damp absorbent kitchen paper dipped in salt. Make shallow diagonal cuts on the fish and rub in salt and five spice powder mixed together. Roll the fish in cornstarch, dusting off any excess.

Cut the scallions in bite-size pieces. Combine the sauce ingredients.

Heat a wok or frying pan, add the peanut oil and when very hot, fry the ginger and scallions for just a few seconds until they are soft but not brown. Remove on a frying spoon and set aside on a plate. Put the fish in the wok, and fry until they are golden brown underneath; then turn them over, lower the heat and fry until the other side is browned too and the fish are cooked through.

Pour off as much oil as possible. Pour the sauce mixture over the fish. Return the ginger and scallions, raise the heat and cook for 1 minute or until the sauce boils. Lift the fish on to a warm serving dish, spoon the sauce over, and serve garnished with cilantro.

Note: Young tender ginger, which has translucent skin and pink tips, is best for this dish. If this is not available, reduce the quantity of ginger by half.
Serves 4

FRIED SHRIMP
Pazoon Kyaw ◆ Burma

16 large shrimp (prawns), shelled
1 teaspoon each salt, ground turmeric, and chili powder
2 tablespoons sesame oil
2 tablespoons peanut oil
thin bamboo skewers

Dust shrimp with mixed salt, turmeric, and chili powder. Bend shrimp into a half circle and thread on skewer through top and tail to keep this shape. Put four shrimp on each skewer, and shallow fry until golden. Serve immediately.
Serves 4 as appetiser

FRIED SHRIMP BALLS WITH CELERY
China

1 lb (500 g) raw shelled and deveined shrimp (prawns)
½ teaspoon crushed garlic
½ teaspoon finely grated fresh ginger
¾ teaspoon salt
3 teaspoons cornstarch (cornflour)
1 stalk celery
1 tablespoon oyster sauce
2 teaspoons light soy sauce
3 tablespoons water
peanut oil for deep frying
3 thin slices fresh ginger

Chop shrimp finely and combine with the garlic, ginger, salt, and two teaspoons cornstarch. With oiled hands, shape into small balls. Slice the celery fairly thinly, holding the knife at a degree angle to give crescent shapes. Blanch the celery for 30 to 40 seconds in lightly salted boiling water until color intensifies. Drain at once and refresh in iced water to set color. Drain once more and set aside. Measure out sauces, combining them in a small bowl with the 3 tablespoons of water and remaining teaspoon cornstarch.

Heat peanut oil in a wok and fry the shrimp balls, a few at a time, until pale golden. Drain on paper towels.

Pour oil from wok, leaving about a tablespoonful. On high heat fry the slices of ginger until golden, then add the celery crescents and stir-fry for 1 minute. Add the sauce and cornstarch mixture and stir until liquid boils and thickens slightly, add shrimp balls and toss together. Serve at once.
Serves 4

FRIED SQUID CURRY
Dhallo Badun ◆ Sri Lanka

about 2 lb (1kg) squid
2 medium onions, finely sliced
2 teaspoons finely chopped garlic
2 teaspoons finely grated fresh ginger
1 teaspoon ground turmeric
1 teaspoon chili powder, optional
2 tablespoons Ceylon curry powder (page 8)
½ teaspoon whole fenugreek seeds
1 cinnamon stick
1 stem fresh lemon grass or 2 strips lemon rind
10 curry leaves
3 tablespoons vinegar
3 cups (24 fl oz, 750 ml) coconut cream
1½ teaspoons ghee or oil for frying

Clean squid, removing ink sac and discarding head. Cut into rings. Put in a deep saucepan with all the ingredients except ghee. Bring to a boil, then simmer for about 1 hour or until squid is tender and the gravy reduced to a small quantity.

Drain pieces of squid from the gravy and, in another pan, heat the ghee and fry the squid. Pour the gravy into the pan in which the squid were fried, simmer for a minute or two longer and serve with white rice and sambols.
Serves 4–6

GARLIC SCALLOPS
China

12 oz (375 g) scallops
½ small green bell pepper (capsicum)
2 large cloves garlic
2 teaspoons light soy sauce
1 tablespoon oyster sauce
1 tablespoon Chinese wine or dry sherry
1 teaspoon cornstarch (cornflour)
1 tablespoon cold water
2 tablespoons peanut oil
1 teaspoon sesame oil
shredded lettuce for garnish

Wash the scallops and remove any dark streaks. If preferred, use scallop meat instead of scallops with coral. Dry the scallops thoroughly on kitchen paper. Dice the bell peppers. Crush or finely chop the garlic. Mix together the soy sauce, oyster sauce, and wine. Mix cornstarch with cold water in a separate container and have all the ingredients assembled before starting to cook.

Heat wok, add the peanut oil and heat again for 30 seconds, then swirl to spread oil. Add garlic and fry over medium heat for a few seconds, stirring. Do not let it brown or it will taste bitter.

Add bell pepper and stir-fry for 1 minute. Add scallops and stir-fry for 1 minute, tossing them so that all surfaces come in contact with the heat. Pour in the mixed seasonings, cover and simmer for a further 2 or 3 minutes. Stir in the cornstarch mixture and continue stirring until the sauce boils and thickens slightly. Sprinkle sesame oil over and mix. Serve at once, garnished with shredded lettuce.

Note: Do not over-cook scallops or they will shrink and toughen.
Serves 4

GARLIC SHRIMP IN COCONUT CREAM
The Philippines

2 lb (1 kg) medium-size raw, shelled and deveined shrimp (prawns)
10 oz (350 g) can thin coconut cream
1 cup (8 fl oz, 250 ml) water
1 tablespoon finely chopped garlic
1 teaspoon finely chopped fresh ginger
2 teaspoons bagoong balayang (fish sauce)
¼ teaspoon ground black pepper

Wash the shrimp and dry well on kitchen paper. In a wok or frying pan, put the coconut cream, water, garlic, ginger, bagoong balayang, and pepper, and bring to a boil, stirring. Reduce heat and simmer uncovered for 10 minutes, stirring frequently. Add shrimp and simmer for 10 more minutes, stirring and mixing through the coconut sauce. Serve with hot white rice.
Serves 6

GOAN CRAB CURRY
India

2 or 3 medium size crabs
3 tablespoons oil or ghee
2 medium onions, finely chopped
2 teaspoons finely grated garlic
2 teaspoons finely grated fresh ginger
2 fresh red chilies, seeded and sliced
2 teaspoons ground coriander
2 teaspoons ground cumin
2 tablespoons ground almonds or white poppy seeds

Garlic scallops (recipe opposite).

2 cassia leaves (tej pattar)
1½ teaspoons salt or to taste
1 cup (12 fl oz, 250 ml) tomato purée
1½ cups (12 fl oz, 375 ml) thin coconut cream
3 tablespoons chopped cilantro (fresh coriander leaves)

Remove large shells of crabs and discard all fibrous tissue from under the shell. Divide each crab into 4 portions, breaking the body in half and separating the large, meaty claws from the body. Legs should be left attached to the body.

Heat the oil in a large saucepan and fry the onions, garlic, ginger, and chilies until onions are soft and golden. Add coriander, cumin, and ground almonds and fry for a minute or so longer. Then add the bay leaves, salt, tomato purée and coconut cream and stir while bringing to a gentle simmer.

Put in the crabs and cook, uncovered, for 15 to 20 minutes or until the crabs are done. If pan is not large enough, cook in two lots. When cooked the shells will turn bright red and the flesh becomes white and opaque. If cooked crabs are used. reduce cooking time by half. Add cilantro during last 5 minutes. Serve with plain boiled rice.

Serves 4–6

GREEN CURRY OF FISH

Thailand

1 lb (500 g) fish steaks
2½ cups (20 fl oz) thin coconut cream
2 tablespoons green curry paste (page 10)
2 sprigs citrus leaves
1 teaspoon salt
1 tablespoon fish sauce
1 or 2 green chilies, seeded and chopped
2 tablespoons finely chopped fresh basil

Wash fish well and trim any spines with kitchen scissors. Bring coconut cream to a boil with the curry paste, stirring constantly. Add fish, reduce heat and simmer with citrus leaves, salt and fish sauce until the fish is cooked through, about 15 minutes.

Add chilies and fresh basil and simmer a few minutes longer, then serve with white rice.

Serves 4

GRILLED FISH WITH SPICES
Ikan Panggang ◆ Indonesia

1 lb (500 g) fish steaks (fresh tuna or other firm fish)
1 onion, roughly chopped
1 fresh red chili or ½ teaspoon sambal ulek
1 clove garlic
½ teaspoon trasi (dried shrimp paste)
½ teaspoon kencur (aromatic ginger) powder
1 teaspoon salt
1½ cups (10 oz, 315 g) thick coconut cream
1 stalk lemon grass or 2 strips lemon rind
2 tablespoons chopped fresh basil
vegetable oil
lemon juice and salt to taste

Wash and dry fish steaks and put in a single layer in glass dish. In blender put onion, chili, garlic, trasi, kencur, and salt with half cup of the coconut cream. Blend until smooth. If blender is not available, grate onion and garlic finely and use sambal or chili powder in place of fresh chili. Crush trasi and combine all these ingredients with the coconut cream.

Marinate fish in the spice mixture for about 1 hour, turning slices once. Preheat broiler (grill) until hot and line tray with foil. Spoon off marinade, leaving only what clings to the fish. Put marinade into a small saucepan with the remaining coconut cream, lemon grass or lemon rind and chopped basil and put on low heat to simmer, stirring frequently to prevent curdling. Do not cover.

Brush fish with oil and put under broiler about 4 in (10 cm) from heat until fish is cooked and touched with brown on one side. Turn fish steaks, brush with more oil and broil other side as before. If steaks are large, divide into serving pieces, removing large middle bone. Arrange fish on serving dish. Taste sauce and add more salt if necessary and lemon juice to taste. Spoon over fish and serve.
Serves 6

GRILLED MACKEREL WITH GREEN CHUTNEY
Bhangra Chatni ◆ India (Goa)

4 small mackerel, about 12 oz (375 g) each, or other small fish
coarse salt
1 cup fresh grated or 3 oz (90 g) unsweetened desiccated coconut
¾ cup chopped cilantro (fresh coriander leaves)
1 small onion, chopped
2 teaspoons chopped garlic
pinch of ground cumin
6 large green chilies, seeded and chopped
2 teaspoons lemon juice
½ teaspoon sugar
1 teaspoon salt

Garnish:
fresh lime

Buy fish gutted and cleaned but with head left on. Scrub cavity with damp kitchen paper dipped in coarse salt and rinse well. With a sharp knife separate flesh from backbone to make a pocket for the green chutney. Score the fish three or four times on each side. Rub over with salt.

If desiccated coconut is used, sprinkle with a little water and mix lightly with fingertips to moisten all the coconut evenly. Put all the ingredients except fish into electric blender and make green chutney by blending to a smooth paste. If necessary, add a little water to facilitate blending. In India these ingredients would be ground on a stone, making a very thick paste, so use only as much water as is necessary.

Fill the pockets and cavities with the green chutney and broil (grill) the fish over coals or under a preheated broiler (grill). Garnish with wedges of fresh lime. Serve hot with rice.
Serves 4

Green curry of fish (page 107).

HOT FISH CURRY WITH SHRIMP PASTE

Indonesia

1 lb (500 g) fish filets
2 tablespoons oil
1 large onion, sliced
1 teaspoon dried shrimp paste
1 teaspoon finely chopped garlic
2 tablespoons ground roasted peanuts or crunchy peanut butter
1 teaspoon ground cumin
4 green chilies, chopped or 2 teaspoons chili powder
1 teaspoon turmeric
1 teaspoon laos powder
½ cup (4 fl oz, 125 ml) hot water
¼ cup (2 fl oz, 60 ml) thick coconut cream
salt to taste

Heat oil in a saucepan and brown sliced onion on medium heat. Add shrimp paste and garlic, lower heat and stir for a few minutes. Add ground peanuts, cumin, chili, turmeric, and laos powder and cook 1 minute longer. Add water, then stir, cover and simmer till mixture smells cooked and the oil comes to the top. Add coconut cream and salt, stir and add fish. Cover and simmer about 10 minutes and serve with steamed rice.
Serves 4

⋖⋗⋘⋙

HOT SHRIMP CURRY

Jhinga Kari ✦ India (Kerala)

2 lb (1 kg) raw shrimp (prawns) in their shells
6 dried red chilis, preferably Kashmiri or Goan
2 medium onions, chopped
3 teaspoons chopped garlic
3 teaspoons chopped fresh ginger
4 tablespoons oil
12 curry leaves
1 teaspoon ground turmeric
1 teaspoon ground coriander
1 teaspoon ground cumin
½ teaspoon ground fennel
2 teaspoons paprika
2 teaspoons salt
2½ cups (20 fl oz, 600 ml) thin coconut cream
lemon juice to taste

Wash the shrimp and remove hard shell from head but leave the legs and body shell on. Drain well. Soak the chilies (discard seeds if a very hot curry is not wanted) in hot water for 5 minutes and put into electric blender with the onion, garlic, and ginger. Blend to a purée.

Heat oil in a heavy saucepan and fry the curry leaves for 1 or 2 minutes then add the blended mixture and fry, stirring constantly, for 5 minutes or until it smells cooked and the oil starts to separate around the edges. Add ground spices and fry for 1 minute, then add shrimp and fry, stirring, until they turn pink. Add the salt and coconut cream and simmer, uncovered, for 10 minutes. Remove from heat, add lemon juice to taste and serve with rice.
Serves 6

⋖⋗⋘⋙

LOBSTER IN BLACK BEAN SAUCE

China

2 fresh lobster tails, medium size
1½ tablespoons canned salted black beans
2 cloves garlic, crushed
1 teaspoon sugar
4 tablespoons peanut oil
½ teaspoon garlic, finely chopped
1 teaspoon fresh ginger, finely chopped
¾ cup (6 fl oz, 180 ml) hot water
1 teaspoon cornstarch (cornflour)
1 tablespoon cold water
2 tablespoons chopped scallions (spring onions)
1 egg, slightly beaten

With a heavy cleaver, chop lobster tails into segments. Rinse black beans in a strainer under cold water for a few seconds, and drain. Mash beans well with crushed garlic and sugar.

Heat oil in a wok or frying pan and fry the chopped garlic and ginger until they start to brown, then add lobster segments, raise heat and stir-fry for 4 or 5 minutes, turning them constantly. Remove cooked lobster tail from wok, add black bean mixture to the oil and fry for 1 minute. Replace the lobster pieces, add the hot water, stir well, cover wok and cook for 3 minutes. Stir in cornstarch mixed with cold water, stir until sauce boils and thickens slightly, then add scallions and egg and stir until egg sets. Serve at once with hot rice.

Note: If using cooked lobster it is not necessary to fry the lobster sections. Make the sauce first and simply heat the lobster in it before adding the cornstarch, egg, and scallions.
Serves 4

LOBSTER SALAD
Noeung Bongkorng ◆ Cambodia & Laos

1 cooked lobster
8 oz (250 g) cellophane noodles
1 or 2 pieces dried wood fungus (cloud ears)
3 cups shredded white Chinese (Napa) cabbage
3 seedless cucumbers, sliced
2 tablespoons peanut oil
1 tablespoon dried garlic flakes
4 oz (125 g) ground (minced) pork
3 tablespoons dried shrimp floss*
3 tablespoons fish sauce
3 tablespoons sugar
4 tablespoons lime juice
⅓ cup (1½ oz, 45 g) chopped toasted peanuts
⅓ cup (1 oz, 30 g) unsweetened desiccated coconut, toasted

Garnish:
3 pickled garlic cloves, finely sliced*
3 mandarins or oranges, segmented
salad greens
sprigs of Vietnamese or Cambodian mint

Remove lobster tail, slit underside, remove meat in one piece and cut into medallions. Shred remaining meat in head. Reserve the shell for garnish.

Boil cellophane noodles for 10 minutes, drain and cut into short lengths. Soak the wood fungus in hot water for 20 minutes. Drain and cut into fine shreds, discarding any woody parts.

Heat the peanut oil in a wok and gently fry the dried garlic flakes until pale golden, remove immediately to absorbent paper. Do not let them brown or they will be bitter. In the same oil stir-fry the ground pork on high heat until browned, add the shrimp floss, 1 tablespoon each of fish sauce and sugar and fry until dry. Remove from wok and cool.

Combine remaining fish sauce and sugar with lime juice, stirring until sugar dissolves. Combine with all the ingredients and toss well, arrange on a dish lined with salad greens. Place medallions of lobster meat in a row and garnish with the lobster shell, segments of mandarin or orange, pickled garlic, and mint sprigs. Serve at room temperature.

*Note: Dried shrimp may be reduced to a floss in electric blender or food processor. Whole heads of garlic, pickled, can be bought in Asian produce stores.
Serves 6

MACKEREL IN VINEGAR MARINADE
Saba No Sutataki ◆ Japan

1 lb (500 g) boned mackerel pieces
salt
½ cup (4 fl oz, 125 ml) mild white vinegar
2 tablespoons cold water
2 tablespoons sugar
4 tablespoons grated white radish
4 tablespoons grated carrot
sprigs of watercress or parsley

Dipping Sauce:
1 teaspoon grated fresh ginger
3 tablespoons Japanese soy sauce
2 tablespoons mild white vinegar
1 tablespoon sugar

Rub mackerel pieces liberally with salt and refrigerate about 3 hours or overnight if more convenient. Rinse off excess salt, then slice fish thinly and marinate in a mixture of vinegar, water, and sugar for about 30 minutes.

Arrange fish slices on individual plates, put a tablespoon each of grated radish and carrot on each plate and garnish with watercress or parsley. Serve accompanied by small bowls of dipping sauce and wasabi.

Dipping Sauce: Combine ginger, soy sauce, vinegar, and sugar, stirring until sugar dissolves.
Serves 4

MADRAS SHRIMP CURRY
India

2 lb (1kg) raw shrimp (prawns)
1 tablespoon unsweetened desiccated coconut
1 tablespoon ground rice
2 cups (16 fl oz, 500 ml) coconut cream
2 tablespoons ghee or oil
12 curry leaves
2 medium onions, finely chopped
2½ teaspoons finely chopped garlic
3 teaspoons finely grated fresh ginger
2 tablespoons Madras curry powder or Madras curry paste
   (page 10)
1 teaspoon chili powder, optional
2 teaspoons paprika
1½ teaspoons salt
2 tablespoons lemon juice

Shell and devein shrimp. Put desiccated coconut into a dry pan and toast over medium heat, shaking pan or stirring constantly until coconut is golden brown. Remove from pan and do the same with the ground rice. Put both into a blender with about 1/2 cup (4 fl oz, 125 ml) of the coconut cream and blend until smooth and coconut is very finely ground.

Heat ghee in a saucepan and fry the curry leaves for 1 minute. Add onions, garlic, and ginger and fry until golden brown, stirring with a wooden spoon. Add curry powder, chili powder, and paprika and fry on low heat, stirring. Do not let the spices burn. Add blended mix, rest of coconut cream and salt, stir while bringing to simmering point. Do not cover. Simmer gently for 15 minutes, stirring occasionally.

Add shrimp, stir to mix, simmer for further 10 to 15 minutes or until shrimp are cooked and gravy thick. Stir in lemon juice. Serve with rice.

Serves 6

⋖⋗⋈⋖⋗

MASALA SHRIMP

Jhinga Masala ◆ India (Goa)

1½ lb (750 g) large raw shrimp (king prawns)
8–10 dried red chilis
2 teaspoons chopped fresh ginger
2 teaspoons chopped garlic
½ teaspoon ground cinnamon
¼ teaspoon ground black pepper
¼ teaspoon ground cloves
1 teaspoon ground cumin
½ teaspoon ground turmeric
¼ cup (2 fl oz, 60 ml) vinegar
⅓ cup (3 fl oz, 90 ml) oil
3 medium onions, finely sliced
1 green bell pepper (capsicum), sliced
3 ripe tomatoes, peeled and chopped
2 tablespoons lemon juice
1½ teaspoons salt or to taste

Wash shrimp and drain but do not remove shells or heads. Soak chilis in hot water for 5 minutes. Put ginger, garlic, chilies, and a little water into blender and blend on high speed until smooth. Mix in the spices and vinegar.

Heat oil and fry the onions and bell pepper until soft. Add shrimp and fry on high heat, stirring, just until they turn pink, then add the blended mixture and fry for about 5 minutes, stirring. Add tomatoes, lemon juice, and salt. Simmer, covered, for 10 minutes.

Serves 4–6

QUICK BOILED FISH WITH FRIED CASHEWS

Yau Pao Yiu Gor Yue Kow ◆ China

1 whole snapper (sea bass) or other white fish, 3 lb (1.5 kg)
salt
1 large onion, sliced
2 stalks celery with leafy tops
1 large carrot, quartered
6 thin slices fresh ginger
½ cup Chinese wine or dry sherry
½ teaspoon whole black peppercorns
1 large chicken stock tablet

For dressing fish:
¼ cup oil for frying
½ cup raw cashews, divided into halves
2 oz (60 g) fat barbecued pork
1 tablespoon soy sauce
2 teaspoons sesame oil
2 scallions (spring onions), cut in thin diagonal slices

Clean and scale fish, but leave head and tail on. Dip a piece of kitchen towel in coarse salt and clean out the cavity of the fish carefully. Trim sharp spines with kitchen scissors.

Into a large wok pour enough water to cover the fish, but don't add the fish yet. Add onion, celery, carrot, ginger, wine or sherry, peppercorns, and stock tablet. Bring slowly to a boil and allow to simmer for 5 minutes to develop flavor, then bring to a fast boil and add the fish. After water comes to a boil again, lower heat and simmer gently for 8–10 minutes or until fish is cooked (test by flaking the thickest part — fish should be milky white and opaque when done). Turn off heat, carefully lift fish out, allow excess liquid to drain for a few seconds, then put fish on a warm platter.

Dressing and Garnish: Heat oil in a wok and fry cashews over medium heat until pale golden. Lift out and drain on absorbent kitchen paper. Pour remaining oil into a heatproof bowl and set aside. In same wok fry the fatty barbecued pork cut into small pieces, stirring frequently until they are crisp. Pour off fat that has collected in wok, return 3 tablespoons of oil in which cashews were fried and heat gently. Combine soy sauce and sesame oil and spoon over fish. Quickly pour over the hot oil from the wok. Garnish with sliced scallions, crisp pork, and cashew nuts and serve immedeatily accompanied by white rice.

Note: The stock from cooking the fish can be strained and served as a soup with the addition of some winter melon or fuzzy melon pieces, cooked until tender but still crisp, or 2 squares of bean curd cut into tiny dice and heated through.

Serves 4–6

RED COOKED FISH
China

1 whole fish, about 3 lb (1.5 kg)
1 teaspoon salt
2 tablespoons cornstarch (cornflour)
1 teaspoon five spice powder
⅛ teaspoon pepper
¼ cup (2 fl oz, 60 ml) dark soy sauce
2 tablespoons dry sherry
1 cup (8 fl oz, 250 ml) water
2 teaspoons sesame oil
2 teaspoons sugar
6 tablespoons peanut oil for frying
6 thin slices fresh ginger
2 cloves garlic, bruised
1 whole star anise
2 scallions (spring onions), cut into short lengths
½ teaspoon cornstarch (cornflour)
2 teaspoons cold water
scallion (spring onion) flowers or sprigs of cilantro (fresh
    coriander leaves) for garnish

Wash and clean fish, leaving head on. Wipe dry with kitchen paper. Score the fish lightly, no more than half-way to the bone, making three or four diagonal slashes on each side. Combine the salt, cornstarch, five spice powder, and pepper by sifting together. Rub the mixture over the fish to coat lightly and dust off excess. Combine liquid ingredients and stir in sugar until dissolved.

Heat a wok or frying pan, pour in the peanut oil and allow the oil time to heat. Lower the fish carefully into the oil and fry over high heat for 2 minutes or until underside of fish is golden brown. Turn the fish, using a large spatula under the thickest part of the fish and helping it with a second spatula. Cook on the second side for a further 2 minutes or until golden. Pour off the oil. Add the soy sauce mixture, pouring it over the fish. Add ginger, garlic, star anise, scallions. Lower heat to let the liquid just simmer gently. Cover and cook for 10 to 12 minutes, basting two or three times with the sauce. Test at thickest part of fish with point of a knife. If flesh is milky white and flakes easily, the fish is cooked.

Carefully lift fish onto a serving plate. Strain sauce left in pan. (This "master sauce" can be used for cooking other seafoods and keeps for months in the freezer.) Heat 1/2 cup (4 fl oz, 125 ml) of the sauce, stir in 1/2 teaspoon cornstarch mixed with 2 teaspoons cold water. When sauce boils and thickens slightly, pour over the fish and serve, garnished with scallion flowers or sprigs of cilantro.
Serves 4–6

RED SHRIMP CURRY
Kaeng Phet Kung ◆ Thailand

1 lb (500 g) raw shrimp (prawns)
2 cups (16 fl oz, 500 ml) thin coconut cream
2 tablespoons red curry paste (page 12)
1–2 tablespoons fish sauce or 1 teaspoon salt
1 fresh red chili, seeded

Shell and devein shrimp, but reserve heads. Wash shrimp heads well, discarding only the hard top shell. Put the coconut cream into a pan with the curry paste, fish sauce and the fresh chili. Bring slowly to simmering point, stirring. Add shrimp and shrimp heads and cook uncovered, stirring frequently, on low heat until shrimp are cooked and the taste has mellowed, about 15 minutes.

This curry is even better prepared ahead and reheated when required. Serve hot with white rice and other accompaniments. The shrimp heads are delicious and may be served as part of the curry.
Serves 4

SASHIMI
Japan

For each serving:
4 oz (125 g) very fresh tuna, salmon, porgy (bream), bonito,
    kingfish, mackerel or halibut (jewfish)
1 tablespoon grated daikon (giant white radish)
1 tablespoon grated carrot
1 teaspoon prepared wasabi (Japanese horseradish)
Japanese soy sauce
mirin or dry sherry

Fish for sashimi must be absolutely fresh, and preferably whole; shop-bought filets are unsatisfactory, and frozen fish is disastrous. Debone the fish and carefully cut away the skin.

With a sharp knife, and handling the fish as little as possible, cut the filet into thin slices and arrange on serving plate. Tuna (and bonito) are preferable cut in small cubes; cut small fish or squid in thin strips.

Serve with grated daikon and grated carrot, decorate with a sprig of watercress and accompany each serving with a dab of wasabi and a sauce dish holding Japanese soy sauce or a mixture of soy sauce and mirin or dry sherry.

SEAFOOD &
VEGETABLES IN FOIL

Sakana No Gingami Yaki ◆ Japan

4 pieces of firm boned white fish
½ teaspoon salt
1 tablespoon sake
8 large raw shrimp (prawns)
4 large dried mushrooms
12 gingko nuts

Wash fish well, dry it, sprinkle lightly with salt and sake and let it marinate for 10 minutes. Remove shrimp heads and cut along the back of the shell with a sharp knife so that the vein can be removed without shelling the shrimp. Soak mushrooms in very hot water for 30 minutes, then cut off and discard stems and slice the caps finely.

Take pieces of foil about 10 in (25 cm) square and lightly oil one side. Put a fish filet, 2 shrimp, a mushroom and 3 gingko nuts on each square of foil. Fold foil to form a parcel and bake in a moderate oven, 350ºF (180ºC, Gas Mark 4), for 20 minutes or cook over coals on a barbecue or under a griller. Serve hot in the foil parcel.
Serves 4

⋖⋗

SHRIMP & BAMBOO
SHOOT CURRY

Burma

1½ lbs (750 g) raw shelled and deveined shrimp (prawns)
9 oz (270 g) canned bamboo shoots
¼ cup (2 fl oz, 60 g) sesame oil
3 medium onions, finely chopped
6 cloves garlic, finely chopped
1 tablespoon finely chopped fresh root ginger
1 teaspoon ground turmeric
1–2 teaspoons chili powder (optional)
1 teaspoon paprika (optional)
2 tomatoes, peeled and chopped
1½ teaspoons salt
1 teaspoon shrimp paste (ngapi or blachan)
1½ cups (12 fl oz, 375 ml) hot water
2 tablespoons chopped cilantro (fresh coriander leaves)
2 tablespoons lemon juice

Drain bamboo shoots and cut into thin strips or small dice.

Heat oil and fry onion, garlic, and ginger until soft and beginning to turn golden. Add turmeric, remove from heat and add chili powder and paprika if used, tomato, and salt. (In Burmese cooking, the amount of chili powder used would be enough to turn the curry red but you can use paprika as a substitute for a portion of it, with chili powder to suit individual taste.)

Wrap shrimp paste in aluminium foil and cook under a hot broiler (grill) for a few minutes on each side. Unwrap, dissolve in hot water and add to the curry. Cook until tomato is soft and pulpy.

Add shrimp and bamboo shoots, cook for a further 20 minutes. Sprinkle with cilantro and lemon juice, mix thoroughly and cook 5 minutes longer. Serve with boiled white rice and accompaniments.
Serves 6

⋖⋗

SHRIMP & BEAN CURD
PUFFS IN OYSTER SAUCE

China

8 oz (250 g) raw shelled and deveined shrimp (prawns)
¼ teaspoon salt
1 tablespoon cornstarch (cornflour)
1 egg
½ teaspoon grated fresh ginger
½ teaspoon sesame oil
8 oz (250 g) fresh bean curd
oil for deep frying

Sauce:
¾ cup (6 fl oz, 180 ml) chicken stock or water
1 tablespoon oyster sauce
1 scallion (spring onion), chopped
1 tablespoon chopped cilantro (fresh coriander leaves)
2 teaspoons cornstarch (cornflour)

Put the shrimp into a food processor with salt, cornstarch, egg, ginger, and sesame oil; process until all ingredients are ground (minced) and the mixture is smooth. Alternatively, the shrimp can be chopped very finely and combined with the other ingredients.

Drain the liquid from bean curd and pat dry with absorbent kitchen paper. Add the shrimp mixture and mix well together with a fork.

Combine the sauce ingredients except cornstarch in a small saucepan, and heat to boiling. Blend the cornstarch with 1 tablespoon of cold water and stir it into the sauce until it boils and thickens.

Heat a wok, add enough oil for deep frying and fry spoon of the shrimp mixture until they are puffy and golden brown all over. This will have to be done in four or five batches. Drain

Shrimp and bean curd puffs in oyster sauce (recipe opposite).

1 stalk lemon grass, bruised
2 tablespoons lemon juice
1 teaspoon sugar, optional
1 tablespoon fish sauce

Peel gourd or cucumbers, cut in halves lengthwise, scoop out seeds and cut in thick slices. Put garlic, onion, and ginger into container of electric blender and blend to a purée. Mix in the ground spices.

Heat oil in a pan and fry the blended ingredients until they are well cooked and the oil starts to show around the edges. Add the shrimp and stir-fry for 3 minutes, then add coconut cream and bring to simmering point. Add sliced gourd or cucumber, remaining seasonings, and stir gently until cooked and tender but not too soft. Serve with rice.
Serves 6

⋰⋱

SHRIMP BALLS WITH BAMBOO SHOOTS
China

8 oz (250 g) raw shelled and deveined shrimp (prawns)
½ teaspoon finely grated fresh ginger
½ teaspoon salt
1 egg yolk
1 teaspoon cornstarch (cornflour)
14 oz (440 g) can braised bamboo shoots
½ cup (4 fl oz, 125 ml) stock from shrimp (prawns)
1 tablespoon soy sauce
1 tablespoon oyster sauce
1 teaspoon extra cornstarch (cornflour), optional

Chop shrimp finely. Combine in a bowl with ginger, salt, egg yolk, and half the cornstarch. With oiled hands shape into small balls. Bring about 1 1/2 cups (12 fl oz, 375 ml) water to a boil in a medium saucepan, put in shrimp balls and simmer gently for 10 minutes. Drain shrimp balls, reserving the liquid for stock, and keep warm.

In another pan heat bamboo shoots in the shrimp stock mixed with the soy sauce and oyster sauce. If a thicker sauce is desired, stir in remaining 1 teaspoon cornstarch mixed with a little cold water and allow to boil. Combine with the shrimp balls, serve with small portions of rice or noodles.
Serves 2

⋰⋱

them well, place on a serving dish and pour the hot sauce over. Serve immediately.
Serves 4

⋰⋱

SHRIMP & SWEET GOURD CURRY
Kari Bonkong Trasak ◆ Cambodia & Laos

1 sweet gourd, tender marrow or 2 green cucumbers
5 cloves garlic
1 small onion, roughly chopped
2 teaspoons finely chopped fresh ginger
½ teaspoon chili powder
½ teaspoon ground fennel
2 teaspoons ground coriander
¼ teaspoon ground turmeric
4 tablespoons oil
1 lb (500 g) large raw shrimp (prawns), shelled and deveined
2 cups (16 fl oz, 500 ml) thin coconut cream

SHRIMP CURRY
Malaysia

1 lb (500 g) large fresh shrimp (prawns)
1 large onion, roughly chopped
6 dried red chilies
2 fresh red chilies
2 teaspoons chopped garlic
1 teaspoon laos powder
1 teaspoon dried shrimp paste
1 teaspoon ground turmeric
2 tablespoons peanut oil
2 tablespoons lemon juice
1 tablespoon sugar
1 teaspoon salt

Garnish:
2 tablespoons chopped cilantro (coriander leaves)

Wash shrimp but do not remove heads and shells. Put onion, dried and fresh chilies, garlic, laos powder, dried shrimp paste, and turmeric in blender and blend to a paste on high speed, using a little water to facilitate blending.

Heat oil in a saucepan and fry the ground spices until they start to smell fragrant. Stir in the lemon juice, sugar and salt, add the shrimp and stir till they turn red. Cover and simmer for 5 minutes, garnish with chopped cilantro and serve with rice.
Serves 4

<figure>❖❖❖</figure>

SHRIMP CURRY WITH GRAVY
Pazoon Hin ◆ Burma

1 lb (500 g) shelled shrimp (prawns)
1 large onion
3 cloves garlic
1 teaspoon finely grated fresh ginger
½ teaspoon ground turmeric
½ teaspoon chili powder
3 tablespoons light sesame oil or corn oil
pinch each of ground cloves, ground cardamom, and
    ground fennel
1 large potato, diced
2 ripe tomatoes, chopped
½ cup (4 fl oz, 125 ml) thin coconut cream
½ cup (4 fl oz, 125 ml) thick coconut cream
1 tablespoon chopped cilantro (fresh coriander leaves)
2 tablespoons chopped scallions (spring onion) leaves
salt to taste

Devein shrimp. Grind the onion, garlic and ginger to a purée. Heat oil in a pan until smoking, add purée with turmeric and chili powder, reduce heat, stir to mix ingredients with oil, then cover and simmer mixture for at least 15 minutes, stirring occasionally. Add ground cloves, cardamom, fennel, potato, and tomato and stir well. Cook for 10 minutes with lid on pan. Add thin coconut cream and gently simmer uncovered for 10 minutes. Then add shrimp and thick coconut cream and simmer, stirring frequently, until shrimp are cooked, about 5 minutes.

Add cilantro and cook a further 2 or 3 minutes, then remove from heat and stir in the scallion leaves. Taste and add more salt if required. Serve hot with white rice and accompaniments.
Serves 4

<figure>❖❖❖</figure>

SHRIMP IN CHILI BEAN SAUCE
Singapore

12 large raw shrimp (prawns), shelled and deveined
1 clove garlic, crushed
½ teaspoon salt
½ teaspoon finely grated fresh ginger
2 teaspoons Chinese wine or dry sherry
1 red bell pepper (capsicum)
1 green bell pepper (capsicum)
1 tablespoon canned salted black beans
1–2 teaspoons Chinese chili sauce
2 teaspoons hoi sin sauce
2 tablespoons peanut oil
scallion (spring onion) brushes and chili flowers to garnish

Put shrimp in a bowl and mix in garlic crushed with the salt. Add ginger and wine and leave to marinate while preparing other ingredients.

Cut bell peppers in small squares. Rinse black beans and drain, then crush or chop finely and mix with chili sauce and hoi sin sauce. Pour oil into a heated wok, stir-fry bell peppers for 2 minutes, then move them to the side of the wok and add shrimp. Fry over high heat until they turn pink, about 2 minutes. Move shrimp to one side and add a little more oil, about half a tablespoon. Add black bean and sauce mixture to oil and stir over heat for 30 seconds, then mix the shrimp and bell pepper into the sauce and fry for a few seconds until coated with the black bean mixture. Garnish and serve at once.
Serves 2–3

<figure>❖❖❖</figure>

SHRIMP IN SPICY SAUCE
Jhinga Baffad ◆ India (Goa)

1 lb (500 g) raw shrimp (prawns), shelled and deveined
4–6 dried red chilies
½ teaspoon cumin seeds
¼ teaspoon ground black pepper
1½ teaspoons chopped garlic
1 teaspoon chopped fresh ginger
1 teaspoon ground turmeric
3 tablespoons oil
2 medium onions, chopped
1 ripe tomato, chopped
1 teaspoon salt
vinegar to taste

Rinse shrimp well and drain in colander. Discard seeds and stalks of chilies, and soak chilies in hot water for 5 minutes. Put chilies, cumin, pepper, garlic, ginger, and turmeric into blender and blend at high speed, adding a little oil to facilitate blending. If blender is not available, substitute 2 teaspoons chili powder for dried chilies, ground cumin for cumin seeds, and finely grate the garlic and ginger. Mix these ingredients together with the turmeric.

Heat oil and fry onions until soft and golden. Add blended mixture and fry for a few minutes, then add the tomato, salt, and vinegar. Cover and cook until tomato is reduced to pulp. Add shrimp, stir well, cover and cook until cooked, about 10 minutes. Serve with white rice.
Serves 4

SHRIMP MUSTARD CURRY
Chingri Kari ◆ India (Bengal)

1 lb (500 g) large raw shrimp (prawns), shelled and deveined
4 dried red chilies, seeded
1 tablespoon black mustard seeds
3 teaspoons cumin seeds
3 medium onions, roughly chopped
2 teaspoons chopped garlic
½ teaspoon ground turmeric
¼ cup (2 fl oz, 60 ml) water
2 tablespoons oil
1 tablespoon ghee
8 dried curry leaves
1½ cups (12 fl oz, 375 ml) hot water
3 tablespoons lemon juice

Rinse shrimp and drain. Soak dried chilies and mustard seeds in hot water for 5 minutes, then drain and put into blender with the cumin seeds, onions, garlic, turmeric, and 1/4 cup water. Blend to a purée.

Heat oil and ghee in a saucepan, fry the curry leaves for a few seconds, then add the blended mixture and fry, stirring, for 5 minutes or until the mixture smells cooked and the oil separates from the mass. Add 1 1/2 cups hot water, cover and simmer for 15 minutes. Add shrimp, simmer 10 minutes, add lemon juice and serve with rice.
Serves 4

SHRIMP VINDALOO
India

1 lb (500 g) large raw shrimp (prawns)
2 medium onions, roughly chopped
2 teaspoons chopped garlic
2 fresh red or green chilies, chopped
2 teaspoons chopped fresh ginger
¼ cup (2 fl oz, 60 ml) white vinegar
1½ teaspoons ground cumin
1 teaspoon garam masala
1 teaspoon ground turmeric
1 teaspoon salt
4 tablespoons oil
1 large onion, finely sliced
3 tablespoons lemon juice

Shell and devein shrimp, wash and drain well. Rub half the turmeric and salt over the shrimp. Put chopped onion, garlic, chilies, ginger, and vinegar in blender and grind to a pulp. If blender is not available crush the garlic, grate ginger finely, and chop onions very fine. Add ground cumin and garam masala, remaining turmeric, and salt.

Heat oil in a saucepan and fry the chopped onion until soft and turning brown. Add the blended mixture and fry, stirring, until it is well cooked and oil separates from the mass. Add the shrimp, bring to a slow simmer and cook for 8 to 10 minutes. Stir in lemon juice and serve with rice.
Serves 4

SHRIMP WITH ASPARAGUS AND WOOD FUNGUS
China

1 lb (500 g) raw shrimp (prawns), shelled and deveined
1 teaspoon crushed garlic
1 teaspoon finely grated fresh ginger
3 tablespoons dried wood fungus (cloud ears)
1 bundle tender asparagus
1 medium size onion
5 tablespoons peanut oil

Sauce:
3 tablespoons light soy sauce
3 tablespoons Chinese wine or dry sherry
3 tablespoons Oriental sweet chili sauce
2 teaspoons sesame oil
1 teaspoon cornstarch (cornflour)

Rinse shrimp in cold water and dry on absorbent kitchen paper. Rub the garlic and ginger over the shrimp and set aside.

Soak the wood fungus in water for 10 minutes. Rinse well and trim away any gritty portions. Leave soaking in fresh cold water until required (but drain before use).

Wash the asparagus thoroughly and trim off any tough ends. If necessary, peel the bottom half of each stalk. Cut into bite-size pieces, keeping the tips whole. Peel the onion, cut in half length wise, then cut each half into six wedge-shaped sections. Mix the sauce ingredients.

Heat a wok and when very hot, add 3 tablespoons of the peanut oil and heat again, swirling to coat the wok. Add the shrimp and stir-fry until they turn pink; then remove from wok.

Add another 1 tablespoon of peanut oil, and stir-fry the drained wood fungus and onion for 1 minute; remove from wok.

Heat the remaining tablespoon of oil and stir-fry the asparagus on high heat for 1 minute; then turn the heat low, add 4 tablespoons of water and cook, covered, for 3 minutes or until the asparagus is tender but still crisp. If the asparagus is mature it may need a little extra liquid and cooking time, but don't let it become limp.

Return the shrimp to the wok, pour in the sauce ingredients and stir until the sauce boils and thickens slightly. Add the wood fungus and onion, toss through quickly, then serve at once with rice or soft fried noodles.

Note: Wood fungus or cloud ears, is a texture ingredient. Having no taste of its own, it needs to be combined with a robust sauce.
Serves 4

SHRIMP WITH BROCCOLI
China

12-16 large raw shrimp (prawns)
1 head firm, fresh broccoli
1 tablespoon peanut oil
½ teaspoon finely grated fresh ginger
¼ teaspoon salt
4 tablespoons water
1 tablespoon Chinese wine or dry sherry
1 teaspoon cornstarch (cornflour)
1 tablespoon cold water
1 tablespoon shredded red chili for garnish (optional)

Shell and devein shrimp, leaving tails on. With point of a sharp knife make a small slit through each shrimp from the underside. Wash broccoli, divide into florets, taking care to keep a length of tender green stalk on each piece. If florets are large, slice with a sharp knife, cutting through stem as well. Pass the end of the stem through the slit in the shrimp so that the floret rests within the curve of the shrimp.

Heat wok, add oil and when oil is hot add ginger and shrimp threaded with broccoli. Stir-fry for 2 minutes. Add salt, water, and wine, reduce heat to simmer, cover and cook for 3 minutes. Push shrimp to side of wok, add cornstarch mixed with water, stir until slightly thickened. Serve at once, garnished with shredded red chili and accompanied by rice.
Serves 4

SHRIMP WITH GREEN BEANS
Saewoo Bokum ◆ Korea

1 lb (500 g) small shrimp (prawns)
1 lb (500 g) tender green (string) beans
2 tablespoons vegetable oil
1 tablespoon sesame oil
1 medium onion, sliced thinly
3 tablespoons light soy sauce
1 teaspoon sugar
3 teaspoons toasted, crushed sesame seeds

Shell and devein shrimp, chop them roughly and set aside. Top and tail the beans, remove strings and with a sharp knife cut into thin diagonal slices. Heat oils in a wok and stir-fry the onion and shrimp together for 2 minutes, add beans and stir-fry for 3 minutes. Add seasonings and mix well, cover and simmer on low heat for 6 to 8 minutes or until beans are just tender. They must not be overcooked. Serve at once with rice.
Serves 6

SICHUAN-STYLE SHRIMP WITH DRIED CHILIES

China

1 lb (500 g) raw shrimp (prawns), shelled and deveined
1 cup (8 fl oz, 250 ml) cold water
½ teaspoon salt
2 teaspoons cornstarch (cornflour)
1 tablespoon water
½ egg white, beaten slightly
½ teaspoon salt

Seasonings and Sauce:
8–10 large dried chilies
1 teaspoon cornstarch (cornflour)
2 teaspoons cold water
1 tablespoon light soy sauce
2 teaspoons Chinese wine or dry sherry
1½ teaspoons honey or sugar
1 teaspoon white vinegar
½ teaspoon salt
¼ teaspoon black pepper
3 tablespoons peanut oil
2 scallions (spring onions), finely chopped
1 teaspoon grated or chopped fresh ginger
2 cloves garlic, crushed

Put shrimp into a bowl and add cold water and salt. Stir and leave for 2 minutes, then rinse under cold tap for 1 minute. Drain well.

Make the marinade by mixing cornstarch with cold water then adding egg white and salt. Add shrimp, mix well, leave for 30 minutes.

Prepare seasonings and sauce. Break or cut tops off chilies, shake out and discard seeds. Mix cornstarch and water in small bowl, then stir in light soy sauce, wine, honey, vinegar, salt, and pepper. Set aside.

Start cooking about 5 minutes before serving, for this is a dish that must be served immediately it is cooked. Heat a wok over medium heat, add the oil and heat again, swirling wok to coat inside with oil. Fry the chilies over medium heat until they are almost black. This takes only a few seconds, and they should be stirred and turned constantly. Remove chilies from wok and drain on absorbent paper.

Drain any excess marinade from shrimp, add shrimp to wok and stir-fry over high heat. They must not be over-cooked, 10 to 20 seconds is enough for very small shrimp, 35 to 40 seconds for large ones. Add scallions, ginger, and garlic and stir-fry briefly. Stir seasoning mixture again to blend the cornstarch smoothly, add to the wok, stirring constantly until sauce boils and thickens. Turn off heat. Return chilies to the wok, stir to mix and serve immediately with small portions of rice.

Note: For a less hot result, discard oil in which the chilies are fried and heat fresh oil for frying the rest of the ingredients.

Serves 6

Shrimp with asparagus and wood fungus (recipe opposite).

SICHUAN–STYLE SQUID
China

1 lb (500 g) tender squid
½ teaspoon salt
1 tablespoon egg white
1½ tablespoons cornstarch (cornflour)
1½ tablespoons peanut oil
1 small red bell pepper (capsicum)
1 clove garlic
6 scallions (spring onions)
½ cup (4 fl oz, 125 ml) chicken stock (page 6) or water
½ teaspoon each salt and sugar
1 teaspoon chili oil
2 teaspoons cornstarch (cornflour)
2 tablespoons cold water
1½ cups (12 fl oz, 375 ml) peanut oil for deep frying
1 tablespoon preserved radish with chili
12 snow peas (mangetout)

Wash squid well. Discard head and inside. Slit body of squid lengthwise and cut into 2 in x 1 in (5 cm x 2.5 cm) pieces. Rinse well. On inner surface make diagonal slits with a sharp knife, first one way and then the other to give a pattern of small diamonds. Be careful not to cut right through. Combine squid with the 1/2 teaspoon salt, egg white, cornstarch, and 1 1/2 tablespoons peanut oil. Mix thoroughly and set aside while preparing other ingredients.

Remove seeds and membranes from bell pepper and cut in thin strips. Chop the garlic finely and cut scallions in bite-size lengths. Have all ingredients prepared, measured and ready before starting to cook. Combine stock with salt, sugar, and chili oil. In a separate bowl mix the cornstarch with the cold water.

Heat peanut oil in wok and when very hot add the squid and fry on high heat for just long enough to cook the squid, about 2 minutes. As it cooks the squid curls, showing the scoring on the inner surface. Do not overcook or it will toughen. Drain contents of wok through wire frying spoon placed over a heatproof bowl.

Return wok to heat with just the oil that clings to the sides. Stir-fry snow peas for 1 minute and remove. Add the garlic, bell pepper, radish, and scallions and stir-fry over high heat for one minute. Return drained squid to wok.

Add stock mixture and as soon as the liquid comes to a boil stir in the cornstarch mixture and stir until it thickens. This should take only a few seconds. Garnish with snow peas and serve immediately with plain white rice.
Serves 4

SIMMERED SEAFOOD & VEGETABLES
Yosenabe ◆ Japan

1 lb (500 g) snapper (sea bass) or porgy (bream) filets
1 lobster tail
1 cup cooked cellophane noodles
8 cups dashi (page 6) or chicken stock
2 tender carrots, sliced
small piece kombu (dried kelp), optional
soy sauce to taste
few young English spinach leaves
6 fresh mushrooms, sliced
6 scallions (spring onions), cut in bite-size lengths

Wash fish and cut into 1 in (2.5 cm) pieces. With a sharp cleaver cut lobster tail into slices, then cut each large slice into halves. Drain cellophane noodles and cut into short lengths, put into a saucepan with the dashi, bring to a boil. Reduce heat and simmer for 5 minutes before adding carrots, kombu and soy sauce. Simmer a further 2 minutes, then add fish and lobster, spinach, mushrooms, and scallions and continue to cook for 5 minutes or until everything is just done. Serve in soup bowls accompanied by small dishes of dipping sauce.
Serves 6

⋘⋙

SOUSED FISH
Nga Tha Lauk Paung ◆ Burma

1 lb (500 g) cleaned whole fish, mackerel or similar, one or
  more according to size
1 medium onion, sliced lengthwise
4 cloves garlic, sliced lengthwise
1 teaspoon finely shredded fresh ginger
5 whole black peppercorns
½ teaspoon salt, or to taste
1 fresh green chili
vinegar as needed

Have fish cleaned and scaled and head, fins and tail removed. Wash well, put in a heatproof dish with a lid and scatter the onion, garlic, ginger, peppercorns, and salt over the fish. Put the chili on top and add vinegar to just cover the fish. Cover and seal the lid with a thick dough of flour and water to prevent moisture escaping. Put in a very slow oven 250ºF (120ºC, Gas Mark 1/2) and cook for six hours. This method of cooking helps to soften the bones. In Burma they use hilsa, a very rich and bony fish.
Serves 4

Squid with green peas in oyster sauce (page 122).

SQUID CURRY

Gulai Cumi–Cumi ◆ Indonesia

1 lb (500 g) fresh squid
1 medium onion, finely chopped
1 teaspoon finely chopped garlic
1 teaspoon finely grated fresh ginger
1 teaspoon salt
1 teaspoon chili powder
½ teaspoon dried shrimp paste
1¾ cups (14 fl oz) coconut cream
4 candlenuts or brazil nuts, grated
1 stem lemon grass, finely sliced or 1 teaspoon grated lemon rind
1 teaspoon sugar
4 tablespoons tamarind liquid or lemon juice to taste

Clean squid, removing head and ink sac. Wash well inside and out and rub away spotted skin from body. Cut each squid in halves lengthwise, then into bitesize pieces. Put all other ingredients except sugar and tamarind or lemon into a saucepan and bring to simmering point, stirring. Allow to simmer, uncovered, until thickened. Stir occasionally. Add squid, simmer for 5 to 6 minutes. Add sugar and tamarind or lemon juice, taste and add more salt if necessary. Serve hot with rice and vegetables.

Serves 4

SQUID WITH GREEN PEAS IN OYSTER SAUCE

Ho Yau Chang Dau Dew Pin ◆ China

1 lb (500 g) tender small squid
1½ cups fresh or frozen peas
2 tablespoons peanut oil
½ teaspoon finely grated fresh ginger
½ cup (4 fl oz, 125 ml) fish or chicken stock (see page 6)
1 teaspoon light soy sauce
1 tablespoon oyster sauce
2 teaspoons cornstarch (cornflour)
1 tablespoon cold water

Wash squid well. On chopping board, put blunt edge of knife at point where head joins body and give a tug to separate tentacles and head from body. Cut just where tentacles start and reserve these. Discard head and inside of squid. Slit body of squid lengthwise and if large cut into pieces. Rinse well and on inner surface make shallow slits with sharp knife in a pattern of squares or diamonds. If using frozen peas, thaw.

Heat 1 tablespoon oil in a wok, add ginger and squid and stir-fry for 2 or 3 minutes. Turn on to dish. Add remaining oil and toss peas in it for a few seconds, then add stock, soy sauce, and oyster sauce. Stir and allow to come to a boil. Mix cornstarch smoothly with cold water and stir into sauce. Return squid and heat through. Serve on a bed of braised Chinese cabbage (page 264).
Serves 6

❖❖❖

STEAMED FISH, VIETNAM-STYLE

Ca Hap ◆ Vietnam

2 lb (1 kg) whole fish or 1½ lb (750 g) firm white boned
    fish
3 oz (90 g) cellophane noodles
8 dried Chinese mushrooms
1 carrot
3 thin slices fresh ginger
1 large clove garlic
½ cup finely sliced cooked pork
2 tablespoons light soy sauce
¼ teaspoon salt
¼ teaspoon black pepper
2 tablespoons fish sauce
6 tablespoons thin coconut cream
2 tablespoons chopped cilantro (fresh coriander leaves)
2 tablespoons finely sliced scallion (spring onion)

Wash fish and clean cavity with kitchen paper dipped in coarse salt. Rinse well again, dry with kitchen paper and trim fins and tail. Slash the flesh diagonally to allow the seasonings to penetrate. Put in a heatproof dish.

Soak noodles in hot water for 30 minutes. Soak mushrooms in hot water 30 minutes. Drain and cut the noodles into short lengths, squeeze out water from mushrooms, cut off and discard stems and slice caps thinly. Scrape carrot and cut into matchstick strips. Cut ginger into thin shreds and finely grate the garlic. Combine all these ingredients in a bowl together with the pork, soy sauce, salt, pepper, and fish sauce. Spread this over the fish, put in a steamer and steam for 30 minutes or until fish is cooked through and milky white right to the bone when flaked with a knife or fork. Filets should take only 15 to 20 minutes. Pour the coconut cream over, garnish with cilantro and scallions and serve at once with white rice.
Serves 6

❖❖❖

STEAMED FISH BALLS WITH SNOW PEAS

China

12 oz (375 g) boned fish pieces
¼ teaspoon finely grated fresh ginger
1 clove garlic, crushed
1½ teaspoon salt
1 egg yolk
1 teaspoon cornstarch (cornflour)
1 tablespoon sesame oil
4 oz (125 g) snow peas (mangetout), strings removed
½ cup (4 fl oz, 125 ml) fish or chicken stock (page 6)
1 teaspoon cornstarch (cornflour)
1 tablespoon cold water
1 tablespoon oyster sauce
½ teaspoon sugar

Remove skin from fish and chop very finely. Combine with ginger, garlic, salt, egg yolk, and 1 teaspoon cornstarch. With oiled hands shape the fish into small balls about 1 in (2.5 cm) across. Place the balls on a plate, put plate on a rack and steam over gently boiling water in a covered pan for 10 minutes.

When fish balls are cooked, heat oil in the wok, and on high heat, toss the snow peas in the oil until they turn bright green. This takes about 1 1/2 minutes. Push peas to side of wok, pour in stock, add remaining teaspoon cornstarch mixed with water and cook, stirring, until clear and thickened, about 1 minute. Stir in oyster sauce and sugar. Stir snow peas into the sauce.

Arrange fish balls on a dish, spoon snow peas and sauce over and serve immediately.

Note: This dish cannot be made with cooked fish. If snow peas are not available, substitute broccoli, sliced celery, or sliced gai choy (Chinese mustard cabbage).

Serves 2

⋙∞⋘

STEAMED FISH WITH HAM & BAMBOO SHOOTS
China

1 whole snapper (seabass) or pearl perch about 2 lb (1 kg)
½ teaspoon salt
1 teaspoon ginger juice
6 dried Chinese mushrooms
1 tablespoon light soy sauce
2 teaspoons sesame oil
2 teaspoons sugar
2 tablespoons Chinese wine or dry sherry
1 tablespoon finely shredded fresh ginger
3 tablespoons each bamboo shoot and cooked ham cut into matchstick strips
2 scallions (spring onions), cut into matchstick strips
sprigs of cilantro (fresh coriander leaves) or scallion (spring onion) flowers for garnish

Wash and clean the fish, wipe with kitchen paper, rub inside and out with salt and ginger juice. Set aside while preparing mushrooms. Wash and soak mushrooms in hot water for 20 minutes, discard stems and cut caps into thin strips. Put the mushroom strips in a small pan with the soy sauce, sesame oil, sugar, and 1/2 cup (4 fl oz, 125 ml) of the mushroom water. Bring to a boil, then cover and simmer for 10 minutes. Drain the mushroom strips and add the wine to the liquid left in the pan.

Lightly oil a heatproof dish and put half the strips of ginger, bamboo, ham, mushrooms, and scallions on the dish. Place the fish on top and spread the remaining ingredients over the fish. Place the dish over gently boiling water, cover and steam for 12 to 15 minutes or until the fish is cooked. Pour the wine mixture over the fish, garnish with sprigs of cilantro or scallion flowers and serve at once. After the top half of the fish has been served, lift the backbone and snap it off near the head, then serve the bottom half of the fish together with the ingredients underneath it and the juices in the dish.

Note: To make ginger juice, grate fresh ginger finely then press out juice through a fine nylon sieve.

Serves 2–4

⋙∞⋘

Steamed fish with ham and bamboo shoots (recipe above).

Steamed fish balls with snow peas (recipe opposite).

STEAMED FISH WITH WALNUTS
China

1 whole snapper (seabass) or pearl perch or other white fish
  about 2 lb (1 kg)
salt
1 teaspoon finely grated fresh ginger
2 tablespoons light soy sauce
¼ cup (2 fl oz, 60 ml) peanut oil
¼ cup peeled walnuts
1 teaspoon sesame oil
3 scallions (spring onions), thinly sliced

Clean and scale fish, but leave head and tail on. Dip a piece of dampened kitchen paper in salt and clean out the cavity of the fish carefully. Rinse well. Trim fins and sharp spines with kitchen scissors. Rub fish all over, inside and out, with the ginger and 1 tablespoon soy sauce. Place on a heat-proof dish, put dish on steaming rack in wok, add 3 cups (24 fl oz, 750 ml) boiling water, cover the wok and steam the fish for 10 to 12 minutes, or until fish is cooked. Test at the thickest part and if flesh is milky white the fish is done.

Lift dish from steamer, cover with foil and keep warm. Dry the wok well, heat oil and fry the walnuts over medium heat until pale golden. (Peeled walnuts are available at Chinese stores and are preferable to ordinary walnuts because there is no thin skin to give a bitter taste.) Lift out walnuts on slotted spoon and drain on absorbent paper. Take 3 tablespoons of the hot oil and pour over the fish. Combine remaining tablespoon soy sauce and sesame oil and pour over the fish also. Garnish with the walnuts and sliced scallions and serve, accompanied by rice.
Serves 4

STEAMED SESAME FISH PARCELS
Burma

1½ lb (750 g) boned fish pieces
8 large lettuce or English spinach leaves for wrapping
¾ cup (2 ½ oz, 75 g) unsweetened desiccated coconut
½ cup (4 fl oz, 125 ml) hot water
2 teaspoons finely chopped garlic
1 tablespoon finely chopped fresh ginger
3 tablespoons toasted sesame seeds
1 teaspoon salt
1 teaspoon ground turmeric

½ teaspoon ground black pepper
½ teaspoon chili powder
juice of half a lemon
2 tablespoons rice flour
3 tablespoons chopped cilantro (fresh coriander leaves)

Wash and dry fish pieces. Place lettuce or spinach leaves in container, pour boiling water over and set aside to soften. Put coconut, hot water, garlic, and ginger in blender, blend until coconut is very finely ground. Turn into a bowl, mix in other ingredients. Divide fish into eight portions, place each on a lettuce or spinach leaf, top with 1 tablespoon of coconut mixture, wrap and arrange on a heatproof plate. Place plate on a rack above boiling water in a wok, cover with lid and steam for 15 minutes. Serve hot with rice.
Serves 4

STEAMED WHOLE FISH WITH MUSHROOMS AND HAM
China

1 whole fish, about 4 lb (2 kg) snapper (seabass) or salmon
  trout
½ teaspoon salt
1 teaspoon ginger juice
6 dried Chinese mushrooms
1 tablespoon light soy sauce
2 teaspoons sugar
1 teaspoon sesame oil
1 tablespoon Chinese wine or dry sherry
2 oz (60 g) ham
2 scallions (spring onions)
1 tablespoon finely grated fresh ginger

Dipping Sauces:
light soy sauce
grated ginger soaked in 4 tablespoons Chinese wine or
  sherry
sesame oil
chili oil

How to deal with a fish too large to fit into your bamboo steamer.

Wash and clean the fish, wipe with kitchen paper. Score the fish six times on one side, cutting diagonally into the flesh down to the bone. Rub the fish inside and out with salt and ginger juice, rubbing into the scorings. Set aside.

Soak the mushrooms in hot water for 30 minutes. Drain, but reserve 5 tablespoons of the water, discard the mushroom stems and slice the caps thinly. Put the mushrooms in a small

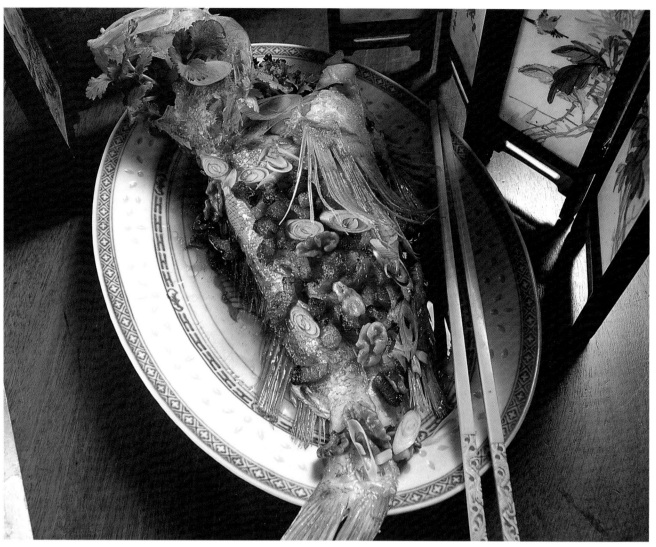

Above, steamed fish with walnuts (recipe opposite).

Steamed whole fish with mushrooms and ham (recipe opposite).

pan; add the soy sauce, sugar, and 5 tablespoons mushroom soaking water. Bring to a boil, then cover the pan and simmer for 10 minutes. Lift out the mushrooms and set them aside. Add the sesame oil and wine to the liquid left in the pan.

Cut the ham and scallions into strips. Lightly oil a heatproof dish and place half the ginger, ham, and scallions on the dish. Place the fish on top, uncut side down. Place the mushrooms and the remaining ginger, ham and scallions in the scorings of fish. Pour the liquid in the pan over the top.

Set a wire rack in a large baking dish and pour in boiling water to a depth of 1/2 in (1.3 cm). Place the dish of fish on the rack, cover all with a large sheet of foil, folding the foil over the rim of the baking dish. Place the baking dish on top of the stove and have the heat medium-high so that there is a lot of steam. Cook the fish for about 20 minutes. Remove foil.

Serve with small bowls for the dipping sauces, so that guests can make their own mixture. If desired, garnish with sprigs of cilantro or scallion curls.

Note: To make ginger juice, finely grate fresh ginger then press out juice through fine nylon sieve.

Serves 6–8

STIR-FRIED HONEY SHRIMP
China

1 lb (500 g) raw shrimp (prawns)
2 tablespoons peanut oil
1 red bell pepper (capsicum), diced
1 green bell pepper (capsicum), diced
½ teaspoon finely chopped fresh ginger
½ cup (4 fl oz, 125 ml) strong chicken stock
1 tablespoon honey
1 tablespoon Chinese wine or dry sherry
1 tablespoon light soy sauce
1 teaspoon cornstarch (cornflour)
2 tablespoons cold water

Shell and devein shrimp, leaving the tails on. Heat wok, add oil and stir-fry red and green bell peppers for 1 minute then push to the side of wok. Add chopped ginger and shrimp and stir-fry on medium heat until they are pink then push up the sides of wok. Add stock, honey, Chinese wine, and soy sauce. Add cornstarch mixed with cold water to wok and stir mixture till it thickens. Bring all ingredients from sides of wok, stir and serve at once accompanied by white rice.

Serves 4

STIR-FRIED LOBSTER WITH RED SAUCE
Chow Loong Har Kau ✦ China

8 oz (250 g) raw lobster tails
½ egg white
2 teaspoons Chinese wine or dry sherry
½ teaspoon salt
2 teaspoons cornstarch (cornflour)
3 tablespoons oil

Sauce:
1 small clove garlic, crushed
½ teaspoon finely grated fresh ginger
¼ cup (1 ½ oz, 45 g) tomato sauce
1 teaspoon chili sauce
¼ cup (2 fl oz, 60 ml) water
1 tablespoon Chinese vinegar or 2 teaspoons cider vinegar
2 teaspoons sugar
2 teaspoons cornstarch (cornflour)
1 tablespoon cold water
½ cup cooked peas, optional

Chop lobster tails into sections and remove shells. Cut lobster meat into bite-size chunks and marinate in a mixture of slightly beaten egg white, wine or sherry, salt, and cornstarch. Set aside for 20 minutes. Heat oil in a wok and when very hot put in pieces of lobster and fry, turning to cook all sides. These should be done in about 2 to 3 minutes, depending on size of lobster chunks. Remove lobster from oil and set aside.

Sauce: Pour off all but about a tablespoon of the oil in which the lobster was fried. On low heat stir-fry garlic and ginger until just beginning to turn golden. Add tomato sauce, chili sauce, water, vinegar, and sugar and stir until sugar is dissolved. When sauce boils add the cornstarch mixed smoothly with cold water and stir until thickened. Return lobster to wok, add green peas and heat through. Serve immediately with rice.

Serves 2–3

Stir-fried scallops with snow peas (recipe below).

STIR-FRIED SCALLOPS WITH SNOW PEAS

Ho Lan Dau Chow Dai Tze ✦ **China**

12 oz (375 g) scallops
2 leeks
4 oz (125 g) snow peas (mangetout)
2 tablespoons peanut oil
1 teaspoon finely grated fresh ginger
2 teaspoons cornstarch (cornflour)
¼ cup (2 fl oz, 60 ml) water
2 teaspoons light soy sauce
salt

Wash and beard scallops and dry well on kitchen paper. Wash leeks thoroughly to get rid of all sand and grit. Slice white part of leeks very fine, diagonally. Remove strings from snow peas.

Heat oil in wok and fry leeks and ginger for 2 minutes over medium heat. Add scallops and fry on high heat, stirring, for 1 minute. Add snow peas and stir-fry for 1 minute longer. Push all ingredients to side of wok, pour in cornstarch mixed with water and soy sauce and stir until thickened, about 1 minute. Stir in scallops and vegetables from side of wok, adjust salt and serve immediately on a bed of braised lettuce.

Note: If leeks are not available, substitute the white part of 10 scallions (spring onions) cut into 1 in (2.5 cm) lengths.

Serves 2–3

STIR-FRIED SHRIMP & CHINESE CABBAGE
China

1 Chinese cabbage (choy sum or gai choy)
¼ cup (2 fl oz, 60 ml) water or stock
1 tablespoon light soy sauce
¼ teaspoon five spice powder
1 tablespoon sherry or Chinese wine
½ teaspoon salt
1 teaspoon cornstarch (cornflour)
1 tablespoon cold water
2 tablespoons peanut oil
1 clove garlic, crushed
½ teaspoon finely grated fresh ginger
12 large raw shrimp (prawns), shelled and deveined

Cut cabbage into bite-sized pieces, using the thick stems and only the tender part of the leaves. In a small bowl combine the water or stock, soy sauce, five spice, sherry and salt. In a separate bowl mix cornstarch with cold water.

Heat oil in a wok. Add garlic, ginger and cabbage and fry for 2 minutes over high heat, stirring constantly. Add shrimp and fry for another minute. Lowerheat to medium, add mixed seasonings, cover and simmer for 5 minutes. Add cornstarch mixture and stir until sauce boils and thickens, about 1 minute. Serve at once with small portions of rice or noodles.

Note: If shrimp are small, simmer for only 2 minutes.
Serves 2

⋯⋯

STIR-FRIED SHRIMP WITH BROCCOLI AND RED GINGER
China

12–16 large raw shrimp (prawns)
1 head firm, fresh broccoli
1 tablespoon peanut oil
½ teaspoon finely grated fresh ginger
1 tablespoon fine strips of red ginger*

Sauce:
¼ cup (2 fl oz, 60 ml) water
2 tablespoons Chinese wine or dry sherry
1 tablespoon light soy sauce
1 tablespoon oyster sauce
½ teaspoon sugar
2 teaspoons cornstarch (cornflour) or arrowroot
1 tablespoon cold water

Shell and devein the shrimp, leaving the tails on. With the point of a sharp knife make a small slit through the underside of the shrimp.

Wash the broccoli and shake dry. Divide into florets, leaving a piece of tender green stalk on each. Pass the end of the stem through the slit in the shrimp so that the floret rests within the curve.

Heat the wok and add the oil. When the oil is hot, add the ginger and stir, then immediately add the shrimp threaded with broccoli. Stir-fry for two minutes. Add all the sauce ingredients mixed together, except the cornstarch and cold water. Turn the head to medium low, cover and simmer for 3 minutes. Push the shrimp to the side of the wok, add the cornstarch mixed smoothly with cold water and stir until thick. Serve at once, garnished with red ginger and accompanied by white rice.

* Note: these are preserved ginger slices colored a deep red.
Serves 4

⋯⋯

SWEET-SOUR SHRIMP
Jhinga Patia ◆ India (Maharashtra Parsi)

1 lb (500 g) raw shrimp (prawns), shelled and deveined
1 teaspoon salt
1 teaspoon ground turmeric
2 teaspoons chili powder, or to taste
6 fresh green chilies
2 teaspoons chopped garlic
1½ teaspoons chopped fresh ginger
3 teaspoons cumin seeds
5 tablespoons light sesame oil
3 medium onions, sliced thinly
2 ripe tomatoes, peeled and chopped
4 tablespoons chopped cilantro (fresh coriander leaves)
1 teaspoon jaggery (palm sugar) or brown sugar
1 tablespoon tamarind pulp or 1 teaspoon instant tamarind
½ cup (4 fl oz, 125 ml) hot water

Sprinkle shrimp with salt, turmeric, and chili powder and set aside.

Grind together in blender two seeded chilis, garlic, ginger, and cumin, adding a little oil if necessary to facilitate blending.

Heat oil in a saucepan and fry the remaining whole chilies and remove. Fry the onions over medium heat, stirring occasionally, until golden. Add the blended spices and cook stirring, for a few minutes. Add tomatoes and half the cilantro. Add shrimp and cook for 10 minutes. Dissolve tamarind pulp in hot water and strain. Alternatively dissolve instant tamarind in hot water. Stir in tamarind liquid and jaggery. Serve garnished with fried green chilies and remaining cilantro.
Serves 4

Stir-fried shrimp and Chinese cabbage (recipe opposite).

THAI-STYLE FRIED FISH
Pla Cian ◆ Thailand

2 lb (1 kg) whole snapper (sea bass) or porgy (bream) or
  1½ lb (750 g) boned fish
¼ cup (2 fl oz, 60 ml) peanut oil
6 scallions (spring onions), cut into 1 in (2.5 cm) pieces
4 cloves garlic, crushed
3 teaspoons finely grated fresh ginger
2 tablespoons light soy sauce
1 tablespoon jaggery (palm sugar) or brown sugar
1 tablespoon tamarind liquid or lemon juice
1 tablespoon fish sauce
¼ teaspoon ground black pepper
2 tablespoons chopped cilantro (fresh coriander leaves)
1 fresh red chili, seeded and sliced

Wash and wipe fish well. Fry in hot oil first on one side and then on the other until lightly browned and cooked through. Remove fish to serving dish and keep warm. Let oil cool slightly, then fry the scallions until soft, add garlic and ginger and cook on low heat, stirring until soft and golden. Add soy sauce, sugar, tamarind liquid, fish sauce, and pepper and simmer for 1 minute. Pour over the fish, garnish with cilantro and chili and serve at once with white rice.

⋙⋘

VELVET FISH WITH OYSTER SAUCE
China

12 oz (375 g) snapper (sea bass) or haddock (gemfish) filet
½ teaspoon salt
pinch pepper
1 teaspoon cornstarch (cornflour)
3 tablespoons peanut oil
1 tablespoon egg white
½ teaspoon finely grated fresh ginger
4 scallions (spring onions), cut into bite-size pieces
2 tablespoons oyster sauce

Skin fish and cut into bite-size pieces. Season with salt and pepper, set aside for 10 minutes. Sprinkle with cornstarch and 1 tablespoon of the peanut oil, mix well to coat fish pieces and leave for 15 minutes. Add egg white, mix again and chill for 30 minutes.

Bring about 5 cups (2 pts, 1.25 L) water to a boil, add a tablespoon of peanut oil to the water and drop in the fish pieces. Return to a boil and cook for 1 minute, then drain.

Heat a wok, add remaining tablespoon oil and swirl to coat inside of wok. Add ginger and scallions and stir-fry on high heat for 1 minute. Add oyster sauce and stir, add the fish pieces and heat through. Serve at once.

Note: The fish may be prepared hours beforehand, or even a day ahead, up to the point where it is drained. It is then only a few minutes' work to assemble the dish.
Serves 2

⋙⋘

WHOLE FRIED FISH WITH GINGER SAUCE
Pla Prio Wan ◆ Thailand

1 whole fish, about 2 lb (1 kg) snapper (sea bass), porgy (bream), halibut (jewfish)
flour, seasoned with salt to taste
oil for frying

Ginger Sauce:
8 dried Chinese mushrooms
6 tablespoons vinegar
6 tablespoons sugar
¾ cup (6 fl oz, 180 ml) water
2 tablespoons soy sauce
2 tablespoons finely chopped scallion (spring onion)
1 tablespoon cornstarch (cornflour)
1 tablespoon cold water
4 tablespoons chopped red ginger (preserved ginger slices colored a deep red)

Buy fish cleaned and scaled, but with head left on. Trim fins and tail with kitchen scissors, and wipe out cavity with kitchen paper dipped in coarse salt. Wash well and dry thoroughly. With a sharp knife slash the fish diagonally on each side almost to the backbone, forming diamond shapes in the flesh. Dip fish in seasoned flour, dusting off any excess. Deep fry in hot oil until golden brown, drain on absorbent paper, then transfer fish carefully to serving dish, spoon sauce over and serve immediately.

Ginger Sauce: Soak mushrooms in hot water for 30 minutes. Slice mushroom caps finely, discarding tough stems. Put mushrooms, vinegar, sugar, water, and soy sauce into a small saucepan and boil for 5 minutes. Add scallion, using most of the green portion as well. Blend cornstarch smoothly with cold water and stir into the sauce. Cook, stirring, until clear and thickened. The sauce can simmer while fish is being fried. Remove from heat, stir in ginger and pour over fish. Garnish with a sprig of cilantro if desired.
Serves 2–3 as a main dish.

Using a wok to cook Sichuan-style squid (page 120).

⨳ Poultry & Eggs ⨳

BALINESE-STYLE FRIED CHICKEN
Ayam Bali ◆ Indonesia

1 onion, roughly chopped
2 cloves garlic
1 teaspoon chopped fresh ginger
3 fresh red chilies, seeded and roughly chopped
4 candlenuts or macadamia nuts
1 tablespoon dark soy sauce
2½ lb (1.25 kg) frying chicken
peanut oil
2 tablespoons palm sugar or brown sugar
2 tablespoons lemon juice
½ teaspoon salt
1 cup (8 fl oz, 250 ml) thin coconut cream

Put onion, garlic, ginger, chilies, nuts, and soy sauce into container of electric blender and blend to a smooth paste. Cut chicken in quarters. Dry well on paper towels. Heat 1/2 cup (4 fl oz, 125 ml) peanut oil in wok or frying pan and fry the chicken pieces quickly until brown. Remove chicken and drain on absorbent paper. Pour off oil, leaving only one tablespoon, and fry the blended mixture for a few minutes, stirring constantly. Add sugar, lemon juice, salt, and coconut cream and keep stirring while mixture comes to a boil. Return chicken and simmer uncovered for 25 minutes or until chicken is tender and gravy thick. Serve with plain white rice, vegetable dishes, and other accompaniments.
Serves 4

⨳

BARBECUE-STYLE ROAST DUCK
Pei Par Ngap ◆ China

3½ lb (1.75 kg) roasting duck
1 clove garlic, crushed
1 teaspoon finely grated fresh root ginger
1 teaspoon hoi sin sauce
1 teaspoon Oriental sesame paste
1 tablespoon corn syrup or honey
1 tablespoon soy sauce
1 teaspoon salt
½ teaspoon pepper

Wash duck inside and out, remove neck and giblets and reserve for stock. Combine all other ingredients in a small saucepan and heat gently until syrup or honey melts and all are smoothly incorporated. Simmer for 2 minutes, adding a spoonful of water if it seems too thick.

Rub marinade all over duck, inside and out. Reserve remaining marinade to serve as a sauce with the duck. Put duck into oven bag or wrap in foil. If using oven bag, follow manufacturer's instructions and do not fail to make 3 or 4 holes in top of bag near the tie.

Turn duck breast side down in baking dish and cook in a moderate oven for 45 minutes. Turn duck breast side up and cook a further 45 minutes to 1 hour. Remove from bag, carve duck and serve hot with reserved marinade, mandarin pancakes (page 301), scallions (spring onions), and plum or red bean sauce.
Serves 4

⨳

BARBECUED CHICKEN
Tandoori Murgh ◆ North India

2 spring chickens, about 1 lb (500 g) each
¾ cup yogurt
1½ teaspoons salt
1½ teaspoons crushed garlic
1½ teaspoons finely grated fresh ginger
½ teaspoon white pepper
½ teaspoon chili powder
1 teaspoon garam masala (page 9)
½ teaspoon ground fenugreek, optional
red food coloring, optional
2 tablespoons ghee for oven method

With a sharp knife cut through the skin of the chickens right down the middle, front and back. Skin, then make slits in the flesh to allow spices to penetrate.

To make marinade combine yogurt with all the other ingredients except ground fenugreek and ghee. Rub marinade all over and inside the chickens, and leave for 2 to 4 hours, or cover and refrigerate overnight.

If cooking on a barbecue, make sure fire has had time to burn down to glowing coals and cut chickens in half lengthwise. Place chickens on a rack above the coals and allow to cook until tender, turning the pieces so they cook on both sides.

If cooking in an oven, use hot oven preheated to 400ºF (200ºC, Gas Mark 6). Melt 2 tablespoons ghee in a baking dish, put the two chickens in the pan, side by side, breasts downwards. Spoon

Chicken shaguti, from India (page 142).

melted ghee over them and bake in oven for 20 minutes. Turn chickens on one side and cook for another 15 minutes, then turn them on the other side, baste again and cook for a further 15 minutes. For the final 10 to 15 minutes of browning, turn the chicken breast upwards and baste every 5 minutes. If oven has a rotisserie, cook the chicken on this. It will still be necessary to baste the chicken as the skin has been removed. Serve hot with parathas (page 304) or naan and sambals (page 18).

Note: If preferred substitute 3 teaspoons tandoori mix (page 13) for the pepper, chili, garam masala (page 9) in the marinade.

Serves 4

BRAISED CHICKEN WITH FIVE FLAVORS
China

2½ lb (1.25 kg) chicken
1 mandarin or orange
1 teaspoon Sichuan peppercorns
3 tablespoons oil
1 tablespoon finely chopped fresh ginger
3 dried red chilies
3 fresh red chilies
3 scallions (spring onions), finely sliced
1 teaspoon salt

Sauce:
2 tablespoons Chinese wine or dry sherry
2 tablespoons dark soy sauce
1 teaspoon sugar
juice from a mandarin or orange
2 teaspoons sesame oil

Cut the chicken in half lengthwise, then chop through the bones into pieces about 1 in (2.5 cm) wide.

Squeeze 3 tablespoons of juice from the mandarin and set this aside for the sauce. Finely shred the orange portion of the rind, first removing all the white pith.

Roast the peppercorns in a dry pan until fragrant. Pound them with a pestle and mortar or with the handle of a cleaver.

Heat wok, add the peanut oil and swirl to coat the sides of the wok. When the oil is hot, put in the ginger, dried and fresh chilies, shredded rind, and half of the scallions. Toss for about 10 seconds. Add half the chicken pieces, brown over high heat and remove from the wok.

Brown the remaining chicken pieces, then return the first batch of chicken to the wok and sprinkle with salt and the Sichuan pepper. Mix together the ingredients for the sauce,

except sesame oil, and pour in. Cover the wok and simmer for 25 to 30 minutes, turning the pieces of chicken every 10 minutes so that they will be evenly browned. Add remaining scallions.

Uncover and, if sauce is thin, cook on high heat for a few minutes, stirring, until it becomes thick and syrupy. Turn off the heat, remove and discard the chilies, add sesame oil and mix well. Serve with hot steamed rice.

If not serving the dish straight away, remove from the wok and reheat before serving.

Serves 6

BRAISED CHICKEN WITH CHINESE MUSHROOMS
China

1 small roasting chicken or 2 small chicken thighs per serving
2 tablespoons Chinese wine or dry sherry
2 tablespoons light soy
1 teaspoon crushed garlic
1 teaspoon finely grated fresh ginger
½ teaspoon five-spice powder
6 dried Chinese mushrooms
2 tablespoons peanut oil
½ cup (4 fl oz, 125 ml) hot stock or mushroom water
12 snow peas (mangetout), optional
1 teaspoon cornstarch (cornflour)

Joint chicken. Cut breast in quarters and if thighs are large, chop each in two. Combine wine, soy, garlic, ginger, and five-spice powder and marinate the chicken in this mixture for 30 minutes. Meanwhile, soak the dry mushrooms in hot water for 30 minutes, then discard stems and slice the caps.

Drain the chicken pieces, reserving the marinade. Heat a wok or cooking pot and pour in the oil. Swirl wok to coat surface with oil. Brown the chicken over high heat, turning the pieces so that all surfaces come in contact with the heat. Add the reserved marinade and stock or mushroom water, and sliced mushrooms. Bring to a boil, then lower heat, cover and simmer for 25 to 30 minutes.

Bring a little lightly salted water to a boil and cook the snow peas for 1 minute. Drain immediately and refresh under cold water. Combine cornstarch with a tablespoon of cold water, stir into juices in pan and allow to boil and thicken. Transfer to serving dish or serve in the cooking pot. Garnish with the snow peas and serve with a small portion of rice.

Note: If snow peas are not available, substitute 1/2 cup sliced celery cooked in the same way.

Serves 2–4

Braised chicken with five flavors (recipe opposite).

BRAISED CHICKEN WITH PLUM SAUCE

China

2 lb (1 kg) chicken thighs and breasts
2 tablespoons oil
1 teaspoon finely chopped garlic
1 teaspoon finely chopped fresh ginger
2 tablespoons Chinese wine or dry sherry
2 tablespoons plum sauce
1 tablespoon light soy sauce
2 teaspoons cornstarch (cornflour)
3 tablespoons cold water
4 scallions (spring onions) cut into 1½ in (4 cm) lengths

Garnish:
2 tablespoons finely shredded red ginger (preserved ginger
  slices colored a deep red)

Braised chicken with Chinese mushrooms (recipe opposite).

Chop chicken into bite-size pieces. Heat a wok, add oil and swirl to coat inside of wok. Add chicken pieces and stir-fry on high heat till brown. Lower heat, add garlic, ginger and stir 1 minute then add wine, plum sauce, and soy sauce. Stir, cover and simmer for 30 minutes, stirring every 10 minutes. Mix cornstarch and cold water and add to wok, raise heat to medium and stir till sauce thickens. Add scallions and stir for 1 minute to mix through chicken. Serve garnished with shredded red ginger.

Serves 4–6

BRAISED DUCK WITH CHESTNUTS
Lut Tze Mun Ngap ◆ China

4 oz (125 g) dried chestnuts
4 lb (2 kg) duck
2 cloves garlic, crushed
1 teaspoon finely grated fresh ginger
1 tablespoon light soy sauce
1 tablespoon Chinese wine or dry sherry
½ cup (4 fl oz, 125 ml) peanut oil
3 tablespoons red bean curd
2 teaspoons sugar
4 scallions (spring onions) cut in lengths
tomato or chili flower to garnish, optional

In a bowl pour boiling water over dried chestnuts and soak for 30 minutes. Pour off, replace with more boiling water, soak a further 30 minutes. Drain off water before using.

If duck has been frozen, allow to thaw completely, rinse and wipe inside and out with absorbent kitchen paper. Combine garlic, ginger, soy, and wine and rub all over duck, inside and out.

Heat oil in a wok and brown duck all over, turning it frequently. Remove duck to a dish and pour off the oil, leaving only a little. Return duck to wok. Add bean curd mashed with the sugar. Pour in hot water to halfway up the duck. Add chestnuts. Bring to a boil, reduce heat, cover wok and simmer duck and chestnuts until duck is tender, about 1 1/4 to 1 1/2 hours. Turn duck during cooking and add more boiling water if necessary. Lift duck onto a wooden board and cut into pieces with a sharp cleaver, Chinese-style. Arrange duck on a serving dish, spoon chestnuts and gravy over and garnish with scallions. If desired, you can also use a tomato or chili flower for garnish.

Note: You can substitute Chinese yam or potato for the dried chestnuts. Peel and cut into cubes, then add to the simmering gravy 30 minutes before duck is cooked.

Serves 6

BRAISED DUCK WITH SWEET POTATOES
China

4 lb (2 kg) duck
2 cloves garlic, crushed
1 teaspoon finely grated fresh ginger
1 tablespoon light soy sauce
1 tablespoon Chinese wine or dry sherry
1½ lb (750 g) sweet potatoes
4 fl oz (125 ml) peanut oil
4 tablespoons red bean curd
2 teaspoons sugar

If the duck has been frozen, allow it to thaw completely, then rinse and wipe inside and out with absorbent kitchen paper. Combine the garlic, ginger, soy sauce, and wine, and rub all over the duck, inside and out. Peel the sweet potatoes, cut them into 2 inch (5 cm) slices and drop into a bowl of cold water.

Heat the oil in a wok and brown the duck all over, turning it frequently. Remove duck to a dish. Pour off all but a little of the oil. Return duck to the wok. Add the bean curd mashed with the sugar. Pour in hot water to come halfway up the duck. Bring to a boil, then reduce heat, cover the wok and simmer for 1 hour. Turn the duck during cooking, adding more boiling water if necessary.

Drain the sweet potatoes, add to the wok, and simmer for a further 15 to 30 minutes or until the duck is tender.

Lift duck onto a wooden board and cut into pieces with a sharp cleaver, Chinese-style. Arrange on a warmed serving dish, spoon the sweet potatoes and gravy over.

Serves 6

CHICKEN ADOBO WITH COCONUT SAUCE
Adobong Manok ◆ The Philippines

3 lb (1.5 kg) roasting chicken
1 tablespoon finely chopped garlic
¾ cup (6 fl oz, 180 ml) white vinegar
1–1½ cups (8–12 fl oz, 250–375 ml) water
1 teaspoon salt
1 bay leaf
½ teaspoon whole peppercorns
few annatto seeds for red coloring
2 tablespoons light soy sauce
oil for frying
½ cup (3½ oz, 100 g) thick coconut cream

Cut chicken into serving pieces, separating drumsticks from thighs and cutting breast into four. Put into a medium saucepan. Add garlic to pan with vinegar, water, salt, bay leaf, peppercorns, and annatto seeds. Liquid should be enough to almost cover the chicken. Bring to a boil, then reduce heat and simmer very gently 25 to 30 minutes. Uncover and simmer about 10 minutes longer. Chicken should be tender but not falling off the bones.

Remove chicken pieces from pan, raise heat, and boil quickly until liquid is thickened and reduced to about 1 1/2 cups (12 fl oz, 375 ml). Strain into a small bowl and refrigerate briefly. Take as much fat as possible off sauce and heat in a frying pan, adding enough oil to cover base of pan. Add chicken pieces in one layer and fry on high heat to brown, then turn and brown other side. Remove pieces of chicken to a heated serving dish as they are done. Heat sauce with coconut cream and pour over. Serve with plain boiled rice.

Serves 6

Braised duck with sweet potatoes (recipe opposite).

Braised duck with chestnuts (recipe opposite).

CHICKEN & HAM ROLLS
So Jar For Tui Gai Guen ✦ China

2 whole large chicken breasts
1 slice ham ½ inch (12 mm) thick
1 teaspoon salt
¼ teaspoon pepper
¼ teaspoon five-spice powder
1 small clove garlic, crushed
2 eggs, beaten
2 tablespoons all-purpose (plain) flour
4 egg (spring) roll wrappers
oil for deep frying

Sauce:
½ cup (4 fl oz, 125 ml) liquid from Chinese mixed pickles
½ cup (4 fl oz, 125 ml) water
1 tablespoon tomato sauce or pinch red food coloring
2 tablespoons sugar
1–2 tablespoons white vinegar
¼ teaspoon salt
¼ cup chopped Chinese mixed pickles
2 teaspoons arrowroot
1 tablespoon cold water

With sharp knife remove skin and bones from chicken breasts. Cut each breast in two down the middle. Remove the small cylindrical pieces of meat next to the bone and reserve for another recipe. Put large pieces of breast meat between two sheets of plastic or wax (greaseproof) paper, and pound until thin with a meat mallet. Meat should be thin, but take care not to tear it. Cut ham into 1/2 in (12 mm) strips the length of the chicken breasts.

Combine salt, pepper, and five-spice. Mix garlic clove with quarter teaspoon of the salt and spice mixture and spread each piece of breast with the merest trace of it. Put stick of ham on the chicken and roll up, covering the ham completely and shaping the chicken flesh to seal.

Dip in beaten egg seasoned with half teaspoon salt and spice mixture, then in flour. Put diagonally on egg roll wrapper, roll over twice, and enclose corners by folding in, envelope-fashion. Seal with a little beaten egg mixed to a thick paste with flour.

Heat oil in wok until it starts to form a haze, but it should not be too hot. Fry rolls over medium heat for 3 1/2 minutes, turning them so they brown evenly. Drain on absorbent kitchen paper. Put on serving dish, on a bed of shredded lettuce if desired, and serve with following sauce.

Sauce: Combine first 6 ingredients in a small saucepan, bring to a boil, stirring to dissolve sugar. Add pickles and the arrowroot mixed smoothly with cold water. Cook, stirring until sauce boils, clears and thickens. Serve in a bowl. If preferred, you can leave out the pickles and pickle liquid. In this case, increase vinegar and salt to taste.
Serves 4–8

CHICKEN & PORK WITH PEANUT SAUCE
Pipi–An ✦ The Philippines

3 lb (1.5 kg) roasting chicken
1 lb (500 g) pork
4 oz (125 g) raw ham
salt and pepper to taste

Sauce:
½ cup (3½ oz, 100 g) uncooked rice
4 tablespoons shortening (lard)
1 teaspoon annatto seeds
1 teaspoon crushed garlic
2 onions, finely chopped
2 tablespoons pork fat, diced
½ cup ground peanuts or peanut butter

Remove skin and bones from chicken. Cut meat into large squares. Cut fat from pork, dice fat finely and reserve 2 tablespoons for use in the sauce. Cut pork into pieces the same size as chicken. Dice the ham. Put meats into wok with water to barely cover. Add salt and pepper to taste. Bring to a simmer, cover and simmer gently until meat is tender. Turn into a dish and wash out wok.

Sauce: Dry wok over heat. Put uncooked rice into wok and roast over low heat, stirring constantly, until golden. Pound with mortar and pestle or grind to a powder in electric blender. Heat shortening in wok and fry annatto seeds over low heat for about 1 minute, by which time oil should have taken on a bright orange color. Cover pan as seeds tend to spatter and jump. Lift out seeds with draining spoon and discard. In the orange oil fry the garlic, onions, and pork fat until soft and golden brown.

Mix the ground rice with enough stock (from cooking chicken and pork) to make a smooth cream. Add to wok with ground peanuts or peanut butter. Cook until sauce boils, adding more liquid as necessary to give the sauce a good pouring consistency. Heat meats through in the sauce and serve with hot rice.
Serves 6–8

Chiken and ham rolls (recipe opposite).

CHICKEN & YOGURT CURRY
India

1 kg (2 lb) roasting chicken
1 medium onion, roughly chopped
3 cloves garlic, peeled
1 teaspoon finely chopped fresh ginger
½ cup (2 oz) fresh coriander or mint leaves
1½ tablespoons ghee or oil
1 teaspoon ground turmeric
1½ teaspoons garam masala (page 9)
1½ teaspoons salt
½ teaspoon chili powder, optional
½ cup (4 fl oz) natural yogurt
2 ripe tomatoes, diced

Garnish:
extra chopped mint or cilantro (coriander leaves).

Cut chicken into serving pieces, or use chicken pieces of one kind — drumsticks, thighs, or half breasts.

Put into container of electric blender the onion, garlic, ginger, fresh coriander or mint. Blend to a smooth purée. Heat oil in a heavy saucepan and fry the blended mixture, stirring, for about 5 minutes. Add turmeric, garam masala, salt, and chili powder and fry for a further minute. Stir in yogurt and tomatoes, and fry until liquid dries up and the mixture is the consistency of thick purée.

Add chicken pieces, turning them in the spice mixture so they are coated on both sides, then turn heat low, cover tightly and cook until chicken is tender. If liquid from chicken has not evaporated by the time the flesh is cooked, uncover and raise heat to dry off excess liquid, stirring gently at the base of pan to prevent burning. Garnish with chopped herbs and serve with rice or chapatis.
Serves 4

CHICKEN CURRY WITH NOODLES
Burma

3 lb (1.5 kg) chicken or chicken pieces
5 cloves garlic
3 medium onions, chopped
1 tablespoon finely chopped fresh ginger
1 teaspoon dried shrimp paste
2 tablespoons peanut oil
1 tablespoon sesame oil

1–2 teaspoons chili powder
2 teaspoons salt
2 cups (16 fl oz, 500 ml) thin coconut cream
2 cups (16 fl oz, 500 ml) thick coconut cream
2 tablespoons chickpea flour
1 lb (500 g) thin egg noodles or cellophane noodles

Cut chicken into serving pieces. Put garlic, onion, ginger, and dried shrimp paste into blender container, cover and blend until smooth, adding 1 tablespoon of peanut oil if necessary. Heat remaining oil and fry blended ingredients for 5 minutes. Add chicken and continue to fry, stirring constantly. Add chili powder, salt, and thin coconut cream. Simmer until chicken is tender, adding a little hot water if mixture becomes too dry. Add thick coconut cream, return to heat and bring slowly to a boil, stirring constantly to prevent mixture from curdling. Mix chickpea flour with a little cold water to a smooth cream, add to curry and cook for a further 5 minutes uncovered (there should be a lot of gravy). If preparing curry a day or two beforehand, refrigerate immediately and reheat when required. Just before serving, cook noodles in a large saucepan of boiling salted water until just tender about 6 minutes. Pour cold water into pan to stop noodles cooking, then drain in colander.

Accompaniments: Finely sliced spring onions, both green and white portions, chopped fresh cilantro (coriander leaves), finely sliced white onion, roasted chick peas finely ground in a blender or crushed with mortar and pestle, crisp fried noodles broken into small pieces, fried onion flakes, thin slices garlic fried in oil until golden, lemon wedges, dried chilies fried in oil 3–4 seconds, chili powder.

Note: Roasted chick peas are sold in Greek delicatessen shops.
Serves 6–8

CHICKEN FRITADA
The Philippines

3 lb (1.5 kg) chicken
2 tablespoons shortening (lard)
5 cloves garlic, peeled and crushed
1 large onion, finely sliced
2 ripe tomatoes, diced
1½ teaspoons salt
½ teaspoon black pepper
1½ cups (12 fl oz, 375 ml) hot chicken stock
1 lb (500 g) new potatoes, scrubbed
1 red bell pepper (capsicum)
1 green bell pepper (capsicum)

Cut chicken into serving pieces. Use neck, back, and wing tips for making stock. Heat shortening in large frying pan and fry garlic and onion until onion is soft. Add chicken pieces and brown on both sides. Add tomatoes, salt, pepper, and stock, cover and cook on medium heat until chicken is half done. Add potatoes (if they are large, halve or quarter) and bell peppers cut into strips. Cook until potatoes are tender. Serve hot with white rice.

Serves 4–6

CHICKEN GRILLED ON SKEWERS

Sate Ayam ◆ Indonesia

1½ lb (750 g) chicken breast
2 red chilies or ½ teaspoon sambal ulek (page 23)
2 medium onions, roughly chopped
3 teaspoons finely chopped fresh ginger
2 tablespoons lemon juice
1½ teaspoons salt
2 tablespoons light soy sauce
2 tablespoons dark soy sauce
2 tablespoons sesame oil
2 tablespoons jaggery (palm sugar) or brown sugar
½ cup (3½ oz, 100 g) thick coconut cream

Bone chicken and remove skin. Cut into small squares. In blender put seeded and roughly chopped chilies, onions, ginger, lemon juice, salt, and soy sauce. Blend until smooth, pour into a bowl and stir in oil and sugar. Add chicken and stir until each piece is well coated with the marinade. Cover and marinate for 1 hour or overnight in the refrigerator. There will be a generous amount of marinade, because this is used as the base for a sauce served with the satay.

Thread pieces of chicken on bamboo skewers which have been soaked for 1 to 2 hours in cold water, leaving at least half the skewer free at the blunt end. Broil (grill) over glowing coals or under a preheated broiler (grill), about 2 in (5 cm) from heat source, for 5 to 8 minutes or until chicken is crisp and brown. Brush with extra oil during broiling, once on each side.

Pour remaining marinade into a small saucepan, add coconut cream and simmer over low heat until smooth and thickened, stirring constantly. Pour into a bowl and serve with the satay.

Serves 6

CHICKEN IN BLACK BEAN SAUCE

China

1 large chicken breast
4 oz (125 g) bean sprouts or 3 stalks celery
2 teaspoons canned salted black beans
1 teaspoon soy sauce
1 clove garlic, crushed
1 tablespoon Chinese wine or sherry
2 teaspoons cornstarch (cornflour)
½ cup (4 fl oz, 125 ml) cold water
1 tablespoon oil

Cut chicken meat off the bone. Save bone for stock. Dice the meat into even-size pieces. Wash and pick over the bean sprouts and leave to drain. Cut celery in thin diagonal slices. Put the black beans in a bowl and mash with a fork. Combine with soy sauce, garlic, wine, and half the water. Mix the cornstarch into the remaining water.

Heat oil in a wok, add the black bean mixture and stir until it boils. Add chicken and cook, stirring, for 2 minutes. Add cornstarch and stir constantly until it boils and thickens, about 1 minute. Add the bean sprouts and toss in the sauce for 1 minute longer. Serve at once.

Serves 2–3

CHICKEN IN COCONUT CREAM

Opor Ayam ◆ Indonesia

3 lb (1.5 kg) roasting chicken or chicken pieces
3 cloves garlic, crushed
1 teaspoon salt
½ teaspoon ground black pepper
1½ teaspoons finely grated fresh ginger
3 candlenuts, macadamia nuts or brazil nuts, finely grated
3 teaspoons ground coriander
1 teaspoon ground cumin
½ teaspoon ground fennel
½ teaspoon laos powder, optional
4 tablespoons oil
2 medium onions, finely sliced
2 cups (16 fl oz, 500 ml) thin coconut cream
2 daun salam or 6 curry leaves
1 stem lemon grass or 3 strips thinly peeled lemon rind
2 in (5 cm) piece cinnamon stick
1½ cups (10 oz, 315 g) thick coconut cream

1 tablespoon lemon juice or tamarind liquid
extra salt to taste

Divide chicken into serving pieces. In a small bowl, combine garlic, salt, pepper, ginger, nuts, coriander, cumin, fennel, and laos powder if used. Mix to a paste, adding a little of the oil if necessary. Rub paste well into the pieces of chicken and leave for 1 hour.

Heat 2 tablespoons of the oil in a frying pan and fry sliced onion slowly until golden brown. Drain from oil and set aside. Add remaining oil to pan and fry the spiced chicken pieces gently, just until they start to brown. Add thin coconut cream, daun salam, lemon grass or rind, and cinnamon stick. Stir until it comes to a boil, then cook uncovered for 30 minutes or until chicken is tender. Add thick coconut cream, stir thoroughly and cook for a further 15 minutes, uncovered. Remove from heat, add lemon juice and season to taste with extra salt. Remove whole spices. Garnish with fried onions and serve the chicken with white rice, vegetables, and sambals.
Serves 4–6

CHICKEN LIVERS WITH BAMBOO SHOOT & CABBAGE
China

1 lb (500 g) chicken livers
2 slices fresh ginger
1 scallion (spring onion)
4 tablespoons dark soy sauce
1 canned winter bamboo shoot
1 bunch gai choy (Chinese mustard cabbage)
1 tablespoon sugar
1 tablespoon Chinese wine or dry sherry
2 tablespoons peanut oil
1 teaspoon cornstarch (cornflour)
2 teaspoons sesame oil
1 tablespoon white cider vinegar

Halve the chicken livers and remove any tubes, connective tissue, and yellow spots. Put livers into a small saucepan with the ginger, scallion cut into three or four pieces, and 2 tablespoons of the soy sauce. Add enough boiling water to just cover the livers. Simmer, covered, over a low heat for 5 minutes. Drain and discard ginger and onion.

Slice the bamboo shoot. Wash the gai choy and slice diagonally; there should be about 12 oz (375 g). Combine the remaining 2 tablespoons of soy sauce, sugar, and wine.

Heat a wok, add the peanut oil and swirl it around the sides of the wok. Toss in the chicken livers and stir-fry for 10

seconds. Add the soy mixture, bamboo shoot, and gai choy, and stir-fry for 2 minutes. Blend the cornstarch with 2 teaspoons of cold water and add this to the livers, stirring until the sauce thickens. Add sesame oil.

Sprinkle the vinegar around the edge of the wok and, as it sizzles into a steam, give the livers a few fast turns. Turn out into a dish to serve.
Serves 4

CHICKEN OMELET
Torimaki ◆ Japan

3 eggs
2 tablespoons dashi (page 6) or water
½ teaspoon salt
1 teaspoon soy sauce
vegetable oil for frying

Filling:
½ cup finely chopped cooked chicken
2 teaspoons Japanese soy sauce
2 teaspoons mirin or dry sherry
1 teaspoon sugar
1 teaspoon finely grated fresh ginger

Beat eggs and add dashi, salt, and soy. Heat omelet pan and grease lightly with a few drops of oil, pour in the egg and cook until set on the bottom, but liquid on top.

Put chicken filling in a neat line across the omelet and roll the egg mixture firmly around it, away from you. Turn onto a plate, cut in two and serve immediately.

This chicken omelet can be rolled in a sudare (bamboo mat), left until cool and firm, then unrolled, sliced and served as an hors d'oeuvre.

Filling: Flavor chicken with soy, mirin, sugar, and juice pressed from the grated ginger.
Serves 2

CHICKEN SHAGUTI
Murgh Shaguti Masala ◆ India

3 lb (1.5 kg) roasting chicken
8 dried red chilies
1 tablespoon ground coriander
1 teaspoon ground cumin
½ teaspoon fenugreek seeds
8 whole black peppercorns

3 teaspoons white poppy seeds or ground almonds
½ cup (2 oz, 60 g) unsweetened desiccated coconut
1 large onion, finely sliced
2 teaspoons chopped fresh ginger
2 teaspoons chopped garlic
½ teaspoon ground cardamom
¼ teaspoon ground cloves
½ teaspoon ground cinnamon
2 teaspoons salt
1 tablespoon ghee
2 tablespoons oil
1 teaspoon ground turmeric
juice of half a lemon

Cut chicken into serving pieces. Remove stalks and seeds from chilies and soak the chilies in hot water for 10 minutes. Meanwhile, roast coriander and cumin in a dry pan over medium heat for a minute or two, until they turn brown and a pleasant aroma is given off. Turn onto a plate. Roast fenugreek seeds and peppercorns for 2 or 3 minutes, stirring constantly or shaking pan. In the same way roast the poppy seeds and the desiccated coconut, separately. Add to the other roasted spices. Put the sliced onion in the pan and dry roast, stirring, until brown.

Put chilies into blender with all the roasted ingredients and the turmeric, cardamom, cloves, and cinnamon. Add some of the water in which the chilies were soaked and grind to a paste.

Heat ghee and oil in a heavy pan and fry the ground mixture and the ginger and garlic, stirring constantly, until oil separates from the mass. Put in the chicken, sprinkle with salt and stir to coat every piece of chicken with the spices.

Add 1/2 cup (4 fl oz, 125 ml) hot water, cover and cook on very low heat, stirring occasionally and adding more water if necessary, until the chicken is tender. Add lemon juice when chicken is cooked. The gravy should be very thick and dark. Serve with rice and accompaniments, such as Onion and Tomato Sambal (page 23) and Beetroot Raita (page 18).
Serves 6

❖

CHICKEN STEW
Dak Jim ◆ Korea

3 lb (1.5 kg) roasting chicken
¼ cup (2 fl oz, 60 ml) light soy sauce
2 tablespoons sesame oil
1 tablespoon finely chopped garlic
½ teaspoon chili powder or cayenne
3 scallions (spring onions), very finely chopped
¼ teaspoon salt

Cut chicken into small serving pieces. Put into a large heavy pan, add all remaining ingredients and mix well so that all the chicken comes in contact with the flavorings. Leave for 2 hours at room temperature then put on low heat and cook, covered, until chicken is tender. Serve with hot rice and pickled Chinese cabbage (page 273).
Serves 4–6

❖

CHICKEN VELVET FU YUNG
China

1 large chicken breast, about 12 oz (375 g)
1 teaspoon salt
2 teaspoons water
water chestnut flour or cornstarch (cornflour)
1 tablespoon Chinese wine or dry sherry
4 eggs, separated
1 stem celery
1 Chinese (Napa) cabbage or lettuce
peanut oil for cooking
1 teaspoon sugar
½ teaspoon salt

Sauce:
stock made with chicken skin and bones
1 teaspoon light soy sauce
1 tablespoon cornstarch (cornflour)

Chicken Velvet Fu Yung (recipe above).

Remove the skin and bones from the chicken breast. When boning, hold a sharp knife close to the bone.

Take the small slice from each side of the breast and, holding the silvery tendon, scrape the flesh finely. Discard tendon.

Place the pieces on the chopping board, with the side that was next to the skin downwards. Again use the sharp chopper to scrape the flesh free of the long fibers that lie against the skin.

Put the skin, bones, and fibers into a small pan with about 12 fl oz (375 ml) cold water to cover, and simmer until chicken stock is reduced to 1 cup (8 fl oz, 250 ml). Strain and season to taste with salt.

Finely chop the chicken meat, first one way and then the other, until it is a fine purée. Gradually add 1 tablespoon of cold water while chopping, to lighten the consistency. Add the salt and wine. Add the chestnut flour or cornstarch mixed smoothly with 1 tablespoon of cold water, stirring to mix.

In a large bowl whip the whites of the eggs until frothy and holding soft peaks. Stir a large spoonful at a time into the chicken mixture until all the egg white is incorporated. Cover and chill for 30 minutes or longer.

Beat the yolks with a little salt and set aside. Cut the celery into thin slices. Cut the cabbage or lettuce into chunky pieces.

Heat a wok, add 1 tablespoon of peanut oil and stir the egg yolk over medium heat until it sets. Do not brown. Remove from heat, cut into small pieces with the sharp edge of a wok chan (spatula).

Heat another tablespoon of peanut oil and stir-fry the celery for 1 minute, not allowing it to brown; set aside.

Heat another 2 tablespoons of peanut oil and stir-fry the cabbage or lettuce for 1 minute. Sprinkle with the sugar and salt. Add 2 tablespoons of water, cover the wok and leave for 30 seconds for lettuce or 2 to 3 minutes for a firmer green vegetable. Spread on the serving dish.

Clean out the wok, return it to the heat and when hot, pour in 1/2 cup (4 fl oz, 125 ml) peanut oil. Do not let the oil become too hot — the aim is to keep the chicken from browning. Pour in the chicken velvet and turn it quickly with the wok chan until it is white. Pour it through a wire strainer and let all excess oil drain out.

Meanwhile, combine the sauce ingredients including the chicken stock, and bring to a boil in a small saucepan, stirring until thick and clear. Toss the chicken velvet with celery and yolk pieces, spread over the green vegetable, and pour the sauce over. Serve at once with rice.

'Chicken velvet' is very finely puréed chicken meat lightened by adding water and egg whites. When cooked, it is similar to a soft custard. ('Velveting' is a method of marinating and coating.) Fu Yung is a white hibiscus and this dish is so named because the chicken should remain white when cooked.

Serves 4

CHICKEN VINDALOO
India

4 lb (2 kg) roasting chicken
2 tablespoons cumin seed
1 tablespoon black mustard seed
3 teaspoons chili powder or to taste
1 tablespoon chopped ginger
1 tablespoon chopped garlic
¾ cup (6 fl oz, 180 ml) vinegar
1 teaspoon ground cinnamon
¼ teaspoon ground cloves
¼ teaspoon ground cardamom
4 tablespoons oil
2 teaspoons salt
½ teaspoon ground black pepper

Cut the chicken into serving pieces. Grind the cumin seeds, mustard seeds, ginger, and garlic in blender with the vinegar. Use high speed so that mixture is finely ground. Add the ground spices.

Heat oil in a heavy saucepan, remove from heat and add the ground mixture to the hot oil. Stir for a few seconds, then add the chicken pieces and stir again so that each piece is coated with the spices. Let it stand for an hour or longer. Return to low heat and bring to simmering point, add salt and black pepper and simmer, covered, until chicken is tender. Stir from time to time so that spices do not catch to the base of pan. Serve with plain white rice.

Serves 6

CHICKEN WITH CASHEW NUTS & SNOW PEAS
China

1½ lb (750 g) chicken breasts
3 teaspoons cornstarch (cornflour) or water chestnut flour
½ teaspoon five-spice powder
½ teaspoon salt
oil for deep frying
1 cup raw cashew nuts
4 tablespoons extra oil
4 oz (125 g) snow peas (mangetout)
1½ teaspoons finely grated fresh root ginger
1 small clove garlic, crushed
2 tablespoons Chinese wine or sherry
1 tablespoon soy sauce
1 teaspoon sugar
2 teaspoons extra cornstarch (cornflour)
2 tablespoons cold water

Bone chicken breasts and cut into small pieces, approximately 1/2 in (1 cm) square. Sieve cornstarch, five-spice powder, and salt over chicken pieces and mix well. Set aside. Heat oil and deep fry cashew nuts over a moderate heat until golden. Lift out and drain on absorbent kitchen paper.

Heat 2 tablespoons of the extra oil in a wok and quickly stir-fry the snow peas over a high heat for 30 seconds, just until they turn a deeper green. Lift onto a plate. Add remaining extra oil to wok, fry ginger and garlic for a few seconds, then add chicken and fry, stirring continuously, over a high heat until chicken turns golden brown. (This will only take a minute or two.) Add remaining ingredients mixed together and stir over heat until liquid boils and thickens. Remove from heat, mix in cashew nuts and snow peas and serve immediately.
Serves 6

CHICKEN WITH CELLOPHANE NOODLES
Ga Xao Bun Tau ◆ Vietnam

1 lb (500 g) chicken meat or 1½ lb (750 g) thighs
* and breasts*
4 oz (125 g) cellophane noodles
2 scallions (spring onions), thinly sliced
1 tablespoon oil
2 tablespoons fish sauce
1 tablespoon light soy sauce
¼ teaspoon ground black pepper
½ cup (4 fl oz, 125 ml) water
2 firm ripe tomatoes
2 white onions
sugar, vinegar, salt, pepper

Remove skin and bone from chicken thighs or breasts and cut the flesh into large bite-size chunks. Reserve bones for soup. Put noodles in a large bowl, pour boiling water over and stand for 10 minutes, then drain and cut noodles into bite-size lengths.

Heat a wok, add oil and swirl to coat inside of wok. Add chicken and scallions, stir-fry for 2 to 3 minutes. Add fish sauce, soy sauce, pepper, and water, bring to a boil and simmer for 3 minutes. Add noodles, return to a boil, stirring constantly, and cook for 3 minutes longer. Serve hot, accompanied by a salad of sliced tomatoes and white onions, dressed with a dash of white vinegar, a sprinkling of sugar, salt and pepper to taste.
Serves 4–6

CHICKEN WITH GINGER SHREDS
Kai Phat Khing ◆ Thailand

1 large chicken breast
½ cup dried wood fungus (cloud ears)
2 tablespoons finely shredded fresh ginger
1 small onion, thinly sliced
1 tablespoon shortening (lard) or oil
3 cloves garlic, finely chopped
1 tablespoon light soy sauce
1 tablespoon fish sauce
1 tablespoon vinegar
1–2 teaspoons sugar
3 scallions (spring onions), finely chopped
2 tablespoons chopped cilantro (fresh coriander leaves)

Remove skin and bones from chicken breast and cut the meat into small dice. Soak wood fungus in hot water for 10 minutes, wash well, remove any gritty parts and cut into bite-size pieces. Soak ginger in lightly salted water for 10 minutes, then squeeze out moisture. This makes the ginger less pungent. To shred ginger, thinly peel off brown skin, cut into very thin slices, then cut slices into long, thread-like strips.

Heat shortening or oil and on medium-low heat fry the onion until soft and translucent, add garlic and stir until garlic starts to turn golden. Add chicken and ginger and stir-fry until chicken turns golden, then add the sauces, vinegar, and sugar. When liquid boils reduce heat, cover and simmer 3 minutes. Do not overcook. Stir in scallions and cilantro and serve immediately.
Serves 2 as a main dish, 4–5 with other dishes

CHICKEN WITH LEMON GRASS
Ga Xao Xa Ot ◆ Vietnam

1 small roasting chicken, about 2 lb (1 kg)
3 or 4 stalks lemon grass or rind of 1 large lemon
3 scallions (spring onions)
1 teaspoon salt
¼ teaspoon ground black pepper
2 tablespoons oil
1 or 2 fresh red chilies, seeded and chopped
2 teaspoons sugar
extra black pepper to taste
½ cup (3 oz, 90 g) roasted peanuts, finely chopped
2 tablespoons fish sauce

Cut chicken into small serving pieces, Chinese-style, chopping through the bones with a sharp cleaver. Remove outer leaves of the lemon grass and finely slice the tender white part at the base of the stalks. Bruise with mortar and pestle or handle of cleaver. Finely slice the scallions, including the green leaves. Mix the chicken with the salt, pepper, lemon grass, and scallions and set aside for 30 minutes. If lemon rind is used instead of lemon grass, shred the thinly peeled rind very finely with a sharp knife.

Heat a wok, add oil and when oil is hot add the chicken mixture and stir-fry for 3 minutes. Add chilies and stir-fry on medium heat for a further 10 minutes or until chicken no longer looks pink. Season with sugar and pepper and add peanuts. Stir well. Add fish sauce and toss to distribute evenly, then serve with rice or noodles.

Note: Dried lemon grass cannot be substituted.

Serves 4–6

⬥⟩⟨⬥

CHICKEN WITH SHRIMP SAUCE
Ayam Petis ◆ Indonesia

3 lb (1.5 kg) chicken
3 tablespoons peanut oil
1 large onion, finely chopped
3–4 cloves garlic, finely chopped
1 teaspoon finely chopped fresh ginger
3 fresh red chilies, seeded and chopped
1 teaspoon ground turmeric
1 teaspoon ground black pepper
½ teaspoon trasi (dried shrimp paste)
½ teaspoon laos powder
1 stalk lemon grass or 2 thinly peeled strips lemon rind
2 teaspoons Chinese shrimp sauce
1½ teaspoons salt
1½ cups (12 fl oz, 375 ml) thin coconut cream
1 tablespoon jaggery (palm sugar) or brown sugar
2 tablespoons lemon juice

Cut chicken into serving pieces. Heat peanut oil and fry the onion, garlic, and ginger until onion is soft. Add the chilies, turmeric, pepper, trasi, and laos powder and fry, stirring, for 1 minute longer. Add the lemon grass or rind, shrimp sauce, salt, and chicken pieces and stir-fry over medium heat until chicken is well coated with the mixture. Add coconut cream and sugar and bring to simmering point on low heat, uncovered, stirring frequently.

Turn heat low, and simmer 30 minutes or until chicken is tender and the gravy has thickened. If necessary cook 15 minutes longer, stirring occasionally. If gravy is still not thick enough, remove chicken pieces to serving dish and reduce gravy over high heat, stirring constantly. Add lemon juice, pour gravy over chicken and serve with rice and sambals.

Serves 6.

⬥⟩⟨⬥

CHICKEN WITH SOTANGHON
The Philippines

3 lb (1.5 kg) chicken
2 tablespoons shortening (lard)
1 onion, sliced
2 cloves garlic, crushed
1 tablespoon fish sauce
2 teaspoons annatto seeds
8 oz (250 g) sotanghon (cellophane noodles) soaked and cut in 2 in (5 cm) lengths
6 large dried Chinese mushrooms, soaked in hot water, de-stemmed and chopped
12 scallions (spring onions), finely sliced
pepper and salt

Put whole chicken in a saucepan, cover with water and bring to a boil. Simmer on low heat, covered, until chicken is almost tender. Lift out chicken and let cool a little, strain stock and reserve. Remove all bones from the chicken and cut meat into large pieces.

Heat shortening in frying pan and fry onion and garlic until soft and golden. Add chicken meat and fish sauce and allow to simmer for a few minutes. Pour 2 tablespoons hot water over annatto seeds, stir until water is bright orange, then strain off water and add to pan with strained chicken broth. Bring to a boil, add sotanghon and chopped mushrooms and simmer 15 minutes. Add scallions and pepper and salt to taste.

Serves 4–6

⬥⟩⟨⬥

CHICKEN WITH SPICY COCONUT CREAM GRAVY
Ayam Lemak ◆ Malaysia

4 lb (1.5 kg) roasting chicken
2½ teaspoons finely grated fresh ginger
2 medium onions, chopped
3 stalks lemon grass or rind of 1 lemon
6 fresh red chilies, seeded, or 2 teaspoons sambal ulek (page 23)
1 teaspoon ground turmeric
3 tablespoons oil
3 cups (20 oz, 600 g) thick coconut cream
3 strips (finger-length) daun pandan or few leaves fresh basil
2 teaspoons salt

Cut chicken into serving pieces. Pound the ginger, onions, lemon grass or rind, and the chilies with a mortar and pestle, or grind in blender with a little oil until they form a paste. Rub chicken pieces with turmeric until they are coated all over. Heat oil in a heavy saucepan and fry the ground ingredients over a low heat, stirring constantly, for 15 minutes or until soft and golden. Add chicken and fry for further 10 minutes. Add coconut cream, pandan or basil leaves, and salt and simmer uncovered until chicken is tender. Serve with white rice.
Serves 6

CHICKEN WITH WALNUTS & BROCCOLI
China

Make Chicken with Cashew Nuts and Snow Peas (see page 144) but substitute an equal quantity of tender broccoli, or thinly sliced green (string) beans for snow peas (mangetout).

They should be fried for approximately 3 minutes. Substitute peeled walnuts for cashew nuts.

CHILI EGGS
Indonesia

4 eggs
3 tablespoons peanut oil
1 medium onion, finely chopped
½ teaspoon finely chopped garlic
½ teaspoon trasi (dried shrimp paste)
1 tablespoon sambal ulek (page 23) or chili sauce
½ teaspoon laos powder
3 candlenuts or macadamia nuts, finely grated, optional
½ teaspoon salt
¼ teaspoon ground black pepper
3 teaspoons brown sugar
½ cup (4 fl oz, 125 ml) canned coconut cream
2 teaspoons lemon juice

Chicken with walnuts and broccoli (recipe above).

Hard-cook (boil) the eggs, stirring for first 5 minutes so the yolks are centered. Heat wok, add oil and fry onion and garlic until they are soft and golden. Add trasi, sambal ulek, laos powder, and grated nuts and fry for 1 minute, crushing the trasi with the frying spoon. Add salt, pepper, sugar, coconut cream, and lemon juice and simmer gently, stirring constantly, until thick and the oil comes to the surface. Add the shelled and halved eggs, spooning the sauce over them. Serve with hot white rice.

Serves 4

❖⤜∞⤛❖

COUNTRY CAPTAIN CHICKEN
Singapore

3 lb (1.5 kg) chicken or chicken pieces
2 cloves garlic, crushed
2 teaspoons salt
1 teaspoon ground turmeric
½ teaspoon ground black pepper
4 tablespoons oil
4 large onions, thinly sliced
2 fresh red chilies, seeded and sliced
½ cup (4 fl oz, 125 ml) water

Cut chicken into serving pieces. Combine garlic, salt, turmeric, and pepper and rub well into chicken. Heat oil in a large saucepan and gently fry half the sliced onion until brown. Remove onion from pan and set aside.

Fry remaining onion and chilies until just starting to turn gold, then add chicken to pan and fry until golden all over. Add water, cover and simmer gently until chicken is tender. Uncover and continue to simmer, allowing any liquid remaining in pan to evaporate. Serve hot, garnished with the reserved fried onion and accompanied by fried potatoes or Ghee Rice (page 234).

Serves 6

❖⤜∞⤛❖

CRISP-FRIED BONELESS DUCK
China

1 duckling, about 3 lb (1.5 kg)
12 fl oz (375 ml) dark soy sauce
4 fl oz (125 ml) Chinese wine or dry sherry
2 whole star anise
2 cloves
2 sticks cinnamon
1 teaspoon fennel seeds
1 teaspoon Sichuan peppercorns
5 slices fresh ginger
2 tablespoons sugar
oil for deep frying

Batter:
3½ oz (100 g) self-raising flour
pinch of salt

For serving:
bottled plum sauce

Wash and dry the duck well. Rub it all over with some of the dark soy sauce and set it aside for at least 30 minutes.

In a large saucepan combine the rest of the dark soy sauce with 12 fl oz (375 ml) water, wine, and the spices knotted in a square of muslin. Add ginger and sugar and bring to a gentle simmer.

Heat at least 2 pts (1.25 L) of oil in a wok for deep frying the duck and when the oil is hot, slide in the duck. Fry first one side and then the other until it is evenly brown all over.

Lift duck out of the wok and put it into the saucepan of soy mixture. Bring to a simmer, turn the heat very low, cover the saucepan and cook for 1 hour or until the duck is tender. Lift duck out of the sauce, drain in a colander, and leave until cold enough to handle

Meanwhile, make a thick batter with the self-raising flour, whisking until smooth with sufficient cold water to give a thick coating consistency. Let stand for at least 1 hour.

Lay the duck on its back on a wooden board and, with a sharp chopper, cut through the skin of the duck, right down the middle. Find the breastbone, right below the neck, and wiggle it out. Spread the skin away from the bones as though unzipping a coat down the front. It is now quite easy to lift out the bony framework (use it for making stock).

Turn the duck over, breast downwards, and make slits in the legs and wings. Loosen the bones and coax them out, twisting them free at the joints. Turn duck over again, feel for the thighbones and remove these as well.

Cut duck in half lengthwise and chop the now boneless duck crosswise into strips 1 in (2.5 cm) wide.

Crisp-fried boneless duck (recipe opposite).

Duck with sweet hot plum sauce (page 150).

Reheat the oil for the second frying, but do not have it too hot. Dip the pieces of duck in the batter and then slide them into the oil, a few at a time. Spoon the oil over while cooking. When golden brown, lift them out and drain. When all the pieces are fried, place them on a serving dish and spoon plum sauce over. Finish with a bright garnish and serve with hot steamed rice or Mandarin Pancakes (page 301).

Note: The liquid in which the duck simmered is now a Master Sauce and may be used for cooking other poultry, meat or seafood. Add a spoonful to sauces. It also freezes well.

Serves 6–8 as part of a meal

DUCK VINDALOO
India

1 x 1.5 kg (3 lb) duck
10 dried red chilies
½ cup (4 fl oz) vinegar
1 tablespoon chopped garlic
1 tablespoon chopped fresh ginger
1 tablespoon ground coriander
2 teaspoons ground cumin
1 teaspoon ground turmeric
½ teaspoon ground black pepper
2–3 tablespoons ghee or oil
2 teaspoons salt
1 tablespoon sugar

Cut the duck into joints. Remove stalks and seeds from dried chilies and soak in vinegar for about 10 minutes. Put chilies, vinegar, garlic, and ginger into blender and blend until smooth.

Scrape mixture out of blender into a large bowl and mix in the ground spices. Add pieces of duck, turn them over in the mixture until they are well coated, cover and leave for 2 hours at room temperature or overnight in the refrigerator.

In a large saucepan heat the ghee or oil and fry the pieces of duck lightly. Add salt and a little hot water together with any marinade left. Cover and simmer on low heat until duck is tender, adding a little more water if necessary during cooking. At end of cooking time stir in the sugar. Serve with rice.
Serves 4–5

⟨≋⟩

DUCK WITH SWEET HOT PLUM SAUCE
China

4 lb (2 kg) duck
1½ teaspoons salt
1 tablespoon light soy sauce
2 teaspoons Chinese wine or dry sherry
1 teaspoon five-spice powder
2 tablespoons cornstarch (cornflour)
oil for deep frying
scallions (spring onions) or cilantro (fresh coriander leaves)
* for garnish*

Sauce:
1 tablespoon oil
1 teaspoon finely grated fresh ginger
½ teaspoon crushed garlic
4 tablespoons bottled plum sauce
1 teaspoon bottled Chinese chili sauce

Wash the duck well. Cut off and discard the tail. Dry inside and out with absorbent kitchen paper. Combine salt, soy sauce, wine, and five-spice powder, and rub all over the duck, inside and out. Leave to marinate for at least 1 hour.

Put the duck on a steamer rack and steam for 1 1/2 to 2 hours or until tender.

Set the duck aside until cool enough to handle, then dry thoroughly with absorbent kitchen paper. Dredge the duck with cornstarch.

Heat oil in a wok and when very hot, gently lower the duck into the oil. Keep ladling hot oil over the top of the duck. Turn it when the underside is done and in the same way fry the other side until the skin is crisp. Lift it out of the oil with a slotted spoon, letting the oil drain back into the wok.

Chop the duck in half lengthwise, then chop each half into bite-size pieces. Arrange on a serving dish and spoon the sauce over.

Sauce: Heat the tablespoon of oil and gently fry the ginger and garlic until fragrant (about 1 minute). Stir in the plum sauce and chili sauce plus 1 tablespoon of water, until the sauce boils. Simmer for 1 minute. Serve with rice and if desired garnish with carrot flowers.
Serves 4

⟨≋⟩

DUCK WITH TANGERINE SAUCE
China

3¾ lb (1.75 kg) duck
½ teaspoon salt
½ teaspoon pepper
1 teaspoon grated fresh ginger
2 tablespoons cornstarch (cornflour)
oil for deep frying

Sauce:
2 tablespoons light soy sauce
1 tablespoon sugar
4 tablespoons Chinese wine or dry sherry
juice of 3 mandarins or 2 oranges
1 piece dried tangerine peel

Garnish:
segments of mandarin or orange

With a sharp cleaver, chop the duck into 12 to 14 pieces. Discard the tail. (Neck and wing tips may be added to the stock pot.) Rub the pieces of duck with salt, pepper, and ginger, and leave for 2 hours.

Blend 1 teaspoon of the cornstarch with 1 tablespoon water and set aside. Toss the duck pieces in the remaining cornstarch.

Deep fry four pieces at a time for 3 to 4 minutes. Drain on absorbent kitchen paper.

In a saucepan, combine the sauce ingredients with 8 fl oz (250 ml) water, bring to a boil and simmer for 2 minutes. Add the duck pieces, cover the saucepan and simmer for 30 to 40 minutes or until the duck is tender. Remove the tangerine peel. Stir the reserved cornstarch and water, and mix it into the sauce until it boils and thickens. Serve garnished with mandarin or orange segments gently heated in the sauce if desired.
Serves 4–6

⟨≋⟩

EGG & COCONUT CURRY
Mootay Molee ◆ India (Kerala)

6–8 eggs
2 tablespoons oil
1 medium onion, finely sliced
1½ teaspoons crushed garlic
1 teaspoon finely grated fresh ginger
2 or 3 fresh green chilies, seeded and sliced
6 curry leaves
1 teaspoon ground turmeric
2 cups (16 fl oz, 500 ml) thin coconut cream
1½ cups (10 oz, 315 g) thick coconut cream
1 teaspoon salt
lemon juice to taste

Put the eggs into cold water, bring slowly to a boil, stirring for the first 5 minutes to center the yolks. Simmer for 10 minutes, then cool quickly under running cold water. Shell the eggs and set aside.

Heat oil in a saucepan and fry the onion, garlic, ginger, chilies, and curry leaves on low heat until onions are soft without letting them brown. Add turmeric and stir, then add the thin coconut cream and simmer uncovered for 10 minutes. Add the thick coconut cream and salt and stir constantly while letting it come to simmering point. Cut the eggs in halves lengthwise and simmer them in the coconut gravy for a few minutes, just until heated through. Remove from heat, stir in lemon juice to taste. Serve with white rice.
Serves 4–6

Duck with tangerine sauce (recipe opposite).

EGGS IN MEATBALLS
Nargisi Kofta ◆ India & Pakistan

Meatballs:
7 small eggs
1 lb (500 g) twice-ground (minced) lamb or beef
1 small onion, finely chopped
2 cloves garlic, finely grated
½ teaspoon finely grated ginger
1 fresh green chili, finely chopped
1 teaspoon salt
1 teaspoon garam masala
½ teaspoon ground turmeric
½ cup (4 fl oz, 125 ml) water
1½ tablespoons besan (chickpea flour)
1 tablespoon yogurt
ghee or oil for frying

Curry:
1 tablespoon ghee or oil
1 medium onion, finely chopped
5 cloves garlic, finely grated
2 teaspoons finely grated fresh ginger
1 teaspoon garam masala
1 teaspoon ground turmeric
½ teaspoon chili powder
2 large ripe tomatoes
1 teaspoon salt
½ cup (3 ½ oz, 100 g) yogurt
½ cup (4 fl oz, 125 ml) hot water
2 tablespoons chopped cilantro (fresh coriander leaves)

Put 6 eggs into a pan of cold water and bring slowly to simmering point. Stir eggs gently for first 5 minutes to center the yolks. Simmer for a further 10 minutes, then run cold water into the pan until the eggs are cold. Shell them and set aside.

Put meat into a saucepan with the onion, garlic, ginger, chili, salt, garam masala, turmeric, and water. Stir well, bring to a boil, then cover and simmer 20 to 30 minutes or until meat is well cooked. Stir in besan and continue cooking until all the liquid has been absorbed. Cool the meat mixture, then knead it until very smooth, adding a little yogurt if necessary to moisten.

Divide into 6 equal portions and shape each one around a hard-cooked (boiled) egg. Beat remaining egg. Dip koftas in beaten egg and fry in hot oil until golden brown all over. Drain on absorbent paper. Cut in halves with a sharp knife, spoon some of the curry over and serve hot.

Curry: Heat ghee or oil and fry onion until soft and pale golden, then add garlic and ginger and fry, stirring, until onions are golden brown. Add garam masala, turmeric, and chili powder, stir for a few seconds, then add tomatoes and salt.

Cover and cook to a pulp, stirring occasionally. Mash the yogurt smoothly, mix with the water and add to the simmering curry. Stir well and cook uncovered until thick. If koftas are prepared beforehand they can be put into the sauce to heat through, then cut in halves and served with rice or chapatis. Garnish with cilantro.
Serves 6

EGGS IN SOY SAUCE
Pindang Telur ◆ Indonesia

2 tablespoons peanut oil
1 small onion, finely sliced
1 fresh red chili, seeded and sliced
1 clove garlic, crushed
½ teaspoon finely grated fresh ginger
½ teaspoon trasi (dried shrimp paste)
1 large ripe tomato, diced
1 tablespoon vinegar
½ teaspoon salt
1 tablespoon palm sugar or brown sugar
3 tablespoons light soy sauce
½ cup (4 fl oz, 125 ml) water
4–6 eggs, hard-cooked (boiled) and shelled

Heat peanut oil in a saucepan and over gentle heat fry the onion, chili, garlic, and ginger, until onion is soft and starts to turn golden. Add trasi and fry, mashing with back of spoon. Add tomato and cook, stirring, until tomato is pulped. Add vinegar, salt, sugar, soy sauce, and water. Cover and simmer until sauce is thickened and smooth. Put in halved eggs and heat through.
Serves 4–6

FRIED CHICKEN WITH SESAME
Goma Yaki ◆ Japan

1 tablespoon white sesame seeds
2 medium-size chicken breasts
4 tablespoons sake
1 teaspoon salt
1 teaspoon Japanese soy sauce
1 tablespoon sesame oil
4 crisp lettuce leaves

In a dry frying pan toast sesame seeds over medium heat, stirring constantly, until they are evenly golden. Turn onto a plate to cool.

Eggs in meatballs, or nargisi kofta (recipe opposite).

Bone the chicken breasts and cut each breast into halves lengthwise. Prick skin several times with a fork. Mix sake, salt, and soy sauce together and dip chicken in the mixture covering both sides, then set aside for 30 minutes.

Heat oil in a frying pan and fry chicken, browning the pieces on both sides. Reduce heat and cook 4 or 5 minutes until done. Cut each piece in slices and put back together in shape. Sprinkle with sesame seeds and serve each half breast on a lettuce leaf.

Serves 4

FRIED EGGS STUFFED WITH PORK & SEAFOOD
Kai Kwam ◆ Thailand

4 large eggs
½ cup chopped raw shrimp (prawns)
½ cup cooked crab meat
½ cup chopped cooked pork
1 teaspoon chopped cilantro (fresh coriander leaves)
⅛ teaspoon ground black pepper
½ teaspoon salt
1 tablespoon fish sauce
1–2 tablespoons thick coconut cream

Batter:
½ cup (2 oz, 60 g) all-purpose (plain) flour
½ cup (4 fl oz, 125 ml) tepid water
2 teaspoons oil
¼ teaspoon salt

Put eggs in a pan of cold water and bring slowly to a boil, stirring frequently with a wooden spoon, and being careful not to crack the shells. Keep stirring until the eggs have been simmering for 3 minutes. This helps center the yolks, leaving an even layer of white all around and making the eggs easy to fill. Simmer for 12 minutes or until hard-cooked (boiled), then run cold water into the pan to cool the eggs quickly. Shell and cut in halves lengthwise.

Scoop out the yolks into a medium-size bowl and mash thoroughly with a fork. Add shrimp, crab meat, and pork, cilantro, pepper, salt, and fish sauce. Mix well, then add as much of the coconut cream as the mixture will take without getting too moist.

Divide the yolk mixture into 8 equal portions and fill the egg whites, shaping filling to a rounded shape so that it looks like a whole egg. Dip in batter and fry in deep hot oil for 3 minutes or until golden brown. Keep filling downwards in the oil when frying. Drain on absorbent paper and serve warm or cold.

Batter: Mix together flour, water, oil, and salt, beating with a wooden spoon until smooth.

Serves 8

GARLIC CHICKEN
Kai Yang ◆ Thailand

3 lb (1.5 kg) roasting chicken or 2 lbs (1 kg) chicken breasts
6 cloves garlic
2 teaspoons salt
2 tablespoons black peppercorns
4 whole plants fresh coriander, including roots
2 tablespoons lemon juice

Cut chicken into serving pieces, or cut breasts in halves. Crush garlic with the salt. Coarsely crush peppercorns with a mortar and pestle or in a blender. Finely chop the well-washed coriander — roots, stems, and leaves. Mix all the seasonings together and rub well into the chicken pieces. Cover and stand for 1 hour at least, or in refrigerator overnight.

Put pieces of chicken on a broiler (grill) tray and put under a hot broiler approximately 6 in (15 cm) from heat. Cook, turning every 5 minutes, until chicken is tender and skin is crisp. (If possible, cook on a barbecue over glowing coals.)

Serve with boiled rice, fresh tomatoes sliced and seasoned with a pinch of chili powder, salt, and lemon juice to taste, or thinly sliced onion.

Serves 4–5

GREEN CURRY OF CHICKEN
Kaeng Khieu Wan Kai ◆ Thailand

1 roasting chicken, 3 lb (1.5 kg)
3½–4 cups thin coconut cream
3 tablespoons green curry paste (page 12)
2 sprigs tender citrus leaves
1 teaspoon salt
2 tablespoons fish sauce
2 tablespoons finely chopped fresh green chilies, seeds removed
4 tablespoons finely chopped fresh basil or cilantro (fresh coriander) leaves

Divide chicken into joints. Heat one cup of coconut cream in a large, heavy saucepan, stirring constantly until it comes to a boil. Lower heat and continue cooking, stirring occasionally, until the cream thickens and oil bubbles around it. By this time it should be reduced to a quarter of the original amount.

Fried eggs stuffed with pork and seafood (recipe opposite).

Add the curry paste and fry the rich, oily cream for about 5 minutes, stirring constantly. The curry paste will smell cooked and oil will separate from it when it is ready.

Add the pieces of chicken and cook over medium-low heat, stirring frequently and turning the pieces, for about 15 minutes. The chicken will change color and have a cooked appearance.

Add the remaining coconut cream, citrus leaves, salt, and fish sauce and stir while the coconut cream comes to a boil.

Turn heat to low and allow to simmer uncovered for 35–45 minutes or until the chicken is well cooked and tender and the gravy rich and oily. (In Thai curries, the aim is not to reduce the liquid to a small amount of thick, almost dry curry, so add extra coconut cream if necessary.) Stir in the chopped fresh chilies and herbs, simmer for 5 minutes longer, then turn into a serving dish. Serve with white rice.

Serves 6

GREEN CURRY OF DUCK
Kaeng Khieu Wan Pet ◆ Thailand

1 roasting duck, 1.5 kg (3 lb)
3½–4 cups (28–32 fl oz) thin coconut cream
3 tablespoons green curry paste (see page 10)
2 sprigs tender citrus leaves
1 teaspoon salt
2 tablespoons fish sauce
2 tablespoons finely chopped fresh green chilies, seeds removed
4 tablespoons finely chopped fresh basil or cilantro (coriander leaves)

Divide duck into joints. Follow the method above, for Green Curry of Chicken, and serve with white rice.

Serves 4.

GRILLED CHICKEN WITH HOT SPICES
Ayam Panggang Pedis ◆ Indonesia

3 lb (1.5 kg) roasting chicken
2 teaspoons salt
3 teaspoons ground black pepper
3 teaspoons sambal ulek (page 23) or ground fresh red chili
2 tablespoons finely grated onion
2 cloves garlic, crushed
2 tablespoons dark soy sauce
2 teaspoons palm sugar or brown sugar

2 tablespoons lemon juice
2 tablespoons peanut oil

Cut the chicken into serving pieces and score the skin and flesh to allow flavors to penetrate. Combine all the other ingredients and rub the chicken well with this marinade, cover and leave for 1 hour or refrigerate and leave for longer. Preheat a broiler (grill) or prepare a barbecue and have the coals glowing hot. Cook chicken at a good distance from the source of heat so that the chicken is cooked right through before skin gets too brown. Brush with marinade or extra oil and keep turning chicken pieces. Test for doneness by piercing thigh joint with a sharp knife. Juice that runs out should be clear, not pink.

Serves 6

GRILLED MARINATED CHICKEN
Tori Teriyaki ◆ Japan

3 lb (1.5 kg) roasting chicken
½ cup (4 fl oz, 125 ml) Japanese soy sauce
½ cup (4 fl oz, 125 ml) mirin or dry sherry
2 tablespoons sugar
1 clove garlic
pinch salt
1½ teaspoons finely grated fresh ginger
few drops sesame or vegetable oil

Joint the chicken and, with a heavy cleaver, cut each drumstick and thigh in half. Cut breast in half lengthwise, then cut each half across into three pieces. Wings are cut in three at the joints and the tips discarded or put into the stock pot. The back may be cut across into four pieces, or used for stock if preferred.

Combine soy sauce, mirin, and sugar in a large bowl. Crush garlic with a good pinch of salt and add to bowl together with ginger and sesame oil. Put chicken pieces one at a time into the marinade, turning them so they are coated all over. Let them stand in the marinade for at least 1 hour, turning them two or three times, or marinate overnight if more convenient.

Preheat oven to 400°F (200°C, Gas Mark 6). Oil a large baking dish and put pieces of chicken in a single layer in the dish. Roast in hot oven for 15 minutes, then turn each piece over with tongs and roast for 10 minutes longer. Turn oven down to moderate, pour away fat from the baking dish, and spoon some of the marinade over the chicken.

Return chicken to oven for a further 20 to 25 minutes, basting with marinade every 10 minutes, until chicken is tender, well glazed and browned. Serve hot with rice, or cold as an appetizer or picnic food.

A Thai classic, green curry chicken (page 154).

Note: To cook chicken teriyaki in a frying pan, drain the pieces of chicken well, reserving marinade. Dry chicken on absorbent paper and pierce the skin a few times with a fork. Heat 2 tablespoons oil in a large, heavy frying pan and put in chicken pieces, skin side down. Brown on one side, then turn with tongs and brown other side. Pour away oil, add half the marinade to pan, turn heat low. Cover and cook for 15 to 20 minutes or until chicken is almost tender. Uncover and cook for a further 5 minutes or until chicken is well glazed and brown and marinade is quite thick.

Serves 6

❖❖❖

HOME-STYLE STEAMED CHICKEN
China

half a 3 lb (1.5 kg) roasting chicken
2 teaspoons light soy sauce
2 teaspoons Chinese wine or dry sherry
2 teaspoons cornstarch (cornflour)
1 teaspoon finely chopped fresh ginger
½ teaspoon salt
½ teaspoon sugar
½ teaspoon sesame oil, optional

Place the half-chicken on a wooden chopping board and separate the thigh and drumstick from the body. Detach the wing, too. With a sharp, heavy cleaver, chop straight through the bones, cutting the chicken into bite-size pieces. Wipe all cut surfaces with damp absorbent kitchen paper to remove any bits of bone.

Put the chicken on a plate, add all the other ingredients and mix well.

Place the plate in a bamboo or other steamer, or on a trivet or upturned bowl in a large pan containing boiling water. Cover the pan with a lid and steam on high heat for 15 minutes.

If desired, place some Chinese vegetables or chunks of peeled pumpkin on the plate with the chicken. Serve hot with steamed rice.

Serves 4 as part of a Chinese meal, serves 2 as a single dish with rice

❖❖❖

HONEY BRAISED CHICKEN WITH TOASTED SESAME
China

1½ lb (750 g) chicken thighs
½ lb (250 g) pork belly, diced
2 tablespoons peanut oil
½ cup (4 fl oz, 125 ml) dark soy sauce
3 tablespoons honey
½ teaspoon five-spice powder
3 tablespoons Chinese wine or dry sherry
½ teaspoon finely chopped garlic
1 teaspoon finely chopped fresh ginger
3 tablespoons toasted sesame seeds

Garnish:
scallion (spring onion) flowers

Chop each chicken thigh into two pieces. Dice pork. Heat wok, add oil and stir-fry the diced pork on high heat for 2 minutes. Add the chicken pieces and stir-fry until browned. Add soy, honey, five-spice, wine, garlic, and ginger and stir well. Reduce heat to low, cover and simmer about 30 minutes or until chicken and pork are tender. Towards end of cooking, stir frequently to make sure the honey glaze does not burn. Sprinkle with sesame seeds and garnish with scallion flowers. Serve warm with hot white rice.

Note: You can use a whole chicken, instead of just the thighs.

Serves 4–6

❖❖❖

HOT CHICKEN CURRY
Malaysia

1.5 kg (3 lb) chicken, jointed
1 tablespoon ground coriander
1 teaspoon ground fennel
1 teaspoon ground black pepper
5 candle nuts or 4 Brazil kernels, chopped
8 dried red chilies
1 teaspoon chopped garlic
½ teaspoon ground turmeric
½ teaspoon ground cinnamon
1 stem fresh lemon grass, finely sliced or rind of half a lemon
1 teaspoon laos powder
2 teaspoons salt
3 tablespoons peanut oil
3 medium onions, finely sliced

3 fresh red chilies, sliced
hot water
½ cup (4 fl oz) thin coconut cream

Place in blender the coriander, fennel, pepper, chopped nuts, chilies, garlic, turmeric, cinnamon, lemon grass, laos, and salt. Blend to a fine paste, adding a little water to facilitate blending.

Heat oil in a large saucepan and fry onions till soft and golden. Add blended mixture and cook stirring, till oil comes to the surface and mixture smells aromatic. Add chicken pieces and sliced chilies and cook, stirring for 5 minutes. Lower heat and cook covered till chicken is tender, stirring occasionally, and adding a little hot water to prevent sticking. Stir in coconut cream, simmer a further 5 minutes and serve with rice and accompaniments.

Serves 6

HUNAN-STYLE CHICKEN
China

2 lb (1 kg) chicken thighs, boned
1 teaspoon Sichuan peppercorns
½ teaspoon salt
2 tablespoons dark soy sauce
2 tablespoons Chinese wine or dry sherry
2 teaspoons sugar
2 tablespoons peanut oil
1 or 2 dried red chilies
2 tablespoons finely chopped scallions (spring onions)
2 teaspoons finely chopped fresh ginger
1 teaspoon finely chopped garlic
1 teaspoon sesame oil
2 tablespoons Chinese black vinegar or 1 tablespoon wine vinegar
1 teaspoon chili bean sauce

Leaving on the skin, lay the chicken pieces on a wooden chopping board, skin side down, and slightly flatten by pounding with the blunt edge of a cleaver or with a meat mallet. Cut into bite-size pieces.

Roast the peppercorns in a dry pan for a few minutes, shaking the pan, until fragrant. Cool, then grind them with a mortar and pestle. Mix with the salt, and sprinkle this over the chicken pieces. Mix and leave for 5 minutes.

Combine the soy sauce, wine, and sugar, stir to dissolve the sugar, and pour over the chicken. Turn the chicken pieces well in the marinade. Leave for 30 minutes.

Heat a wok, add the peanut oil and swirl to coat the sides of the wok. Fry the dried chilies for 1 minute. Add the scallions,

ginger, and garlic and stir-fry for 10 seconds. Add the chicken with the marinade and on high heat, stir-fry for a few minutes, just until all the chicken has come into contact with the hot pan. Turn the heat to low, cover the wok and simmer for about 5 minutes or until the chicken is tender.

Meanwhile, mix together the sesame oil, vinegar, and chili bean sauce.

Uncover the wok and if liquid is not thick, raise the heat and turn the chicken pieces over and over using a wok chan (spatula). The sauce will thicken and coat the chicken.

Add the sesame oil combination and mix quickly but thoroughly. Transfer to a serving dish immediately and, if desired, discard the dry chilies. Serve with rice and a dish of vegetables.

Serves 4–6

JAVANESE CHICKEN CURRY
Indonesia

1 x 1.5 kg (3 lb) roasting chicken
1 medium onion, chopped
1 teaspoon finely chopped garlic
1 teaspoon chopped fresh ginger
3 fresh red chilies or 1 teaspoon sambal ulek (page 23)
2 candle nuts or Brazil nuts
¾ cup (6 fl oz) thin coconut cream
1 tablespoon desiccated or fresh grated coconut
2 teaspoons ground coriander
1 teaspoon laos powder, optional
½ teaspoon ground turmeric
1½ teaspoons salt
1 stem fresh lemon grass, or 3 strips thinly peeled lemon rind
2 daun salam or 6 curry leaves

Cut chicken into serving pieces.

Put onion, garlic, ginger, chilies, and nuts in blender with half the coconut cream and the desiccated coconut. Cover and blend on high speed for approximately 30 seconds or until smooth. Rinse blender with remaining coconut cream and add to pan. Add all remaining ingredients, and bring slowly to a boil, stirring. Cook, uncovered, until chicken is tender and gravy thick and almost dry.

Serve with white rice and a sayur (vegetable cooked in coconut cream) or a curry with plenty of gravy.

Serves 4–6

LAOTIAN CHICKEN
Kai Lao ◆ Laos

3 lb (1.5 kg) roasting chicken
1½ teaspoons salt
2 cloves garlic, crushed
1 tablespoon oil
2 medium onions, finely chopped
8 oz (250 g) ground (minced) pork
½ teaspoon salt
½ teaspoon ground black pepper
1 fresh red chili, finely chopped
1 tablespoon chopped cilantro (fresh coriander leaves)
½ cup (2½ oz, 100 g) uncooked rice
1 cup (6½ oz, 200 g) thick coconut cream
2 cups (16 fl oz, 500 ml) thin coconut cream
1 tablespoon fish sauce

Wash and dry chicken well, then rub it inside and out with salt and half the crushed garlic. Heat oil in frying pan, fry remaining garlic and onions with the pork. Season with salt, pepper, and chili. When pork is well fried, add coriander, rice, and thick coconut cream. Bring to simmering point, then reduce heat, cover and cook for 10 minutes or until liquid is absorbed. Remove from heat and leave until cool enough to handle. Stuff chicken with pork mixture. Put chicken in a large saucepan with thin coconut cream and fish sauce, cover and simmer for 1 hour or until chicken is tender.
Serves 6

⋖≫⋗

LEMON CHICKEN WITH OLIVE NUTS OR PINE NUTS
China

1½ lb (750 g) chicken thighs or 1 lb (500 g) chicken breasts
1 teaspoon salt
½ teaspoon grated fresh ginger
2 egg yolks
4 teaspoons cornstarch (cornflour)
peanut oil for deep frying
1 oz (30 g) Chinese olive nuts or pine nuts
6 lemon slices
1 teaspoon sesame oil

Lemon Sauce:
4 teaspoons lemon juice
2 tablespoons sugar
2 teaspoons light soy sauce
2 drops yellow food coloring
4 teaspoons cornstarch (cornflour)

Garnish:
sprigs of cilantro (fresh coriander leaves)
additional lemon slices

Bone the chicken and remove the skin. Cut the chicken into finger-width strips. Place the pieces in a bowl, add the salt, ginger, and egg yolks; mix well. Sprinkle the cornstarch over and mix again. Cover the bowl and chill for at least 30 minutes.

Combine sauce ingredients in a small bowl, with 12 tablespoons of water.

Heat a wok, add about 14 fl oz (450 ml) peanut oil and when hot, drop in the chicken, one piece at a time until one-third of the pieces have been added. Fry over medium heat until the chicken meat is cooked through but do not allow to brown — cut a piece of chicken in half to test. Drain the cooked pieces, then cook remaining chicken meat in the same way.

When chicken has been removed from the wok, turn the heat very low and fry the olive nuts to a pale gold. Lift out onto absorbent kitchen paper. Drain the oil into a heatproof container.

Return the wok to the heat, pour in the sauce mixture, first giving it a little stir to ensure that the cornstarch has not settled at the bottom. Stir until it boils and thickens. Add the lemon slices and sesame oil. Return the chicken meat and olive nuts, toss quickly to coat, and serve immediately. Garnish with cilantro and extra lemon slices.
Serves 4–6

⋖≫⋗

MARINATED FRIED CHICKEN
Tatsuta Age ◆ Japan

1 lb (500 g) boned chicken
3 tablespoons Japanese soy sauce
2 tablespoons sake
2 teaspoons sugar
4 tablespoons cornstarch (cornflour)
oil for deep frying

Cut chicken into bite-size squares and marinate in a mixture of soy, sake, and sugar for at least 1 hour. Drain chicken, roll pieces in cornstarch and set aside for 10 minutes.

Heat oil in a deep pan and fry chicken in small batches for about 2 to 3 minutes or until golden brown and crisp. Drain on absorbent paper and serve hot.
Serves 4

⋖≫⋗

Lemon chicken with olive nuts or pine nuts (recipe opposite).

MILD CHICKEN CURRY
Panthe Kowshwe ✦ **Burma**

3 lb (1.5 kg) chicken or chicken pieces
5 cloves garlic, chopped
3 medium onions, chopped
1 tablespoon finely chopped fresh root ginger
1 teaspoon ngapi or blachan (shrimp paste)
2 tablespoons peanut oil

1 tablespoon sesame oil
1–2 teaspoons chili powder
2 teaspoons salt
2 cups (16 fl oz, 500 ml) thin coconut cream
2 cups (13 oz, 400 g) thick coconut cream
2 tablespoons besan (chickpea) flour
1 lb (500 g) thin egg noodles

Accompaniments (see recipe for Cellophane Noodles, page 224)

Cut chicken into serving pieces. Put garlic, onion, ginger, and ngapi into blender, cover and blend until smooth, adding 1 tablespoon of the peanut oil if necessary. Heat remaining oil and fry the blended ingredients for 5 minutes. Add chicken and continue to fry, stirring constantly. Add chili powder, salt, and thin coconut cream. Cover and simmer until chicken is tender, adding a little hot water if mixture becomes dry. Add thick coconut cream, return to the heat and bring slowly to a boil, stirring continuously to prevent the mixture from curdling. Mix besan with a little cold water to a smooth cream, add to the curry and cook for a further 5 minutes, uncovered. (There should be a lot of gravy.)

Just before serving, cook noodles in a large saucepan of boiling salted water until just tender, approximately 5 to 6 minutes. Pour cold water into pan to stop noodles cooking, drain in a colander.

Serve noodles in a large bowl and the curry in a separate bowl. Serve accompaniments in small bowls. Each person takes a serving of noodles, ladles on a generous amount of the curry, and sprinkles various accompaniments over the top.
Serves 6–8

⌁⌁⌁

MOSLEM CHICKEN CURRY
Thailand

1 roasting chicken about 1.75 kg (3½ lb)
4 cups (32 fl oz, 1 L) thin coconut cream
1 cup (5 oz) roasted, unsalted peanuts
2 tablespoons fish sauce
15 cardamom pods
1 stick cinnamon, about 5 cm (2 in)
1 quantity Moslem curry paste (page 12)
3 tablespoons tamarind liquid
2 tablespoons lime or lemon juice
1–2 tablespoons sugar
extra fish sauce if necessary

Cut chicken into serving pieces. Put into a saucepan with the coconut cream, peanuts, fish sauce, cardamom pods, and cinnamon. Bring slowly to simmering point, stirring frequently with a wooden spoon. Turn heat low and allow to simmer, uncovered, until meat is tender. This should take about 35–40 minutes. Do not cover at any stage or the coconut cream will curdle. Stir occasionally during this initial cooking.

Meanwhile, make the curry paste. When the chicken is just tender lift it out and simmer the coconut cream a little longer, until it is reduced by about a third. If it has already reduced considerably, do not give it this further cooking. Stir in the curry paste, tamarind liquid, lemon juice, and sugar. Return chicken

to pan and continue simmering until the gravy is thickened slightly. Taste and add more fish sauce if necessary. Serve with white rice.
Serves 6–8

⌁⌁⌁

OMELET CURRY
Sri Lanka

Omelets:
6 eggs
1 small onion, finely chopped
1 fresh green chili, seeded and finely chopped
2 teaspoons fresh dill, finely chopped or ½ teaspoon dried dill weed
salt and pepper to taste
ghee or butter

Gravy:
3 cups (24 fl oz) thin coconut cream
1 medium onion, finely sliced
2 fresh chilies, seeded and split
½ teaspoon ground turmeric
1 teaspoon finely sliced garlic
½ teaspoon finely grated fresh ginger
1 stick cinnamon
4 dried rampé leaves
2 stems fresh lemon grass, bruised
8 curry leaves
salt to taste
1 cup (12 fl oz, 250 ml) thick coconut cream

Omelets: Beat eggs together, add onion, chili, dill, salt, and pepper. Heat a little ghee in a frying pan and make 2 omelettes with mixture. Cut each omelet in 3 pieces. Heat through in prepared gravy and serve with boiled rice and accompaniments.

Gravy: Place all ingredients, except thick coconut cream, in a large saucepan and simmer gently, uncovered, for approximately 10 minutes. Add thick coconut cream, stir and simmer 5 minutes longer.
Serves 4

⌁⌁⌁

Parsi scrambled eggs (page 164).

PADANG DUCK CURRY
Indonesia

1.5 kg (3 lb) duck, jointed
3 daun salam or 6 curry leaves
2 cups (16 fl oz, 500 ml) thick coconut cream
3 medium onions, roughly chopped
1 teaspoon laos powder
2 teaspoons chopped garlic
1 teaspoon chopped fresh ginger
½ teaspoon dried shrimp paste
1 teaspoon ground turmeric
4 dried red chilies
1 stem fresh lemon grass, finely sliced or rind of ½ lemon
5 candle nuts or 4 Brazil kernels, chopped
2 teaspoons salt
2 teaspoons tamarind paste
½ cup hot water

Place in container of blender the onions, laos, garlic, ginger, shrimp paste, turmeric, chilies, lemon grass, and candle nut kernels. Blend to a fine paste, adding a little hot water to facilitate blending.

Put duck, daun salam, and coconut cream in a saucepan, add blended ingredients and bring to a boil. Add the salt and tamarind paste dissolved in hot water, reduce heat and simmer, stirring frequently, until coconut cream is absorbed and the oil comes to the surface. Add sufficient hot water to prevent catching, stir and cook until duck is tender. Serve with rice.

Serves 4–5

PARSI SCRAMBLED EGGS
Akoori ◆ India

6–8 eggs
4 tablespoons milk
¾ teaspoon salt
¼ teaspoon ground black pepper
2 tablespoons ghee (clarified butter)
6 scallions (spring onions), finely chopped
2–3 fresh red or green chilies, seeded and chopped
1 teaspoon finely grated fresh ginger
⅛ teaspoon ground turmeric
2 tablespoons chopped cilantro (fresh coriander leaves)
1 ripe tomato, diced, optional
½ teaspoon ground cumin
tomato wedges to garnish
sprig of cilantro (fresh coriander leaves) to garnish

Beat eggs until well mixed. Add the milk, salt, and pepper. Heat ghee in a large, heavy frying pan and cook the scallions, chilies, and ginger until soft. Add turmeric, cilantro, and tomato if used and fry for a minute or two longer, then stir in the egg mixture and the ground cumin. Cook over low heat, stirring and lifting the eggs as they begin to set on the base of the pan. Mix and cook until the eggs are of a creamy consistency — they should not be cooked until dry. Turn onto a serving plate and garnish with tomato and cilantro. Serve with chapatis or parathas.

Serves 4–6

PIQUANT FRIED CHICKEN
Ayam Goreng Asam ◆ Indonesia

3 lb (1.5 kg) roasting chicken
3 cloves garlic
1½ teaspoons salt
1 teaspoon ground black pepper
1 teaspoon palm sugar or brown sugar
2 teaspoons ground coriander
1 teaspoon ground cumin
½ teaspoon ground turmeric
⅓ cup (3 fl oz, 90 ml) tamarind liquid
oil for frying

Cut chicken into small serving pieces, as for curry. Crush garlic with salt to a smooth paste and combine with pepper, sugar, coriander, cumin, turmeric, and tamarind liquid. Rub over the chicken pieces and leave for one hour, or cover and marinate in refrigerator overnight. Heat enough oil in a large, heavy frying pan to cover base of pan. Take chicken pieces from marinade and drain on absorbent paper to get rid of excess moisture. Put pieces into the frying pan and cook over medium heat for 2 minutes on each side, turning with tongs until golden brown. Reduce heat, cover pan and cook for 10 to 12 minutes longer, turning pieces halfway through. Drain on absorbent paper and serve warm.

Serves 6–8

RED COOKED CHICKEN & MUSHROOMS
China

8–10 large dried Chinese mushrooms
3 lb (1.5 kg) chicken
1½ cups (12 fl oz, 375 ml) dark soy sauce
⅓ cup (3 fl oz, 90 ml) Chinese wine or dry sherry
sesame oil
2 in (5 cm) piece fresh ginger, peeled and sliced
1 clove garlic, peeled
1 whole star anise
2 tablespoons sugar
1 tablespoon peanut oil
Chinese (Napa) cabbage

Soak the mushrooms in 1 1/2 cups (12 fl oz, 375 ml) boiling water for 30 minutes. Drain and reserve the liquid.

Wash the chicken under cold running water and drain well. Cut off the mushroom stems and put them into the cavity of the chicken. These will be discarded after cooking.

Choose a saucepan into which the chicken will just fit so that the liquid will cover as much of the bird as possible. Put the chicken into the saucepan breast down, then add the liquid from the mushrooms, the soy sauce, wine, 2 teaspoons of sesame oil, ginger, garlic, star anise, sugar, and the mushroom caps. Bring slowly to a boil, then turn the heat low, cover the saucepan and simmer very gently for 15 minutes.

Using tongs, turn chicken over, replace lid and simmer for 20 minutes more. Baste chicken with liquid every 5 minutes.

Remove from the heat and leave covered in the saucepan until cool. Lift the chicken onto a chopping board and cut it in half lengthwise. Discard the mushroom stems. Brush over the chicken with 2 teaspoons of sesame oil, then cut each half into bite-size pieces through the bones, using a cleaver.

Bring a large saucepan of lightly salted water to a boil, add the peanut oil. Boil 6 to 8 leaves of cabbage for 2 minutes uncovered. The leaves should be bright and the texture still crisp. Drain, and place them on chopping board in a neat pile. Cut across into bite-size sections.

Arrange the cabbage around the edge of a serving plate. Remove the mushroom caps from the sauce with a slotted spoon and place on top. Arrange the chicken pieces in the middle of the plate. Some of the sauce may be served in small bowls as a dipping sauce.

Red cooking is done in quite a large amount of soy sauce, but it must be dark soy or the dish will not have its rich color and the proper flavor. The remaining cooking liquid is a Master Sauce. It can be frozen and used over and over again to simmer meats and poultry.

Serves 4–5

ROAST SPICED CHICKEN
Ayam Panggang ◆ Indonesia

3 lb (1.5 kg) roasting chicken
2 tablespoons dark soy sauce
1 tablespoon lemon juice
1 medium onion, roughly chopped
2 cloves garlic
½ teaspoon sambal ulek (page 23) or chili sauce
½ teaspoon ground black pepper
½ teaspoon trasi (dried shrimp paste)
½ cup (4 fl oz, 125 ml) water or thin coconut cream

Cut chicken in half lengthwise, or split it open down the breast and open it out flat. Wash chicken and dry well with kitchen paper. Put soy sauce, lemon juice, onion, and garlic into blender and blend until smooth. If blender is not available grate onion and garlic finely and mix with the sauce and lemon juice. Add sambal ulek, pepper, and crushed trasi to the onion mixture and rub all over the chicken. Leave for 30 minutes or longer. If blender is used, wash out container with the water or coconut cream.

Put the liquid into a large frying pan or wok and cook the chicken, skin side upwards, for 10 minutes over medium heat. Turn and cook for 10 minutes over low heat. Do not cover during cooking, and baste with the marinade and juices in the pan. Meanwhile, preheat oven to moderately hot. Put chicken, skin side upwards, on a rack in a baking dish with 1/2 in (12 mm) of water in it. Spoon marinade over chicken. Roast for 30 minutes or until skin is crisp and brown. Turn and cook other side 20 to 25 minutes. Serve hot.

If finishing chicken over hot coals, position rack 4–5 in (10–13 cm) away from heat so that chicken can cook through before skin gets too brown.

Serves 4

ROASTED SPICED CHICKEN
China

3 lb (1.5 kg) roasting chicken
¼ cup (2 fl oz, 60 ml) soy sauce
2 tablespoons peanut oil
2 tablespoons Chinese wine or dry sherry
½ teaspoon crushed garlic
½ teaspoon finely grated fresh ginger
2 teaspoons five-spice powder
1 tablespoon hoi sin sauce
¼ teaspoon ground black pepper

Wash chicken and dry on kitchen paper. Mix together the remaining ingredients and rub it well all over the chicken. Spoon some of the marinade into the cavity. Cover and marinate in refrigerator overnight, or at room temperature for at least 1 hour.

Preheat oven to 350°F (180°C, Gas Mark 4). Place chicken in an oiled baking dish and roast for 1 hour 20 minutes, basting or brushing with the marinade every 20 minutes. Turn the chicken first on one side, then on the other and finish cooking breast upwards.

This chicken may be served warm or at room temperature. To carve Chinese-style, place chicken on a chopping board and cut in two lengthwise with a sharp cleaver. Then place each half cut side downwards and chop into strips, reassembling them on a serving dish. Alternatively, carve the chicken into joints.

Note: If preferred, prepare this dish with chicken drumsticks or wings instead of a whole chicken. Cooking time will be 45 minutes to 1 hour. Arrange marinated chicken in baking dish in one layer and turn pieces halfway through cooking.

Serves 6

⋖≫∞≪⋗

ROLLED OMELET

Dashimaki Tamago ✦ Japan

5 eggs
2 teaspoons sugar
¼ teaspoon salt
½ cup dashi (page 6)
2 teaspoons Japanese soy sauce
vegetable oil for cooking
parsley sprigs for garnish

Beat eggs until well mixed. Dissolve sugar and salt in the dashi, stir in soy sauce, then mix with beaten eggs.

Heat omelet pan and grease with a few drops of oil. Pour in a third of the egg mixture and tilt pan so it covers entire surface. Cook on low heat (omelet must not brown) until it is set, then roll the omelet away from you.

When omelet is completely rolled up, lightly grease pan again, slide omelet towards you and grease the part of the pan where omelet was. Pour in half the remaining mixture and lift the egg roll so the uncooked egg can cover the base of pan. Cook as before and roll again, this time rolling the first omelet within the second one.

Repeat as before, using the remaining beaten egg. Turn the omelets onto a sudare (bamboo mat) or a clean cloth and roll the omelet firmly. Leave it for 10 minutes, then remove mat and cut the rolled egg into thick slices. Serve garnished with parsley.

Japanese omelet pans are rectangular. If you can get one it will make your rolled omelets easier to handle, but a round pan can be used quite successfully.

Serves 4

SATAY-FLAVORED ROAST CHICKEN

Singapore

3 lb (1.5 kg) roasting chicken
1 medium onion, roughly chopped
1 clove garlic
2 fresh red chilies, seeded and chopped
2 cups (16 fl oz, 500 ml) thin coconut cream
2 teaspoons ground coriander
1½ teaspoons ground cumin
½ teaspoon ground fennel
½ teaspoon ground turmeric
½ teaspoon laos powder, optional
½ teaspoon finely grated lemon rind
2 candlenuts or brazil kernels, finely grated
1½ teaspoons salt
1 tablespoon lemon juice
2 tablespoons oil or ghee

Wash chicken well and dry inside and out with kitchen paper. Put onion, garlic, and chilies into blender and blend to a smooth paste, adding 2 tablespoons of the coconut cream if necessary. Mix in the ground spices, lemon rind, and grated nuts.

Heat oil or ghee in pan and fry the mixed ingredients, stirring constantly, until they darken and oil separates from the mixture. It should smell cooked and come away cleanly from the pan. Remove from heat and mix in salt and lemon juice. Rub the mixture inside and outside the chicken, truss it and put it in a baking dish breast upwards. Pour the coconut cream around the chicken. Roast in a preheated moderate oven, basting after 15 minutes. After a further 15 minutes, turn the chicken breast downwards, baste again and continue cooking until tender, basting every 20 minutes. If coconut cream shows signs of drying up, add about 1/2–1 cup more. Turn chicken breast upwards for 15 minutes longer or until golden brown and cooked through. Carve chicken and serve with the thick coconut cream gravy spooned over. Serve with rice and accompaniments.

Serves 4–5

⋖≫∞≪⋗

SHANGHAI FRIED EGGS
China

2 oz (60 g) cellophane noodles
oil for frying
3 egg whites
1 canned bamboo shoot, diced
7 oz (220 g) canned crab meat, flaked and drained
1 tablespoon Chinese wine or dry sherry
¼ cup (2 fl oz, 60 ml) chicken stock
½ teaspoon sesame oil
1 teaspoon light soy sauce
⅛ teaspoon ground black pepper
4 sprigs of cilantro (fresh coriander leaves)

Heat wok, add 1 cup (8 fl oz, 250 ml) oil and deep fry cellophane noodles on both sides till crispy and puffed. Remove noodles from wok, drain on kitchen paper and arrange on serving dish.

Beat egg whites till frothy and combine with bamboo shoot, crab meat, wine, stock, sesame oil, soy sauce, and pepper.

Heat wok and add 2 tablespoons oil. When hot, add half the egg mixture and when middle sets, turn over and fry the other side. Remove and place on noodles. Fry rest of egg mixture and arrange on noodles, garnish with sprigs of cilantro and serve immediately.
Serves 4

⋘⋙

SICHUANESE-STYLE ROAST DUCK
Sze Chuen Shiu Ngap ♦ China

6 lb (3 kg) roasting duck
3 teaspoons salt
3 teaspoons black peppercorns or Sichuan pepper
1 whole fresh coriander plant
1½ teaspoons finely grated fresh ginger
4 scallions (spring onions), chopped into 2 in (5 cm) lengths
½ teaspoon five-spice powder
1 tablespoon honey
1 tablespoon Chinese wine or dry sherry
2 teaspoons sesame oil
1 tablespoon light soy sauce
½ teaspoon red food coloring

Remove neck and giblets from body cavity, wash duck inside and out and dry thoroughly with absorbent kitchen paper. Pick off any pin feathers or quills that remain. Rub all over with salt.

Roast the pepper in a dry pan for a few minutes, then crack coarsely with mortar and pestle or rolling pin. Wash and dry fresh coriander, chop leaves and stem. Reserve the well-washed root. Combine all seasonings and the red coloring and rub well inside and outside duck. Put any coarse scallion leaves and the coriander root inside the duck. Cover with plastic wrap (film) or foil and refrigerate overnight, or at least 4 hours.

Preheat oven to moderate. Half-fill a roasting pan with hot water and put a rack in the pan; the water should not reach the rack. Put duck on rack, breast upwards, and roast in oven for 30 minutes. Cover with foil and continue cooking for another 30 minutes. Reduce heat to 300°F (150°C, Gas Mark 2), turn duck breast downwards, put foil over duck and roast for a further 30 minutes. Turn duck breast upwards again and continue cooking for 30 minutes, remove foil and allow duck to brown for 15 to 20 minutes. Carve duck and serve with mandarin pancakes (page 301), plum sauce, and scallions fringed to form brushes. Rub the sauce on the pancakes with the 'brush', put on a piece of meat, put the scallion on the meat, and roll all up in the pancake. Eaten in the style of Peking duck.
Serves 4–5

⋘⋙

SKEWERED BARBECUED CHICKEN
Murgh Tikka ♦ India & Pakistan

1 lb (500 g) chicken breasts or thighs
1 medium onion, roughly chopped
1 clove garlic, sliced
2 teaspoons finely chopped fresh ginger
2 tablespoons lemon juice
1 teaspoon ground coriander
½ teaspoon ground cumin
1 teaspoon garam masala
3 tablespoons yogurt
1 teaspoon salt
2 tablespoons chopped cilantro (fresh coriander leaves) or mint leaves

Bone the chicken and remove skin. Cut chicken meat into bite-size pieces. In blender put the onion, garlic, and ginger and blend until smooth, adding the lemon juice if more liquid is required. Mix with the ground spices, yogurt, and salt and marinate the chicken in this mixture for at least 2 hours at room temperature, or refrigerate overnight if possible. Thread chicken on bamboo skewers and cook over glowing coals or under a preheated broiler (grill) until cooked through. Serve with Onion and Tomato Sambal and puris or chapatis.
Serves 4–6

SMOKED TANGERINE CHICKEN
China

3 lb (1.5 kg) roasting chicken
1 tablespoon light soy sauce
1 teaspoon salt
1 teaspoon sugar
1 tablespoon Chinese wine or dry sherry
1 piece dried tangerine peel about the size of a rose leaf
1 whole star anise
3 tablespoons brown sugar
cilantro (fresh coriander leaves) to garnish

Wipe chicken inside and out with kitchen paper. Combine soy sauce, salt, sugar, and wine and rub inside and outside the chicken. Marinate for 20 minutes, then put in a steamer and steam for 15 minutes.

In a mortar and pestle crush the tangerine peel and star anise as finely as possible and mix with brown sugar. Take a heavy saucepan with a well-fitting lid, large enough to hold the whole chicken. Line the base of the pan with heavy-duty foil, bringing it a little way up the side of the pan. Sprinkle sugar and spice mixture evenly over foil, then put a trivet or wire rack in pan and put chicken on it. Cover pan tightly, stand over medium heat and when smoke starts escaping under lid turn heat very low and smoke chicken for 15 minutes or until done.

This chicken dish can be served hot, at room temperature, or cold. Slice the flesh off the bones and arrange on a dish, or chop through bones into small serving pieces. Garnish with sprigs of cilantro.
Serves 4–5

SPICED GRILLED CHICKEN
Singgang Ayam ◆ Indonesia

3 lb (1.5 kg) roasting chicken
1 large onion, roughly chopped
3 cloves garlic
3 fresh red chilies or 1½ teaspoons sambal ulek or chili sauce
2 teaspoons chopped fresh ginger
2 strips lemon rind or 1 stalk lemon grass
½ teaspoon ground turmeric
1 teaspoon ground black pepper
2 teaspoons ground coriander
1½ teaspoons salt
2 daun salam or 4 curry leaves
2 lime or lemon leaves, optional
3 cups (24 fl oz, 750 ml) thin coconut cream

Split chicken and spread out flat. Put onion, garlic, chilies, ginger, and lemon rind into blender with 2 or 3 tablespoons of the coconut cream, and blend to a smooth paste. Add turmeric, pepper, coriander, and salt and a spoon more cream if necessary and blend again for a few seconds.

Spread some of this spice paste over the chicken inside and out and let it marinate for half an hour or longer. Put the remaining spice mixture in a wok or large pan with the leaves and the coconut cream (wash out the blender container with some of the coconut cream) and bring slowly to simmering point, stirring constantly.

Lower the chicken into this gravy and continue simmering, occasionally stirring and ladling the gravy over the chicken. Turn chicken after 10 minutes and continue cooking until chicken is done. Lift chicken from pan and broil (grill) over coals or under a preheated broiler (grill), a good distance away from the heat source, until chicken is touched with brown. In the meantime, continue simmering gravy, stirring occasionally, until thick. When chicken has been broiled on both sides transfer to a serving plate and spoon a little of the gravy over. Serve the rest of the gravy separately.
Serves 6–8

STEAMED CHICKEN & MUSHROOMS WITH FISH SAUCE
Vietnam

2 lb (1 kg) chicken breasts
6 dried Chinese mushrooms
1 tablespoon finely shredded ginger
4 scallions (spring onions), sliced diagonally
¾ teaspoon ground black pepper
2 tablespoons fish sauce
1 tablespoon light soy sauce
1 teaspoon finely chopped garlic
1 teaspoon salt
2 teaspoons sesame oil
2 cups, soaked and drained, cellophane noodles
4 tablespoons chopped cilantro (fresh coriander leaves)

Pour hot water over cellophane noodles in a bowl, let stand for 15 minutes, then drain. Pour hot water over Chinese mushrooms and soak for 30 minutes. Squeeze out excess water, cut off and discard mushroom stems and cut the caps into thick slices. Chop chicken breasts into bite-size pieces, place in a bowl and add mushrooms, ginger, scallions, black pepper, fish sauce, soy, garlic, salt, and sesame oil and mix well.

Chop the cellophane noodles into bite-size lengths and place in a heatproof dish. Sprinkle half the cilantro over the noodles then spread the chicken mixture over. Place dish on a rack over boiling water in a wok, cover and steam for 35 minutes, adding more boiling water as necessary. Garnish with remaining cilantro and serve hot.

Serves 4–6

⟨≈⟩⋈⟨≈⟩

STEAMED CHICKEN WITH MUSHROOMS
Nam Dong Co Tiem Ga ✦ Vietnam

6 dried Chinese mushrooms
1 small roasting chicken, about 2 lb (1 kg)
1 tablespoon finely shredded fresh ginger
3 scallions (spring onions), sliced diagonally
good grinding of black pepper
2 teaspoons fish sauce
1 small glove garlic, crushed
¼ teaspoon salt
1 teaspoon sesame oil

Pour hot water over mushrooms and leave to soak at least 20 minutes. Cut off and discard stems, cut mushroom caps into thin slices. With a sharp knife bone the chicken. Use the bones for stock, and cut the flesh (together with skin) into bite-size pieces. Put these into a heatproof bowl with the mushroom slices, ginger, scallions, pepper, fish sauce, garlic, salt, and sesame oil. Mix well.

Bring water to a boil in a large saucepan, deep frying pan or wok. Put the bowl in the pan — water should come a third of the way up the bowl. Cover and steam for 25 to 30 minutes or until chicken is cooked. Check periodically to ensure that water has not boiled away, and add more boiling water if it is getting low. Serve with rice, noodles, or cellophane noodles.

Serves 4

⟨≈⟩⋈⟨≈⟩

STEAMED CHICKEN WITH TOMATOES
Ga Hap Ca ✦ Vietnam

1½ lb (750 g) chicken pieces (breast and thighs)
3 ripe tomatoes, cut in thin wedges
3 scallions (spring onions), finely sliced
3 thin slices fresh ginger, cut in thin strips
2 tablespoons fish sauce
½ teaspoon salt
½ teaspoon sugar
ground black pepper to taste
2 teaspoons sesame or other vegetable oil

Bone the chicken and cut flesh into bite-size pieces. Reserve bones for stock. Put chicken into a heatproof bowl or other deep dish. Add tomatoes, scallions, and ginger. Add seasonings and oil and mix thoroughly. Put the dish in a pan with water almost halfway up the dish. Cover and steam for 25 to 35 minutes or until chicken is tender. Serve with rice and nuoc cham (page 14).

Serves 4

⟨≈⟩⋈⟨≈⟩

STEAMED EGG CUSTARD WITH SEAFOOD
Chawan Mushi ✦ Japan

4 dried mushrooms
2 tablespoons Japanese soy sauce
1 tablespoon sugar
4 small shrimp (prawns), shelled and deveined or 8 slices
*   kamaboko (fish cake)*
4 fresh oysters

Custard:
4 eggs
2½ cups dashi (page 6)
1½ teaspoons salt
1 tablespoon Japanese soy sauce
2 tablespoons sake, mirin or dry sherry

Soak mushrooms in hot water 30 minutes, cut off and discard stems and simmer the caps in a small saucepan with 1/2 cup (4 fl oz, 125 ml) water, 1 tablespoon of soy, and the sugar for 10 minutes.

Custard: Beat eggs, then mix in all other ingredients. When mixture has been poured into cups, carefully skim off the bubbles on the top of the mixture.

Into each custard cup or ramekin put a mushroom, a shrimp or 2 slices kamaboko, and an oyster. Fill cups with custard mixture and place on a rack in a wok with hot water to 1 in (2.5 cm) below rack. Cover each cup with foil, pressing it close over the side of the cup. Cover wok with the lid and bring water to a boil. Lower heat and simmer 15 minutes or until set. Serve hot or cold.

Note: If preferred, substitute thinly sliced chicken breast for the seafood. You will need half a large chicken breast, skin and bones removed.

Serves 4

⟨≈⟩⋈⟨≈⟩

STEAMED EGG WITH MUSHROOMS
Trung Hap ✦ Vietnam

4 dried Chinese mushrooms
½ cup soaked cellophane noodles
4 oz (125 g) crab or shrimp (prawn) meat
4 oz (125 g) cooked pork
5 eggs
2 scallions (spring onions), finely chopped
2 teaspoons finely chopped cilantro (fresh coriander leaves)
½ teaspoon salt
⅛ teaspoon black pepper

Soak mushrooms in hot water 30 minutes. Discard stems, squeeze excess water from caps and slice finely. Soak a small amount of cellophane noodles in hot water for about 10 minutes, then measure half cup. Flake crab meat and discard any bony bits, or chop the shelled and deveined shrimp into small pieces. Chop pork finely.

Beat eggs until yolks and whites are well mixed but not frothy. Stir in the scallions, coriander, salt, and pepper and the prepared mushrooms, noodles, seafood, and pork. Put into a heatproof dish and steam until firm, exact time depending on the depth of the mixture in the dish. Serve with rice and nuoc cham (page 14).
Serves 3–4

⋘⋙

STIR-FRIED CHICKEN & ASPARAGUS
China

1 large chicken breast
2 teaspoons light soy sauce
½ teaspoon crushed garlic
12 fresh green asparagus spears
half a medium-size red bell pepper (capsicum)
half a medium-size onion
2 teaspoons oyster sauce
2 teaspoons Chinese wine or dry sherry
2 tablespoons water or stock
2 tablespoons peanut oil

Remove skin and bones (reserve for the stock pot) and cut the chicken meat into thin slices. Cut the slices into bite-size pieces. In a bowl stir together the light soy sauce and crushed garlic, add the chicken and thoroughly mix by hand.

Wash the asparagus thoroughly, trimming off any tough ends. Thinly peel about 1 inch (2.5 cm) of bottom ends of the stalks. Slice stalks diagonally keeping tips whole. Cut bell pepper into strips. Cut onion into 4 wedges, divide each wedge in half crosswise and separate layers. In a small bowl combine the oyster sauce, wine, and water.

Heat a wok, add 1 tablespoon of peanut oil and swirl to coat the wok. Add the marinated chicken and stir-fry on high heat for 1 minute or until chicken turns golden. Remove to a plate. Stir-fry bell pepper and onion for 1 minute adding an extra teaspoon of oil if necessary, remove to plate. Add remaining oil to wok and stir-fry the asparagus on high heat for 1 minute, turn heat low, add combined liquid ingredients, cover and simmer for 3 minutes when the asparagus will be tender but still crisp. Return chicken and other vegetables and stir only until heated through. Serve at once.

Note: When asparagus is unavailable substitute 1 cup sliced broccoli or 1/2 cup thinly sliced green (string) beans.
Serves 2

⋘⋙

STIR-FRIED CHICKEN & HAM
China

1 large chicken breast
2 teaspoons cornstarch (cornflour)
¼ teaspoon salt
3 tablespoons peanut oil
half an egg white
1 ham steak, ½ in (1 cm) thick
1 cup sliced celery, sliced in thin crescent shapes
1 medium onion
½ teaspoon grated fresh ginger
½ teaspoon crushed garlic
2 teaspoons oyster sauce or light soy sauce

Skin and bone the chicken breast. Cut the meat into bite-size pieces and roll them in the cornstarch and salt mixed together. Pour 1 tablespoon oil over and mix well by hand. Set aside for 10 minutes, then add the unbeaten egg white and mix again by hand so all the pieces are well coated. Chill for 20 to 30 minutes.

Cut ham into thin strips about 2 in (5 cm) long. Cut onion into 4 wedges, divide each wedge in half crosswise and separate layers.

Heat a wok until very hot, add remaining two tablespoons of oil and swirl to coat wok. Add ginger and garlic, stir briefly, add ham strips and celery slices and toss over high heat for 1 minute. Move ham and celery to side of wok and let the oil run to the middle.

Add the chicken to the oil and turn the pieces over until all the chicken has turned white. Add the onions and stir-fry the entire contents of the pan for 1 minute. Add the oyster sauce

or soy sauce, mix thoroughly and serve at once, garnished with scallion (spring onion) curls or carrot flowers.
Serves 2–4

STIR-FRIED CHICKEN WITH MUSHROOMS
Moan Chua Noeung Phset Kream
Cambodia & Laos

6 dried Chinese mushrooms
1 small roasting chicken
4 cloves garlic, crushed
½ teaspoon finely grated fresh ginger
2 tablespoons shortening (lard) or oil
1 cup (8 fl oz, 250 ml) water
2 tablespoons fish sauce
2 teaspoons sugar
2 tablespoons chopped cilantro (fresh coriander leaves)

Soak mushrooms in hot water for 30 minutes. Squeeze dry, cut off and discard stems, cut caps into quarters if they are large. Cut chicken into small pieces with cleaver, chopping through bones as well. Fry garlic and ginger in the hot shortening or oil for a few seconds, then add chicken and stir-fry until color changes. Add mushrooms, water, fish sauce, and sugar, cover and simmer until chicken is cooked. Sprinkle with chopped cilantro and serve with rice.
Serves 4–6

STIR-FRIED GINGER CHICKEN WITH BAMBOO SHOOT
Thailand

2 large chicken breasts
½ cup dried wood fungus (cloud ears)
4 tablespoons finely shredded fresh ginger
1 canned bamboo shoot, shredded
1 medium onion, thinly sliced
2 tablespoons shortening (lard) or peanut oil
2 teaspoons garlic, finely chopped
1 tablespoon light soy sauce
2 tablespoons fish sauce
1 tablespoon vinegar
2 teaspoons sugar
5 scallions (spring onions), finely chopped
4 tablespoons cilantro (fresh coriander leaves), chopped

Remove skin and bones from chicken breasts and cut the meat into dice. Soak wood fungus in hot water for 15 minutes, wash well to remove any grit and cut into bite-size pieces. To shred ginger, thinly peel off outer skin, cut into very thin slices, then cut slices into long thread-like strips. Soak ginger in lightly salted water for 10 minutes, then squeeze out moisture. This makes the ginger less pungent.

Heat wok, add shortening or oil and on medium low heat fry the onion until soft. Add garlic and stir until garlic starts to turn golden. Add the chicken meat, ginger, and bamboo shoot and stir-fry for 2 minutes, on medium high heat. Now add the sauces, vinegar, and sugar, and when liquid boils reduce heat, cover and simmer 3 minutes. Stir in wood fungus, scallions, and cilantro and serve with hot white rice.
Serves 4

STIR-FRIED MARINATED CHICKEN
Japan

2 tablespoons sesame seeds
1 lb (500 g) boned chicken meat
2 tablespoons Japanese soy sauce
2 tablespoons sake or dry sherry
2 teaspoons sugar
4 tablespoons cornstarch (cornflour)
1 tablespoon peanut oil
1 tablespoon sesame oil
4 crisp lettuce leaves

In a dry wok, toast sesame seeds over medium low heat, stirring constantly, until they are evenly golden. Turn onto a plate to cool.

Cut chicken meat into bite-size pieces and marinate in a mixture of soy, sake, and sugar for 1 hour. Drain chicken well, roll pieces in cornstarch and set aside for 10 minutes.

Heat both oils in a wok, and stir-fry chicken on medium high heat for about 2 to 3 minutes or until golden brown and crisp. Drain on kitchen paper, place on lettuce leaves and serve hot sprinkled with toasted sesame seeds.
Serves 4

WHOLE CHICKEN IN SPICES & YOGURT

Murgh Musallam ◆ North India & Pakistan

3 lb (1.5 kg) roasting chicken
¼ teaspoon saffron strands
1 tablespoon hot water
½ teaspoon each ground black pepper, ground turmeric, ground cumin, and chili powder
¼ teaspoon each ground cardamom, cloves, cinnamon, and mace
2 cloves garlic, crushed
1½ teaspoons salt
2 tablespoons yogurt
3 tablespoons ghee or oil
2 medium onions, finely sliced
1¼ cups (10 fl oz, 300 ml) hot water or stock

Wash and dry chicken inside and out, removing neck and giblets and cutting off wing tips. These can be used for making stock.

Soak saffron strands in hot water 10 minutes, pressing saffron strands between the fingers. Mix saffron and soaking water, all the ground spices, and the garlic crushed with salt, into the yogurt. Rub a tablespoon of the mixture inside the cavity of the chicken. Rub some of the mixture over the chicken. Leave chicken to marinate for 1 hour.

Heat ghee in a large, heavy saucepan and fry onions until golden. Remove onions to a plate, put in the chicken and brown it lightly on all sides. Return onions to the pan and stir remaining chicken marinade into the hot water or stock, pour into pan and bring to a boil. Turn heat low, cover and cook for 45 minutes or until chicken is very tender. Turn chicken from time to time so it cooks first on one side and then the other, on its back and, for the last 10 minutes, breast downwards. Liquid should evaporate almost completely. Serve hot with parathas and raita or salad.

Serves 6

Opposite: whole chicken in spices and yogurt (recipe above).

Meats

BANQUET FIREPOT
Sin Sul Lo ◆ Korea

1 lb (500 g) filet steak
2 medium onions, peeled and sliced
8 oz (250 g) boned white fish
8 oz (250 g) calf's liver
3 eggs, separated
all-purpose (plain) flour
vegetable oil for frying
4 scallions (spring onions)
1 carrot
6–8 cups (2½–3 pts, 1.5–2 L) beef stock (page 6)
½ cup each walnuts and pine nuts
sesame seed sauce (see end of recipe for Ghanghwe, page 42)
*   or other dipping sauce*

Partially freeze steak, then cut into paper-thin slices. Put beef and onions into sin sul lo pot (pictured) or individual pots. Slice fish into bite-size pieces. Slice liver very thinly into pieces of similar size. Season both fish and liver with pepper and salt. Dip the slices of liver into the beaten yolk of 1 egg, then in flour. Slightly beat the white of the egg and dip fish slices in it, then in flour. Heat just enough oil to cover the base of a frying pan and quickly saute the pieces of fish and liver until just cooked. Put these in the pot on top of the beef and onions.

Beat remaining 2 egg yolks and make a flat omelet, turn out on a plate to cool. Do the same with the remaining egg whites. On a wooden board cut the yellow and white omelet into strips just long enough to fit across the moat of the firepot. Do the same with the scallions. Slice the carrot thinly and cut into strips of the same size. Arrange these over the beef, fish, and liver, then garnish with walnuts and pine nuts. The recipe may be prepared up to this point, covered and refrigerated.

At serving time carefully ladle boiling stock into the moat without disturbing the arrangement of the food. Replace cover on pot and with tongs put glowing coals into the chimney. Bring to the table and allow broth to simmer for a few minutes and heat the contents of the pot thoroughly.

Remove cover and let guests help themselves from the pot with chopsticks. They dip the food in individual bowls of sesame seed sauce before eating. Serve with boiled rice and at the end of the meal serve the stock as soup.
Serves 6

BARBECUED PORK
China

2 lb (1 kg) pork filet
1 teaspoon finely chopped garlic
1 teaspoon salt
½ teaspoon finely grated fresh ginger
2 tablespoons dark soy sauce
2 tablespoons honey
1 tablespoon Chinese wine or dry sherry
½ teaspoon five-spice powder
1 tablespoon bottled hoi sin sauce

In China barbecued pork is cooked in special barrel-shaped ovens. Here are two ways to get almost the same effect in your own oven at home.

Cut the pork lengthwise into three or four strips. Crush the garlic with the salt and combine with all the remaining ingredients in a large bowl. Add the pork and mix well together so that the meat is covered on all sides with the mixture. Allow it to marinate for 15 minutes or longer if convenient.

Cooking method 1: Remove all racks from oven except one, which should be on the highest level. Put a baking dish with a little water in it on the bottom shelf.

Preheat the oven to 400º F (200º C, Gas Mark 6). Insert a butcher's hook in the end of each strip of pork and hang it from the rack. Roast for 15 minutes in the hot oven, then reduce the temperature to 375º F (190º C, Gas Mark 5), brush the meat with the marinade and continue roasting for a further 30 minutes or until the pork is cooked.

Remove from oven, allow to cool for at least 10 minutes, then cut in thin slices crosswise.

Cooking method 2: Half-fill a baking dish with hot water and put a wire rack across the top of the pan. Place the strips of pork on the rack (reserving the marinade) and roast in an oven preheated to 400º F (200º C, Gas Mark 6) for 15 minutes, then turn the pork, brush with marinade and continue roasting for 15 minutes. Turn the meat again and baste it, and roast for another 15 minutes or until the pork is tender and well glazed.

Barbecued pork may be served hot or cold as an hors d'oeuvre or part of a meal, or the meat can be used in other dishes such as fried rice. Stir-fried with snow peas (mangetout) or fresh green (string) beans, it makes a quick, light meal. On its own, serve with plum sauce and steamed bread.
Serves 4–6

Japanese pork cutlet (page 192).

BARBECUED PORK SPARERIBS
China

3 lb (1.5 kg) pork spareribs
2 large cloves garlic, crushed
1 teaspoon salt
1 teaspoon fresh root ginger, finely grated
2 tablespoons soy sauce
1 tablespoon hoi sin sauce
2 teaspoons purchased sesame sauce
1 tablespoon honey
1 tablespoon Chinese wine or dry sherry

Cut rack of bones into lengths of about 4 or 5 bones each and, using a sharp knife, cut between the bones but do not separate them.

Combine garlic, crushed with salt, and all other ingredients in a bowl and beat well together with a spoon. The sesame sauce should be stirred well in the jar before measuring the required amount as the oil floats on top and the paste settles at the bottom. Pour marinade over the pork and rub on all sides and between the bones. Marinate for an hour or more.

Half fill baking dish with water and place a rack in the pan or across the top. Water should not touch rack. Place the marinated pork on the rack and cook in a hot oven for 20 minutes, then reduce heat to moderate, turn pork and cook a further 25 minutes. Pork may require further cooking. When barbecued pork is ready it should be reddish brown all over, touched with dark brown here and there, as if barbecued over open coals. Cooking time will be between 45 minutes and 1 hour, depending on thickness of pork
Serves 6–8

❖⟡❖

BARBECUED SPICED MUTTON
Mutton Sula ◆ India (Rajasthan)

1 lb (500 g) boneless lamb
1 teaspoon ajowan seeds
1 teaspoon chili powder
1 teaspoon ground turmeric
2 teaspoons ground coriander
pinch of ground cloves
1 teaspoon crushed garlic
1 teaspoon salt
1 teaspoon finely grated fresh ginger
1 cup yogurt

Garnish:
lemon slices
1 medium onion, finely sliced

Cut lamb into small cubes. Crush the ajowan seeds and combine with the other spices. Crush garlic with salt. Mix spices, salt, garlic, and ginger with the yogurt, pour over the lamb and mix well. Marinate the lamb in this mixture for at least 5 hours.

Thread the pieces of meat on skewers and broil (grill) over charcoal fire or under preheated broiler (grill), turning the skewers frequently, until the meat is well done.

Push the meat off the skewers onto the serving plate, garnish with lemon slices and finely sliced onions. This is usually served with naan, fresh mint chutney (page 21), and pickles.
Serves 4

❖⟡❖

BEEF & CARDAMOM CURRY
India

1 lb (500 g) lean stewing steak
2 tablespoons peanut oil
1 large onion, sliced
1 teaspoon finely chopped garlic
1 teaspoon finely chopped fresh ginger
½ teaspoon turmeric
2 teaspoons ground cardamom
1 teaspoon ground coriander
1 teaspoon ground cumin
1 x 2 in (5 cm) cinnamon stick
pinch of ground cloves
1 teaspoon chili powder
1 tablespoon lemon juice
6 curry leaves
salt to taste
½ cup (4 fl oz, 15 ml) warm water

Cut meat into 2 in (5 cm) squares. Heat oil in a saucepan, add onions and fry, stirring occasionally, until golden brown. Add meat, raise heat, and brown all over. Add all other ingredients except the water, mix with the meat and cook for 3 minutes.

Add water, lower heat, cover and simmer till meat is tender, adding more water if necessary. Stir occasionally to prevent meat catching to base of saucepan. Serve with boiled rice and accompaniments.

❖⟡❖

BEEF & POTATO CURRY
Burma

1½ lb (750 g) beef
¾ lb (375 g) potatoes
2 large onions
5 large cloves garlic
2 teaspoons chopped fresh ginger
1 teaspoon chili powder
8 tablespoons light sesame oil or corn oil
½ teaspoon ground cumin
½ teaspoon ground coriander
1½ teaspoons salt or to taste
2 cups (16 fl oz, 500 ml) water

Cut beef into large squares. Peel and cut potatoes into quarters. Fry the onion, garlic and ginger in oil until soft, then add chili powder. When cooked and sizzling, add cumin and coriander, then add meat and fry, stirring for a few minutes. Add salt, about 2 cups (16 fl oz, 500 ml) water, potatoes, and simmer slowly until meat is tender and potatoes are cooked.

Note: Some cooks prefer to rub the cumin, coriander, and salt into the beef before cooking. Care must be taken to fry on low heat so spices will not burn.
Serves 4–6

BEEF & PORK BALLS SIMMERED IN STOCK
Almondigas ◆ **The Philippines**

8 oz (250 g) ground (minced) pork
8 oz (250 g) ground (minced) beef
1 teaspoon salt
¼ teaspoon pepper
1 small egg
1½ tablespoons oil
2 cloves garlic, finely chopped
1 medium onion, finely chopped
2 ripe tomatoes, diced
4 cups broth or rice water
2 teaspoons soy sauce

Combine pork, beef, salt, pepper, and egg thoroughly and form into balls. Heat oil and fry garlic and onion until golden brown, then add tomatoes and fry, stirring, until soft. Add broth or water from washing rice, bring to a boil, then add meat balls one by one and let them simmer slowly until well cooked. Serve hot.
Serves 4

Barbecued pork (page 174).

BEEF & SQUASH CURRY
Ametha Net Shwephayone Thee Hin ◆ **Burma**

1½ lb (750 g) beef
1 lb (500 g) squash (pumpkin)
2 large onions
5 large garlic cloves
2 teaspoons chopped fresh ginger
1 teaspoon ground turmeric
1 teaspoon chili powder
8 tablespoons light sesame oil or corn oil
1 cup (8 fl oz, 250 ml) water
1½ teaspoons salt or to taste

Cut beef into large squares. Peel and cut squash into 2 in (5 cm) squares. Fry the onion, garlic, and ginger in oil until soft, then add turmeric and chili powder. When cooked and sizzling, add meat and fry slowly, stirring for a few minutes. Add water and cook slowly with cover on pan until meat is nearly done. Add salt and squash and continue cooking until meat is tender and squash is soft.

Note: In place of squash the following vegetables can be used: tomatoes, green (string) beans, potatoes, eggplant (aubergines), peas, split peas, okra (ladies' fingers), cauliflower, kohlrabi, lima (broad) beans.
Serves 4–6

BEEF & TOASTED COCONUT CURRY
Malaysia

2 lb (1kg) lean stewing steak, thinly sliced
3 tablespoons peanut oil
3 tablespoons unsweetened desiccated coconut
1 stem lemon grass, chopped or rind of half a lemon
4 dried red chilies
1 teaspoon chopped garlic
1 teaspoon chopped fresh ginger
1 medium onion, roughly chopped
1 teaspoon dried shrimp paste
4 tablespoons tamarind liquid
2 teaspoons salt

Roast coconut in a dry pan until golden brown. Remove to a plate and when cool put into blender together with rest of ingredients and blend to a smooth paste adding a little hot water to facilitate blending.

Heat oil in a saucepan then add blended spices and cook, stirring till oil comes to the surface and spices smell aromatic. Add meat and stir until browned, then cover and simmer until meat is tender, stirring occasionally. Add more water if necessary.

Serve with rice and accompaniments.
Serves 4–6

BEEF & VEGETABLE STEW
Kari-Kari ◆ The Philippines

4 lb (2 kg) oxtail, jointed
2 lb (1 kg) shin of beef on bone, sliced
3 teaspoons salt
3 tablespoons vegetable oil
2 teaspoons annatto seeds
2 large onions, very finely sliced
4 large cloves garlic, finely chopped
8 cups (64 fl oz, 2 L) water
¼ teaspoon ground black pepper
½ cup (3 ½ oz, 100 g) uncooked rice
½ cup roasted skinned peanuts
12 oz (375 g) tender green (string) beans
2 medium eggplants (aubergines)
2 tablespoons sliced scallions (spring onions)
2 tablespoons chopped celery leaves
2 tablespoons fish sauce, or to taste

Put oxtail and shin of beef into pressure cooker with just enough water to cover and 2 teaspoons salt. Cook under pressure for 1 hour. Allow to cool to lukewarm and strain. Chill stock in refrigerator so fat may be lifted from surface. If no pressure cooker is available, simmer meat until almost tender.

Wipe pieces of meat on absorbent paper so no moisture remains. Heat 1 tablespoon oil in a large, deep saucepan or heatproof cooking pot and brown pieces of meat, putting in a few at a time and turning with tongs to ensure even browning. Remove each batch from pan to a plate. Pour off fat from pan and heat remaining oil, not making it too hot. Add annatto seeds, cover pan because they are inclined to pop and spatter, and warm on very low heat for 1 minute. Remove from heat, lift out seeds with a perforated spoon.

Fry onions and garlic on medium heat in the annatto oil until soft, about 10 minutes. Return meat to pan, remove fat from stock and reheat it, then make up to 8 cups with hot water. Pour into pan, add pepper, bring to a boil then turn heat low and simmer, with lid on pan, but allowing a little steam to escape, until meat is tender.

While meat is simmering, put uncooked rice into a heavy frying pan and roast over medium heat, stirring frequently and shaking pan so grains color evenly. When they are deep golden allow to cool slightly, then grind to a powder in electric blender. Tip ground rice into a bowl and blend peanuts until they too are reduced to powder. If some particles are large, sift and use only the fine ground nuts.

Test tenderness of meat. Meat should be easily pierced with a fork, but not falling off the bone, and there should be sufficient liquid in pan to cover the meat. If necessary add more hot water. Stir in rice and peanut powder with a wooden spoon, stirring until smooth. String and cut beans into large bite-size lengths. Wash eggplants, remove stems and cut in 8 lengthwise wedges, then cut wedges into 3, crosswise. Stir into the stew and cook, uncovered, for 10 minutes or until vegetables are tender but not mushy. Add 1 tablespoon fish sauce, or more if liked. Serve from pot or ladle into a large soup tureen. Sprinkle scallions (including green portion) and celery leaves over and serve hot with white rice. If desired, accompany with extra fish sauce, soy sauce, and a hot sambal sauce.
Serves 6–8

BEEF CURRY
Harak Mas Curry ◆ Sri Lanka

3 lb (1.5 kg) stewing beef steak
3 tablespoons ghee or oil
2 large onions, finely chopped
1 tablespoon finely chopped fresh ginger
3 teaspoons finely chopped garlic
4 tablespoons Ceylon curry powder (page 10)
1 teaspoon ground turmeric

2 teaspoons black mustard seeds
2 teaspoons salt
1 tablespoon vinegar
2 fresh red chilies, seeded and chopped
3 ripe tomatoes, peeled and chopped

Cut steak into 2 in (5 cm) squares. Heat ghee in saucepan and gently fry onions, ginger and garlic until just beginning to turn golden. Add curry powder, turmeric, mustard seeds and fry over low heat for 2 to 3 minutes. Add salt and vinegar and stir well. Add steak and fry, stirring to coat meat well. Add chilies and tomatoes, cover pan and simmer on very low heat for about 2 hours. Serve with rice and other accompaniments. If gravy is too thin when meat is tender, cook over high heat, uncovered, until reduced.
Serves 8–10

BEEF IN SOY SAUCE & CHILIES
Empal Jawa • Indonesia

1 lb (500 g) topside, round or rump steak
3 tablespoons peanut oil
1 onion, finely chopped
3 cloves garlic, crushed
1½ teaspoons sambal ulek (page 23) or 2 fresh red chilies,
*   seeded and finely chopped*
½ teaspoon trasi (dried shrimp paste)
½ teaspoon laos powder
1 teaspoon finely chopped lemon rind or ½ teaspoon sereh
*   powder*
2 tablespoons dark soy sauce
¼ cup (2 fl oz, 60 ml) stock
1 teaspoon palm sugar or brown sugar

Put the meat, trimmed of all fat, into a medium saucepan with just enough water to cover. Bring to a boil, then simmer for 15 minutes. Allow meat to cool to lukewarm in the stock. When cool enough to handle, slice meat into thin strips. Heat peanut oil in a wok or frying pan and fry onions over low heat until soft and transparent. When starting to turn golden add garlic, chilies, trasi, laos powder and lemon rind. Crush trasi in the pan with the back of a wooden spoon and stir-fry for a minute. Add beef and stir-fry for about 3 or 4 minutes on medium heat.

Add soy sauce, stock, and sugar, stir and continue to cook on low heat until liquid has almost evaporated and oil separates from the rest of the gravy. The oil should have a reddish colour from the chilies. Serve hot with boiled rice and vegetable dishes.
Serves 6

BEEF PEPPER CURRY
Kuruma Iraichchi • Sri Lanka

2 lb (1 kg) lean stewing steak
2 teaspoons salt
2–4 teaspoons ground black pepper
1 tablespoon ground coriander
2 teaspoons ground cumin
1 teaspoon ground fennel
½ teaspoon ground turmeric
2 medium onions, finely chopped
1½ teaspoons finely chopped garlic
1½ teaspoons finely grated fresh ginger
2 fresh red chilies, seeded and sliced
8 curry leaves
2 strips daun pandan (rampé leaf)
1 stem fresh lemon grass or 2 strips lemon rind
2 tablespoons vinegar
2 cups (16 fl oz, 500 ml) thin coconut cream
1 tablespoon ghee or oil
1 cup (8 fl oz, 250 ml) thick coconut cream

Cut the meat into 2 in (5 cm) squares and beat lightly with a meat mallet. Season with salt and pepper and mix well. Roast separately in a dry pan the coriander, cumin, and fennel. Add coriander to meat and set aside the cumin and fennel. Put meat into a saucepan with spices and all other ingredients except roasted cumin, fennel, ghee, and the thick coconut cream.

Bring slowly to a boil, reduce heat and simmer covered, until meat is tender. If gravy thickens too quickly add a little water. Pour gravy into another pan, then add the ghee or oil to the meat left in the pan and fry it for a few minutes, stirring. Add the cumin and fennel to the thick coconut cream and mix with the cooked gravy. Return everything to pan with the meat and continue to simmer uncovered over a very low heat until the gravy is thick and the various ingredients are well blended. Serve with rice and other accompaniments.
Serves 8

BEEF SMOORE
Mas Ismoru • Sri Lanka

3 lb (1.5 kg) fresh silverside or other stewing steak, in one piece
2 medium onions, finely chopped
3 teaspoons finely chopped garlic
1 tablespoon finely chopped fresh ginger
1 stick cinnamon
10 curry leaves
1 stem fresh lemon grass or 2 strips lemon rind

3 tablespoons Ceylon curry powder (page 10)
½ teaspoon fenugreek seeds
½ cup (4 fl oz, 125 ml) vinegar
½ pickled lime or lemon or ½ cup tamarind liquid
2 cups (16 fl oz, 500 ml) thin coconut cream
1 teaspoon ground turmeric
2 teaspoons chili powder, or to taste
2 teaspoons salt, or to taste
1 cup (8 fl oz, 250 ml) thick coconut cream
2½ tablespoons ghee

Pierce the meat well with a skewer and put in a large saucepan with all the ingredients except the thick coconut cream and ghee. Cover and simmer gently until meat is tender, approximately 1 1/2 to 2 hours. Add thick coconut cream and cook, uncovered for 15 minutes longer.

Lift meat out on to a serving dish and if gravy is too thin, reduce by boiling rapidly uncovered. Transfer gravy to a bowl. Rinse pan to remove any gravy, return to stove and heat ghee in it. Fry meat on all sides, pour gravy over meat and heat through.

To serve, cut meat into thick slices and spoon gravy over.

Serves 6–8

❖

BEEF STRIPS, BALINESE-STYLE

Dagang Masak Bali ◆ Indonesia

1½ lb (750 g) blade steak
1 medium onion, roughly chopped
3 cloves garlic
1 tablespoon finely chopped fresh root ginger
4–6 fresh chilies, seeded
½ teaspoon trasi or blachan (dried shrimp paste)
3 tablespoons oil
1 cup (8 fl oz, 250 ml) water
2 tablespoons tamarind liquid
2 tablespoons soy sauce
salt to taste

Cut beef into thin strips. Place onion, garlic, ginger, chilies, and trasi into blender container, cover and blend until smooth. Heat oil in a saucepan and fry mixture for approximately 5 minutes, stirring constantly. Add beef strips and continue to stir-fry until browned. Add water, tamarind liquid, and soy sauce, cover and simmer gently until beef is tender. Uncover and cook until liquid has almost evaporated. Season to taste with salt. Serve with boiled white rice, vegetables, and sambals.

Serves 6

BEEF TERIYAKI

Japan

1½ lb (750 g) filet steak
2 teaspoons finely grated fresh root ginger
1 clove garlic, crushed
½ cup (4 fl oz, 250 ml) soy sauce
2 tablespoons mirin or sherry
1 tablespoon sugar
1 tablespoon sesame oil
2 teaspoons cornstarch (cornflour)

Cut filet into thin steaks. Mix all remaining ingredients together except cornstarch and marinate the steak for at least 2 hours. Heat broiler (grill), hibachi, or electric frypan. Before starting to cook the meat, mix 2 tablespoons of the marinade with an equal quantity of water. Mix cornstarch to a smooth paste with a little of the mixture. Bring remaining mixture to a boil and stirring continuously, add the blended cornstarch and cook until clear and thickened. Set aside.

Broil (grill) or fry slices of steak for a few minutes on each side. Pour a spoonful of the glaze on each one and cut in strips before serving (making it easier to eat with chopsticks). Serve with boiled white rice.

Serves 4

❖

BEEF WITH BAMBOO SHOOTS,

Bo Xao Mang ◆ Vietnam

12 oz (375 g) rump or filet steak
2 tablespoons peanut oil
extra 2 tablespoons of peanut oil
1 large can bamboo shoots, sliced
6 scallions (spring onions), sliced
1 tablespoon fish sauce
½ teaspoon salt
1 clove garlic, crushed
4 tablespoons sesame seeds, toasted and crushed

Cut beef into very thin slices about 2 in (5 cm) long. Heat peanut oil in wok, stir-fry beef quickly for only about 1 minute. Remove from wok while meat is still pink. In same wok heat extra oil and fry well-drained sliced bamboo shoots and scallions for about 2 minutes. Add fish sauce and salt and fry for a further 5 minutes. Add crushed garlic, stir and fry for a further minute, then return beef to wok and stir-fry for a minute. Add sesame seeds and mix well. Serve hot with rice.

Note: Do not double this recipe. If a larger quantity is needed, make two lots.

Serves 3–4

Beef smoore (page 179).

BRAISED BEEF SHORTRIBS WITH SESAME SAUCE

Korea

3 lb (1.5 kg) shortribs of beef
1 tablespoon peanut oil
2 tablespoons dark soy sauce
2 teaspoons sesame oil
4 scallions (spring onions), finely chopped
1 teaspoon finely chopped garlic
1 teaspoon finely chopped fresh ginger
2 tablespoons sugar
3 tablespoons rice wine or dry sherry
2 tablespoons toasted, ground sesame seeds
2 cups (16 fl oz, 500 ml) hot water
1 teaspoon cornstarch (cornflour)
1 tablespoon cold water
scallion (spring onion) flowers
few sprigs cilantro (fresh coriander leaves), optional

You can buy the ribs already cut into short lengths at many supermarkets, or ask your butcher to chop spareribs across into short lengths of about 2 in (5 cm). Separate them with a sharp cleaver, heat oil in a wok and brown the ribs over high heat. Combine all other ingredients (except cornstarch and cold water) and add to wok, bring to a boil, then cover and simmer 50 to 60 minutes or until tender. Add cornstarch mixed with cold water and stir constantly over medium heat until gravy boils and thickens. Garnish with scallion flowers and if desired, sprigs of cilantro and serve with hot white rice.

To make scallion flowers, cut into short lengths and split one or both ends several times with a sharp knife. Soak in iced water for a few minutes until the ends curl.

Serves 4

BRAISED HONEY PORK

China

2 lb (1 kg) boneless loin of pork
1 tablespoon canned black beans
1 teaspoon crushed garlic
1 teaspoon salt
2 teaspoons finely grated fresh ginger
3 tablespoons honey
3 tablespoons Chinese wine or dry cherry
½ teaspoon five-spice powder
4 tablespoons dark soy sauce
3 tablespoons peanut oil

Remove rind from the pork and cut the pork into strips 2 in x 1 in (5 cm x 2.5 cm).

Wash the black beans well under running cold water. Drain and chop. Combine all ingredients except peanut oil and mix with the pork. Leave for at least 15 minutes to marinate.

Heat wok, add the peanut oil and swirl to coat the wok. Add the pork pieces (reserving the marinade) and stir-fry until they are browned. Then add the reserved marinade. Swirl 3/4 cup (6 fl oz, 180 ml) hot water in the marinating bowl and add that too.

Reduce the heat, cover the wok and simmer for 30 to 40 minutes until pork is tender. Stir occasionally and add more hot water if the liquid seems to be drying up. Be careful that the sweet marinade does not burn. The heat should be very low throughout the cooking.

When the pork is tender, remove from heat. If it is not to be served straight away, it may be reheated at serving time. Serve on a bed of Braised Chinese Cabbage (page 264) with plain rice and garnish with cilantro (fresh coriander leaves).

Serves 6

BRAISED PORK WITH BLACK BEANS

Singapore

1½ lbs (750 g) loin of pork (rind and bone removed)
2 teaspoons finely chopped garlic
1 teaspoon finely chopped fresh ginger
2 tablespoons Chinese wine or dry sherry
½ teaspoon five-spice powder
2 tablespoons black beans, chopped
1 tablespoon chili sauce
1 tablespoon peanut oil
hot water or stock
1 red bell pepper (capsicum) cut into 1 in (5 cm) dice
5 scallions (spring onions) cut into 1 in (2.5 cm) lengths

Cut pork into strips 2 in (5 cm) long and 1 in (2.5 cm) wide. Combine garlic, ginger, wine, five-spice powder, black beans, chili sauce and rub over the pork. Set aside to marinate for 20 minutes. Heat wok, add oil and swirl to coat wok. Add the pork pieces, reserving marinade. Stir-fry the pork over high heat until browned, then add reserved marinade, washing out the bowl with 1/2 cup (4 fl oz, 125 ml) hot water and adding that to wok.

Reduce heat, cover and simmer for 40 minutes until pork is tender. Stir occasionally and add more hot water if liquid looks like drying up. Ten minutes before serving, add bell pepper and scallions and mix through the pork. Serve with hot boiled rice.

Serves 4–6

Beef with bamboo shoots, a Vietnamese dish (page 180).

BRAISED PORK WITH CHESTNUTS

Lut Gee Hoong Shiu Ju Yook ✦ **China**

1½ lb (750 g) skinless pork belly
2 cloves garlic, crushed
1 teaspoon salt
1 tablespoon light soy sauce
1 tablespoon Chinese wine or brandy
4 oz (125 g) dried chestnuts
2 tablespoons peanut oil
2½ cups (20 fl oz, 600 ml) hot water
2 teaspoons cornstarch (cornflour)
2 tablespoons cold water
scallions (spring onions) to garnish, optional

Cut pork into thin slices, then into small dice. Mix with garlic crushed with salt, soy sauce, and wine or brandy. Marinate for 1 hour. Pour boiling water over dried chestnuts in a bowl, allow to soak for 30 minutes. Pour off water and replace with more boiling water. Soak for a further 30 minutes. Drain off water before using.

Heat oil in a wok and fry marinated pork, stirring constantly, until brown. Add chestnuts and stir well, then add hot water, cover and simmer for 35 to 40 minutes. Mix cornstarch with cold water. Push pork and chestnuts to side of pan and add cornstarch mixture to liquid in pan. There should be about 1 cup (8 fl oz, 250 ml) cooking liquid. If not, make up quantity with water. Cook until thick, stirring constantly. If desired garnish with pieces of scallion. Serve with rice.

Serves 4–6

CHILI BEEF WITH BITTER MELON

China

12 oz (375 g) piece of stewing steak
½ teaspoon baking soda (bicarbonate of soda)
1 large bitter melon
1 teaspoon salt
1 tablespoon canned Chinese salted black beans
1 tablespoon dark soy sauce
2 teaspoons chili bean sauce
1 teaspoon sugar
1 teaspoon cornstarch (cornflour)
6 tablespoons peanut oil
1 teaspoon crushed garlic

Remove any fat from the meat and slice thinly across the grain. Dissolve the baking soda in 4 tablespoons of hot water. Add to the meat and knead well until the meat absorbs all the liquid. Cover and refrigerate for 2 hours or longer.

Halve the bitter melon lengthwise. Scoop out and discard the spongy middle and seeds. Cut the melon into 1/2 in (12 mm) slices. Sprinkle 1 teaspoon of salt over the melon pieces and lightly mix through. Leave for 30 minutes or longer.

Rinse the melon pieces under a cold tap, and drain. Rinse the black beans under cold water, drain, and chop. Combine the soy sauce, chili bean sauce, sugar, and cornstarch with 5 tablespoons of water.

Heat the wok, add 3 tablespoons of the oil and when hot, add the beef and stir-fry over high heat, tossing and stirring until brown. Remove to a plate.

Add a further tablespoon of oil to the wok and when hot stir-fry the bitter melon for 2 minutes. Remove.

Heat the remaining oil, add garlic and stir-fry for a few seconds. Add black beans and fry, stirring for a few seconds more. Stir the sauce mixture, add it to the wok and stir until it boils and thickens. Return the melon to the wok, simmer for 5 minutes. Then stir in the beef until reheated through. Serve immediately, garnished with chili flowers.
Serves 4

CHILI BEEF WITH SHRIMP PASTE

Indonesia

1 lb (500 g) topside or round steak
3 tablespoons peanut oil
1 large onion, finely chopped
2 teaspoons finely chopped garlic
2 teaspoons sambal ulek (page 23) or 3 fresh red chilies, seeded and finely chopped
1 teaspoon trasi (dried shrimp paste)
2 teaspoons finely chopped lemon rind
2 tablespoons dark soy sauce
¼ cup (2 fl oz, 60 ml) stock (page 6)
2 teaspoons palm sugar or brown sugar

Put the meat, trimmed of all fat, into a saucepan with enough water to cover. Bring to a boil, and simmer for 15 minutes. Allow meat to cool in the stock. When cool enough to handle, slice meat into thin strips.

Heat peanut oil in a wok and fry onion over low heat until soft and transparent. When onion starts to turn golden add garlic, chilies, trasi, and lemon rind. Crush trasi in the wok, using the back of a wooden spoon, and stir-fry for 1 minute. Add beef and stir-fry for about 3 to 4 minutes on medium heat. Add soy sauce, stock, and sugar, stir and continue to cook on low heat until liquid has almost evaporated and oil separates from the rest of the gravy. The oil should have a reddish colour from the chilies. Serve hot with boiled rice and vegetables.
Serves 4

COLD STEAMED LAMB WITH PUNGENT SAUCE

China

2½ lb (1.25 kg) lamb shoulder, boned but not rolled
1 tablespoon ground bean sauce
3 tablespoons dark soy sauce
2 scallions (spring onions) chopped
1 teaspoon finely grated garlic
1 teaspoon finely grated fresh ginger
1 star anise
1 tablespoon Chinese wine or dry sherry
1 tablespoon sugar
1 teaspoon red bean curd

Combine the bean sauce, soy sauce, scallions, garlic, ginger, star anise broken into pieces, wine, sugar, and bean curd. Place the lamb in a bowl that will fit in your steamer, pour the sauce mixture over the lamb and rub it well into the meat. Leave for 30 minutes.

Cover and steam for 1 1/2 hours, adding more boiling water to the steamer to replace the water that boils away.

Pour the liquid from the lamb into a saucepan and simmer until reduced and syrupy. Pour it over the lamb and chill.

To serve, cut the meat into thin slices and arrange them on a dish. This dish is also delicious hot. If serving hot, lift the lamb out of the steamer and slice it. Reduce the sauce by quick cooking, then spoon it over the lamb, and serve.

Serves 6

Chili beef with bitter melon (recipe opposite).

Cold steamed lamb with pungent sauce (recipe opposite).

CURRIED MEATBALLS, KASHMIRI-STYLE

Kashmiri Kofta Kari ◆ **India**

1½ lb (750 g) lean ground (minced) lamb
1 teaspoon finely grated fresh ginger
2 fresh chilies, finely chopped
1 teaspoon ground coriander
½ teaspoon chili powder
2 teaspoons garam masala
2 teaspoons salt
½ cup yogurt
3 tablespoons ghee
1 tablespoon dried milk
1 teaspoon sugar
½ teaspoon ground black pepper
¼ teaspoon ground cardamom

Put the lamb into a bowl with ginger, chilies, coriander, chili powder, and 1 teaspoon each of the garam masala and salt, adding 1 tablespoon of the yogurt to moisten the spices and help distribute them evenly. A teaspoon or so of the ghee can also be added if the lamb is very lean. Mix well and form into small oval shapes.

Heat ghee in a heavy saucepan, add the dried milk, sugar, remaining yogurt, garam masala, and salt. Fry in the ghee, then add half cup (4 fl oz, 125 ml) hot water, bring to a boil and add the koftas. Simmer, covered, until no liquid remains. Turn koftas over, add half cup more hot water and the pepper, cover and simmer until liquid is absorbed once more. Sprinkle the dish with cardamom and serve with Indian breads or rice. Cover after adding cardamom so its fragrance will not dissipate.

Serves 6

DRY-FRIED BEEF CURRY
Rendang Daging ✦ Indonesia

3 lb (1.5 kg) stewing steak
2 medium onions, roughly chopped
6 cloves garlic
1 tablespoon chopped fresh ginger
6 fresh red chilies, seeded
2 cups (13 oz, 400 g) thick coconut cream
1½ teaspoons salt
1 teaspoon ground turmeric
3 teaspoons chili powder, optional
2 teaspoons ground coriander
2 daun salam or 6 curry leaves
1 stem fresh lemon grass or 3 strips thinly peeled lemon rind
1 teaspoon laos powder
½ cup (4 fl oz, 125 ml) tamarind liquid
2 teaspoons sugar

Cut beef into strips about 1 in (2.5 cm) wide and 2 in (5 cm) long.

Put onion, garlic, ginger, and chilies in blender container with half cup (3 1/2 oz, 100 g) of coconut cream. Cover and blend until smooth. Pour into a large saucepan and wash out blender with remaining coconut cream. Add to saucepan with all remaining ingredients except tamarind liquid and sugar. Mix well, add meat and bring quickly to a boil.

Reduce heat to moderate, add tamarind liquid and cook uncovered, until gravy is thick, stirring occasionally. Turn heat to low and continue cooking until gravy is almost dry, stirring frequently to ensure mixture does not catch to pan. At end of cooking time, approximately 2 1/2 hours, when oil separates from the gravy, add sugar and stir constantly. Allow meat to fry in the oily gravy until it is dark brown. Serve with white rice, one or two vegetable dishes, sambals, and prawn crisps.
Serves 8

✦

DRY-FRIED KIDNEY CURRY
Rendang Ginjal ✦ Indonesia

1½ lb (750 g) ox kidney
1 teaspoon finely grated fresh ginger
1 teaspoon finely chopped garlic
1 teaspoon salt
3 tablespoons peanut oil
2 onions, finely chopped or sliced
1 teaspoon ground turmeric
2 teaspoons ground coriander
1 teaspoon ground cumin
½ teaspoon ground fennel

½ teaspoon ground black pepper
1 teaspoon chili powder or 2 fresh red chilies, seeded and chopped
3 candlenuts, finely grated
2 cups (16 fl oz, 500 ml) coconut cream
1 small stick cinnamon
2 tablespoons tamarind liquid
2 teaspoons sugar

Wash kidneys, remove and discard core. Cut kidneys into small dice. Rub with ginger and garlic crushed with salt and set aside.

Heat oil and fry onions until they are soft and start to turn golden, stirring frequently. Add turmeric, coriander, cumin, fennel and pepper and stir-fry for 1 minute. Add chilies, candlenuts and kidneys, continue to fry, stirring constantly, until kidneys are browned. Add coconut cream and cinnamon and simmer gently, uncovered, until gravy is thick and reduced. This will take almost 2 hours of gentle simmering. Stir occasionally during simmering period. As mixture thickens it will be necessary to stir more frequently. Add tamarind liquid and sugar, stir and cook for a few minutes longer. Serve hot.
Serves 6

✦

DRY MEAT CURRY
Rendang ✦ Indonesia

2 lb (1 kg) beef or mutton
2 medium onions
2 cloves garlic
1 tablespoon chopped fresh ginger
3 tablespoons peanut oil
1 small stick cinnamon
4 or 5 whole cloves
3 teaspoons ground coriander
1 teaspoon ground cumin
1 teaspoon ground black pepper
1 teaspoon chili powder, or to taste
½ teaspoon ground fennel
½ teaspoon ground kencur (aromatic ginger)
3 tablespoons unsweetened desiccated coconut, toasted
4 cups (32 fl oz, 1 L) thin coconut cream
2 teaspoons salt
¼ cup (2 fl oz, 60 ml) tamarind liquid
1 cup (6 ½ oz, 200 g) thick coconut cream

Cut meat into large cubes. Finely slice one onion and set aside. Roughly chop the other onion and put into blender container with garlic and ginger. (If blender is not available, finely grate the onion, garlic, and ginger.) Blend to a smooth purée, adding

Curried meat balls (page 185).

2 tablespoons of thin coconut cream if necessary. Put meat into a bowl, mix well with ground ingredients and set aside.

In a large saucepan heat the oil and fry sliced onion and whole spices, stirring occasionally, until onion is soft and starts to turn golden. Add meat and fry until meat browns. Add ground spices, coconut, thin coconut cream and salt. Stir while bringing to a boil and continue stirring for about 10 minutes. Simmer uncovered until meat is almost tender. Add tamarind liquid, stir well and simmer until liquid is almost dry. Add thick coconut cream, stirring constantly, and allow to simmer again until oil separates from gravy and curry is very dry.
Serves 8

⬦⬦⬦

DUTCH FORCEMEAT BALLS
Frikkadels ✦ Sri Lanka

1 tablespoon butter
1 small onion, finely chopped
1 lb (500 g) ground (minced) steak
½ cup soft white breadcrumbs
1½ teaspoons salt
½ teaspoon ground black pepper
2 teaspoons chopped fresh dill or ½ teaspoon dried dill weed
¼ teaspoon ground cinnamon
½ teaspoon ground cloves
1 clove garlic, crushed
½ teaspoon finely grated fresh root ginger
2 teaspoons worcestershire sauce or lemon juice
1 egg, beaten
dry breadcrumbs for coating
oil or ghee for deep frying

Heat butter in a small frying pan and gently fry onion until soft. Combine with ground steak, breadcrumbs, salt, pepper, chopped dill, cinnamon, cloves, garlic, ginger, and worcestershire sauce, Mix thoroughly and form into small balls (approximately 1 in (2.5 cm) in diameter). Dip into beaten egg and coat with dry breadcrumbs. Deep fry in hot oil until golden brown. Drain on absorbent paper before serving.
Makes approximately 40

⬦⬦⬦

FRIED BEEF & LONG BEANS
China

12–15 long (snake) beans
12 oz (375 g) Scotch filet or rump steak
1 clove garlic, crushed
½ teaspoon finely grated fresh ginger
½ teaspoon salt
½ teaspoon five-spice powder
2 teaspoons cornstarch (cornflour)
1 tablespoon cold water
2 tablespoons oyster sauce
1 tablespoon soy sauce
2 tablespoons peanut oil
½ cup (4 fl oz, 125 ml) stock

Wash and cut beans into 2 in (5 cm) lengths. Shred beef finely and mix well with the garlic, ginger, salt, and five-spice powder. Mix cornstarch smoothly with water, stir in oyster sauce and soy sauce.

Heat oil in a wok or heavy frying pan, add beef and beans and stir-fry over high heat for 2 minutes. Add stock and allow to simmer until beans are just tender, then stir in cornstarch and sauce mixture and stir constantly until it boils and thickens. Toss the beef and beans in the sauce and serve at once.
Serves 3–4

❖

FRIED MEAT BALLS
Tod Man Nuer ◆ Thailand

4 oz (125 g) ground (minced) beef
4 oz (125 g) ground (minced) pork
¼ teaspoon ground black pepper
scant ½ teaspoon ground nutmeg
2 tablespoons finely chopped cilantro (fresh coriander leaves)
4 cloves garlic, crushed
½ teaspoon salt
1 scallion (spring onion), finely chopped
2 teaspoons fish sauce
1 tablespoon beaten egg
all-purpose (plain) flour
shortening (lard) for frying

Mix together the ground beef and pork. If the pork is very lean add a tablespoon of finely diced pork fat. Combine with all other ingredients except flour and shortening. Make small balls the size of a filbert (hazelnut) in its shell. Roll in flour and fry in hot shortening over medium low heat for 5 minutes or until cooked through and golden brown. Drain on absorbent paper.
Makes about 30 small balls

FRIED PORK & CRAB ROLLS
Vietnam

½ cup soaked cellophane noodles
1 small onion, finely chopped
6 scallions (spring onions), finely chopped
8 oz (250 g) ground minced pork
6 oz (185 g) crab meat, frozen or canned
½ teaspoon salt
1 tablespoon fish sauce
¼ teaspoon ground black pepper
half packet Chinese egg (spring) roll pastry
oil for deep frying

For Serving:
lettuce leaves
sprigs of mint and cilantro (fresh coriander leaves)
cucumber cut in julienne strips

Soak a small amount of cellophane noodles in hot water for 10 minutes, then drain and measure 1/2 cup. Roughly chop and put into a bowl with the onion, scallions, pork, flaked crab meat, salt, fish sauce, and pepper. Mix well. Cut each egg roll wrapper in half and put 2 teaspoons of filling on one end, shaping it into a neat roll. Roll up, turning in the sides so that the filling is completely enclosed. Moisten edge of wrapper with a little water or egg white to stick. Heat oil in a wok and fry a few rolls at a time on medium heat until they are crisp and golden. Do not have oil too hot or the filling will not cook through. Drain on kitchen paper.

To serve: Wrap each roll in a lettuce leaf including a sprig of mint, some cilantro and a strip of cucumber. Dip in nuoc cham sauce and eat immediately.

Nuoc cham sauce: Combine 1 teaspoon crushed garlic with 1 tablespoon chili sauce, 1 teaspoon sugar, 1 tablespoon lemon juice, 1 tablespoon vinegar, 1 tablespoon water, and 4 table-spoons fish sauce.
Makes about 24

❖

The meat dish in this Indonesian selection is dry meat curry or rendang, (page 186). In the background are vegetables in coconut gravy, (page 283) and in the foreground green bean sambal, (page 22).

FRIED PORK CURRY
Ooroomas Badun ◆ Sri Lanka

2 lb (1 kg) pork
3 tablespoons oil
10 curry leaves
¼ teaspoon fenugreek seeds, chopped
4 cloves garlic, finely chopped
1½ teaspoons finely grated fresh ginger
3 tablespoons Ceylon curry powder (page 8)
1–2 teaspoons chili powder
2 teaspoons salt
1 tablespoon vinegar
1 tablespoon tamarind pulp
1½ cups hot water
2 inch (5 cm) cinnamon stick
4 cardamom pods
1 cup thick coconut cream

Cut pork into large cubes. Heat oil in a large saucepan and fry curry leaves and fenugreek, if used, until they start to brown. Add onion and garlic and fry over a low heat until onion is soft and golden. Add ginger, curry powder, chili powder, salt, vinegar and pork. Fry on high heat, stirring thoroughly until meat is well coated with spice mixture. Squeeze tamarind pulp into hot water, strain and discard seeds. Add tamarind liquid, cinnamon and cardamom, cover and cook on low heat until pork is tender, about 1 hour. Add coconut cream and cook 10 minutes or more, uncovered.

Pour gravy into another saucepan, return pork to heat and allow to fry in its own fat. (If pork is not fat enough, add 1 teaspoon of oil of ghee to pan.) When pork is nicely brown, return gravy to pan and cook, uncovered, until gravy is thick. Serve hot with boiled rice.

Serves 6–8

FRIED PORK WITH SWEET-SOUR SAUCE
China

1 lb (500 g) pork filet
1 tablespoon light soy sauce
1 tablespoon Chinese wine or dry sherry
½ teaspoon salt
¼ teaspoon pepper
¼ teaspoon five-spice powder
1 cup (4 oz, 125 g) all-purpose (plain) flour
¾ cup (6 fl oz, 180 ml) warm water
1 tablespoon peanut oil

1 egg white
extra peanut oil for frying

Sweet-Sour Sauce:
1 tablespoon light soy sauce
2 tablespoons Chinese wine or dry sherry
3 tablespoons tomato sauce
1 tablespoon white vinegar
2 tablespoons white sugar
½ cup (4 fl oz, 125 ml) water
1 tablespoon cornstarch (cornflour)
1 tablespoon water
1 small onion
2 tablespoons peanut oil
1 clove garlic, crushed
¼ teaspoon finely grated fresh ginger
2 tablespoons preserved melon shreds

Cut pork into 1/2 in (12 mm) slices, then into 1 in (2.5 cm) squares. Mix with soy sauce, wine, salt, pepper, and five-spice powder. Refrigerate while preparing batter.

Mix flour and warm water to a smooth batter with a wooden spoon, stir in oil and allow to stand for 30 minutes. Beat egg white until stiff and fold in. Heat wok and add oil. When oil is hot, dip pieces of pork in batter and deep fry a few at a time over medium heat, until pork is cooked and batter golden. Drain on kitchen paper and set aside. Make sauce.

Sweet-Sour Sauce: Combine soy sauce, wine, tomato sauce, vinegar, sugar, and water in a bowl and stir until sugar dissolves.

Mix cornstarch smoothly with about 1 tablespoon cold water. Peel onion, cut into four lengthwise, then cut each quarter across into two. Separate layers of onion. Heat oil, add garlic, ginger and fry for 1 minute. Add combined sauce mixture, bring to a boil, then stir in cornstarch and cook, stirring constantly, until thickened. Remove from heat, stir in melon shreds.

Shortly before serving, reheat oil and once more fry pork, a few pieces at a time, on high heat for just a few seconds. This second frying makes the batter very crisp. Drain on kitchen paper and set aside. When all the pork is fried, arrange on a serving dish, pour hot sauce over and serve immediately, with hot white rice.

Serves 4–6

GOANESE KEBAB CURRY
Goani Kebab ◆ India

1 lb (500 g) lean lamb
1 lb (500 g) pork
thin slices fresh ginger
2 tablespoons ghee or oil
1 large onion, finely chopped
4 cloves garlic, finely chopped
2 fresh red or green chilies, seeded
1 tablespoon ground cumin
2 tablespoons black mustard seed, ground
2 teaspoons chili powder, or to taste
2 teaspoons garam masala
½ cup (4 fl oz, 125 ml) vinegar
½ cup (4 fl oz, 125 ml) water
2 teaspoons salt
½ teaspoon ground black pepper

Cut both meats into cubes and thread on bamboo skewers alternately with thin slices of tender ginger. Heat ghee or oil in a saucepan and fry the onion, garlic, and chilies until onion is soft and golden brown. Add the ground spices and continue stirring and frying for 1 minute. Add vinegar, water, salt, and

Fried pork and crab rolls (page 188).

Fried pork curry (page 190).

pepper. Let the mixture come to a boil, then put in skewers of meat, turn to coat in the spice mixture, cover and cook on very low heat, until meat is tender. Stir and turn kebabs once or twice during cooking. When meat is tender, cook uncovered until gravy is thickened and dark. Serve with white rice and accompaniments.

Serves 6

GROUND MEAT &
POTATO CURRY
North India

3 tablespoons oil or ghee
2 medium onions, finely chopped
1 teaspoon finely chopped garlic
1 teaspoon finely grated fresh ginger
½ teaspoon ground turmeric
2 teaspoons ground coriander
1 teaspoon ground cumin
½ teaspoon chili powder, optional
2 teaspoons salt
2 tablespoons lemon juice or vinegar
1 lb (500 g) ground lamb or beef
1 lb (500 g) potatoes, peeled and quartered
1 cup (8 fl oz, 250 ml) hot water
1 teaspoon garam masala (page 9)

Garnish:
2 tablespoons chopped fresh mint or cilantro (fresh coriander leaves)

Heat oil in a heavy saucepan and fry the onions, garlic, and ginger until soft and golden. Add turmeric, coriander, cumin, and chili powder and fry, stirring, for 1 minute. Add the salt and lemon juice and when it starts to sizzle fry the meat, stirring constantly, until all the meat is browned and any lumps broken up.

Add the potatoes and hot water, bring to simmering point, cover and cook on low heat until potatoes are done and meat tender, about 30 minutes. Stir occasionally towards end of this time to ensure curry does not catch to base of pan. Sprinkle the garam masala over, stir gently, then garnish with the chopped herbs. Serve with rice or Indian breads.

Serves 4–6

HOT BEEF CURRY
Malaysia

1 lb (500 g) stewing steak
5 red or green chilies
1 large onion, roughly chopped
1 teaspoon chopped garlic
1 teaspoon chopped fresh ginger
¼ cup (1 oz, 300 g) roasted peanuts
½ teaspoon ground nutmeg
½ teaspoon ground black pepper
1 teaspoon salt
1 tablespoon lemon juice
1 cup (8 fl oz, 250 ml) warm water
2 tablespoons peanut oil
1 tablespoon light soy sauce
3 daun salam or curry leaves

Cut meat into 2 in (5 cm) squares. Into an electric blender put chilies, onion, garlic, ginger, peanuts, nutmeg, black pepper, salt, and lemon juice. Blend to a paste, adding a little warm water to facilitate blending.

Heat oil in a saucepan, add contents of blender and cook for 5 minutes, stirring occasionally. Add meat and cook for a further 5 minutes. Add soy sauce, daun salam, and rest of warm water, stir well, cover and simmer until meat is tender and oil comes to the top. Stir occasionally to prevent meat catching to base of saucepan. Adjust seasoning and serve with hot rice and a sambal.

Serves 4

JAPANESE PORK CUTLET
Tonkatsu ◆ Japan

4 slices pork filet, cut as for schnitzel
4 tablespoons Japanese soy sauce
4 tablespoons mirin or dry sherry
1 clove garlic, crushed
pinch of sansho (Japanese pepper) or ground black pepper
1 egg, beaten
1 tablespoon finely chopped scallion (spring onion)
1 cup soft white breadcrumbs
oil for shallow frying
shreds of pickled ginger (shoga)

Marinate pork in mixture of soy, mirin, garlic, and pepper for 30 minutes. Mix egg and scallion together. Dip pork in egg and then in breadcrumbs, pressing them on firmly. Chill for 1 hour or longer.

Heat oil in a large, heavy frying pan and fry crumbed slices over medium heat until golden brown on both sides. Drain on absorbent paper, cut each one in slices and assemble again in original shape.

Serve on white rice and garnish with pickled ginger. A tempura-style dipping sauce may be served separately.

Serves 4

⋖⋗∞⋖⋗

JAVANESE-STYLE FRIED MEATBALLS

Pergedel Goreng Jawa ◆ Indonesia

1 lb (500 g) finely ground (minced) lean beef
2 medium onions, finely chopped
2 cloves garlic
1 teaspoon salt
2 fresh red chilies or 1 teaspoon sambal ulek (page 23)
1 lb (500 g) floury potatoes
1 tablespoon dark soy sauce
1 tablespoon lemon juice
2 teaspoons palm sugar or brown sugar
½ teaspoon trasi (dried shrimp paste)
3 tablespoons ground coriander
2 teaspoons ground cumin
1 teaspoon ground nutmeg or mace
1 egg, beaten
peanut oil for frying

Put ground beef into a large bowl. Add onions, garlic crushed with salt, and the chilies, which have been seeded and chopped very finely or, preferably, pounded to a paste with a mortar and pestle. Boil the potatoes, drain well, and dry them off in the pan before mashing until smooth. Add to the bowl. In the soy and lemon juice dissolve the sugar and trasi and mix in the coriander, cumin, and nutmeg. Pour over the ingredients in bowl together with the beaten egg. Mix very thoroughly with the hand and shape into small meatballs. Allow to stand for an hour.

Banquet firepot or sin sul lo from Korea (page 174).

Heat sufficient oil in a wok or frying pan to deep fry the balls. Add no more than 6–8 at a time to the hot oil and fry on medium heat until brown. This should take only 3 or 4 minutes. Drain on absorbent paper. Serve hot or as a cold snack.
Makes about 60–70 meatballs

KIDNEYS IN BLACK BEAN SAUCE
China

1 lb (500 g) pork, lamb or veal kidneys
1 red bell pepper (capsicum)
2 tablespoons canned salted black beans
2 cloves garlic
1 teaspoon sugar
2 tablespoons peanut oil
1 teaspoon finely grated fresh ginger
¼ cup (2 fl oz, 60 ml) water

Wash the kidneys, remove core and cut them into paper-thin slices. If the slices are large, cut to bite-size. Wash the kidneys under running cold water, then put into a large bowl, cover with cold water and leave to soak for half an hour. Drain, wash well once more until there is no trace of blood in the water. Drop into a saucepan of lightly salted boiling water, boil for 1 minute. Drain well and blot on absorbent paper.

Discard seeds and membrane and cut bell pepper into thin slices. Mash beans with fork. Crush garlic with sugar and mix with the mashed beans. Heat peanut oil and stir-fry the ginger and bell pepper for a few seconds, then add the bean mixture and fry for a few seconds longer. Add the water and stir while bringing to a boil, then add kidneys and cook, stirring, until they are coated with the bean sauce. Serve at once with small portions or rice.
Serves 4–6

KOFTA CURRY
North India

Koftas:
1½ lb (750 g) finely ground lamb
1 medium onion, finely chopped
½ teaspoon crushed garlic
½ teaspoon finely grated fresh ginger
1 red or green fresh chili, seeded and finely chopped
3 tablespoons chopped cilantro (fresh coriander leaves) or fresh mint

1½ teaspoons salt
1 teaspoon garam masala (page 9)
1½ teaspoons salt

Gravy:
3 tablespoons ghee or oil
2 medium onions, finely chopped
1 teaspoon finely chopped garlic
1 tablespoon finely chopped fresh ginger
1 teaspoon ground turmeric
1 teaspoon garam masala
1 teaspoon chili powder
2 ripe tomatoes, peeled and chopped
1 teaspoon salt
2 tablespoons chopped cilantro (fresh coriander) or mint
lemon juice to taste

Koftas: Mix ground lamb thoroughly with all the other ingredients. Shape into small balls.
Gravy: Heat ghee in a large, heavy saucepan, brown the koftas, remove from pan and set aside. In the same pan fry the onion, garlic, and ginger until soft and golden. Add turmeric, garam masala, and chili powder, fry for 1 minute. Add tomato, salt, and koftas, cover and simmer for 25 minutes or until gravy is thick and koftas tender. Stir in chopped herbs and lemon juice. Serve with rice or chapatis and various accompaniments.
Serves 6

LAMB & APRICOTS WITH POTATO STRAWS
Sali Jardaloo Boti ◆ India

8 oz (250 g) dried apricots
3 lb (1.5 kg) lean lamb or mutton
10 dried red chilies, seeds removed
1 tablespoon chopped fresh ginger
1 tablespoon chopped garlic
2 teaspoons ground cumin
3 tablespoons ghee or oil
2 large onions, finely chopped
1 teaspoon ground cinnamon
½ teaspoon ground cloves
½ teaspoon ground black pepper
½ teaspoon ground cardamom
1 lb (500 g) ripe tomatoes, peeled, seeded and chopped
2½ teaspoons salt
1 tablespoon jaggery or brown sugar
2 tablespoons malt vinegar

Lamb and apricots with potato straws (recipe opposite).

Garnish:
2 tablespoons chopped fresh coriander
1 cup potato straws

Soak apricots in water 30 minutes, drain. Cut meat into small cubes, discarding any fat. Soak chilies in hot water for 10 minutes. In an electric blender grind ginger, garlic, cumin, and chilies to a paste, adding a little water to facilitate blending. Marinate the meat in half this paste for 1 hour.

Heat ghee or oil in heavy saucepan and fry the onions until golden brown. Add remaining ground paste and the dry ground spices and stir well. Add meat and fry until browned, then add the tomatoes and salt, cover and cook on low heat until meat is tender, adding a little water if necessary. Lastly add jaggery or sugar, then vinegar and apricots, and simmer on very low heat for 15 minutes. Serve garnished with chopped coriander and potato straws.

Serves 6

LAMB & LENTIL PATTIES
Shami Kebab ◆ India (Uttar Pradesh)

1½ lb (750 g) finely ground (minced) lamb
1 medium onion, finely chopped
3 tablespoons mattar dhal (yellow split peas) or masoor dhal (red lentils)
1 teaspoon finely grated fresh ginger
1½ teaspoons finely chopped garlic
1½ teaspoons salt
2 cups (16 fl oz, 500 ml) water
½ teaspoon garam masala (page 9)
1 tablespoon yogurt or heavy (double) cream
1 small egg, beaten
ghee or oil for shallow frying

Filling:
1 fresh green chili, seeded and finely chopped
1 tablespoon finely chopped cilantro (fresh coriander leaves)
1 scallion (spring onion), including green leaves
½ teaspoon finely grated fresh ginger

Put lamb, onion, dhal, ginger, garlic, salt, and water into a heavy saucepan and bring to a boil, stirring. Cover and cook over low heat until meat, lentils, and onions are soft, about 45 minutes. Then uncover and cook, stirring now and then, until all the liquid has been absorbed. This may take at least 1 hour. Leave to cool, then mix in the garam masala and yogurt or cream. Add 1 tablespoon of beaten egg and mix well. If mixture is not very moist add more of the beaten egg. Knead very well for 10 minutes or until mixture is completely smooth.

Divide into 8 portions and form each into a flat circle. Put 1/2 teaspoonful of filling in the middle, close the meat mixture around it, pinching edges together. Flatten gently to form a small round patty. Shallow fry on a heavy griddle or frying pan lightly greased with ghee or oil. Serve hot. If serving these as cocktail snacks and making them bite-size, it is easier not to use a filling but to serve with fresh mint chutney (page 21) for dipping.

Filling: Chop scallion very finely. Mix all the ingredients together.
Makes 8 large or 24 cocktail-size patties

LAMB & POTATO CURRY
India

Make Lamb Curry (see below). For last 30 minutes of cooking time, add 2–3 cups (16–24 fl oz, 500–750 ml) hot water and 1 lb (500 g) potatoes, peeled and cut into quarters.

LAMB CURRY
India

3 lb (1.5 kg) boned shoulder of lamb
2 tablespoons ghee or oil
3 large onions, chopped
3 cloves garlic, chopped
1 tablespoon finely chopped fresh root ginger
2 tablespoons curry powder
3 teaspoons salt
2 tablespoons vinegar or lemon juice
3 large tomatoes, chopped
2 fresh red or green chilies
2 tablespoons chopped fresh mint
1 teaspoon garam masala
1 tablespoon chopped cilantro (fresh coriander leaves) or
*   extra mint*

Cut lamb into squares. Heat ghee in a saucepan and gently fry onion, garlic, and ginger until soft and golden. Add curry powder, salt, vinegar, stir thoroughly. Add lamb and cook, stirring continuously, until lamb is coated with the spice mixture. Add tomatoes, chilies, and mint, cover and cook over a very low heat for 1 1/4 hours or until lamb is tender, stirring occasionally. The tomatoes should provide enough liquid for the meat to cook in, but if necessary, add a little hot water, approximately 1/2 cup (4 fl oz, 125 ml), just enough to prevent meat from catching to saucepan. Add garam masala and chopped cilantro for last 5 minutes of cooking time.
Serves 6–8

LAMB KORMA
India

2 lb (1kg) boned leg of lamb
2 medium onions
1 tablespoon chopped fresh ginger
2 teaspoons chopped garlic
2–6 dried chilies, seeded
2 teaspoons ground coriander
1 teaspoon ground cumin
¼ teaspoon ground cinnamon
¼ teaspoon ground cardamom
¼ teaspoon ground cloves
½ teaspoon saffron strands or ¼ teaspoon powdered saffron
2 tablespoons boiling water
1 tablespoon ghee
2 tablespoons oil
2 teaspoons salt
½ cup (4 fl oz, 125 ml) natural yogurt
2 tablespoons chopped cilantro (fresh coriander leaves)

Cut lamb into large cubes, trimming off any excess fat. Peel onions, slice one finely and set aside. Chop other onion roughly and put into an electric blender with ginger, garlic, cashews, and chilies. Add 1/2 cup (4 fl oz, 125 ml) water to blender, cover and blend on high speed for a minute or until all ingredients are ground smoothly. Add all the ground spices and blend for a few seconds longer.

Put saffron strands into a small bowl, pour the boiling water over and allow to soak while starting to cook the masala (ground spice mixture).

Heat ghee and oil in a large saucepan and when hot put in the finely sliced onion and fry, stirring frequently with a wooden spoon, until soft and golden. Add the blended mixture and continue to fry, stirring constantly until the masala is well cooked and the oil starts to separate from the mixture. Wash out blender with an extra 1/4 cup (2 fl oz, 60 ml) water, add to pan together with salt and continue to stir and fry until the liquid dries up once more.

Add the meat and stir over medium heat until each piece is coated with the spice. Stir the saffron, crushing the strands against side of the bowl, then add to the pan. Stir to mix well. Add yogurt and stir again until evenly mixed. Reduce heat to low, cover and cook at a gentle simmer for 1 hour or until meat is tender and gravy thick. Stir occasionally, taking care that the spice mixture does not catch to base of pan. When lamb is tender, sprinkle with cilantro, replace lid and cook for 5 minutes longer. Serve hot with rice.

Serves 6

✦※✦

LAMB WITH SPICES AND YOGURT
Roghan Josh ◆ India & Pakistan

1½ lb (750 g) lean lamb
3 dried red chilies, seeded
½ cup hot water
6–8 cloves garlic
1 tablespoon finely grated fresh ginger
2 tablespoons dessicated coconut, toasted
2 tablespoons blanched almonds
1 tablespoon ground coriander
1 teaspoon ground cumin
1 teaspoon poppy seeds
½ teaspoon ground fennel
½ teaspoon ground cardamom
¼ teaspoon ground cloves
¼ teaspoon ground mace
½ teaspoon ground black pepper
4 tablespoons ghee or oil
1 medium onion, finely chopped
4 cardamom pods, bruised
½ teaspoon ground turmeric
½ cup yogurt
2 ripe tomatoes, peeled and chopped
1½ teaspoons salt
1 teaspoon garam masala (page 9)
2 tablespoons chopped cilantro (fresh coriander leaves)

Cut the lamb into large cubes. Soak chilies in the hot water for 5 minutes. Put garlic, ginger, coconut (shake in a dry pan over medium heat to toast), almonds, and chilies together with 2 tablespoons of the soaking water in a blender. Put ground coriander, cumin, poppy seeds, and fennel in a small pan and shake over low heat for a few minutes until spices darken slightly in color and give off an aromatic smell. Add to the ingredients in blender. Blend for a few seconds until smooth. Remove from blender container and add the ground cardamom, cloves, mace, and pepper. Set aside.

Heat ghee in a large heavy saucepan and fry the chopped onion, stirring, until onion is golden brown. Add bruised cardamoms, turmeric and the blended spice mixture and fry, stirring until well cooked and the ghee starts to separate from the spices. Add the yogurt, a spoonful at a time and stir it in. Add tomatoes and salt, stir and fry for a further 5 minutes, then add the cubed lamb and cook over high heat, stirring and turning meat so that each piece is coated with the spice. Turn heat very low, cover and cook for 1 hour or longer. Lamb should be very tender and liquid almost absorbed. Stir occasionally to ensure that spices don't catch to base of pan. Sprinkle with garam masala, replace lid and cook 5 minutes longer. Serve sprinkled with cilantro and accompanied by plain rice or a pilau.

Serves 6

✦※✦

LIVER CURRY
Malaysia

2 lb (1 kg) calves' liver, diced
2 tablespoons unsweetened desiccated coconut
2 teaspoons chopped garlic
4 candlenuts or 3 brazil kernels, chopped
4 fresh red chilies
2 teaspoons ground coriander
1 teaspoon ground cumin
1 teaspoon ground fennel
1 stem lemon grass chopped or 2 strips lemon rind
2 teaspoons dried shrimp paste
1½ teaspoons salt
4 tablespoons peanut oil
1 large onion, thinly sliced
½ cup (4 fl oz, 125 ml) thin coconut cream

Roast desiccated coconut in a dry pan until golden brown. Remove to a plate and when cool put into blender with the garlic, nuts, chilies, coriander, cumin, fennel, lemon grass, shrimp paste, and salt. Blend to a smooth paste adding a little hot water to facilitate blending.

Heat oil in a saucepan and fry onion till soft and golden. Add blended spices and fry till they smell aromatic and oil comes to the surface. Add diced liver and coconut cream and simmer till cooked, stirring contents occasionally. Serve with rice and accompaniments.

Serves 4–6

MADURESE-STYLE LAMB SATAY

Sate Kambing Madura ◆ Indonesia

1 lb (500 g) boneless lamb from leg
1 small onion, grated
2 cloves garlic, crushed
½ teaspoon salt
*1 teaspoon sambal ulek (page 23), or 2 fresh red chilies, seeded
    and crushed*
½ teaspoon trasi (dried shrimp paste)
1 tablespoon tamarind liquid
1 tablespoon dark soy sauce
2 tablespoons fresh grated or unsweetened desiccated coconut

Cut lamb into small cubes. Combine grated onion with all other ingredients. If using desiccated coconut, moisten with a tablespoon of hot water. Mix marinade well into the meat, cover and leave at room temperature for 2 hours or longer in refrigerator. Thread on bamboo skewers. Broil (grill), turning frequently and taking care that the coconut does not burn. Serve with rice and spicy satay sauce (page 16).
Serves 4–6

***

MALAY SATAY

Malayasia

2 lb (1 kg) rump steak
1 medium onion, chopped
1 tablespoon finely chopped fresh root ginger
3 cloves garlic
1 tablespoon lemon juice or tamarind liquid
2 teaspoons salt
1 tablespoon ground coriander
1 teaspoon ground cumin
1 teaspoon ground curry leaves
¼ teaspoon ground cardamom
½ teaspoon ground cinnamon
½ teaspoon ground black pepper
1 tablespoon ground rice

Cut steak into small cubes. Place onion, ginger, garlic, lemon juice, and salt into blender container, cover and blend on high speed until smooth. Heat coriander and cumin in a dry frying pan until they darken slightly, stir or shake constantly to prevent burning. Combine blended mixture, coriander and cumin, and remaining ingredients in a mixing bowl. Add meat and rub the mixture well in. Marinate for at least 1 hour. (If possible, prepare the previous day, cover and refrigerate.)

   At serving time, thread meat on bamboo skewers and cook over glowing coals or under a hot broiler (grill) until meat is tender. Place on a serving plate and serve with Peanut Sauce (page 16).
Serves 8–10

***

MEAT & COCONUT PATTIES

Rempah-Rempah ◆ Indonesia

8 oz (250 g) unsweetened desiccated coconut
6–7 tablespoons hot water
1 lb (500 g) finely ground (minced) beef
½ teaspoon trasi (dried shrimp paste)
2 cloves garlic
1½ teaspoons salt
½ teaspoon ground black pepper
1½ teaspoons ground coriander
1 teaspoon ground cumin
½ teaspoon ground kencur (aromatic ginger)
2 eggs, beaten
peanut oil for deep frying

Put coconut into a bowl and sprinkle hot water over. Mix well until all the coconut is moistened. Put into a large bowl with the ground beef. Crush trasi with back of spoon and dissolve in a tablespoon of hot water. Crush garlic and salt to a smooth paste. Add all the spices, the garlic, and trasi to the beaten eggs and mix well. Pour over the meat and coconut in the bowl. Mix and knead well with the hands so that spices are evenly distributed and mixture becomes smooth. Shape into small hamburger shapes or into small balls. Shallow fry the hamburger shapes, or deep fry the balls, until they are crisp and golden brown all over. Drain on absorbent paper and serve as an accompaniment to a rice dish or as a snack by themselves. Serve cold at picnics. The balls, made small enough, are ideal to serve with drinks.
Makes 30 flat hamburger shapes or 60 small balls

***

MEAT & POTATO CURRY

India

3 lb (1.5 kg) hogget or beef
¼ cup (2 fl oz, 60 ml) oil or 2 tablespoons ghee
1 teaspoon black mustard seeds
½ teaspoon fenugreek seeds
3 teaspoons finely chopped garlic
1 tablespoon finely chopped fresh ginger
3 medium onions, finely sliced

1½ teaspoons ground turmeric
2 tablespoons ground coriander
1 tablespoon ground cumin
2 teaspoons chili powder
3 teaspoons salt
2 tablespoons vinegar
2 teaspoons garam masala (page 9)
2 tablespoons extra vinegar
1½ lb (750 g) potatoes, peeled and cubed
2 tablespoons chopped cilantro (fresh coriander leaves)

Trim fat and gristle from meat and cut into small cubes. Heat oil in a large saucepan and fry the mustard seeds until they pop. Add fenugreek seeds, garlic, ginger, and onion and fry over medium heat, stirring occasionally with a wooden spoon, until onions just begin to brown. Add turmeric and fry for a minute longer. Add coriander, cumin, and chili powder and stir for a minute or so, then add salt and vinegar and stir until liquid dries up. Sprinkle in the garam masala and mix well. Add the cubed meat, stirring so that all the pieces are coated with the spice mixture. If some of the spice begins to catch to the base of the pan, add the extra vinegar and stir, scraping as much as possible from the base of the pan.

Reduce heat, cover with well-fitting lid and let meat and spice mixture simmer for 1 1/2 to 2 hours or until meat is tender. Depending on the type of meat used, it may be necessary to add a little water. Add the cubed potatoes, cover once more and cook for 20 to 25 minutes or until done. Sprinkle with cilantro and serve hot with rice or Indian bread.
Serves 6–8

⪻⪼

MEAT WITH PALM SUGAR

Jaggery Satay ◆ Sri Lanka

1½ lb (750 g) round, blade or other lean steak
2 tablespoons tamarind pulp
1 cup (8 fl oz, 250 ml) hot water
2 teaspoons chili powder, or to taste
½ teaspoon ground black pepper
½ teaspoon salt or to taste
¼ cup chopped jaggery (palm sugar) or 2 tablespoons black or brown sugar
⅓ cup (3 fl oz, 90 ml) oil

Cut meat into 3/4 in (2 cm) cubes. Soak the tamarind pulp in hot water for 10 minutes, then squeeze to release all the pulp from the seeds. Strain. If more pulp is left on the seeds, add a little more water and dissolve this too. Strain again, preferably through a fine nylon sieve. Add chili powder, pepper, salt, and

sugar and stir to dissolve sugar.

In a small frying pan heat the oil until very hot and fry a small portion of the meat at a time (divide meat into 5 or 6 portions) until the cubes are lightly browned. This generally takes only 1 minute if the oil is hot enough and not too much is put in at one time. Lift out with slotted spoon and put into a saucepan. Wait until oil stops spitting, then add and fry next batch. Repeat until all the meat has been fried, putting each batch into a saucepan.

Pour the tamarind mixture over the beef, bring to a boil, then allow to simmer, covered, until meat is tender and the gravy very much reduced. Thread on skewers and serve with white rice.
Serves 6

⪻⪼

MEATBALLS WITH WATER CHESTNUTS & CELERY

China

1 lb (500 g) ground (minced) topside of beef or ground pork and veal
½ teaspoon crushed garlic
1 teaspoon finely grated fresh ginger
½ teaspoon salt
½ teaspoon pepper
1 tablespoon light soy sauce
2 teaspoons cornstarch (cornflour)
1 small egg, beaten
2 tablespoons finely chopped water chestnuts
2 tablespoons peanut oil
1 tablespoon dark soy sauce
1 tablespoon Chinese wine or dry sherry
½ teaspoon sesame oil
¼ cup (2 fl oz, 60 ml) water
1 cup finely sliced celery
5 water chestnuts, sliced into rounds
3 scallions (spring onions), cut in bite-size lengths
½ cup sliced bamboo shoot, optional

Combine ground meat with garlic, ginger, salt, pepper, and soy sauce mixed with cornstarch. Add egg and chopped water chestnuts and mix thoroughly. Form into 20 small balls.

Heat peanut oil in a wok or frying pan and brown the meatballs lightly, a few at a time. Remove to a dish. When all the meatballs have been browned, pour off oil and wipe out pan with kitchen towels. Return meatballs to pan and add the dark soy sauce, sherry, sesame oil, and water. Cover and simmer for 10 minutes, turning the meatballs over halfway through. Add celery, water chestnuts, scallions, and bamboo shoot and cook on high heat, stirring, for 1 minute. Serve hot.
Serves 4–6

MONGOLIAN LAMB
China

2 lb (1 kg) boned leg of lamb
1 tablespoon sugar
1 teaspoon salt
2 tablespoons dark soy sauce
1 egg
¼ teaspoon baking soda (bicarbonate of soda)
1 oz (30 g) cornstarch (cornflour)
4 tablespoons peanut oil
1 teaspoon finely chopped garlic
1 scallion (spring onion), finely sliced
¼ teaspoon five-spice powder
1 heaped tablespoon hoi sin sauce
1 teaspoon hot bean sauce
1 tablespoon Chinese wine or dry sherry

Trim away all fat, skin, and gristle and cut the lean meat into bite-size, paper-thin slices. Soak in cold water for 30 minutes. Rinse until water runs clear, then drain well and squeeze out excess water. Add sugar, salt, soy sauce, egg, baking soda (for tenderizing), and cornstarch. Mix well, then add 1 tablespoon of the peanut oil and mix again. Leave to marinate at least 2 hours.

Heat a wok, add 2 tablespoons peanut oil, and on very high heat stir-fry the lamb till browned. Remove lamb from wok. Heat remaining 1 tablespoon oil over low heat, add garlic and scallion and cook gently until they start to turn golden. Add the five-spice powder, hoi sin sauce, and bean sauce, return lamb to wok, and toss over high heat. Add wine, mix and serve at once.
Serves 4–6

※

MOSLEM BEEF CURRY
Thailand

2 lb (1 kg) stewing beef
2 tablespoons peanut oil
2 teaspoons finely chopped garlic
1 large onion, sliced
2 tablespoons Moslem curry paste (page 12)
2 tablespoons basil leaves or 2 teaspoons dried basil
1 teaspoon chili powder
2 teaspoons sugar
2 in (5 cm) cinnamon stick
2 teaspoons salt
1 cup (8 fl oz, 250 ml) warm water
4 tablespoons thick coconut cream

Garnish:
½ cup (2 oz) chopped, roasted peanuts

Cut beef into 2.5 cm (1 in) squares. Heat oil in a saucepan and add garlic and sliced onion and fry till golden brown. Add meat and brown on high heat, stirring frequently.

Stir in the curry paste, basil leaves, chili powder, sugar, cinnamon, and salt. Add water and bring to a boil, cover and simmer till meat is tender and oil comes to the surface. Stir in the coconut cream, simmer 2 minutes longer uncovered and serve garnished with chopped peanuts.
Serves 6–8

MU SHU PORK
China

8 oz (250 g) boneless lean pork
2 teaspoons light soy sauce
2 teaspoons Chinese wine or dry sherry
2 teaspoons cornstarch (cornflour)
4 dried Chinese mushrooms
30 dried lily buds
2 tablespoons dried wood fungus (cloud ears)
1 piece canned winter bamboo shoot
2 scallions (spring onions)
1 whole egg and 1 egg yolk
½ teaspoon salt
3 tablespoons peanut oil
1 teaspoon sesame oil

Sauce:
1 tablespoon oyster sauce
1 tablespoon Chinese wine or dry sherry
1 tablespoon light soy sauce

For serving:
hoi sin or sweet chili sauce
scallion (spring onion) tassels
Mandarin Pancakes (page 301)

Partially freeze the pork until it is firm enough to cut into very thin slices, then into shreds. Use a very sharp knife for slicing. Mix with soy sauce, wine, and 1 teaspoon of the cornstarch. Refrigerate for at least 30 minutes.

Meanwhile, put the dried mushrooms and lily buds into a bowl, cover with very hot water and soak for 30 minutes. Drain, discard the mushroom stems and cut the mushroom caps into thin strips. Discard the hard tips of the lily buds and tie each bud into a knot.

Soak the wood fungus in cold water for 10 minutes. Drain,

Meatballs with water chestnuts and celery (page 199).

pinch off any hard, gritty portions and cut into smaller pieces.

Shred the bamboo shoot into matchstick strips. Finely slice the scallions. Combine the sauce ingredients with 4 tablespoons of water. Beat the egg and yolk together with the salt.

Heat a wok, add 1 tablespoon of the peanut oil and pour in the beaten egg. Swirl the pan, then stir and cook until the egg is firm without browning. Remove from heat and cut into small pieces with a wok chan (spatula). Immediately turn out onto a dish. Wipe the wok with absorbent paper.

Reheat the wok, add another tablespoon of peanut oil and stir-fry the bamboo shoot and scallions on high heat for 1 minute. Remove to plate.

Heat the remaining tablespoon of peanut oil. On high heat, stir-fry the pork, mushrooms, and lily buds until the pork browns. Add the sauce mixture, cover the wok and cook for 3 minutes. Mix the remaining teaspoon of cornstarch with 1 tablespoon of cold water and stir into the sauce until it boils and thickens.

Return the scallions, bamboo shoot and wood fungus to the wok. Drizzle the sesame oil over and stir rapidly together. Remove from heat and fold in the cooked egg.

Serve hot with scallion tassels and Mandarin Pancakes (page 301).

Serves 4

Mu shu pork, from China (recipe opposite).

⋘⋙

MUTTON & LENTIL RISSOLES
Shami Kebab ◆ **Malaysia**

4 oz (125 g) red lentils or yellow split peas
2 cups (16 fl oz, 500 ml) water
8 oz (250 g) lean finely ground (minced) mutton, lamb, or
  beef
2 medium onions, finely chopped
¼ teaspoon ground cinnamon
¼ teaspoon ground cardamom
⅛ teaspoon ground cloves
1 teaspoon salt
½ teaspoon ground black pepper
1 egg, beaten
2 tablespoons finely chopped mint
oil for frying

Wash the red lentils or split peas well and put into a saucepan with the water. Bring to a boil, add meat and onions, cook on medium low heat, stirring occasionally until lentils are cooked. Stir as mixture becomes dry and continue cooking until liquid is completely absorbed. Turn into a bowl and when cool enough to handle mix in the spices and seasonings, egg, and mint. Mix thoroughly, then shape into flat round patties. Fry in shallow hot oil until golden brown on both sides. Drain and serve hot.
Serves 4

⋘⋙

MUTTON CURRY
Mutton Bohlapuri ◆ **India (Maharashtra)**

2 lb (1 kg) lean mutton
6 green chilies, seeded and roughly chopped
3 tablespoons chopped cilantro (fresh coriander leaves)
3 teaspoons chopped garlic
1 tablespoon chopped fresh ginger
1 teaspoon ground turmeric
4 tablespoons ghee or oil
4 medium onions, finely chopped
1 cup (8 fl oz, 250 ml) water
2 teaspoons salt
2 tablespoons unsweetened desiccated coconut
1 teaspoon fennel seeds
1 teaspoon white poppy seeds, optional
1 tablespoon ground coriander
1 tablespoon ground cumin
¼ teaspoon grated nutmeg

8 oz (250 g) tomatoes, peeled and chopped
8 oz (250 g) potatoes, peeled and cubed
1 cup (8 oz, 250 ml) thin coconut cream
Garnish:
1 large onion
pakorha batter (see Savory Vegetable Fritters, page 58)
oil for deep frying

Trim off any fat and cut mutton into cubes. Grind chilies, coriander, garlic, ginger, and turmeric to a paste in electric blender, adding as little water as necessary to facilitate blending. Marinate the meat in this mixture for 2 hours or longer.

Heat ghee or oil in a large, heavy saucepan and fry the onions, stirring, until golden brown. Add meat and fry on high heat until browned. Add water and salt and simmer, covered, until meat is tender, about 30 minutes. Meanwhile roast the coconut, fennel seeds, and white poppy seeds (if used) separately in a dry pan until golden brown, stirring constantly. Grind very fine in blender or pound with a mortar and pestle. Add to pan together with the coriander, cumin, nutmeg, tomatoes. Stir well, cover and cook for 20 minutes. Add the potatoes and a little water if necessary, continue cooking for a further 20 minutes or until potatoes are cooked. Stir in coconut cream and cook uncovered for a further 10 minutes. Serve hot, garnished with onion ring pakorhas (fritters) and accompanied by rice or puris.

Garnish: Cut onion into fairly thick slices and separate into rings. Dip in pakorha batter and deep fry in hot oil. Drain on absorbent paper.
Serves 6–8

⋘⋙

MUTTON KEBAB
Botee Kebab ◆ **India & Pakistan**

1 lb (500 g) mutton
2 tablespoons unsweetened desiccated coconut
1 large onion, roughly chopped
2 cloves garlic, peeled
1 teaspoon chopped fresh ginger
¼ teaspoon each ground nutmeg, cinnamon, cloves, and
  cardamom
½ teaspoon coarsely ground black pepper
1 teaspoon poppy seeds
½ cup yogurt

Trim mutton of excess fat but leave a thin layer, for it gives a delicious crisp layer when broiled (grilled). Cut meat into bite-size cubes.

Toast the coconut in a dry frying pan over medium heat,

stirring constantly, until golden brown. Set aside to cool.

Put onion, garlic, and ginger into container of electric blender and grind to a smooth purée. Add spices, toasted coconut, poppy seeds, and yogurt and blend again for 1 minute or until coconut is finely ground. Pour over the pieces of meat in a bowl and rub well into the meat so that every piece is well covered with the spice marinade. Cover and leave in the refrigerator overnight or at room temperature for 2 hours. Thread the pieces on bamboo skewers and cook under a preheated broiler (grill) or over glowing coals until brown. Serve with chapatis, parathas or rice, accompanied by onion sambal or other salad type of relish.

Serves 4–6

<hr>

MUTTON KOFTAS IN SAFFRON SAUCE

Rista ✦ India (Kashmir)

2 lb (1 kg) boneless lamb
½ teaspoon ground cardamom
1 teaspoon garam masala
2 teaspoons salt
3 tablespoons arrowroot
2 tablespoons cold water
1 teaspoon ground turmeric
3 teaspoons chili powder, or to taste
2 tablespoons ghee
2 tablespoons oil
4 oz (125 g) finely sliced French shallots or brown onions
2 teaspoons finely chopped fresh ginger
4 whole brown cardamoms or small green cardamoms, bruised
4 whole cloves
1 small stick cinnamon
2 teaspoons paprika
2 teaspoons tomato paste
¼ teaspoon saffron strands
2 tablespoons boiling water

Cut the meat into 1 in (2.5 cm) cubes and divide into four portions. Process one portion at a time in food processor, using steel chopping blade, until it is a smooth, thick paste. Mix in the ground cardamom, garam masala, salt, and the arrowroot mixed smoothly with the cold water. Form into large balls and parboil in lightly salted water for 10 minutes, adding half the turmeric and chili powder to the water.

Heat ghee and oil, fry the onions and whole spices. Add remaining turmeric, chili powder, paprika, and tomato paste. Add the meat balls and the stock in which they were cooked. Cover

and simmer until tender. Dissolve saffron in the boiling water and add towards end of cooking. Serve hot with plain white rice.

Serves 6

MUTTON WITH FENUGREEK

Methi Maaz ✦ India (Kashmir)

2 bunches fresh fenugreek or 1 bunch spinach
1 lb (500 g) lamb
3 tablespoons ghee or mustard oil
1 large onion, finely chopped
1 teaspoon finely chopped garlic
2 teaspoons finely chopped fresh ginger
1 teaspoon chili powder, or to taste
1 teaspoon ground turmeric
2 ripe tomatoes, peeled and chopped
2 teaspoons salt
1 teaspoon garam masala (page 9)

Wash the greens well and discard any tough stalks. Cut the meat into small cubes. Heat ghee or oil and gently fry onion, garlic, and ginger until soft and golden. Add chili powder and turmeric, stir, then add meat to the pan and fry, stirring, until it browns. Add tomatoes and salt and a little water. Cover and simmer on very low heat until meat is almost tender. If liquid evaporates, add a little hot water. Add the fenugreek, sprinkle with garam masala and continue cooking until greens are cooked to a pulp, the meat completely tender and oil comes to the surface. Serve hot with rice or chapatis.

Note: If you cannot get fresh fenugreek herb, use spinach as a substitute, adding 2 tablespoons of dried fenugreek leaves.

Serves 6

<hr>

NONYA SPICED SPARERIBS

Malaysia

3 lb (1.2 kg) pork spareribs
4 cloves garlic
1½ teaspoons salt
½ teaspoon ground black pepper
½ teaspoon five-spice powder
1 tablespoon honey
1 tablespoon sesame oil
3 tablespoons soy sauce
½ cup hot water

Separate the spareribs with a sharp knife or ask the butcher to do it for you. Crush garlic with salt, combine with pepper, five-spice powder, honey, sesame oil, and soy sauce. Rub well over the spareribs. Place spareribs in a roasting pan and cook in a moderate oven. After 30 minutes, turn spareribs, add hot water to pan and continue roasting, basting with liquid every 10 minutes, for a further 30 minutes.

Alternatively, heat 1–2 tablespoons peanut oil in a large heavy frying pan and brown spareribs. Add water, cover and simmer for 30–35 minutes or until tender.

Serve hot with boiled rice and plum sauce.

Serves 6

PORK & BAMBOO SHOOT IN BLACK BEAN SAUCE
China

1½ lbs (750 g) pork belly
1 teaspoon salt
1 bamboo shoot, canned
2 tablespoons canned salted black beans
1 tablespoon Chinese wine or dry sherry
1 tablespoon soy sauce
2 cloves garlic
2 tablespoons oil
2 cups (16 fl oz, 500 ml) hot water

With a sharp knife remove and discard skin and cut pork into 1 in (2.5 cm) squares. Sprinkle 1/2 teaspoon salt over pork, mix well and set aside. Cut bamboo shoot into thin slices, then into pieces about 1 in (2.5 cm) across. Rinse beans in a strainer, running cold water through for a few seconds. Drain beans, put on chopping board and mash with a fork. Combine in a bowl with the wine and soy sauce. Crush garlic with remaining 1/2 teaspoon salt and add.

Heat oil in a wok and fry the pork on high heat for 3 or 4 minutes or until brown, stirring all the time. Add bamboo shoot and bean mixture and fry for a few minutes longer. Then add hot water, stir once, cover and simmer 40 minutes. Serve with boiled rice.

Serves 6

PORK & SHRIMP BALLS
Almondigas ◆ The Philippines

8 oz (250 g) ground (minced) pork
8 oz (250 g) raw shrimp (prawns)
1 scallion (spring onion), finely chopped

½ teaspoon salt
1 tablespoon oil
1 medium onion, finely chopped

2 cloves garlic, crushed
½ teaspoon Chinese shrimp sauce
3 cups hot water
salt and pepper to taste
½ cup meesua (fine wheat noodles)

Shell and devein shrimp and chop very finely. Combine shrimp, pork, scallion and salt, mix well and form into balls the size of a large marble. Heat oil and fry onion and garlic gently until goden brown. Add shrimp sauce and water, bring to a boil and drop in the balls a few at a time, keeping the water boiling. Simmer 8 minutes or until the balls are cooked, drop in the noodles and remove from heat. Cover and stand 5 minutes, then add pepper and salt to taste and serve hot.

Note: If meesua are not available, use rice vermicelli but allow to cook for 1 minute before removing from heat.

Serves 4

PORK COOKED WITH SUGAR
Thit Heo Kho Kho ◆ Vietnam

2–2½ lb (1–1.25 kg) pork belly or loin
2 tablespoons oil
3 scallions (spring onions), finely chopped
good pinch ground black pepper
2 teaspoons sugar
½ teaspoon salt
4 cups (1¾ pts, 1 L) water
2 tablespoons fish sauce

Cut pork into large cubes. Do not discard fat, for this is a delicious way of cooking it. Heat oil in a large saucepan and fry the scallions gently until golden. Add pork and fry, stirring, until pork loses its pinkness, then add sugar, salt, and pepper, and continue stirring until meat is browned. Add water and simmer without covering pan for 1 hour. Add fish sauce and continue to simmer until the pork is almost dry, taking care to stir frequently as liquid reduces or the pork may burn. Serve with plain white rice.

Serves 6–8

PORK CURRY
Sri Lanka

2 lb (1kg) pork belly
8–10 large dried chilies
1½ cups (12 fl oz, 375 ml) hot water
1 tablespoon tamarind pulp
½ teaspoon ground turmeric
1 medium onion, roughly chopped
5 cloves garlic
1½ teaspoons chopped fresh ginger
2 in (5cm) cinnamon stick
2 teaspoons salt
1 stem lemon grass or 2 strips lemon rind
10 curry leaves
¼ teaspoon fenugreek seeds
1 strip daun pandan or rampe leaf, optional
½ cup (4 fl oz, 15 ml) thick coconut cream
1 tablespoon oil or melted ghee
1 small onion, finely sliced
2 tablespoons lemon juice

Cut the pork into 2 in (5 cm) pieces and put into a saucepan. Remove stalks and seeds from dried chilies and soak them in half the hot water for 10 minutes. Soak and dissolve tamarind pulp in remaining hot water, strain out seeds and fibers. Put chilies and soaking water into blender with the turmeric, roughly chopped onion, garlic, and ginger and blend until smooth. Pour over pork in pan, add cinnamon and strained tamarind water. Add salt, half each of the lemon grass, curry leaves, fenugreek seeds, and pandan or rampé leaf. Bring to a boil, then turn heat low, cover and simmer until pork is tender. Add coconut cream and simmer, uncovered, for 10 minutes longer.

In another pan heat the oil or ghee and fry the sliced onion and the remaining lemon grass, curry leaves, fenugreek seeds, and pandan or rampé. When onion is golden brown, transfer to the cooked pork mixture and add the lemon juice, stir and simmer on very low heat for about 5 minutes. Serve with rice and accompaniments.
Serves 8

PORK SATAY
Sate Babi ◆ Indonesia

2 lb (1 kg) pork filet or boned pork loin
1 medium onion, roughly chopped
1 clove garlic
1 teaspoon chopped fresh ginger
3 tablespoons tamarind liquid or lemon juice

2 tablespoons dark soy sauce
1 teaspoon sambal ulek (page 23) or 2 fresh red chilies, seeded and chopped
½ teaspoon salt
1 teaspoon palm sugar or brown sugar
2 tablespoons peanut oil

Ask butcher to remove rind from pork loin. Cut pork into small cubes about 3/4 in (2 cm) square. Put onion, garlic, ginger, tamarind liquid, soy sauce, sambal ulek or chilies, salt, and sugar into blender container and blend until smooth. Pour into a bowl, stir in oil, then add cubed pork and stir until all the pieces are well coated with marinade. Leave for at least 1 hour or longer in the refrigerator. Thread 5 or 6 pieces on skewers – don't push them too close together and leave the end of skewer free for holding. Leaving space between pieces enables them to cook more evenly. Broil (grill) over glowing coals or under preheated broiler (grill) for 6 or 7 minutes on each side, or until pork is well cooked through and brown on all sides. Do not put too close to source of heat or outside will be brown before pork is cooked through.

Note: Soak bamboo skewers in water for a few hours before using. This helps prevent the ends of the skewers burning.
Serves 6

PORK STRIPS, DRY-COOKED
Thit Heo Kho Tieu ◆ Vietnam

1½ lb (750 g) lean pork chops
2 tablespoons water
2 tablespoons fish sauce
1 tablespoon sugar
3 scallions (spring onions), thinly sliced
¼ teaspoon ground black pepper

Remove skin and bones from pork chops, and cut meat into thin strips. Put into a small, deep saucepan – the little liquid there is must not be allowed to evaporate over a large surface area. Add all other ingredients and bring to a boil over high heat. Stir, cook for 2 minutes on high heat, then reduce heat to medium and boil for 20 minutes or until liquid is completely absorbed. Stir towards end of cooking time so that meat does not burn. It will turn brown. Serve with white rice and a green vegetable or salad.
Serves 6–8

PORK VINDALOO
South India

2 lb (1kg) pork
6–8 large dried red chilies
1 cup (8 fl oz, 250 ml) vinegar, preferably coconut vinegar
2 teaspoons chopped fresh ginger
4 teaspoons chopped garlic
2 teaspoons ground cumin
½ teaspoon ground black pepper
½ teaspoon ground cinnamon
½ teaspoon ground cardamom
¼ teaspoon ground cloves
¼ teaspoon ground nutmeg
2 teaspoons salt
2–3 tablespoons ghee or oil
2 medium onions, finely chopped
1 tablespoon brown sugar

Cut pork into cubes. Soak chilies in vinegar for 10 minutes. If available use coconut vinegar for authentic taste, but any kind of vinegar may be substituted, diluting it if it is very strong. Put chilies and vinegar, ginger, garlic, all the ground spices, and salt into blender and blend until chilies are finely ground. Pour this mixture over the pork in an earthenware bowl, cover and marinate for 2 hours.

Heat enough ghee or oil to cover base of an enamel or stainless steel saucepan. (This dish is cooked in earthenware pots in India and if one is available it would be an advantage.) Fry the onions on low heat until soft and golden, stirring frequently. Drain pork from the marinade and fry on medium high heat, stirring, until lightly brown. Pour in marinade, cover pan and simmer on low heat until pork is tender, about 1 1/2 hours. Stir in sugar. Serve with plain white rice.
Serves 6–8

PORK WITH ABALONE, SICHUAN-STYLE
China

8 oz (250 g) lean pork filet
16 oz (500 g) canned abalone
2 tablespoons peanut oil
1 teaspoon finely chopped fresh ginger
1 clove garlic, finely chopped
1 teaspoon cornstarch (cornflour)
1 tablespoon cold water
1 teaspoon chili sauce

Cut pork into very thin slices. Drain canned abalone, reserving liquid from can. Cut abalone into paper-thin slices.

Heat oil in wok with ginger and garlic, add pork and stir-fry over high heat until browned. Add 1/2 cup (4 fl oz, 125 ml) liquid from can of abalone, cover and simmer for 10 minutes. Add cornstarch mixed with cold water, stir until boiling and thickened, then stir in chili sauce. Mix well. Add abalone slices and leave only just long enough to heat through, about 1 minute. Abalone must not be overcooked or it will be tough. Serve with small portions boiled rice or noodles.
Serves 4–6

PORK WITH BRAISED ENGLISH SPINACH
Korea

1 bunch fresh English spinach
8 oz (250 g) pork shoulder
2 tablespoons peanut oil
1 teaspoon finely chopped garlic
2 tablespoons light soy sauce
¼ teaspoon ground black pepper
1 cup diced canned bamboo shoot
5 scallions (spring onions), finely chopped
½ teaspoon sesame oil
3 tablespoons toasted, crushed sesame seeds

Wash spinach well, remove tough stem and break leaves into large pieces. Dice the pork very small. Heat wok, add oil and when hot fry the pork and garlic, stirring constantly, until pork is golden. Add spinach and toss well, season with soy sauce and pepper. Cover and simmer on low heat until pork is tender. Add bamboo shoot, scallions, and sesame oil and stir well over medium heat for 2 minutes. Sprinkle with sesame seeds and serve hot with rice.
Serves 4

PORK WITH SWEET CUMQUATS
China

12 oz (375 g) pork filet or lean pork chops, boned
1 tablespoon Chinese wine or dry sherry
1 tablespoon light soy sauce
1 teaspoon grated fresh ginger
1 tablespoon cornstarch (cornflour)
3 scallions (spring onions)
peanut oil for deep frying
8 sweet cumquats preserved in syrup

Sauce:
2 tablespoons Chinese wine or dry sherry
1 tablespoon sugar
1 tablespoon light soy sauce
2 tablespoons white vinegar
1 tablespoon cumquat syrup
1 teaspoon cornstarch (cornflour)

Cut the pork into small squares. Marinate in wine, soy sauce, and ginger for 20 minutes.

Stir the cornstarch into the pork and marinade. Cut the scallions diagonally into short lengths. Combine the sauce ingredients with 1 tablespoon of water.

Heat a wok, add oil for deep frying and when hot, fry the pork in three or four batches until brown and cooked through. Drain. Pour the oil from the wok into a heatproof bowl and reserve for future use.

Return 1 tablespoon of the oil to the wok and gently cook the scallions. Add the pork and sauce mixture, stirring constantly until heated through. Lastly stir in the cumquats. Serve immediately on a bed of stir-fried lettuce (page 282).
Serves 4

RED COOKED BEEF
See Yo Ngau Yook ♦ China

3 lb (1 kg) shin of beef in one piece
3 cups (24 fl oz, 750 ml) cold water
1½ cups (12 fl oz, 375 ml) soy sauce
¼ cup (2 fl oz, 60 ml) chinese wine or dry sherry
2 in (5 cm) piece fresh root ginger, peeled and sliced
2 whole cloves garlic, peeled
2 whole star anise
2 tablespoons sugar
1 tablespoon sesame oil

Put beef in a saucepan just large enough to hold it. Add all other ingredients, bring to a boil, then turn heat low so that it simmers very gently. Cover and simmer for 3 hours or until beef is very tender. Test by piercing with a skewer – it should be able to penetrate easily. Turn beef once or twice so that all of it is immersed in the liquid at some time during cooking. Uncover pan and cook for a further 15 minutes, pouring sauce over the beef with a ladle every 5 minutes. Let the beef cool in the sauce, turning it over after an hour. Chill until serving time, then place on a board and with a sharp Chinese chopper, cut into very thin slices. Arrange on a dish.

Note: Save the master sauce, as the cooking liquid is now called, and freeze it for future use. A spoonful added to a dish in place of stock will give a rich, delicious flavor. If whole star anise is difficult to obtain, use about 16 of the broken sections.
Serves 10–12 as part of a meal

Pork with sweet cumquats (recipe this page).

RED CURRY OF BEEF
Thailand

2 lb (1 kg) stewing steak
2 cups (16 fl oz, 500 ml) thick coconut cream
3 tablespoons red curry paste (page 12)
2 cups (16 fl oz, 500 ml) thin coconut cream
2 sprigs tender citrus leaves
1 tablespoon dried makrud rind, soaked
1 teaspoon salt
2 tablespoons fish sauce
2 fresh red chilies, seeded and sliced

Trim the meat and cut into cubes. Use undiluted canned coconut cream, checking the label to ensure it does not have a stabilizer. Simmer this in a large saucepan, stirring constantly, until it comes to a boil, then cook over a low heat until the cream thickens and the oil starts to show around the edges. Add the curry paste and fry for 5 minutes or so, stirring constantly.

When done, the curry paste will smell fragrant and mellow, and oil will start to separate from the mass again. Add beef and stir well, then add thin coconut cream. Add all remaining ingredients. Stir while bringing to a boil, then lower heat and simmer uncovered until beef is tender. If the beef is not yet tender and the gravy seems to be cooking away, add a little more coconut cream or hot water and stir. The gravy should be rich and red, and there should be quite a lot of it. Serve with white rice and side dishes.
Serves 6

SEARED FILET STEAK
IN PLUM SAUCE
China

1 lb (500 g) filet steak
2 tablespoons light soy sauce
1 tablespoon Chinese wine or dry sherry
1 teaspoon grated ginger
1 teaspoon sugar
1 clove garlic, crushed in ½ teaspoon salt
1 Chinese (Napa) cabbage
peanut oil for deep frying
½ teaspoon sugar
6 scallions (spring onions)
2 tablespoons oil
4 tablespoons plum sauce

Trim the beef, removing all fat and gristle. Cut into 1/2 in (12 mm) slices. Press each slice of meat with the palm of your hand to flatten it slightly. Combine the soy sauce, wine, ginger, sugar, and garlic. Add the beef and turn the slices to coat them. Leave to marinate for 1 hour or longer.

Meanwhile shred the green leaves of the cabbage very finely. Heat oil in a wok for deep frying and when hot, add the shredded cabbage. Scoop it out with a wire spoon almost immediately. Drain and sprinkle it with the sugar to keep crisp.

Cut the scallions into 1 inch (2.5 cm) lengths.

Heat a wok, add 1 tablespoon of the oil and when hot, fry half of the beef, pressing the slices against the wok and turning to brown both sides. Remove and set aside. Add the remaining tablespoon of oil to the wok and when hot, cook the remaining beef. Add the scallions and first lot of meat and toss together.

Stir in plum sauce and about 1 tablespoon of water. Cook for about 1 minute until thoroughly heated. Serve on a bed of crisp-fried Chinese cabbage.
Serves 4–6

SESAME LAMB ON
CRISP NOODLES
China

1 lb (500 g) lean lamb chops
1 teaspoon sugar
½ teaspoon salt
1 tablespoon light soy sauce
1 egg white
peanut oil
2 teaspoons cornstarch (cornflour)
3 scallions (spring onions)
1 small red bell pepper (capsicum)
½ teaspoon crushed garlic
2 oz (60 g) bean starch (transparent) noodles or rice vermicelli

Sauce:
4 teaspoons purchased sesame sauce
3 tablespoons dark soy sauce
3 tablespoons Chinese wine or dry sherry
1 teaspoon sugar
½ teaspoon chili oil (optional)

Trim all the fat from the lamb and remove the bones. Cut the meat into very thin slices. Mix with the sugar, salt, and soy sauce. Leave for 10 minutes

Add the egg white, 1 tablespoon of peanut oil and the cornstarch. Mix well and chill for 30 minutes.

Seared filet steak with plum sauce (recipe opposite).

SHREDDED BEEF WITH ASPARAGUS
China

12 oz (375 g) lean steak
½ teaspoon baking soda (bicarbonate of soda)
2 onions
1 bunch asparagus
5 tablespoons peanut oil

Marinade:
2 teaspoons dark soy sauce
2 teaspoons cornstarch (cornflour)
½ teaspoon sugar
1 tablespoon Chinese wine or dry sherry

Sauce:
1 tablespoon light soy sauce
1 tablespoon bottled oyster sauce
1 tablespoon water
2 teaspoons cornstarch (cornflour)

Cut the scallions into bite-size pieces. Slice the pepper into strips.

Heat a wok, add 3 tablespoons of peanut oil. When hot, add the garlic, scallions, and bell pepper, and stir-fry for 10 seconds. Then add the meat and stir-fry until it browns. Remove and set aside.

Add all ingredients for the sauce to the wok, add 3 tablespoons of water and stir over low heat until it is smooth. Return the lamb and vegetables to the wok and stir until heated. Serve on a bed of fried noodles.

To prepare the noodles: Heat 12 fl oz (375 ml) of peanut oil in a wok and when hot, add about a quarter of the noodles at a time. They will puff and turn white instantly. Drain on absorbent kitchen paper. They may be done beforehand, but store them in an airtight container until served.
Serves 4

Cut the meat into fine shreds, discarding any fat. Dissolve the baking soda in 4 tablespoons of water, pour this over the meat and knead well until the meat absorbs the liquid. Refrigerate for 2 hours or longer if possible. This tenderizes economical cuts of meat. If time is short, use a tender cut of beef and omit this step.

Peel the onions and cut them in half lengthwise, then cut each half into six wedges. Snap off any tough ends of asparagus and discard; cut the stalks into 2 in (5 cm) lengths.

Combine the marinade ingredients, add to the meat and mix well. Leave to marinate for about 20 minutes. In a small bowl, mix the sauce ingredients.

Heat a wok, add 2 tablespoons of the peanut oil and stir-fry the onions over high heat for 1 minute. Remove the onions to a plate.

Add 2 tablespoons of peanut oil to the wok and when very hot, add the meat and toss over high heat until browned. Put the meat aside with the onions.

Wipe out the wok and heat the remaining tablespoon of peanut oil. Stir-fry the asparagus for 1 minute. Then add 2 fl oz (60 ml) hot water, cover the wok and cook for 3 minutes or until the asparagus is tender but still crisp.

Add the sauce ingredients and stir until boiling and slightly thickened. Then return the beef and onions to the wok and toss together until heated through. Serve hot.
Serves 3–4

SHREDDED BEEF WITH HOT SESAME SAUCE

Vietnam

12 oz (375 g) rump steak
3 tablespoons peanut oil
1 teaspoon finely chopped garlic
2 tablespoons dark soy sauce
½ cup (4 fl oz, 125 ml) beef stock
3 teaspoons cornstarch (cornflour)
2 tablespoons cold water
1 tablespoon sesame paste
1 table Chinese chili sauce

Garnish:
3 tablespoons chopped cilantro (fresh coriander leaves)

Shred rump steak into very thin strips. Heat peanut oil in a wok, add garlic and meat and stir-fry over high heat until meat has browned, about 2 minutes. Add soy sauce and stock and bring to a boil, then stir in cornstarch mixed smoothly with cold water, stirring until it boils and thickens. Turn off heat, stir in sesame paste and chili sauce. Garnish with cilantro and serve with hot white rice.
Serves 2–3

❧

SHREDDED FIVE-SPICE BEEF WITH BROCCOLI

China

1 lb (500 g) beef filet or rump
1 clove garlic, crushed
1 teaspoon salt
½ teaspoon fresh ginger, grated
3 teaspoons cornstarch (cornflour)
½ teaspoon five-spice powder
8 oz (250 g) broccoli
2 tablespoons water
1 tablespoon soy sauce
3 tablespoons peanut oil
2 teaspoons sesame oil

Cut beef into very thin slices, then cut slices into fine shreds. Remove any fat. Crush the garlic with the salt and rub garlic and ginger into beef, mixing thoroughly. Mix 2 teaspoons cornstarch and the five-spice powder together and sprinkle over beef. Toss to distribute evenly. Slice broccoli thinly, or divide into small sprigs. Mix together the remaining cornstarch, water, and soy sauce.

Heat oils in a wok and when hot add the beef and fry, over high heat, stirring constantly, for 2 minutes or until meat is browned. Add broccoli and fry for 3 minutes, stirring and tossing ingredients together all the time. Add cornstarch mixture and stir until it boils and thickens, then stir well to coat beef and broccoli with sauce. Serve immediately with boiled rice or noodles.
Serves 4–5

❧

SKEWERED BEEF & MUSHROOMS

Sanjuck ✦ Korea

8 oz (250 g) lean rump or round steak
2 tablespoons sesame oil
1 tablespoon soy sauce
2 teaspoons toasted, crushed sesame seeds
1 clove garlic, crushed
½ teaspoon sugar
pinch ground pepper
½ teaspoon crushed fresh chili
6 oz (185 g) fresh mushrooms
12 scallions (spring onions)
all-purpose (plain) flour for dipping
2 large egg, beaten
oil for frying

Cut slice of steak into 1/4 in (6 mm) strips, then cut strips into 2 in (5 cm) lengths. Combine oil, soy sauce, sesame seed, and garlic crushed with sugar, pepper, and chili. Pour mixture over the meat in a bowl, mix and leave to marinate while preparing other ingredients. Slice mushrooms thickly if large, or cut into halves if small. Wash and trim scallions to where the green leaves start to separate, then cut the solid part into 2 in (5 cm) lengths. On bamboo skewers thread alternately pieces of meat, onion, and mushrooms. Cut skewers in half if they are too long to fit into your frying pan, but thread two lots of ingredients on before you cut them so you have the pointed end for easy threading.

Dip skewers in flour, then in beaten egg. Heat enough oil to cover base of frying pan. Oil should be hot, but not smoking. Put skewers in pan and cook until brown and crisp, 2 or 3 minutes on each side. Serve immediately with white rice.
Serves 4–5

❧

SPICED RIBS OF LAMB

Tabak Maaz ◆ India (Kashmir)

3 lb (1.5 kg) ribs of lamb
1 teaspoon chopped garlic
3 tablespoons chopped cilantro (fresh coriander leaves)
½ cup (4 fl oz, 125 ml) milk
1½ cups (12 fl oz, 375 ml) water
1 teaspoon ground turmeric
1 teaspoon chili powder
½ teaspoon ground cardamom
½ teaspoon ground fennel
¼ teaspoon ground black pepper
2 teaspoons salt
1½ cups (12 fl oz, 375 ml) water
1 teaspoon ghee
1 tablespoon oil

Remove all excess fat and cut the lamb ribs in short lengths, two or three ribs to a piece.

Combine the garlic, coriander, and milk in a blender, mix in the ground spices and salt. Put into pressure cooker with meat and water. Bring to pressure and cook for 15 minutes. Turn off heat, allow pressure to drop, then open pan and cook until almost all liquid has evaporated. Alternatively, put in saucepan with water to cover and cook until tender. Take ribs from pan and allow to drain. In a heavy frying pan heat the ghee and oil and shallow fry the pieces of lamb ribs, pressing them down against the pan with a frying slice so that they get nicely browned. Drain on absorbent paper, serve hot. The ends of the ribs may be decorated with silver foil. Any liquid left after boiling the ribs may be reduced to make a delicious sauce once the fat has been spooned off.

Serves 6–8

SPICY MUTTON CURRY

Gulai Kambing ◆ Malaysia

1½ lb (750 g) lamb or mutton
4 tablespoons unsweetened desiccated coconut
¼ cup (2 fl oz, 60 ml) tamarind liquid
2 large onions, roughly chopped
2 teaspoons chopped garlic
1 tablespoon roughly chopped fresh ginger
2 teaspoons ground coriander
1 teaspoon each ground cumin and turmeric
½ teaspoon each ground cinnamon, fennel, nutmeg, and black pepper
¼ teaspoon each ground cloves and cardamom

4 candlenuts
4–8 dried red chilies, or to taste
2 tablespoons peanut oil
2 ripe tomatoes, chopped
1½ cups (12 fl oz, 375 ml) thin coconut cream
1½ teaspoons salt
1 stem fresh lemon grass, finely sliced, or 1 grass, finely sliced, or 1 teaspoon finely chopped lemon rind.

Cut meat into small cubes. Brown the coconut in a dry frying pan, stirring constantly over medium low heat for 4 or 5 minutes or until it is a rich golden-brown color. Set aside. Pour 1/4 cup (2 fl oz, 60 ml) very hot water over a walnut-size piece of dried tamarind pulp and leave for 5 minutes. Squeeze the tamarind in the water to dissolve. Strain through a fine sieve.

In a blender put the tamarind liquid and onions and blend to a smooth, thick liquid. Add garlic and ginger and blend again. Add the spices, candlenuts, dried chilies, and, last of all, the toasted coconut. Blend until smooth and well combined.

Heat the oil in a large saucepan and fry the blended mixture for 5 minutes, stirring frequently at the beginning and constantly at the end. Add meat and fry for 3 minutes, stirring well so that each piece is coated with spices. Add tomato and fry for a further 3 minutes. Add coconut cream, salt, and lemon grass and bring slowly to a boil. Reduce heat to very low and simmer, uncovered, until meat is tender, stirring now and then. This may take from 1 1/2 to 2 hours.

Serve with white rice.

Serves 6

SPICY SATAY

Sate Bumbu ◆ Indonesia

1 lb (500 g) lean steak, topside, round or blade
2 tablespoons dark soy sauce
2 tablespoons tamarind liquid
1 medium onion, roughly chopped
2 cloves garlic
½ teaspoon laos powder
½ teaspoon sambal ulek (page 23)
½ teaspoon ground black pepper
½ teaspoon trasi (dried shrimp paste)
2 tablespoons peanut oil
½ cup (4 fl oz, 125 ml) thin coconut cream
1 daun salam or 3 curry leaves
1 stalk lemon grass or 2 strips lemon rind
2 teaspoons palm sugar or brown sugar

Trim meat and cut into long strips 3/4–1 in (2–2.5 cm) wide and about 1/4 in (6 mm) thick. Put soy sauce, tamarind liquid, onion, and garlic into container of blender and blend to a smooth paste. (If blender is not available, finely grate onion and garlic, then mix with the liquid.) Mix in laos powder, sambal ulek, pepper, and crushed trasi. Heat peanut oil in a wok or frying pan and fry the blended mixture, stirring constantly until it turns brown and comes away from sides of pan. Add meat and fry, stirring, for a minute or so, until browned. Add coconut cream, curry leaves, lemon grass, and sugar. Stir, reduce heat and simmer uncovered until sauce is very thick and almost dry.

Thread the meat on bamboo skewers, one strip to each skewer, looping it like a ruffled ribbon. Keep meat at pointed end of skewer, leaving the rest of the skewer for holding. It may be wise to wrap strips of foil around exposed end of skewer. Broil (grill) over hot coals or under preheated broiler (grill) until lightly touched with brown. If there is any leftover sauce in pan, spoon it over the satay to serve.
Serves 4–5

⋘⋙

STEAMBOAT DINNER
China

1 lb (500 g) filet or rump steak
1 lb (500 g) lean pork filet
8 oz (250 g) fresh or frozen scallops
16 oz (500 g) canned abalone
4 oz (125 g) snow peas (mangetout) or sliced green (string)
  beans
4 squares fresh bean curd
8 oz (250 g) fresh bean sprouts
12 oz (375 g) Chinese cabbage (gai choy or choy sum)
1 lb (500 g) fresh raw shelled and deveined shrimp (prawns)
8–10 cups (3–4 pts, 2–2.5 L) chicken stock

Trim all fat from beef and place in the freezer until partially frozen and firm enough to cut into paper-thin slices. Arrange on plate. Do the same with the pork.

Thaw scallops if frozen and wash well, removing any sandy tracts. Drain canned abalone, reserving liquid from can to add to stock. Cut abalone into paper-thin slices.

String snow peas and leave whole, or string beans and cut into thin diagonal slices. Cut squares of bean curd into thin slices. Wash bean sprouts and pinch off any straggly brown tails. Wash Chinese cabbage and cut stems into bite-size pieces. Arrange ingredients, including shrimp, on separate plates or two large plates.

Set each place with a plate, chopsticks, bowl, porcelain spoon, and small sauce dish. Prepare steamboat, filling the moat three-quarters full with hot stock, place it on the table and let the stock come to a boil before removing the cover of the steamboat.

Guests select their food and hold it in the bubbling stock, about 30 seconds for a slice of steak to 90 seconds or so for a medium-size shrimp. Abalone needs to be heated only for a few seconds – long immersion in the stock will toughen it. It is best to cook one type of food at a time.

When all the meats and seafood have been cooked and eaten, add the vegetables to the broth, replace the lid and simmer for a few minutes, then ladle the soup into bowls.
Serves 6

⋘⋙

STEAMED BEEF WITH SNOW PEAS
China

12 oz (375 g) lean steak
½ teaspoon finely grated fresh ginger
2 teaspoons min sze jeung (bean sauce)
1 tablespoon Chinese wine or dry sherry
1 teaspoon sesame oil
2 oz (60 g) snow peas (mangetout)

Cut steak into paper-thin slices, across the grain of the beef. Combine the ginger, bean sauce, wine, and sesame oil and marinate the beef in the mixture for at least 1 hour. This may be done beforehand and the meat refrigerated.

Put meat into a heatproof dish, cover and steam over boiling water for 30 to 40 minutes, until beef is almost tender. Add snow peas and steam for a further few minutes. Serve with a vegetable dish or small portions of rice.
Serves 2–4

⋘⋙

STEAMED FIVE-FLOWERED PORK
Jing Ng Far Nam ◆ China

2 lb (1 kg) lean, skinless pork belly
4 tablespoons dark soy sauce
2 tablespoons Chinese wine or dry sherry
½ teaspoon five-spice powder, optional
1 clove garlic, crushed
½ cup (3 ½ oz, 100 g) uncooked rice

Cut pork into large squares and marinate in a mixture of soy sauce, wine, five-spice powder, and garlic for at least an hour, preferably longer.

Roast uncooked rice in a heavy frying pan over medium low heat, stirring constantly, for 15 minutes or until the grains are golden. Put into container of blender and blend on high speed until ground to powder. If blender is not available, pound a little at a time using a mortar and pestle.

Roll pieces of pork, one at a time, in the rice powder and put them into a heatproof dish. Steam over rapidly boiling water for 2 hours or until the pork is so tender it can easily be broken with chopsticks. Serve hot, accompanied by steamed white rice.

Serves 6

⋘∞⋙

STIR-FRIED CUCUMBERS WITH BEEF
Oyi Jikai ◆ Korea

8 oz (250 g) lean rump or filet steak
2 teaspoons sesame oil
1 tablespoon light soy sauce
½ teaspoon salt
½ teaspoon sugar
¼ teaspoon cayenne
2 large green cucumbers
1 tablespoon vegetable oil
2 tablespoons toasted, crushed sesame seeds

Freeze the beef for a short time until firm enough to cut into paper-thin slices. Slices should be about 2 in (5 cm) long and 1/2 in (12 mm) wide. Put beef in a bowl and add sesame oil, soy, salt, sugar, and cayenne. Mix well with the hand.

Peel cucumbers, leaving a thin strip of green skin at intervals for decorative effect. Cut in halves lengthwise, scoop out seeds, then cut crosswise into medium-thin slices.

Heat the oil in a wok, swirl wok to coat with oil, add beef and stir-fry on high heat for 1 minute. Add cucumbers and toss for a further minute, then let mixture simmer until cucumber is half cooked. It should be tender but still crisp. Garnish with sesame seeds and serve hot with white rice.

Serves 4

⋘∞⋙

STIR-FRIED BEEF & VEGETABLES IN OYSTER SAUCE
China

1 lb (500 g) filet or rump steak
2 tablespoons soy sauce
½ teaspoon salt
1 tablespoon Chinese wine or dry sherry
1 lb (500 g) mixed vegetables (see note below)
3 tablespoons peanut oil
1 large clove garlic, finely chopped
½ teaspoon fresh root ginger, finely grated
½ cup (4 fl oz, 125 ml) stock or water
3 teaspoons cornstarch (cornflour)
2 tablespoons cold water
2 tablespoons oyster sauce
4 scallions (spring onions)

Slice meat very, very thinly against the grain and cut into shreds approximately 1 1/2 in (3.5 cm) long. Combine soy sauce, wine, salt, and mix well with the beef. Let it stand while preparing the vegetables.

Use any combination of vegetables and cut them into pieces the same size as the beef. Heat 1 tablespoon of the oil in a wok, add ginger, and garlic, stir for 3 or 4 seconds, then add all the vegetables and stir constantly over high heat for 2 1/2 to 3 minutes. Remove from heat and turn into a bowl, together with any liquid in wok.

Heat wok again, add remaining 2 tablespoons oil and when very hot put in the beef and stir-fry over high heat about 2 minutes or until browned. Add stock and bring to a boil, then add cornstarch mixed smoothly with the cold water and return to a boil, stirring constantly. Cook until liquid thickens, about 1 minute. Stir in oyster sauce, return fried vegetables and toss well together. Add scallions, and serve immediately with boiled rice.

Serves 4

⋘∞⋙

STIR-FRIED BEEF WITH BELL PEPPERS

China

1 lb (500 g) beef filet or rump
1 clove garlic
1 teaspoon salt
1 teaspoon finely grated fresh ginger
½ teaspoon five-spice powder
1 large red bell pepper (capsicum)
1 large green bell pepper (capsicum)
2 teaspoons cornstarch (cornflour)
5 tablespoons cold water
2 tablespoons dark soy sauce
2 teaspoons sesame oil
2 tablespoons peanut oil

Trim off all fat from the beef. Leave in the freezer for about 2 hours, long enough for it to be firm enough to cut into paper-thin slices.

Crush garlic with salt, and rub into beef with the ginger and five-spice, mixing well.

Remove stem, seeds, and membranes from bell peppers and cut into thin slices. In a small bowl, mix the cornstarch, water, soy sauce, and sesame oil, together.

Heat a wok and when hot, add 1 tablespoon of the peanut oil and heat for a further 30 seconds, swirling the wok to coat the surface. Add the pepper strips and stir-fry over high heat for 1 minute. Remove from wok.

Add the remaining tablespoon of peanut oil and heat again, then add the beef and fry over high heat for 2 minutes, stirring constantly, until the beef browns. Add the cornstarch mixture and stir until it boils and thickens. Then return the pepper strips to the wok and combine with beef.

Serve immediately accompanied by rice or noodles.

Serves 4–6

⬥⬥⬥

STIR-FRIED BEEF WITH CELLOPHANE NOODLES

Korea

8 oz (250 g) tender steak
1 teaspoon sugar
1 tablespoon soy sauce
2 teaspoons finely chopped scallions (spring onions)
1 teaspoon finely chopped garlic
1 teaspoon finely chopped fresh ginger
1 teaspoon ground toasted sesame seeds

¼ teaspoon ground black pepper
2 tablespoons sesame oil
2 oz (60 g) cellophane noodles
4 oz (125 g) white Chinese (Napa) cabbage
4 oz (125 g) canned bamboo shoot
1 medium-size carrot
1 medium-size onion
1 large cucumber
few leaves English spinach
peanut oil for stir-frying
soy sauce, sugar, salt, and pepper to taste

Garnish:
2 eggs

Cut beef into paper-thin strips and marinate in a bowl with a mixture of the sugar, soy sauce, scallion, garlic, ginger, sesame seeds, pepper, and sesame oil.

Soak cellophane noodles in hot water for 20 minutes, then drain and cut into 4 in (10 cm) lengths. Cut cabbage into thin strips and the bamboo shoot and carrot into matchstick strips. Peel the onion, cut in half and slice finely. Peel the cucumber, cut in half lengthwise and scoop out seeds, then cut into thin strips. Wash the spinach well, steam until soft and cut into shreds.

Garnish: Separate eggs and beat yolks and whites separately with a fork. Lightly grease a wok with oil, preferably sesame oil, and pour in the beaten yolks. Swirl pan to make a very thin omelet. When set, turn and cook other side. Do not allow to brown. Turn onto a plate. Repeat with egg whites. Cut yellow and white omelet into fine strips.

Heat a tablespoon of oil and stir-fry the vegetables, each one separately, until cooked but still crisp. Remove vegetables to a plate. Heat remaining oil, stir-fry the beef and noodles. Mix all together on a large plate, season to taste with soy, sugar, salt, and pepper according to taste. Garnish with omelet strips and serve very hot.

Serves 4

⬥⬥⬥

STIR-FRIED GARLIC BEEF & MUSTARD CABBAGE

China

12 oz (375 g) flank (skirt) steak
½ teaspoon baking soda (bicarbonate of soda)
1 teaspoon sugar
1 teaspoon cornstarch (cornflour)
6–8 dried Chinese mushrooms
1 small bunch gai choy (Chinese mustard cabbage), about
* 8 oz (250 g)*

Stir-fried beef with bell peppers (recipe opposite).

Stir-fried garlic beef & mustard cabbage (recipe opposite).

4 cloves garlic
1 teaspoon salt
4 tablespoons peanut oil
2 teaspoons sesame oil

Sauce:
1 tablespoon Chinese wine or dry sherry
1 tablespoon dark soy sauce
2 tablespoons oyster sauce

Remove any fat from the meat. Slice the meat thinly across the grain.

In a bowl, dissolve the baking soda in 5 tablespoons of water. Add the sugar, cornstarch, and sliced meat and knead the liquid well into the meat until the liquid is absorbed. Refrigerate for 2 hours or overnight.

Soak the mushrooms in hot water for 30 minutes. Discard the mushroom stems, and cut the caps into halves (or quarters, if large).

Wash the gai choy and drain it well, then slice diagonally, discarding any tough ends of outer leaves.

Crush the garlic in the salt. Combine the ingredients for the sauce in a small bowl.

Heat a wok, add 3 tablespoons of the peanut oil and swirl the wok to coat its sides. Add beef and stir-fry over high heat until browned. Remove to a plate.

Add the remaining 1 tablespoon of peanut oil to the wok. When hot add the gai choy, garlic, and mushrooms, and stir-fry for 1 minute. Return the meat to the wok and continue to cook for 30 seconds. Add the sauce mixture and stir through. Turn off the heat and stir in the sesame oil. Serve immediately with boiled rice.
Serves 3–4

STIR-FRIED LAMB WITH CHILI & GARLIC

China

1 lb (500 g) lamb leg steaks (or shoulder chops)
1 tablespoon light soy sauce
2 teaspoons grated fresh ginger
2 teaspoons cornstarch (cornflour)
1 tablespoon Chinese wine or dry sherry
1 teaspoon sugar
3 scallions (spring onions)
8 oz (250 g) canned water chestnuts
4 oz (125 g) snow peas (mangetout)
2 teaspoons crushed garlic
2 teaspoons bottled chili bean sauce
5 tablespoons peanut oil

Sauce:
2 tablespoons dark soy sauce
1 tablespoon sugar
1 tablespoon Chinese wine or dry sherry
2 teaspoons cornstarch (cornflour)
2 teaspoons Chinese black vinegar
4 tablespoons water

Trim and discard the skin, fat, and bones from the steaks. Cut the meat into strips. Combine the soy sauce, ginger, cornstarch, wine, and sugar. Add the lamb strips and mix well. Leave to marinate for 30 minutes.

Finely chop the scallions. Drain the water chestnuts and halve them. Combine the sauce ingredients in a small bowl. String and wash the snow peas. Combine the garlic and the chili bean sauce.

Heat a wok until very hot. Add 4 tablespoons of the peanut oil and swirl to coat the wok. Add the lamb and stir-fry over high heat until the meat browns. Add the scallions, water chestnuts, and snow peas, and fry for about 30 seconds.

Push the meat and vegetables to one side of the wok, add the remaining tablespoon of peanut oil in the middle, and fry the garlic and chili bean sauce, stirring, for a few seconds until it smells fragrant.

Stir the sauce ingredients again because the cornstarch will have settled at the bottom, add this to the wok and stir until the sauce is thick and clear. Toss the meat and vegetables in the sauce, and serve at once. Garnish with sliced cucumber and scallion flowers.

Serves 6

⪻∞⪼

STIR-FRIED PORK WITH CELLOPHANE NOODLES
China

4 oz (125 g) cellophane noodles
6 dried Chinese mushrooms
8 oz (250 g) pork
2 tablespoons Chinese wine or dry sherry
1 tablespoon light soy sauce
1 teaspoon salt
1 cup (8 fl oz, 250 ml) stock or mushroom liquid
1 teaspoon cornstarch (cornflour)
3 tablespoons peanut oil
5 scallions (spring onions), finely chopped
2 teaspoons finely chopped fresh ginger
2 tablespoons chili bean sauce
2 fresh red chilies, seeded and finely chopped
4 tablespoons chopped cilantro (fresh coriander leaves)

Put the noodles in a large bowl, pour over boiling water to cover, and leave to soak 10 minutes. Strain noodles and cut into short lengths and set aside. Soak mushrooms in hot water for 30 minutes, squeeze dry, cut off and discard stems, dice caps finely and reserve soaking water. Cut pork into paper-thin, bite-size strips. Mix wine, soy, salt, stock, and cornstarch together in a small bowl and set aside.

Heat wok, add oil and swirl to coat wok. When oil is hot, add the pork and mushrooms and stir-fry until cooked and brown. Add scallions and ginger, stir-fry for 1 minute, then add bean sauce and red chilies and cook over medium heat for 2 minutes.

Add the sauce mixture and stir until it comes to a boil, then add noodles and simmer, stirring until liquid is reduced. Stir in cilantro and serve at once.

Serves 4

⪻∞⪼

STIR-FRIED PORK WITH WALNUTS & LOTUS ROOT
China

12 oz (375 g) pork filet or escalopes
2 teaspoons light soy sauce
1 teaspoon Chinese wine or dry sherry
½ teaspoon salt
½ teaspoon crushed garlic
½ teaspoon finely grated fresh ginger
1 canned lotus root
2 oz (60 g) peeled walnut halves
oil for frying
2 teaspoons cornstarch (cornflour)

Sauce:
½ cup (4 fl oz, 125 ml) stock or water
2 teaspoons bottled oyster sauce
1 tablespoon Chinese wine or dry sherry
1 teaspoon sesame oil
1 teaspoon chili oil (optional)

Freeze the pork until it is firm enough to cut into paper-thin slices.

Combine the soy sauce, wine, salt, garlic, and ginger in a bowl. Add the sliced pork, mix well and leave to marinate.

Slice the lotus root thinly and set aside. Peeled walnuts are not always easy to find, but it is better to remove the fine skin as this becomes bitter when the walnuts are fried. An easy way to do this is to bring a small pan of water to a boil, add the walnut halves and simmer for 7 minutes. Drain, then spread on absorbent paper. The thin skin peels off easily.

Heat about 1 cup (8 fl oz, 250 ml) oil in a wok and deep fry the nuts on low heat, stirring and turning them constantly, just until golden brown (this should take less than a minute). Drain on absorbent paper.

Mix all the sauce ingredients together.

Reheat the wok, add 1 tablespoon of oil and swirl to coat the wok. When the oil is very hot, add the marinated pork mixture and stir-fry on high heat until the pork is browned. Add the sauce mixture and when it boils lower the heat, cover the wok and simmer for 5 minutes.

Blend the cornstarch with 1 tablespoon of cold water and stir into the pork mixture. When the sauce boils and thickens

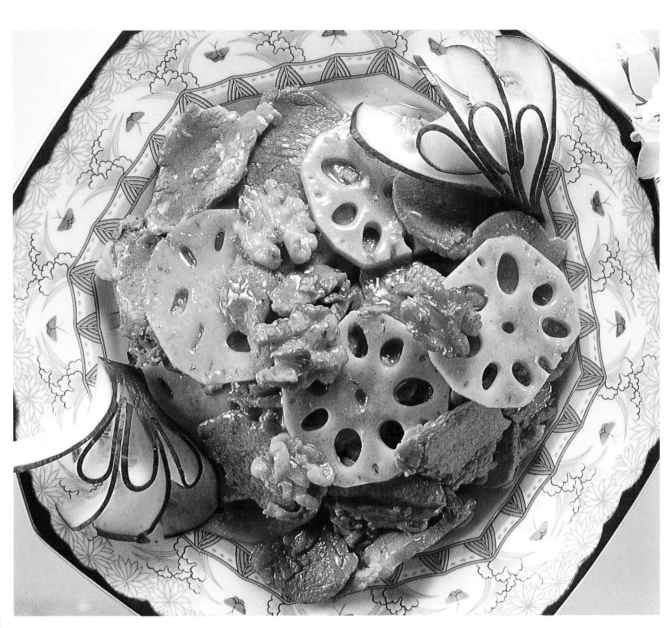

Stir-fried pork with walnut and lotus root (recipe opposite).

slightly, add the lotus root and heat through. Arrange on a dish and sprinkle the walnut halves over. Garnish with cucumber.
Serves 4

STIR-FRIED VEAL & VEGETABLES
China

12 oz (375 g) veal schnitzel
1 teaspoon crushed garlic
1 teaspoon finely grated fresh ginger
2 tablespoons light soy sauce
2 teaspoons Chinese wine or dry sherry, optional

1 large stalk celery
1 small green bell pepper (capsicum)
1 small red bell pepper (capsicum)
1 small winter bamboo shoot, optional
4 scallions (spring onions)
1 small, firm lettuce
2 tablespoons peanut oil
salt to taste

Slice the veal into thin strips. Mix half the garlic and ginger with 1 tablespoon of the soy sauce and the wine, if used. Pour it over the veal and set aside. String celery and cut into thin strips. Remove stalks and seeds from bell peppers and cut into thin strips. Cut bamboo shoot into thin strips, and scallions into bite-size lengths. Have these vegetables ready on a plate. Cut the lettuce in half lengthwise, then cut each half into three strips and across into three again so there are nine chunky pieces in each half. Keep lettuce separate from other vegetables.

Heat 1 tablespoon oil in a wok and when very hot swirl to coat wok. Add the remaining garlic and ginger and the mixed vegetables and stir-fry over high heat for 1 minute or until all the vegetables have come in contact with the oil and heat. At the most this step should take 2 minutes. Add the lettuce, stir-fry for a further 30 seconds, then sprinkle with remaining tablespoon of soy sauce, turn heat low, cover and allow to steam for 1 minute. Remove all the vegetables to a dish. Wipe out pan with paper, heat remaining tablespoon oil and when very hot add the marinated veal and stir-fry on high heat until meat changes color. Turn heat to medium, allow to simmer for 1 minute, then return vegetables and toss together. Taste, and add salt if necessary. Serve at once.
Serves 4

⬧⟵∗⟶⬧

SUMATRAN BEEF CURRY
Indonesia

2 lb (1kg) lean stewing steak
1 large onion, roughly chopped
2 teaspoons chopped garlic
2 teaspoons ground coriander
2 teaspoons ground cumin
2 teaspoons dried shrimp paste
6 candlenuts or 4 brazil nuts, chopped
8 dried red chilies
1 teaspoon laos powder
1 teaspoon ground turmeric
2 teaspoons salt
½ teaspoon ground black pepper
3 tablespoons peanut oil
1 cup (8 fl oz, 250 ml) thin coconut cream
4 tablespoons tamarind liquid

Cube the steak and set aside in a bowl. Place onion, garlic, coriander, cumin, shrimp paste, nuts, chilies, laos powder, turmeric, salt, and pepper in container of electric blender and blend to a smooth paste, adding a little water to facilitate blending. Marinate meat in this mixture for 30 minutes.

Heat oil in a saucepan, stir in meat and marinade and cook till meat is browned. Cover and simmer on very low heat till meat is tender, stirring occasionally. Juices from the meat should provide sufficient liquid, but if necessary add a little water.

Add coconut cream and continue stirring till oil comes to the surface. Stir in tamarind liquid, cook a few more minutes uncovered and serve with rice and accompaniments.
Serves 4–6

SWEET SATAY
Sate Manis ◆ Indonesia

1½ lb (750 g) filet or rump steak, or pork filet
1 tablespoon palm sugar or brown sugar
1 clove garlic, crushed
½ teaspoon salt
2 tablespoons dark soy sauce
1 tablespoon oil
1 teaspoon ground cumin

Satay Sauce:
½ cup (4 fl oz, 125 ml) peanut sauce (page 16)
2 tablespoons tamarind liquid or lemon juice
2 teaspoons sambal of your choice
3–4 tablespoons water

Cut beef or pork into 3/4 in (2 cm) cubes. Thread 4 or 5 cubes on each bamboo skewer, not pushing them too close together. If skewers have been soaked in cold water for an hour or so beforehand, it prevents them burning when satay is cooked. Combine sugar with garlic, salt, soy sauce, oil, and cumin. Stir until sugar dissolves. Pour into a long shallow dish and put satay in the marinade, turning each one so the marinade coats the meat. Cover and refrigerate for a few hours.

Cook over glowing coals or under a hot broiler (grill) for approximately 15 minutes, not too close to the source of heat for pork must be well done. Turn skewers every 5 minutes, and brush with marinade. Serve hot accompanied with satay sauce.

Satay Sauce: Combine all ingredients and serve in a bowl. The sauce is spooned over the satay before eating.
Serves 4–6

⬧⟵∗⟶⬧

Opposite: This wonderful array is for a Chinese steamboat dinner (page 212).

AGAR-AGAR &
NOODLE SALAD
China

½ oz (15 g) refined agar-agar strands
8 oz (250 g) egg noodles
2 eggs, beaten
½ teaspoon salt
2 scallions (spring onions)
2 tablespoons peanut oil
½ teaspoon crushed garlic
8 oz (250 g) fresh bean sprouts
strips of cold, cooked chicken
2 tablespoons sesame oil
4 tablespoons light soy sauce
4 tablespoons chopped cilantro (fresh coriander leaves)
4 tablespoons sliced scallions (spring onions)
matchstick strips of ham, optional

Soak the agar-agar for at least 2 hours in cold water. Drain well and cut into finger-length strips. Cook the noodles in plenty of lightly salted boiling water until just tender, testing every now and then to make sure they don't overcook. Run cold water into the pan and drain in a colander.

Combine the beaten eggs with salt and scallions. Heat a small heavy frying pan and lightly grease the base with a piece of absorbent kitchen paper soaked in a tablespoon of peanut oil. Pour in just enough egg mixture to make a thin omelet; cook on low heat just until set, without browning, then turn out onto a plate. Continue until all the egg is used. Allow to cool.

Heat a wok, add the remaining 1 tablespoon of peanut oil and fry the garlic for a few seconds, not long enough to brown it. Add the bean sprouts, toss for 30 seconds, then remove from heat. Allow to cool.

In a large serving bowl, toss together the agar-agar, noodles, bean sprouts, and chicken.

Combine sesame oil and soy sauce to make a dressing, pour it over the ingredients in the bowl, and toss to distribute the dressing.

Roll up the omelets, cut them into narrow slices, and add to the bowl. Cover and refrigerate. Just before serving, garnish with cilantro, scallions and strips of ham.

You can make a meatless version of this salad, substituting strips of bean curd for the chicken, or simply omitting it.
Serves 6

❧

BEAN CURD &
BEAN SPROUTS
Taukwa Dan Taugeh ◆ Malaysia

2 squares yellow bean curd
8 oz (250 g) fresh bean sprouts
2 cloves garlic, crushed
2 tablespoons oil
salt and pepper to taste
soy sauce to taste

Cut the bean curd in slices. Wash and drain bean sprouts pinching off any brown "tails".

Fry garlic in oil until turning golden, add bean curd and bean sprouts and stir-fry for 3 to 4 minutes. Add seasonings to taste and serve immediately.
Serves 6

❧

BEAN CURD IN
BARBECUE SAUCE

Chu Hau Jeung Mun Dau Fu ◆ China

2 tablespoons oil
6 squares fresh bean curd
2 tablespoons barbecue sauce or marinade as for barbecued pork (page 174)
¾ cup (6 fl oz, 180 ml) light stock or water
1 cup cooked peas or chopped scallions (spring onions)

Opposite: Pulses are of major importance in some Asian diets, especially Indian. Beans, peas, and lentils are the chief source of protein for vegetarians in India, where they are known as 'dhal' (meaning a seed that has been split in half and had the skin removed). The basket top left contains green and yellow split peas (mattar ki dhal), with black-eyed beans in the basket underneath. Grouped in small baskets on the right are, clockwise from top, red kidney beans (rajma), whole green or brown lentils (malka masoor), and whole chickpeas. Below the green and yellow split peas is a basket of Bengal gram (channa dhal) and clockwise from this are red lentils (masoor dhal), mung beans or whole green gram (moong saboot) with split and husked mung beans (moong dhal), husked black gram (urad dhal), and red gram dhal (toor dhal or arhar dhal).

Heat oil and gently fry the bean curd for a few minutes, turning once. Mix marinade with stock or water and add to pan. Simmer for 3 minutes. Add peas or scallions and heat through. Serve with boiled rice or noodles.

Serves 3

BEAN CURD IN SALTED SOY BEAN PASTE
Taukwa Tauceo ◆ Malaysia

3 squares yellow bean curd
2 cloves garlic
3 fresh red chilies
2 teaspoons salted soya bean paste
8 oz (250 g) raw shrimp (prawns) or ½ cup crab meat
2 tablespoons peanut oil
¼ cup (2 fl oz, 60 ml) water
1 tablespoon light soy sauce
salt to taste
2 tablespoons chopped celery leaves
2 tablespoons chopped scallions (spring onions)

Cut bean curd into dice, grate garlic finely, seed and shred chilies. Chop shrimp or flake crab meat. Heat oil and fry garlic and chilies until garlic starts to turn brown, then add soy bean paste and fry for 1 minute, stirring. Add shrimp or crab meat and stir until cooked, add bean curd and fry, stirring. Add water and soy sauce and cook until liquid dries up. Taste and add salt if necessary. Remove from heat, mix in celery and scallions and serve.

Serves 6

BEAN PANCAKES
Bindae Duk ◆ Korea

1 cup mung dhal (dried mung beans split and husked)
1 cup (8 fl oz, 250 ml) water
2 eggs, beaten
4 oz (125 g) ground (minced) pork
1 small onion, finely chopped
1 scallion (spring onion), finely chopped
2 cloves garlic, crushed
1 teaspoon salt
¼ teaspoon ground black pepper
1 teaspoon finely grated fresh ginger
½ cup fresh bean sprouts, chopped
½ cup kim chi or shredded white Chinese (Napa) cabbage
2 tablespoons sesame oil

Wash mung dhal and soak in cold water overnight. Rinse and drain well, then put in a blender with 1 cup water. Blend until smooth. Pour into a bowl, add all other ingredients and mix well. Heat a griddle or heavy frying pan and drop tablespoonfuls of the mixture on the hot surface. Cook until golden brown underneath, turn and cook other side. Serve hot or cold.

Makes about 20

BEAN STARCH NOODLES WITH PORK
China

4 oz (125 g) cellophane (bean starch) noodles
6 dried Chinese mushrooms
6 oz (185 g) boneless pork
1 tablespoon Chinese wine or dry sherry
1 tablespoon light soy sauce
1 teaspoon salt
6 fl oz (180 ml) light stock
1 teaspoon cornstarch (cornflour)
4 tablespoons peanut oil
4 scallions (spring onions), finely chopped
2 teaspoons finely grated fresh ginger
3 tablespoons chili bean sauce
1 large fresh red chili or red bell pepper (capsicum), seeded and finely chopped
4 tablespoons chopped cilantro (fresh coriander leaves)

Put noodles in a large bowl, cover with boiling water and leave for 20 minutes or until soft and transparent. Strain and cut into short lengths with a sharp knife.

Soak the mushrooms in hot water for 30 minutes, squeeze dry, discard stems, dice finely.

Cut the pork into small dice. Mix the wine, soy sauce, salt, stock, and cornstarch together in a small bowl.

Heat a wok over high heat, add the peanut oil and swirl it around the wok. When the oil is hot, add the pork and mushrooms and stir-fry until cooked and brown. Add the scallions and ginger, stir for a few seconds; add the chili bean sauce and the chopped chili, and cook over medium heat for a minute or until the mixture looks and smells cooked.

Add the seasonings and sauce mixture, and stir until it comes to a boil. Then add the noodles and simmer, stirring until all the liquid has cooked down. Stir in the cilantro and serve at once.

If desired, garnish with a chili flower and extra cilantro.

Serves 4–6

Bean starch noodles with pork (recipe opposite).

BOILED NOODLES
China

Allow 1 bundle egg noodles for each person. Soak noodles in hot water for about 10 minutes. The strands will separate allowing the noodles to cook evenly. Meanwhile, bring a large saucepan of water to a boil and add a spoonful of peanut oil. Drain the soaked noodles and drop them into the boiling water. When water returns to a boil, cook fine noodles for 2 to 3 minutes, wide noodles for 3 to 4 minutes. Do not overcook. Like properly cooked spaghetti, noodles should be tender but still firm to the bite.

At end of cooking time drain noodles in a large colander, then run cold water through the noodles to rinse off excess starch and cool so they don't continue to cook in their own heat. Drain thoroughly and serve with stir-fried dishes or use in soups and braised noodle dishes.

BRAISED NOODLES WITH CHICKEN
China

4 bundles wide egg noodles
1 lb (500 g) chicken, boned
3 cups bok choy (chard) or gai choy (mustard cabbage)
12 snow peas (mangetout)
1 tablespoon soy sauce
1 tablespoon Chinese wine or dry sherry
1 tablespoon cornstarch (cornflour)
2 tablespoons cold water
1 tablespoon oyster sauce
½ teaspoon salt
2 tablespoons peanut oil
2 cloves garlic, crushed
1 teaspoon finely grated fresh root ginger
1 cup (8 fl oz, 250 ml) chicken stock

Soak noodles in hot water for 10 minutes. Drain. Bring plenty of water to a boil in a large saucepan, drop in bundles of egg noodles and loosen bundles with chopsticks or a fork as they cook. Boil for 3 to 4 minutes or until they are cooked but still firm. Do not overcook. Drain in a colander and hold under running cold water to rinse and stop cooking. Drain.

Cut chicken into small squares and pour the soy sauce and sherry over. Mix and allow to marinate while preparing vegetables. Cut stalks of bok choy into bite-size pieces. Remove strings from snow peas. Mix cornstarch with cold water, oyster sauce, and salt, and set aside.

Heat oil in a wok and gently fry garlic and ginger for a few seconds. Add chicken and stir-fry over high heat for 2 minutes or until it begins to turn golden. Add bok choy, snow peas, and fry, stirring, for 1 minute longer. Add stock, bring to a boil, add cornstarch mixture and stir until thick. Add well-drained noodles and heat through, tossing to mix evenly.
Serves 4–5

BROWN LENTIL & TOMATO CURRY
India

1 cup brown lentils
2 teaspoons ghee
2 tablespoons peanut oil
1 medium onion, thinly sliced
3 tablespoons chopped cilantro (coriander leaves)
2 medium tomatoes, chopped
2 teaspoons finely chopped garlic
1 teaspoon finely chopped fresh ginger
2 teaspoons ground cumin
1 teaspoon chili powder
1 teaspoon turmeric
salt to taste
1 tablespoon lemon juice
½ teaspoon garam masala

Soak lentils for 2 hours and boil in 4 cups (32 fl oz, 1 L) water till cooked but still firm. Drain and set aside. Heat ghee and oil and fry onion till soft and golden. Stir in chopped coriander, tomatoes, garlic, ginger, and cumin and cook further 3–4 minutes.

Add chili powder, turmeric, salt, and lemon juice and cook till mixture smells aromatic, stirring occasionally. Add lentils, mix thoroughly and cook further 4 minutes. Sprinkle with garam masala and serve with chapatis or rice, and accompaniments.
Serves 4

CELLOPHANE NOODLES
Throughout Asia

These fine noodles are also known as transparent bean starch noodles, bean threads, silver threads, spring rain noodles, harusame, or fenszu. For a crisp garnish, fry in the same way as rice vermicelli, straight from the packet. For use in soups or braised dishes, soak in hot water or cook in boiling water for 15 minutes or until tender.

Bean starch is also available in large round sheets, which are made of mung bean flour and water paste rolled into thin sheets and dried, ready for use. Soak, cut into strips, and cook in boiling water as directed in recipes.

CELLOPHANE NOODLES
Kyazan ◆ Burma

12 oz (375 g) cellophane (bean starch) noodles
Mild Chicken Curry (page 161) or Mohinga (page 238)
accompaniments (see below)
lemon wedges

Prepare mild chicken curry (page 161).

Bring a large saucepan of salted water to a boil, drop in the noodles and cook for 20 minutes. Drain. Serve in a large bowl. (Serving is easier if the noodles are cut into shorter lengths with a sharp knife.)

Guests place some noodles in a bowl, ladle chicken curry or Mohinga over and add whichever accompaniments they please. Everything is mixed together and a lemon wedge squeezed over to add piquancy. The crisp fried chilies are held by the stalk and bitten into (with caution please, if this is your first experience) when a hot mouthful is desired.

Accompaniments:
Finely sliced scallions (spring onions), both green and white portion.
Chopped cilantro (fresh coriander leaves).
Finely sliced white onions.
Roasted garbanzos (chickpeas), finely ground in a blender, or crushed with a mortar and pestle.
Crisp fried noodles, broken into small pieces.
Fried onion flakes.
Thin slices of garlic, fried in oil until golden.
Lemon wedges.
Dried chilies, fried in oil for 3 to 4 seconds.
Chili powder.
Note: Roasted garbanzos are sold in Greek delicatessen shops.
Serves 6–8

CELLOPHANE NOODLES WITH PORK
Yook Nup Fun See ◆ China (Sichuan)

4 oz (125 g) cellophane (bean starch) noodles
4 dried Chinese mushrooms
6 oz (185 g) pork
1 tablespoon Chinese wine or dry sherry
1 tablespoon light soy sauce
1 teaspoon salt
¾ cup (6 fl oz, 180 ml) light stock or water
1 teaspoon cornstarch (cornflour)
3 tablespoons oil for frying
4 scallions (spring onions), finely chopped

Cellophane noodles (recipe opposite), fried chilies and mild chicken curry, from Burma (page 161).

2 teaspoons finely grated fresh ginger
2 tablespoons hot bean sauce
1 large fresh red chili or red bell pepper (capsicum), seeded and finely chopped
2 tablespoons chopped cilantro (fresh coriander leaves)

Put noodles in a large bowl, pour over boiling water to cover, then leave 10 minutes or until soft and transparent. Strain and cut into short lengths with a sharp knife. Soak mushrooms in hot water for 30 minutes, squeeze dry, discard stems, dice finely. Cut pork into small dice. Mix all sauce and seasoning ingredients together in a small bowl.

Heat a wok over high heat, add oil and swirl around wok. When oil is hot add the pork and mushrooms and stir-fry until cooked and brown. Add scallions and ginger, stir for a few seconds, then add bean sauce, red chili and cook over medium heat for a minute or until the mixture looks and smells cooked.

Add the seasonings and sauce mixture and stir until it comes to a boil; add noodles and simmer, stirring, until all the liquid has cooked down. Stir in cilantro and serve at once. Garnish with a chili flower and extra cilantro if desired.

Traditionally, this dish is seasoned with hot bean sauce. If not available substitute with an equal amount of canned salted yellow beans, rinsed briefly in a fine strainer, then mashed with a fork. Stir in 1 teaspoon Chinese chili sauce to each tablespoon of beans.
Serves 4–6

CHICKEN & PORK FRIED RICE
Burma

2 cups (14 oz, 440 g) short grain rice
2 Chinese sausages
3 tablespoons peanut oil
3 eggs, beaten
1 teaspoon finely chopped garlic
1–2 teaspoons shrimp paste
1 red bell pepper (capsicum), finely diced
4 scallions (spring onions), finely chopped
1 cup small cooked shrimp (prawns)
½ cup cooked pork, diced
1 cup cooked chicken breasts, boned and diced
2 tablespoons dark soy sauce
2 tablespoons water
2 teaspoons chili sauce
1 teaspoon sesame oil

Garnish:
½ cup cilantro (fresh coriander) leaves
omelet strips (see method)

Put 3 1/2 cups water in a saucepan, add rice and Chinese sausages and bring to a boil. Cover with well-fitting lid, turn heat to low and cook for 20 minutes without lifting the lid. When cooked, turn rice onto tray and leave to cool. Separate sausages, slice thin diagonally and set aside. Grease a wok lightly and make 3 omelets with beaten eggs. Cut into strips and set aside.

Heat remaining oil in wok, add garlic, shrimp paste, bell pepper, half the scallions, and stir-fry for 1 minute. Add cooked rice to wok and stir-fry until warmed through. Add shrimp, pork, chicken and sausage, and stir until heated through. In a bowl mix together soy, water, chili sauce and sesame oil, and pour over rice in the wok. Raise heat, add remaining scallions and half the omelet strips, stir and blend well. Serve hot, garnished wtih chopped cilantro leaves and remaining omelet strips.
Serves 6–8

CHILI FRIED RICE
Khao Phat Prik ◆ Thailand

3 tablespoons peanut oil
1 large onion, finely chopped
1 fresh red chili and 1 fresh green chili, seeded and sliced
1 tablespoon red curry paste (page 12)
1 pork chop, finely diced
1 lb (500 g) raw shrimp (prawns), shelled and deveined
4 cups (24 oz, 750 g) cold steamed rice
2 eggs, beaten
pepper and salt to taste
3 tablespoons fish sauce or light soy sauce
1 cup chopped scallions (spring onions) including green tops
½ cup chopped cilantro (fresh coriander leaves)
chili flowers for garnish

Heat oil in wok, fry onion and sliced chilies until soft. Add the curry paste and fry until the oil separates from the mixture. Add pork and fry until cooked, then add shrimp (chopped into pieces if they are large). Fry for a minute or two longer, until they turn pink, then add cooked rice and toss thoroughly until coated with the curry mixture and heated through. Push rice to side of wok, season beaten eggs with salt and pepper, and pour into the middle. Stir until eggs start to set, then mix the rice through, tossing on high heat until eggs are cooked. Sprinkle fish sauce evenly over the rice and mix well, then remove from heat. Stir the scallions through. Garnish with cilantro and chili flowers and serve.
Serves 4.

Chicken and pork fried rice (recipe opposite).

COCONUT RICE

Nasi Lemak ◆ **Singapore**

1 lb (500 g) medium or long grain rice
1¼ cups (10 fl oz, 300 ml) coconut cream (milk)
2½ teaspoons salt

Soak rice in cold water overnight. Drain rice, spread in top part of a steamer and steam over rapidly boiling water for 30 minutes. Halfway through steaming, stir rice and turn it so that the rice on the bottom comes to the top and vice versa.

Gently heat the coconut cream with the salt in a large saucepan, stirring. Do not boil. Add the steamed rice, stir well, cover tightly and let stand for a further 30 minutes, by which time the cream should be completely absorbed. Once more spread the rice in top of steamer, bring water back to a boil and steam for 30 minutes, starting on high heat and gradually turning heat lower until in the end the water merely simmers. Serve hot with meat, poultry, fish, or vegetable dishes.
Serves: 4–5

COMBINATION CHOW MEIN

Jahp Wui Chow Min ◆ **China**

8 oz (250 g) fine wheat noodles
1 chicken breast, skinned and boned
4 oz (125 g) barbecued pork (page 174)
4 oz (125 g) bean sprouts
4 oz (125 g) snow peas (mangetout)
1 teaspoon crushed garlic
1 teaspoon finely grated fresh ginger
4 oz (125 g) shredded bok choy (chard)
6 scallions (spring onions) in bite-size lengths
1 canned winter bamboo shoot, cut into strips
peanut oil

Sauce:
6 fl oz (180 ml) chicken stock
3 tablespoons light soy sauce
3 tablespoons oyster sauce
2 teaspoons sesame oil
1 tablespoon cornstarch (cornflour)

Cook the wheat noodles as described on page 258. Drain, toss with oil, and spread on a tray to dry.

Cut the chicken breast into fine shreds. Cut the barbecued pork into narrow strips. Wash and drain the bean sprouts, discard loose skins and pinch off any straggly tails. String the snow peas. Have all meat and vegetable ingredients ready.

CHILLED NOODLES

Zaru Soba ◆ **Japan**

7 oz (220 g) soba (buckwheat noodles)
1 sheet nori (dried laver seaweed)
1 tablespoon finely grated fresh ginger
3 scallions (spring onions), very finely sliced

Dipping Sauce:
2 cups dashi (page 6)
½ cup (4 fl oz, 125 ml) Japanese soy sauce
½ cup (4 fl oz, 125 ml) mirin or dry sherry
salt or sugar, optional

Bring a large saucepan of water to a boil and add noodles. When water returns to a boil add 1 cup (8 fl oz, 250 ml) cold water. Bring to a boil again and cook until the noodles are just tender, about 2 minutes. Drain in a colander and hold under running cold water until they are quite cold. Drain well.

Toast sheet of nori over gas or electric burner or under broiler (grill) until crisp. Put noodles on plates and crumble the nori over.

Mix ginger with scallions and put a small portion on each plate. Pour dipping sauce into individual sauce dishes for each person. The ginger mixture is stirred into the sauce and the noodles are dipped in the sauce before eating.

Dipping Sauce: Put ingredients into a small pan and bring to a boil. Remove from heat and cool. Taste and add salt or sugar as desired.
Serves 4

In a bowl, combine the stock, soy sauce, oyster sauce, and sesame oil. In a separate bowl combine cornstarch smoothly with 2 tablespoons of cold water.

Heat a large heavy frying pan and when hot, add 4 tablespoons of peanut oil and fry the noodles on medium heat until crisp and golden on one side (about 5 minutes). Turn them and fry the other side. Remove from heat and keep warm in the frying pan.

Heat a wok, add 3 tablespoons of peanut oil and swirl to coat the wok. Add garlic and ginger, and stir for a few seconds. Add the chicken, and stir-fry until it turns golden. Add the pork and vegetables, and toss for a further 2 minutes. Add the mixed sauce ingredients, and bring to a boil.

Add cornstarch mixture to wok and stir until the sauce boils. Pour over noodles and serve hot.
Serves 4

❖

COMBINATION FRIED NOODLES

The Philippines

1 lb (500 g) shelled and deveined cooked shrimp (prawns)
1 lb (500 g) thin egg noodles
2 tablespoons each oil, and shortening (lard)
3 teaspoons finely chopped garlic
3 medium onions, finely sliced
1 cup diced cooked chicken
1 cup cooked pork, cut in thin strips
¾ cup ham, cut in thin strips
1 cup shredded bok choy (chard)
3 tablespoons light soy sauce
1 cup (8 fl oz, 250 ml) hot stock or water
salt and pepper to taste

Garnish:
lemon wedges

Cut shrimp into pieces if large. Soak noodles in warm water while bringing a large pan of water to a boil. Drain noodles and drop them into the fast-boiling water, bring back to a boil and cook for 2 minutes. Do not overcook. Drain immediately, spread on a large baking tray lined with kitchen paper and allow to dry for at least 30 minutes, sprinkling a little oil over to prevent sticking together.

Heat wok, add 1 tablespoon of oil and shortening mixture and when very hot fry noodles, a handful at a time, until golden on both sides, adding more oil mixture to the wok as necessary. Remove noodles from wok. Heat a little more oil mixture and fry separately the garlic, onion, shrimp, chicken, pork, and ham.

Set aside some of each for garnishing the dish and return the rest to the wok together with bok choy, soy sauce, hot stock, salt, and pepper. Cook uncovered until almost dry, then return noodles and heat through, stirring and tossing well to mix. Arrange on serving dish and garnish with the reserved ingredients and wedges of lemon.
Serves 6–8

❖

CRAB & PORK FRIED RICE

Bokum Bahb ◆ Korea

2 tablespoons peanut oil
1 clove garlic, crushed
1 teaspoon finely grated fresh ginger
½ cup flaked cooked crab meat
½–1 cup chopped cooked pork
4 cups (24 oz, 750 g) cooked rice
½ cup finely sliced scallions (spring onions)
1 teaspoon salt or to taste

Heat oil in a wok and fry garlic, ginger, crab, and pork together, stirring. Add rice and continue to stir and toss until rice is fried. Add scallions and sprinkle salt over. Toss to mix thoroughly, taste for seasoning. Serve hot.
Serves 4

❖

CRISP FRIED VERMICELLI

Mee Krob ◆ Thailand

7 oz (200 g) rice vermicelli
3 cups (24 fl oz, 750 ml) peanut oil for deep frying
4 oz (125 g) minced pork or chicken
4 oz (125 g) shelled and deveined raw shrimp (prawns), chopped
1 cup finely diced firm beancurd
⅓ cup white vinegar
⅓ cup sugar
⅓ cup fish sauce
3 eggs beaten
½ teaspoon ground black pepper
2 whole heads pickled garlic, finely sliced
3 red chilies, seeded and sliced
¾ cup chopped cilantro (fresh coriander leaves)
¼ cup chopped garlic chives

Dip the rice noodles briefly in cold water or run the cold tap over them. Shake off excess water and leave in a breezy place about

30 minutes. (When these noodles are fried, they will not puff up as spectacularly as when fried straight from the packet, but will hold their crispness longer.) Heat the oil in a wok and when a light haze rises from the surface, test the heat of the oil with a few strands of the vermicelli. It should puff and swell immediately. If it sinks to the bottom it means the oil is not hot enough and the vermicelli will be tough and oily instead of light and crisp.

Fry the vermicelli in small handfuls, and remove from the oil as soon as it puffs and becomes pale golden in color. Drain on absorbent kitchen paper and allow to cool completely. May be stored airtight and kept for a few hours.

Pour off the oil into a metal bowl, leaving a small amount in the wok, about 1/4 cup. Reheat this oil and fry the minced pork on high heat, stirring and pressing it against the hot wok, until it has lost its pinkness. Add the prawns and fry for 1 minute, add bean curd and toss until heated through.

Stir vinegar, sugar, and fish sauce in a bowl until sugar dissolves, pour into the wok and bring to a boil. Pour in the beaten eggs seasoned with pepper, stirring until the eggs are set and firm. Prepare ahead up to this stage if convenient, but do not leave the mixture in wok or it will develop unpleasant flavors because of the acid.

Just before serving, heat the cooked mixture, add the fries noodles, the sliced pickled garlic, and most of the sliced chilies and chopped herbs. Mix well. Serve in individual bowls or a serving dish and sprinkle with chopped coriander, garlic chives, and chilies. Urge your guests to eat Mee Krob without delay.
Serves 6

⬦⬦⬦

CURRIED DRIED BEANS
India

250 g (8 oz) dried beans
water
2 teaspoons salt
1½ tablespoons ghee or oil
1 large onion, finely chopped
1 teaspoon finely chopped garlic
1 tablespoon finely chopped fresh ginger
1 teaspoon ground turmeric
1 teaspoon garam masala (page 9)
2 large ripe tomatoes, chopped
1–2 fresh green chilies, seeded and chopped
2 tablespoons chopped fresh mint
2 tablespoons lemon juice

Soak dried beans in plenty of cold water overnight. Drain, rinse and put beans into a large saucepan with water to cover and

1 teaspoon salt. Bring to a boil, cover and cook until tender. Add more hot water during cooking if necessary. Drain and reserve cooking liquid.

Heat ghee in large saucepan and gently fry the onion, garlic and ginger until soft and golden, then add turmeric, garam masala, tomatoes, chilies, mint, remaining teaspoon salt, and lemon juice. Add the beans and stir well over medium heat for 5 minutes. Add 1 cup (12 fl oz, 250 ml) reserved liquid, cover and cook over low heat until tomatoes and chilies are soft and the gravy thick. Serve with rice or Indian breads as part of a vegetarian meal.
Serves 4

⬦⬦⬦

FESTIVE SPICED RICE
Rajasthani Pilau ◆ India

3 tablespoons ghee or oil
2 medium onions, finely sliced
2 sticks cinnamon
6 cardamom pods, bruised
6 whole cloves
2½ cups (18 oz, 550 g) long grain rice
4 cups (32 fl oz, 1 L) hot stock or water
2½ teaspoons salt

Garnish:
red and green food coloring
carrots and tomatoes

Heat ghee or oil in a large, heavy saucepan and fry the sliced onion with the cinnamon, cardamoms, and cloves until the onions are golden, stirring frequently so that they brown evenly. Add the rice and fry for about 3 minutes, then pour in the stock or water. Add the salt and stir well while bringing quickly to a boil. Turn heat very low, cover tightly and cook without lifting lid for 25 minutes. Uncover, allow steam to escape for a few minutes, remove whole spices.

Take 1/2 cup (3 oz, 90 g) cooked rice and color bright red; color an equal amount bright green. Garnish the dish with tomato and carrot roses and the colored rice. Serve hot with mutton dishes.
Serves 6

⬦⬦⬦

FRAGRANT RICE
Nasi Gurih ✦ Indonesia

4½ cups (36 fl oz, 1 L) thin coconut cream (milk)
½ teaspoon ground black pepper
1 teaspoon finely grated lemon rind or 1 stalk fresh lemon grass
½ teaspoon ground nutmeg or mace
¼ teaspoon ground cloves
1 daun salam or 3 curry leaves
2½ teaspoons salt
1 lb (500 g) long grain rice

Put the coconut cream with all ingredients except the rice into a large saucepan with a well-fitting lid, and bring slowly to a boil, uncovered. Stir in the rice and return to a boil, then turn heat very low, cover and steam for 20 minutes. Uncover, fork the rice lightly from around sides of pan, mixing in any coconut cream that has not been absorbed, and replace lid for 5 minutes. Serve hot with fried chicken or curries and hot sambals.
Serves 6

FRIED BEAN CURD WITH PEANUTS
Tahu Goreng Kacang ◆ Indonesia

5 cakes hard yellow bean curd
peanut oil for frying
½ cup raw peanuts
1 large clove garlic, crushed
½ teaspoons trasi (dried shrimp paste)
½ cup crushed roasted peanuts, or crunchy peanut butter
2 tablespoons dark soy sauce
3 tablespoons tamarind liquid
½ teaspoon sambal ulek (hot chili paste, page 23)
1 teaspoon palm sugar or brown sugar
½ cup (4 fl oz, 125 ml) thin coconut cream (milk)
1 cup shredded cabbage
1 cup fresh bean sprouts
4 scallions (spring onions), finely sliced, to garnish

Wipe bean curd thoroughly on paper towels. Cut cakes of bean curd into 9 dice each. Heat peanut oil in a wok or frying pan and fry the bean curd, taking care not to stir or break the dice, until they are golden brown on all sides. Drain on absorbent paper. In the same oil fry peanuts for 3 or 4 minutes, drain, rub off skins. Set aside.

Make the sauce by pouring off all but a tablespoon of oil and frying the garlic and trasi over low heat, stirring constantly and crushing the trasi with back of the spoon. Add crushed peanuts, soy sauce, tamarind liquid, sambal, and sugar. Stir until well mixed. Remove from heat. Gradually add the coconut cream until sauce is of a thick pouring consistency.

Put bean curd on a dish, cover with the shredded cabbage and then with the bean sprouts. Spoon sauce over and garnish with scallions and fried peanuts.
Serves 4

FRIED NOODLES
Mie Goreng ✦ Indonesia

8 oz (250 g) fine egg noodles
1 large pork chop
8 oz (250 g) shelled and deveined shrimp (prawns), raw or cooked
4 tablespoons peanut oil
1 onion, finely chopped
3 cloves garlic, finely chopped
1 fresh red chili, seeded and sliced
½ teaspoon trasi (dried shrimp paste)
2 stalks celery, finely sliced
small wedge of cabbage, finely shredded
1 teaspoon salt
½ teaspoon pepper
1–2 tablespoons light soy sauce

Garnish:
fried onion flakes (page 22), optional
4 scallions (spring onions)
thinly sliced cucumber

Soak noodles in hot water, while bringing large saucepan of water to a boil. Drain noodles and drop into the boiling water, return to a boil and boil from 1 to 3 minutes, depending on the noodles. Some take a little longer to cook than others. Test a strand every half minute or so; do not overcook. Drain in colander and run cold water through them until cool or they will continue to cook in their own heat. Drain well.

Cut away rind and bone from pork chop and cut into small dice. Heat peanut oil in a wok or large deep frying pan and fry onion, garlic, and chili until onion is soft and starts to turn golden. Add trasi. Add the pork and shrimp and stir-fry until cooked through. Add celery, cabbage, salt, and pepper and fry for a further minute or just until tender. Vegetables should retain their crispness. Add noodles and keep turning the mixture so that it all gets heated through. Season with soy sauce to taste. Pile into a serving dish and sprinkle onion flakes over the top. Chop the scallions, including green leaves, and sprinkle over. Arrange cucumber slices around edge of dish. Serve hot.
Serves 4

FRIED NOODLES, SINGAPORE-STYLE
Singapore

2 lb (1 kg) fresh rice or yellow wheat noodles
1 lb (500 g) boiled pork
1 lb (500 g) small raw shrimp (prawns)
8 oz (250 g) fresh bean sprouts
6 cloves garlic
1 tablespoon canned salted black beans or bean sauce
¼ cup (2 fl oz, 60 ml) water or stock
1 teaspoon salt, or to taste
½ cup (4 fl oz, 125 ml) oil
3 stalks celery, finely chopped

Garnish:
4 eggs
pepper and salt to taste
8 scallions (spring onions)
3 or 4 fresh red chilies
few sprigs cilantro (fresh coriander leaves)
10 cloves garlic

If using rice noodles, cut into 1/4 in (5 mm) strips and pour boiling water over to soften and separate the layers. Drain in a colander. If using yellow wheat noodles, rinse in hot water and drain.

Slice the pork finely, then cut into narrow strips. If small prawns are not available, cut large prawns into pieces. Wash bean sprouts, rinsing away any skins, and pinch off straggly tails. Crush garlic, rinse salted beans and mash with a fork or chop finely. Bean sauce can be used straight from the jar.

At serving time heat a wok, pour in oil and when oil has heated stir-fry the garlic on low heat until just starting to turn golden. Add beans or bean sauce and stir-fry for 30 seconds. Turn heat to high, add pork and fry for 1 minute, then add shrimp and continue to stir-fry for 2 minutes. Add water or stock, bring to a boil and add salt. Cook quickly, uncovered, for 1 minutes, then add celery and bean sprouts and toss for a further minute. Add the noodles and keep tossing until all the ingredients are thoroughly mixed and noodles heated through.

Turn onto a large flat dish and sprinkle the top of the noodles with all of the prepared garnishes. Serve immediately, accompanied with a bowl of cucumber salad if desired.

Garnish: Beat eggs and season with pepper and salt. Heat a frying pan and grease lightly with oil. Fry the mixture, a little at a time, into thin round omelets. Do not fold but turn them onto a plate as they are cooked. When cool, roll up and cut into thin strips.

Cut scallions, including green leaves, into 2 in (5 cm) lengths. Seed the chilies, then slice finely. Wash the cilantro and chop leaves and stalks. Finely chop or pound garlic, rinse in cold water, squeeze dry in kitchen paper and fry over low heat until pale golden. Drain and crumble into small pieces.
Serves 8–10

✥

FRIED NOODLES WITH MEAT & VEGETABLES
Kowshwe ◆ Burma

1 cup (8 oz, 250 g) shortening (lard) or bacon fat
4 medium onions, sliced
½ medium cabbage, shredded
3 lb (1.5 kg) chicken, cut into joints
8 oz (250 g) pork, cut into fine strips
2 teaspoons salt or to taste
1 cup (8 fl oz, 250 ml) water
1 teaspoon chili powder, optional
1 lb (500 g) egg noodles

Accompaniments (see recipe for Cellophane Noodles, page 224)

Heat shortening in a large saucepan and fry the onion and cabbage until soft. Add chicken and pork and fry, stirring continuously, for 10 minutes. Add salt, water, and chili powder if used. Cover and cook over a low heat for 35 to 40 minutes or until chicken is tender. Uncover pan and cook until liquid evaporates and oil separates from mixture. Lift out chicken pieces.

Cook noodles in boiling salted water until just tender, pour some cold water into pan to stop noodles cooking and drain thoroughly in a colander. Add noodles to pan of cabbage and pork mixture and toss to combine ingredients thoroughly.

Arrange chicken pieces on top and serve hot. Pass accompaniments separately.
Serves 6–8

✥

FRIED NOODLES WITH MIXED MEATS

Pancit Guisado ◆ The Philippines

1 lb (500 g) raw shrimp (prawns)
1 lb (500 g) thin egg noodles
3–4 tablespoons shortening (lard) or oil
5 cloves garlic, crushed
2 onions, finely sliced
1 cup flaked cooked chicken
1 cup cooked pork, cut in thin strips
½ cup ham, cut in thin strips
1 cup shredded cabbage
3 tablespoons light soy sauce
salt and pepper to taste
lemon wedges for garnish

Cook shrimp in a little lightly salted water, cool, then shell and devein. Cut into pieces if large. Reserve 1 cup (8 fl oz, 250 ml) of the shrimp stock. Soak noodles in warm water while bringing a large pan of water to a boil. Drain noodles and drop them into the fast-boiling water, bring back to a boil and cook for 2 minutes or until just tender. Do not overcook. Drain immediately, spread on a large baking tray lined with kitchen paper and allow to dry for at least 30 minutes, sprinkling a little oil over to prevent sticking.

Heat a tablespoon of shortening in a large wok and when very hot fry noodles, a handful at a time, until golden on both sides, adding more shortening to the wok as necessary. Remove noodles from wok. Heat a little more shortening or oil and fry separately the garlic, onion, shrimp, chicken, pork, and ham. Set aside some of each for garnishing and return the rest to the pan together with cabbage, soy sauce, shrimp stock, salt, and pepper. Cook uncovered until almost dry, then return noodles and heat through, tossing well to mix. Arrange on serving dish and garnish with the reserved ingredients and wedges of lemon.
Serves 6–8

⋙※⋘

FRIED RICE

Nasi Goreng ◆ Indonesia

3 eggs
salt and pepper to taste
oil for frying
2 medium onions
2 cloves garlic
½ teaspoon trasi or blachan (dried shrimp paste)
5 tablespoons extra oil

1 lb (500 g) lean steak or pork
8 oz (250 g) raw shrimp (prawns), shelled and deveined
6 scallions (spring onions), chopped
4 cups (24 oz, 750 g) cold boiled rice
2 tablespoons soy sauce
3 tablespoons dried onion flakes, fried until golden brown in oil
1 green cucumber, thinly sliced

Beat eggs with salt and pepper to taste. Heat a little oil in a frying pan and make an omelet with half the beaten eggs. Turn onto a plate to cool (do not fold). Repeat process with remaining beaten eggs. When cool, place one omelet on top of the other, roll up and cut into thin strips.

Chop onions roughly and place in blender container with garlic and trasi. Cover and blend to a paste. (If blender is not available, finely chop onions and garlic and dissolve trasi in a little hot water. Combine these ingredients.)

Heat 3 tablespoons of the extra oil in a large frying pan or wok and fry the blended ingredients until cooked. Cut steak or pork into fine strips. Add shrimp and meat to pan and fry, stirring continuously, until they are cooked. Add remaining 2 tablespoons of extra oil, and when hot, stir in the scallions and rice, mixing thoroughly and frying until it is very hot. Sprinkle with soy sauce and mix evenly.

Serve the fried rice garnished with strips of omelet, fried onion flakes, and very thin slices of cucumber.

Note: Fry dried onion flakes for a few seconds only. Remove from heat at once as they burn easily.
Serves 6–8

⋙※⋘

FRIED RICE WITH MIXED VEGETABLES

China

1 lb (500 g) short grain rice
3 cups (24 fl oz, 750 ml) water
12 dried Chinese mushrooms
1 or 2 large leeks
4 stalks celery
8 oz (250 g) green (string) beans
4 oz (125 g) fresh bean sprouts
2 medium carrots
1 piece canned bamboo shoot
3 tablespoons peanut oil
1 tablespoon sesame oil
1 teaspoon finely grated fresh ginger
1 teaspoon finely grated garlic
1 cup finely sliced scallions (spring onions)

Fried rice with mixed vegetables (recipe opposite and below).

½ cup (4 fl oz, 125 ml) mushroom liquid
2 tablespoons light soy sauce
salt to taste

Put rice and water into a heavy saucepan, bring to a boil over high heat, then turn heat very low, cover pan tightly with a close-fitting lid and cook for 20 minutes. Turn out of pan, spread on large tray or baking dish and allow to cool. Refrigerate. This should be done some hours before rice is to be fried, or even the day before.

Soak mushrooms in hot water for 30 minutes, then squeeze out as much liquid as possible and reserve liquid. With a sharp knife cut off and discard stems. Cut mushroom caps into thin slices and if they are large mushrooms cut the slices across so that slices are not too long.

Wash leeks well in cold water, making sure all the grit between the leaves is washed away. Cut into thin slices, using all the white portion and about 2–3 in (5–7 cm) of the green leaves. String celery and green beans and cut into very thin diagonal slices. Wash and drain bean sprouts and pinch off any straggly brown tails. Grate carrots coarsely and cut bamboo shoot into matchstick strips.

Heat peanut oil and sesame oil in a large wok, add ginger and garlic and fry over medium low heat, stirring well, for 30 seconds. Add mushrooms, leeks, celery, beans, and carrots and stir-fry over high heat for 3 minutes. Add bean sprouts and bamboo shoot and fry 1 minute longer.

Add rice, toss and fry over high heat until all the grains are heated through. Add scallions. Mix mushroom liquid and soy sauce together and sprinkle evenly over rice. Continue stirring to mix well together and season to taste with salt. Serve hot.
Serves 6

GHEE RICE
Sri Lanka

2 cups (14 oz, 440 g) basmati or other long grain rice
2½ tablespoons ghee
1 large onion, finely sliced
4 cloves
6 cardamom pods, bruised
3 in (8 cm) piece cinnamon stick
3½ cups (28 fl oz, 875 ml) hot beef, chicken or mutton
    stock or water and stock cubes
2½ teaspoons salt

Wash rice well and drain for at least 30 minutes. Heat ghee in a saucepan and fry onion until golden, add spices and drained rice. Fry, stirring with slotted metal spoon, for 5 minutes over a moderate heat. Add hot stock and salt and bring to a boil.

Reduce heat to very low, cover pan tightly with lid and cook for 15 to 20 minutes without lifting lid. At end of cooking time, uncover and allow steam to escape, stand for 5 minutes. Gently fluff up rice with fork, removing whole spices.

When transferring rice to a serving dish, again use a slotted metal spoon to avoid crushing grains of rice. Serve hot, accompanied by curries of meat and vegetables, pickles, and sambals.
Serves 4–5

GLUTINOUS YELLOW RICE
Nasi Kunyit ◆ Malaysia

1 lb (500 g) glutinous rice
2 cups (16 fl oz, 500 ml) water
2 teaspoons salt
1 clove garlic, crushed
1 teaspoon ground turmeric
½ teaspoon ground black pepper
1 daun pandan (pandanus leaf) or curry leaf
2 cups (16 fl oz, 500 ml) hot coconut cream (milk)

Garnish:
crisp fried onion flakes (page 22)

Wash rice and drain. Put into a saucepan with water, salt, garlic, turmeric, pepper, and pandanus leaf for flavoring. Bring to a boil, reduce heat, cover tightly and steam for 10 minutes.

Uncover, add coconut cream (which should be very hot), and with a long-pronged fork stir gently so that the rice is mixed with the coconut cream. Cover and cook 10 minutes longer. Serve garnished with onion flakes and accompanied by curries and other dishes.
Serves 6

GOLDEN SAFFRON RICE
India

8 cups (3½ lb, 1.75 kg) long grain rice
5 tablespoons ghee
4 medium onions, finely sliced
2 teaspoons ground turmeric
2 good pinches powdered saffron or ½ teaspoon saffron
    strands
7 cups (56 fl oz, 1.75 L) chicken stock
2 tablespoons salt
1 teaspoon ground cardamom
2 cinnamon sticks
8 cloves
1 teaspoon peppercorns
½ cup (3 oz, 90 g) golden raisins (sultanas)
1 cup (4 oz, 125 g) almonds, fried until golden brown
    in oil
2 cups peas, cooked

Wash rice in 4 or 5 changes of water and drain thoroughly. Do this approximately 1 hour before starting to cook.

Melt ghee in a large, heavy saucepan and gently fry onion until starting to turn golden. Add turmeric, saffron, and rice. Stir and toss rice with a metal spoon until well coated with the ghee. Fry until rice is just golden, approximately 5 minutes. Add boiling stock, salt, and spices, stir well. Bring back to boiling point, turn heat to very low, cover pan tightly and cook for 20 minutes. Do not lift lid or stir during cooking time. Turn off heat and leave uncovered for 10 minutes to allow steam to escape.

Just before serving, fluff up rice with a long-pronged fork. Garnish with golden raisins, almonds, and peas.

Note: For each person allow 1/3 cup (2 1/2 oz, 75 g) raw rice. Just remember the rule, allow 2 cups (16 fl oz, 500 ml) of water to the first cup of rice and 1 1/2 cups (12 fl oz, 375 ml) water to each additional cup of rice. If you do not have a pan large enough, divide recipe in half and cook it in two saucepans.
Serves 20–25

JAPANESE RICE
Japan

2½ cups (17½ oz, 540 g) short or medium grain rice
3 cups (24 fl oz, 750 ml) cold water

Wash rice several times in cold water. Drain in a colander for at least 30 minutes. Put rice in a heavy-based saucepan with a well-fitting lid, add cold water and bring rapidly to a boil. Cover pan, turn heat low and cook for 15 minutes without lifting lid. Turn heat high for 20 seconds and, still without lifting lid, remove pan from heat and allow to stand for 10 minutes before serving.

White rice cooked by the absorption method is the staple food of Japan, and short or medium grain varieties are preferred.

Serves 6

❧❧❧

LENTIL CAKES IN YOGURT
Dahi Bhalas ◆ India (Punjab)

1½ cups urad dhal (split black gram lentils)
1½ teaspoons salt
½ teaspoon finely grated fresh ginger, optional
pinch asafoetida, optional
oil or ghee for deep frying
1 cup (6 ½ oz, 200 g) yogurt
1 cup (8 fl oz, 250 ml) buttermilk
1 teaspoon cumin seed
½ teaspoon chili powder
2 tablespoons chopped cilantro (fresh coriander leaves)
1 fresh green chili, seeded and chopped

Wash lentils thoroughly in several changes of water, then soak in cold water overnight. Drain well, put into electric blender and blend at high speed, adding only as much water as is necessary to facilitate blending. It should form a thick, smooth paste. Add 1 teaspoon salt. Add finely grated fresh ginger and a pinch of asafoetida to the dhal if desired. With wet hands form mixture into flat patties about 2 in (5 cm) across, and as each one is made drop it into hot oil or ghee. Fry, turning with slotted spoon, until pale golden — do not allow patties to brown. Drain on kitchen paper and when cool immerse in cold water for about 10 minutes. Press out excess moisture gently between palms, taking care not to break them.

Combine yogurt, buttermilk and 1/2 teaspoon salt. Immerse the patties in this mixture and chill thoroughly. Roast the cumin seeds in a dry pan, stirring constantly until dark brown. Crush and sprinkle over the dish together with chili powder, chopped cilantro and fresh chili. Serve cold as an accompaniment to rice or parathas.

Serves 6

❧❧❧

LENTIL PURÉE
Dhal ◆ India

250 g (8 oz) red lentils
2 tablespoons ghee or oil
1 onion, finely sliced
2 cloves garlic, sliced
1 teaspoon finely chopped fresh ginger
½ teaspoon ground turmeric
3 cups (24 fl oz) hot water
1 teaspoon salt, or to taste
½ teaspoon garam masala, optional

Wash lentils, discarding those that float. Drain well. In a saucepan heat ghee or oil and fry onion, garlic and ginger until golden brown. Add turmeric and stir for a few seconds, then add the drained lentils and fry for a minute. Add hot water and bring to a boil, reduce heat. Cover and simmer until lentils are soft before adding salt and garam masala. Continue cooking until the consistency of porridge.

Serves 4–5

❧❧❧

LENTILS, SRI LANKAN–STYLE
Paripoo ◆ Sri Lanka

2 cups red lentils
2 cups (16 fl oz, 500 ml) thin coconut cream (milk)
1 dried red chili, broken into pieces
2 teaspoons pounded Maldive fish
1 teaspoon ground turmeric
1 tablespoon ghee or oil
6 curry leaves
2 medium onions, finely sliced
2 in (5 cm) strip pandanus leaf
2 in (5 cm) stick of cinnamon
small stalk lemon grass or strip of lemon rind
½ cup (3½ oz, 100 g) thick coconut cream
salt to taste

Wash lentils well until water is clean. Remove and discard lentils that float on the surface of the water or any that are discolored. Put drained lentils in a saucepan with the thin coconut cream, chili, Maldive fish, and turmeric. Bring to a boil, then cover and cook slowly until lentils are soft.

In another saucepan heat the oil and fry the curry leaves, onions, pandanus, cinnamon, and lemon grass until onions are brown. Reserve half the onions for garnishing the dish and turn the lentil mixture into the saucepan. Add thick coconut cream, salt to taste, and simmer uncovered until lentils are

very soft and the consistency of runny porridge. Serve with rice and curries.
Serves 6

MILK RICE
Kiri Bath ◆ Sri Lanka

2 cups (14 oz, 440 g) white short grain rice
3 cups (24 fl oz, 750 ml) water
2 cups (13 oz, 400 g) thick coconut cream
2 teaspoons salt
1 cinnamon stick, optional

Put rice and water in a saucepan and bring to a boil. Cover and cook for 15 minutes. Add coconut cream, salt, and cinnamon, stir well with the handle of a wooden spoon. Cover pan and cook over a low heat for a further 10 to 15 minutes, when all the cream will be absorbed. Remove cinnamon stick. Cool slightly. Turn out onto a flat serving plate. Cut into large diamond shapes and serve with hot sambals.
Serves 4–5

MIXED FRIED NOODLES
Kaukswe Kyaw ◆ Burma

1 lb (500 g) egg noodles
½ cup (4 fl oz, 125 ml) oil
1 lb (500 g) chicken meat
1 chicken liver
1 chicken gizzard, parboiled
5 medium onions, chopped
5 cloves garlic, chopped
2 tablespoons soy sauce
¼ cabbage, shredded
2 stalks celery, sliced and shredded
¼ white Chinese (Napa) cabbage, shredded
4 or 5 dried Chinese mushrooms, soaked and sliced
6 scallions (spring onions), finely sliced
4 eggs, beaten
salt and pepper to taste

Soak noodles in warm water while bringing water to a boil in a large saucepan. Add drained noodles and cook until just tender. Drain and spread on large dish or tray. Pour 2 tablespoons oil evenly on noodles and toss gently. This prevents noodles sticking to each other and gives a glossy appearance. Finely slice chicken meat, liver, and gizzard. Heat

oil in wok. Fry onions and garlic till soft. Add meat, liver, and gizzard and fry. Add soy sauce. Cover and simmer gently till meat is tender. Add shredded vegetables and continue frying and tossing till done. Remove from wok and set aside. Put noodles in wok, toss gently for about 3 minutes and remove. In the same wok, scramble the eggs, adding a little oil if necessary. Add salt and pepper to taste. When ready to serve, spread noodles on dish, then cover with meat and vegetables. Garnish with scrambled eggs. Serve hot or cold.
Serves 6

MIXED FRIED VERMICELLI
Phat Sen Mee ◆ Thailand

8 oz (250 g) rice vermicelli
10 dried Chinese mushrooms
6 oz (185 g) pork filet
8 oz (250 g) raw shelled and deveined shrimp (prawns)
2 leeks or 6 scallions (spring onions)
1 canned bamboo shoot
2 tender carrots
3 large cloves garlic
2 fresh red chilies, optional
2 tablespoons peanut oil
2 tablespoons fish sauce
1 tablespoon white vinegar
1 teaspoon salt
2 teaspoons sugar
½ teaspoon black pepper
fried onion flakes (page 22), optional
3 tablespoons chopped cilantro (fresh coriander leaves)

Soak vermicelli in hot, not boiling, water for 10 minutes, then drain in a colander. Soak mushrooms in hot water for 20 minutes, squeeze out water, slice mushroom caps thinly and discard stems. Cut the pork into very thin shreds. Cut the shrimp into pieces if large. Wash leeks well, making sure there is no sand left among leaves. Use the white portion and about 2 in (5 cm) of the green leaves. Slice very finely. If scallions are used, cut into short lengths. Cut bamboo shoot and carrots into julienne strips. Chop garlic finely and slice the chilies diagonally, flipping out the seeds with point of knife.

Heat oil in wok or large frying pan and fry the garlic and chilies on gentle heat until soft. Move to side of pan, raise heat to medium and add the pork. Stir-fry for 3 or 4 minutes, until cooked. Add shrimp, leeks, bamboo shoots, and carrots and stir-fry for a further 3 minutes. Add all the seasonings mixed together and simmer for 1 minute, then add the vermicelli and

Mixed fried vermicelli (recipe opposite).

toss until well mixed and heated through. Serve on a long dish and garnish with finely chopped cilantro and crisp-fried onion flakes if desired.

Serves 4

✧✦✧

MOHINGA
Burma

4 tablespoons peanut oil
2 tablespoons sesame oil
4 medium onions, sliced
4 cloves garlic, chopped
2 fresh chilies, seeded and chopped
1 teaspoon ngapi or blachan (dried shrimp paste)
4 cups (32 fl oz, 1 L) thin coconut cream (milk)
4 fresh boneless fish pieces or 7 oz (220 g) can herrings in
  tomato sauce
2 teaspoons salt
9 oz (270 g) canned bamboo shoots
3 tablespoons besan (lentil flour)
2 cups (13 oz, 400 g) thick coconut cream
2 tablespoons lemon juice
extra salt to taste
1 lb (500 g) egg noodles

Heat peanut and sesame oil and fry onion and garlic until soft. Add chilies and ngapi and fry 2 minutes longer. Add thin coconut cream, fish, and salt. (If using canned fish, add liquid from can as well.) Drain bamboo shoots, cut in half lengthwise and across into very thin slices, add to mixture. Bring to a boil, lower heat and simmer 15 minutes. Stir in besan mixed to a smooth cream with a little cold water, simmer 5 minutes longer. Add thick coconut cream and lemon juice. Season to taste with extra salt if necessary.

Cook noodles in boiling salted water until just tender, drain well. Serve in a bowl.

Serve fish soup in a separate bowl or tureen. Provide deep bowls rather than plates. Noodles are served first and soup ladled over the top. Mohinga must be served piping hot. Serve with a variety of accompaniments (see recipe for Cellophane Noodles, page 224).

Note: In Burma this traditional dish is made with slices from the heart of a banana tree. Bamboo shoots are a suitable substitute.

Serves 8

✧✦✧

NOODLES WITH BRAISED BEEF
China

4 bundles wide egg noodles
1 lb (500 g) rump or scotch filet steak
1 clove garlic, crushed
½ teaspoon salt
¼ teaspoon finely grated fresh root ginger
¼ teaspoon five-spice powder
2 tablespoons peanut oil
1 cup (8 fl oz, 250 ml) Master Sauce (see Note below)
2 teaspoons cornstarch (cornflour)
1 tablespoon cold water
10 scallions (spring onions)

Soak noodles in hot water for 10 minutes, drain, then drop noodles into a large pan of boiling water and cook for 3 minutes or until just tender. Drain in colander, rinse under cold water and drain once more.

While noodles are draining, cut beef into paper-thin shreds. Rub garlic crushed with salt, ginger, and five-spice powder into beef.

Heat oil in a wok and quickly stir-fry the beef over high heat until it browns. Add the Master Sauce and bring to a boil. Add cornstarch mixed to a smooth paste with cold water and stir until it boils and thickens. Add noodles and heat through. Stir in the scallions cut into bite-size pieces and keep turning and mixing noodles and beef in the sauce for a further minute. Serve at once.

Note: If Master Sauce is not available, substitute 1/2 cup (4 fl oz, 125 ml) soy sauce and 1/2 cup (4 fl oz, 125 ml) water or stock.

Serves 4

✧✦✧

OIL RICE
See Htamin ◆ Burma

2 cups (16 oz, 500 ml) glutinous rice
3 large onions
1½ teaspoons turmeric
6 tablespoons oil
4 cups (32 fl oz, 1 L) hot water
2 teaspoons salt
4 tablespoons toasted sesame seeds

Wash rice well and leave to drain and dry. Slice onions thinly, keeping them uniform in thickness. Sprinkle turmeric over onions and mix lightly. Heat oil in a medium-size saucepan and fry onions until brown. Remove two-thirds of the onions and set aside for garnish. Add rice to pan and stir until it is well mixed with the oil. Add water and salt, stir well and bring to a boil. Turn heat very low, cover tightly and cook for 20 minutes by which time the rice should be cooked and the water completely absorbed.

Serve hot, garnished with fried onion and accompanied by the sesame seed lightly bruised and mixed with a little salt.

Note: Some people like a crust on the rice. To encourage a crust to form leave the rice on low heat for 5 to 10 minutes longer until a slight crackling sound is heard.

Serves 4–6

✧⚬✧

POT ROASTED RICE
Com Chien ◆ Vietnam

2 cups (14 oz, 440 g) medium grain rice
2 tablespoons peanut oil or shortening (lard)
1¾ cups (14 fl oz, 450 ml) hot water

Wash rice well and drain for 30 minutes or until dry. Heat oil or melt shortening in a heavy saucepan with a well-fitting lid. Fry rice, stirring gently with a metal spoon, for 10 to 15 minutes or until rice becomes opaque and turns golden. Add hot water, bring to a boil, then reduce heat to very low. Cover tightly and cook for 20 minutes. Serve with garlic, chili and fish sauce (nuoc cham, page 14), and other dishes.

Note: The amount of water in this recipe gives short or medium grain rice a dry, fluffy result with firm grains. If using long grain rice, increase hot water to 2 1/2 cups (20 fl oz, 600 ml) for the same result because the long grain variety has a greater absorbency.

✧⚬✧

PILAU RICE
India

1 lb (500 g) chicken pieces
4 cardamom pods
10 peppercorns
4½ teaspoons salt
2 bay leaves
1 onion
3 cloves
2½ cups (16 ½ oz, 540 g) basmati rice
5 tablespoons ghee
1 large extra onion, finely sliced
good pinch powdered saffron or ¼ teaspoon saffron strands
2 cloves garlic, crushed

½ teaspoon finely grated fresh root ginger
½ teaspoon garam masala
½ teaspoon ground cardamom
3 tablespoons rose water
¼ cup golden raisins (sultanas)

Garnish:
¼ cup fried almonds
1 cup hot cooked peas
4 hard-cooked (boiled) eggs, cut in halves

Make a strong, rich-tasting chicken stock by simmering chicken in water to cover with cardamom pods, peppercorns, 2 teaspoons salt, bay leaves, and the onion stuck with cloves. Simmer for approximately 2 hours. Cool slightly, strain stock and measure 4 cups (1 3/4 pts, 1 L). Remove chicken meat from bones, cut into bite-size pieces and set aside. Instead of home-made stock you can combine 4 cups (1 3/4 pts, 1 L) of boiling water and 4 large chicken stock cubes, thoroughly mixed together.

Wash rice thoroughly in water, drain in a colander and allow to dry for at least 1 hour. Heat ghee in a large saucepan and fry sliced onion until golden. Add saffron, garlic, and ginger and fry for 1 minute, stirring continuously. Add rice and fry 5 minutes longer over a moderate heat, stirring with a slotted metal spoon. (This prevents breaking the long delicate grains of rice.) Add hot stock, garam masala, cardamom, remaining salt, rose water, golden raisins, reserved chicken pieces, stir well. Cover pan with a tightly fitting lid and cook over a very low heat for 20 minutes. Do not uncover saucepan or stir rice during cooking time.

When rice is cooked, remove from heat and stand, uncovered, for 5 minutes. Gently fluff up rice with a fork and place in a serving dish, again using a slotted metal spoon. Garnish with almonds, hot peas, hard-cooked eggs.

Serves 4–5

✧⚬✧

RICE BALLS
Musubi ◆ Japan

hot cooked rice
goma sio (black sesame seeds and salt) or powdered nori (seaweed)
raw or smoked fish, optional

Cook rice and when cool enough to handle take about 1/2 cup (3 oz, 90 g) rice and , with wet hands, roll into firm balls about 3 in (7.5 cm) in diameter. If using fish cut it into very thin strips and push a strip into the middle of each rice ball, shaping the rice around it. Roll the rice balls lightly in goma sio or powdered nori.

Note: In Japan, rice takes the place of sandwich bread,

hamburger buns, and hot dog rolls. Rice balls are sometimes filled with pieces of fish, raw or smoked, or simply flavored with sesame seeds or seaweed.

⋞⋙∞⋘⋟

RICE CONGEE
China

8 oz (250 g) short or medium grain rice
4 cups (1¾ pts, 1 L) water
2 cups (16 fl oz, 500 ml) stock
salt and white pepper to taste
12 oz (375 g) boned haddock (gemfish) or boned chicken breast
2 teaspoons sesame oil
1 teaspoon salt
½ teaspoon finely grated ginger

Accompaniments:
finely chopped scallions (spring onions)
fresh red chilies, seeded and sliced
finely chopped cilantro (fresh coriander leaves)
light soy sauce
crisp-fried onions

Wash and drain the rice, put in a saucepan with the water and stock, and bring to a boil. Reduce heat, cover saucepan and simmer for 1 hour or until the rice is very soft.

Skin the fish, cut into thin slices and mix with the sesame oil, salt, and ginger. If using chicken breast, cut into fine shreds and marinate as for the fish.

When rice porridge is cooked to a thick, creamy consistency, stir in the fish or chicken and cook for 1 minute or just long enough to turn slices white and opaque. Ladle into bowls and let each person choose the accompaniments preferred. This is the traditional Chinese breakfast.

Crisp-fried onions: Finely slice red onions (small purple shallots) in plenty of oil, stirring constantly, until golden brown. Drain, and save the oil to use as a flavoring in many dishes. Sometimes available at Chinese stores.
Serves 6

⋞⋙∞⋘⋟

RICE COOKED IN COCONUT CREAM WITH SPICES
Nasi Uduk ◆ Indonesia

1 lb (500 g) long grain rice
4½ cups (36 fl oz, 1.25 l) thin coconut cream
2½ teaspoons salt
1 onion, finely chopped
1 teaspoon finely chopped garlic
1 teaspoon ground turmeric
1 teaspoon ground cumin
2 teaspoons ground coriander
½ teaspoon dried shrimp paste
¼ teaspoon kencur (galangal, lesser) powder
1 teaspoon finely chopped lemon rind, or 1 stem of lemon grass, chopped

If rice needs washing, wash and drain well. Put all ingredients except rice into a saucepan with a well fitting lid, and bring slowly to a boil, uncovered, stirring frequently.

Add the rice, stir and bring back to a boil. Turn heat as low as possible, cover pan tightly and steam for 20 minutes. Uncover, fork rice lightly from around sides of pan, mixing in any coconut cream that has not been absorbed, replace lid and steam for 5 minutes longer. Serve hot with Indonesian or Malaysian curries and accompaniments.
Serves 6

⋞⋙∞⋘⋟

RICE ROLLS WITH SPICY FILLING
Lemper ◆ Indonesia

1 lb (500 g) ketan (glutinous rice)
2 cups (16 fl oz, 500 ml) water
1 cup (6 ½ oz, 200 g) thick coconut cream
8 oz (250 g) ground (minced) pork or finely chopped chicken
½ teaspoon salt
½ teaspoon ground black pepper
2 tablespoons oil
2 cloves garlic, crushed
2 daun salam or curry leaves
2 teaspoons ground coriander
1 teaspoon ground cumin
½ teaspoon ground turmeric
½ teaspoon trasi (dried shrimp paste)
squeeze of lemon juice
squares of banana leaf or aluminum foil

RICE VERMICELLI PILAU
Sri Lanka

1 lb (500 g) rice vermicelli
5 tablespoons ghee
3 large onions, finely sliced
10 curry leaves
1 good pinch powdered saffron or ½ teaspoon saffron
  strands
1 teaspoon ground turmeric
1 teaspoon ground cardamom
salt and pepper to taste
4–5 eggs, hard-cooked (boiled)
1 cup peas, cooked
¼ cup cashew nuts or almonds, fried until golden brown
  in oil

Cook rice vermicelli in a large quantity of lightly salted boiling water for 3 minutes, no longer. Drain in a large colander.

Heat ghee in a large saucepan and fry onion and curry leaves until onion is golden. Add saffron, turmeric, and cardamom and stir well. Add rice vermicelli and toss ingredients together until well mixed and evenly colored. Season to taste with salt and pepper.

Serve garnished with eggs cut into slices or quarters, peas, and nuts.

Note: The hard-cooked eggs may be rubbed with ground turmeric and fried in a little hot oil until golden.

Rice congee (recipe opposite).

RICE VERMICELLI WITH BEEF AND LONG BEANS
Ngau Yook Dau Kok Chow Mi Fun • China

8 oz (250 g) rice vermicelli
12 oz (375 g) lean steak
12 oz (375 g) long (snake) beans
3 tablespoons peanut oil
1 clove garlic, crushed
½ teaspoon finely grated fresh ginger
1 cup beef stock (page 6)
1 teaspoon salt
2 tablespoons light soy sauce
few drops chili oil, optional

Wash rice and drain. Put in a saucepan with water and bring to a boil, then turn heat very low, cover pan tightly and steam for 15 minutes. Mix 3/4 cup (5 oz, 155 g) of the coconut cream with 1/2 cup (4 fl oz, 125 ml) water in a small saucepan and heat without boiling. Add to rice, stir gently with a fork, cover and steam for 5 to 10 minutes, until coconut cream has been absorbed. Leave to cool.

Season pork or chicken with salt and pepper. Heat oil in a wok or medium-size saucepan and fry the garlic and daun salam for 1 minute. Add ground spices and trasi and fry, stirring, for a minute longer, crushing the trasi with the spoon. Add pork or chicken and fry until it turns golden. Add remaining coconut cream and simmer, uncovered, on low heat until well cooked and quite dry. Add lemon juice to taste, check seasoning and add more salt and pepper if necessary. Cool.

To make lemper: Take a large tablespoonful of rice and flatten on a piece of banana leaf or foil till 1/2 in (12 mm) thick. Put a good teaspoon of the filling in the middle and shape the rice around into a cylinder. Roll up in the banana leaf and secure with wooden toothpicks, or roll in the foil to make a neat parcel. Heat over a barbecue or steam for 15 minutes, then allow to cool once again. They are served at room temperature as a snack.

To prepare banana leaves: Strip the leaves from the thick middle rib with a sharp knife. They are inclined to split, but this doesn't matter, for they have to be cut into pieces anyway. Wash the leaves to remove any dust, then pour boiling water over, making them pliable enough to fold without splitting. Ti leaves or bamboo leaves (from Chinese stores) can be used instead, or heavy-duty aluminum foil.

Soak rice vermicelli in a large bowl of cold water for 10 minutes. Slice beef very thinly, cut beans into 2 in (5 cm) lengths. Heat oil in wok, stir-fry beans for 2 minutes, remove from wok. Add garlic, ginger, and beef, stir-fry until beef browns, then add stock, salt, and soy sauce. Add well-drained rice vermicelli and toss until heated through. Cover and cook on fairly low heat for

3 minutes. Return beans to wok, toss with other ingredients for 1 minute and serve at once. Chili oil can be served separately for sprinkling on individual servings.

Serves 4–5

❖❖❖

RICE VERMICELLI WITH SHRIMP
China

8 oz (250 g) rice vermicelli
6 leaves gai choy (mustard cabbage)
1 lb (500 g) raw shelled, deveined shrimp (prawns)
1 clove garlic, crushed
1 teaspoon finely grated fresh ginger
1 tablespoon Chinese wine or dry sherry
1 teaspoon oyster sauce
1 tablespoon light soy sauce
4 fl oz (125 ml) stock
salt to taste
4 tablespoons peanut oil
1 teaspoon sesame oil

Soak the vermicelli for 10 minutes in hot water; drain in a colander. Wash the gai choy, trim off and discard the leaves, and cut the leaf ribs into thin strips. If the shrimp are large, cut in two lengthwise. Mix together the garlic, ginger, wine, oyster sauce, light soy, and stock.

Heat a wok, add the peanut oil and swirl to coat the sides of the wok. Add the shrimp, stir-fry until they turn pink, then transfer them to a bowl containing the sesame oil. Mix thoroughly.

Reheat the oil in the wok, add the sliced cabbage and stir-fry for 1 minute. Add the mixed liquids and cook for a further 2 minutes.

Add the vermicelli and toss until heated through. Return the shrimp to the wok, toss to mix well, and serve immediately.

Serves 4

❖❖❖

RICE WITH CHICKEN & MUSHROOMS
Oboro ◆ Japan

2½ cups (17 ½ oz, 540 g) short grain rice
8 shiitake (dried mushrooms)
4 tablespoons Japanese soy sauce
4 tablespoons mirin or dry sherry
2 tablespoons sugar

12 oz (375 g) boned chicken breast, thinly sliced
2 eggs, beaten
⅛ teaspoon salt
1 cup cooked green peas

Wash rice well and let it drain in a colander for 30 minutes. Pour boiling water over the shiitake and soak for 30 minutes. Cut off and discard stems and put caps in a small saucepan with 1/2 cup (4 fl oz, 125 ml) of the soaking water and half each of the soy, mirin, and sugar. Bring to a boil, cover and cook until liquid is almost completely evaporated. Remove shiitake from pan and cool.

Into same saucepan put remaining soy, mirin, sugar, and about 1/4 cup (2 fl oz, 60 ml) mushroom liquid. Add sliced chicken and bring to a boil, turn heat low, cover and simmer gently for 3 minutes. Turn off heat and leave covered.

Put rice into a saucepan with 3 cups (24 fl oz, 750 ml) water, bring to a boil, turn heat very low, cover pan and cook for 20 minutes without lifting lid or stirring.

While rice is cooking beat eggs slightly with salt and in a lightly greased frying pan make 2 or 3 large, flat omelets, taking care not to brown them. Turn onto a flat plate and when cool cut into narrow strips.

When rice is cooked spoon it into a large domburi or earthenware bowl with lid, spread chicken over surface of rice and spoon the liquid in which the chicken was cooked over the rice. Slice shiitake and spread them over chicken. Decorate top with omelet strips and green peas and serve hot.

Serves 6

❖❖❖

RICE WITH CHICKEN & SEAFOOD
Arroz a la Paella ◆ The Philippines

3 lb (1.5 kg) roasting chicken, cut into serving pieces
salt and pepper to taste
1 lb (500 g) pork chops
2 chorizos (hot Spanish sausages)
1 raw lobster tail, optional
1 lb (500 g) raw shrimp (prawns)
1 lb (500 g) fresh mussels
olive oil for frying

Sofrito:
3 tablespoons olive oil
2 large onions, finely chopped
½ teaspoon saffron strands
5 cloves garlic, finely chopped
2 large ripe tomatoes or 1 cup canned tomatoes

5 weeks of fitness

5 weeks of fitness with Leisureactive

leisure & culture DUNDEE

Join from 14 September
to get up to 5 weeks of Fitness*

Platinum Membership

- Over 120 Group Exercise Classes
- 8 Fitness Studios across Dundee
- 5 Swimming pools
- 2 Saunas, 1 Steam room

£20

Junior & Teen Membership

£10

- Swimming, 9 Hole Golf, Fitness Studios,
  Sports Centre Activity Programmes, Ice Skating (Mon -Fri 10am - 12noon).

*This promotion does not include holiday programmes or swimming lessons. Child admission policy applies.
Please check centre timetables for any changes to availability. Fitness studios can only be accessed by age 14+
who have underwent a youth induction.*

All members receive discounted entry to; Dundee Ice Arena, Camperdown
Wildlife Centre & 20% off group activities at Ancrum Outdoor Centre.

Memberships can be taken out at any Leisureactive Site.
Platinum memberships can also be taken out
via: www.leisuredundee.com/JoinAtHome

*All memberships will end on 19 October 2018.

*Member Loyalty points accrued during the promotion must be redeemed for a reward (if eligible) by this date. If a further
membership is taken out within 2 weeks of this date, accrued Member Loyalty points will remain on the member record.*

For more info please call 01382 432328 or email: Leisureactive@leisureandculturedundee.com

Leisure & Culture Dundee is a Scottish Charitable Incorporated Organisation No. SC042421

www.leisureandculturedundee.com

Rice vermicelli with shrimp (recipe opposite).

3 teaspoons salt
3 teaspoons paprika
2½ cups (17½ oz, 540 g) long grain rice
4½ cups (36 fl oz, 1.2 L) chicken or fish stock
1 cup green peas
1 red bell pepper (capsicum), seeded and cut in strips

Dry chicken on kitchen paper and season well with salt and pepper. Cut pork chops into dice, discarding skin and bones. Pierce chorizos in a few places with a sharp knife, put into a saucepan with water to cover and bring to a boil. Reduce heat and simmer for 5 minutes, drain and slice into rounds.

Chop lobster tail into large slices, including shell. Wash shrimp but do not remove shells. Scrub mussels with a stiff brush, beard them, and discard any that are not tightly closed.

Heat enough olive oil in a large, heavy frying pan to cover base of pan and brown the pieces of chicken on all sides. Remove to a plate. Add lobster and cook for a minute or two until shell turns pink. Transfer to plate. Brown chorizo slices, drain on absorbent paper. Brown the pork quickly, drain. Discard oil in pan.

Sofrito: In a large frying pan or heavy saucepan heat olive oil and fry onions over medium heat until soft and golden. While onions are cooking pour 2 tablespoons boiling water over saffron and leave to soak. Add garlic, soaked saffron, peeled and chopped tomatoes, and fry, stirring, until tomatoes are soft and pulpy. Add salt and paprika and stir well. Add rice and stir over medium heat for 3 or 4 minutes, then add hot stock and stir well.

When stock comes to a boil add chicken, pork, chorizo, and lobster, cover and cook on very low heat for 15 minutes. Add shrimp and mussels, pushing mussels into the mass of rice so they will cook in the steam. Do not stir. Scatter peas over top. Cover and cook for a further 15 minutes, when rice should be cooked through and liquid absorbed. Decorate top of paella with strips of red capsicum and serve.
Serves 6–8

⋘∞⋙

RICE WITH FRIED CHICKEN
Yakitori Domburi • Japan

1 small roasting chicken, cut into serving pieces
½ cup (4 fl oz, 125 ml) Japanese soy sauce
½ cup (4 fl oz, 125 ml) mirin or dry sherry
2 cloves garlic, crushed
1 teaspoon finely grated fresh ginger
3 cups (24 fl oz, 750 ml) chicken stock
¼ cup (2 fl oz, 60 ml) vegetable oil
2½ cups (15 oz, 470 g) cooked short grain rice
3 teaspoons sugar
3 scallions (spring onions), finely sliced

Marinate chicken in a mixture of soy, mirin, garlic, and ginger for 30 minutes. Use chicken back and wing tips to make a stock.

Drain pieces of chicken well, reserving marinade. Heat oil and fry chicken until golden brown, cool slightly, then cut meat into bite-size pieces.

Arrange hot cooked rice in a large bowl or individual bowls and put chicken pieces on top of rice. Add reserved marinade to the stock, bring to a boil with sugar. As it comes to a boil stir in the scallions. Pour over the rice and chicken and serve immediately.
Serves 6

⋘∞⋙

RICE WITH FRESH PEAS
Mattar Pilau • India (Uttar Pradesh)

1½ cups (10 ½ oz, 320 g) long grain rice
1 tablespoon ghee
4 whole cloves
1 small cinnamon stick
3 or 4 cardamom pods, bruised
1 teaspoon cumin seeds
½ teaspoon ground turmeric
1½ cups shelled green peas
2½ teaspoons salt
3¼ cups (26 fl oz, 810 ml) hot water

Wash the rice well and leave to soak in cold water for 30 minutes, then drain well. Heat the ghee in a heavy saucepan and fry the cloves, cinnamon, cardamom pods, and cumin seeds, for 1 minute. Add turmeric and rice and stir over medium heat for about 3 minutes. Add peas, salt, and hot water. Bring quickly to a boil, then turn heat very low, cover with a well-fitting lid and cook for 25 to 30 minutes without lifting lid or stirring. Uncover at end of cooking time to allow steam to escape for about 3 minutes. Remove whole spices, fork rice grains lightly and serve hot with meat or vegetable curries.
Serves 4–5

⋞⋙∞⋘⋟

RICE WITH FRIED BEAN CURD

Kitsune Domburi ◆ Japan

2½ cups rice
4 sheets aburage (fried bean curd)
2½ cups (20 fl oz, 600 ml) dashi (page 6) or chicken stock
½ cup (4 fl oz, 125 ml) Japanese soy sauce
½ cup (4 fl oz, 125 ml) mirin or dry sherry
1 tablespoon sugar
6 scallions (spring onions), finely sliced diagonally

Cook rice by absorption method. While it is cooking pour half a kettle of boiling water over the aburage in a colander to make it less oily. Cut each sheet in half lengthwise, then cut across into strips the width of a pencil.

Put the dashi, soy, mirin, and sugar into a pan with strips of bean curd and bring to a boil, reduce heat and simmer for 10 minutes. Add sliced scallions, simmer covered for 1 minute.

Put the rice into one large bowl or six individual bowls and ladle the hot soup over. Serve hot.
Serves 6

⋞⋙∞⋘⋟

RICE WITH KAPI

Khao Kluk Kapi ◆ Thailand

1 tablespoon dried shrimp (prawns)
4 or 5 large cloves garlic, finely chopped
2 fresh bird's eye chilies (very hot, tiny chilies)
2 eggs, beaten
pepper and salt to taste
1 tablespoon kapi (dried shrimp paste)
4 tablespoons shortening (lard) or oil
½ cup finely diced cooked pork
4 cups (24 oz, 660 g) hot cooked rice
2–3 tablespoons fish sauce
4 tablespoons chopped cilantro (fresh coriander leaves)

Soak shrimp in hot water for 10 minutes, then drain. Remove sandy vein and chop shrimps. Seed and chop the chilies. Beat eggs and season with salt and pepper. In a flat frying pan lightly greased with oil make 2 or 3 flat omelets and cut them into thin strips. Wrap kapi in foil and broil (grill) for 5 minutes. Heat oil in a wok and fry the garlic and chilies on low heat until golden. Do not have oil too hot when the garlic is put in or it will brown too quickly. Add the shrimp and kapi and fry, stirring constantly, for 2 or 3 minutes. Add pork and fry for 1 minute. Add the rice and toss together with other ingredients until heated through. Season with fish sauce to taste, pile on a dish and garnish with omelet strips and cilantro. More hot chilies may be used for garnish if desired.
Serves 6

⋞⋙∞⋘⋟

RICE WITH LENTILS & TAMARIND

Bisi Bellha Hoolli Annam ◆ India (Karnataka)

½ cup toor dhal (red lentils)
1 cup (7 oz, 220 g) long grain rice
2¾ cups (22 fl oz, 700 ml) water
¼ teaspoon ground turmeric
1½ teaspoons salt
3 tablespoons oil
½ teaspoon asafoetida, optional
2 tablespoons coriander seeds
4 dried red chilies, stalks and seeds removed
small piece cinnamon stick
20 cloves
3 tablespoons freshly grated or unsweetened desiccated
  coconut
1 lb (500 g) green (string) beans
¼ cup tamarind pulp or 2 teaspoons instant tamarind
1½ tablespoons mustard seed
12 curry leaves
2 tablespoons ghee
¼ cup raw cashews

Wash the dhal and rice, drain well, then put into a saucepan with water, turmeric, and salt, bring to a boil, cover and cook until water is absorbed, about 20 minutes.

Meanwhile heat 3 teaspoons oil and fry the asafoetida (if used) for about 3 minutes. Remove the asafoetida and fry the coriander and chilies for 3 or 4 minutes. Put asafoetida, coriander, chilies, cinnamon, cloves, and coconut into electric blender, add just enough water to facilitate blending and blend until spices are finely ground.

Top and tail beans and cut into small pieces. Cook in lightly salted boiling water until almost tender. Drain, reserving liquid.

Rice with chicken and seafood, from the Philippines (page 242).

Soak the tamarind pulp in 1/2 cup (4 fl oz, 125 ml) of this liquid, and squeeze to dissolve the pulp, then strain and discard seeds and fibers. If using instant tamarind, dissolve in the hot liquid.

Heat remaining oil in saucepan and fry the mustard seeds and curry leaves until the seeds pop. Add beans, tamarind liquid, ground spice, and coconut mixture and bring to a boil, cover and simmer 5 minutes. Add the cooked dhal and rice and stir well, taking care not to mash the grains. Heat the ghee in a small pan and fry the cashew nuts until golden. Pour the ghee over the rice and mix. Serve hot, garnished with fried cashews.

Note: Slices of fried eggplant (aubergine) and potato are sometimes added to this dish.

Serves 4–5

❖❖❖

RICE WITH MIXED LENTILS
Bhuna Kitchri ◆ India (Uttar Pradesh)

1 cup moong dhal (green lentils)
½ cup masoor dhal (red lentils)
1½ cups (10½ oz, 320 g) basmati or other long grain rice
1 lb (500 g) fresh peas
1 tablespoon ghee
3 tablespoons vegetable oil
6 cardamom pods, bruised
1 small stick cinnamon
4 small bay leaves
4 whole cloves
4 large onions, finely sliced
1 tablespoon finely grated fresh ginger
1 fresh green chili, seeded and sliced
½ teaspoon cumin seeds
½ teaspoon ground turmeric
1 teaspoon ground cumin
4 cups (1¾ pts, 1 L) hot water
3½ teaspoons salt

Garnish:
2 tablespoons chopped cilantro (fresh coriander leaves),
  optional

In a dry pan roast the moong dhal, stirring constantly, until evenly golden brown. Turn into a bowl and wash well, then leave to drain. Wash masoor dhal separately and leave to drain. Wash rice well and leave to drain for at least 30 minutes. Meanwhile, shell the peas. There should be about 3/4 cup of shelled peas.

Heat the ghee and oil in a heavy saucepan. Add the cardamom pods, cinnamon, bay leaves, cloves, and the sliced onions. Fry over medium heat, stirring frequently, until the onions are golden brown. Remove to a plate with a slotted spoon. To the oil left in the pan add the ginger, chili, and cumin seeds. Fry, stirring, until ginger is golden. Add the rice and masoor dhal and fry, stirring, for 3 minutes. Add the turmeric, ground cumin and fry for a further 2 minutes. Add fresh peas, moong dhal, water, and salt, stir and bring to a boil. Return the cardamoms, cinnamon, bay leaves, and cloves to the pan. Turn heat very low, cover and cook for 30 to 35 minutes or until liquid is absorbed and peas tender. Transfer to serving dish with a metal spoon and garnish with fried onions and cilantro, if used.

Serve with an accompaniment of peeled, diced tomatoes dressed with a pinch of chili powder and salt to taste. Pickles or chutneys and a bowl of yogurt complete the meal.

Serves 4–5

❖❖❖

RICE WITH SESAME SEEDS
Til Bhath ◆ South India

2½ cups (14 oz, 540 g) long grain rice
4 cups (1¾ pts, 1 L) water
2½ teaspoons salt
2 tablespoons light sesame oil
1 teaspoon mustard seeds
12 curry leaves
1 cup sesame seeds
lemon juice to taste

Put rice, water, and salt into a heavy saucepan, bring to a boil. Cover with well-fitting lid, turn heat very low and cook for 20 minutes. Turn off heat and leave while preparing seasoning.

Heat sesame oil in small saucepan and fry the mustard seeds and curry leaves until leaves are brown and mustard seeds pop. Add the sesame seeds and keep stirring over medium heat until the seeds are evenly golden brown. Mix this seasoning together with the hot cooked rice and add a little lemon juice to taste. Serve with curried vegetables, fresh chutney, and fried pappadams.

Serves 4–6

❖❖❖

RICE WITH SPICED LAMB IN YOGURT

Korma Pilau ◆ India & Pakistan

1 quantity lamb curry (page 196)
1 quantity pilau (page 239) using lamb stock or water in
place of chicken, and cooking rice for 15 minutes only

Extra ingredients:
¼ teaspoon saffron strands
¾ cup (6 fl oz, 180 ml) hot milk
2 tablespoons rose water or few drops rose extract (essence)
3 drops kewra extract (essence), optional
ghee
slices of firm ripe tomato
1 cucumber, thinly sliced
1 onion, thinly sliced
2 fresh green chilies, thinly sliced
3 hard-cooked (boiled) eggs, sliced or quartered
3 tablespoons slivered fried almonds

Prepare lamb curry. While pilau is cooking soak the saffron strands in the hot milk and press to diffuse as much as possible of the yellow color. Mix in the flavorings.

Grease a large, ovenproof cooking pot with ghee and arrange pilau and lamb curry in layers. Sprinkle each layer of rice with the saffron and milk mixture. Finish with a layer of rice. Cover the pot and cook in a slow oven for 30 minutes. Garnish top with the remaining ingredients and serve hot.

Alternatively, cook pilau for full 20 minutes. Remove two-thirds of the rice from pan in which it was cooked, sprinkle the rice left in the pan with a third of the milk. Put in half the lamb curry, spreading it to sides of pan. Cover with half the rice, sprinkle rice with half the remaining milk. Make a layer of the remaining korma and cover that with the rest of the rice. Sprinkle remaining milk over, cover tightly and leave on very low heat for 25 to 30 minutes.
Serves 6–8

RICE WITH YOGURT

Thair Sadam ◆ South India

2½ cups (14½ oz, 540 g) long grain rice
4 cups (1¾ pts, 1 L) water
2½ teaspoons salt
2 tablespoons ghee or oil
1 teaspoon black cumin seeds
1 teaspoon black mustard seeds

1 teaspoon urad dhal (black split lentils)
¼ teaspoon asafoetida, optional
3 fresh red or green chilies, seeded and sliced
3 cups yogurt
salt to taste

Put well washed and drained rice into a saucepan with the water and salt. Bring quickly to a boil, then cover tightly, turn heat very low and cook for 20 minutes without lifting lid.

In another pan heat the ghee and fry the black cumin, mustard, dhal, asafoetida (if used), and chilies until the mustard seeds pop and the dhal is golden brown. Remove from heat, stir into the yogurt and add a little salt to taste. Mix thoroughly with the cooked rice.
Serves 4–6

SAVORY BLACK-EYED PEAS

Lobia ◆ India (Punjab)

1 cup black-eyed peas (beans)
3 bay leaves
2 cardamom pods, bruised
2 teaspoons chopped garlic
½ teaspoon ground turmeric
1 teaspoon salt
2 medium onions, roughly chopped
2 teaspoons chopped fresh ginger
2 dried red chilies, seeded
2 tablespoons oil or ghee
1 teaspoon ground cumin
½ cup (3½ oz, 100 g) yogurt
½ teaspoon garam masala

Garnish:
2 tablespoons chopped cilantro (fresh coriander leaves)

Wash peas well and soak overnight in cold water to cover. Drain, cover with fresh water and bring to a boil with the bay leaves, cardamoms, 1 teaspoon chopped garlic, turmeric and salt. Cover and simmer until tender, or pressure-cook for about 15 minutes. Drain, reserving liquid.

Put the onions, remaining teaspoon garlic, ginger, and chilies in blender and blend to a purée. Heat oil or ghee and fry the blended mixture, stirring. When it begins to brown add the cumin and fry, stirring, for a few seconds longer. Add the drained peas and the yogurt blended with 1/2 cup (4 fl oz, 125 ml) of the liquid in which the peas cooked. Cook for a further 5 minutes or until the gravy thickens. Sprinkle with garam masala and coriander and serve with chapatis or rice.
Serves 4

SAVORY CHICKPEAS
Chole ◆ India (Punjab)

1 cup dried chickpeas
2 teaspoons salt
2 bay leaves
2 tablespoons ghee or oil
2 large onions, finely chopped
2 teaspoons chopped garlic
2 teaspoons finely chopped fresh ginger
½ teaspoon ground turmeric
1 teaspoon garam masala
2 large ripe tomatoes, peeled and chopped
1 fresh green chili, seeded and sliced
*2 tablespoons chopped fresh mint or cilantro (fresh
    coriander leaves)*
lemon juice to taste

Soak chickpeas in cold water to cover overnight, or better still, for 24 hours. Drain, rinse and put the chickpeas with just enough water to cover in a pressure cooker or heavy saucepan. Add salt and bay leaves and cook until just tender, about 20 minutes in pressure cooker. Drain, reserving liquid.

Heat ghee or oil in a heavy saucepan and fry the onion, garlic, and ginger until golden, stirring frequently. Add turmeric and fry for a few seconds. Add the garam masala, tomatoes, chili, and half the fresh herbs. Add peas and stir well, then add the reserved cooking liquid, cover and simmer on low heat until peas are quite tender and the tomatoes have become a puree. Add lemon juice to taste and sprinkle with remaining fresh herbs. Serve with bread.
Serves 4

SAVORY FRIED RICE
Malaysia

2½ tablespoons ghee or oil
*3 large leeks, finely sliced or 12 scallions (spring onions),
    chopped*
1 medium onion, finely sliced
2 or 3 fresh chilies, seeded and sliced
8 oz (250 g) ham or bacon, chopped
6 eggs
1 teaspoon salt
½ teaspoon freshly ground black pepper
4 cups (24 oz, 660 g) cold cooked rice
2 tablespoons light soy sauce

In a large wok heat ghee and fry leeks, onion, chilies, and ham until leeks and onion are golden. Beat eggs with salt and

pepper, pour into pan and stir over medium heat until eggs are creamy and almost set. Add rice and mix thoroughly. Cook, stirring and tossing, until heated through. Sprinkle with soy sauce, mixing well. Serve as a light meal, by itself or accompanied by pickles or chutneys.
Serves 4

SAVORY RICE
Malaysia & Singapore

2½ tablespoons ghee
3 large leeks, sliced or 12 scallions, chopped
1 medium onion, finely sliced
2 fresh chilies. seeded and sliced
8 oz (250g) ham or bacon, chopped
6 eggs
salt and pepper to taste
4 cups (24 oz, 660 g) cold boiled rice

Heat ghee and fry leeks, onion, chilies, and ham until leeks and onion are golden. Beat eggs with salt and pepper to taste, pour into pan and stir until eggs are creamy and almost set. Add rice and mix thoroughly. Cook, stirring continuously, until heated through.

This is a meal in itself and accompaniments are hardly necessary, but crisp pappadams, and hot pickles or chutneys are suitable.
Serves 4

SCALLION & SOY FRIED RICE
Ching Choong Chow Fan ◆ China

2 tablespoons peanut oil
3–4 cups (18–24 oz, 555–660 g) cold cooked rice
1 tablespoon light soy sauce
1 tablespoon mushroom soy sauce
6 scallions (spring onions), sliced diagonally

Heat oil in wok until very hot. Add rice and stir-fry until grains are all separate and pale gold. Sprinkle with sauces and toss to mix evenly. Add sliced scallions and toss over heat for 1 minute longer. Serve hot.

Note: You can vary this recipe to make it more elaborate. Add one or more of the following ingredients, which should be fried before combining with the rice: chopped ham or bacon; chopped cooked pork; sliced lap cheong (Chinese sausages); small cooked shrimp (prawns), shelled; beaten eggs, seasoned; cooked green peas.
Serves 3–4

SIMPLE FRIED RICE
China

1 cup (6 oz, 185 g) cold cooked rice
4 dried Chinese mushrooms
2 scallions (spring onions)
2 tablespoons peanut oil
1 teaspoon sesame oil
½ teaspoon finely grated fresh ginger
1 clove garlic, crushed
1 tablespoon soy sauce
salt to taste

The trick to making good fried rice is to cook the rice the day before or some hours ahead and allow it to cool completely. With the fingers, separate grains and spread out on a tray. Refrigerate if time permits — this gives a firm texture to the fried rice.

Soak mushrooms in hot water for 30 minutes, then squeeze out as much liquid as possible. With a sharp knife cut off and discard stems, cut mushroom caps into thin slices. Finely chop the scallions, including green leaves.

Heat a wok, add both kinds of oil and fry the ginger and garlic, stirring, until golden. Add mushrooms and fry for a minute longer, then add rice and stir-fry until it is heated through. Add the scallions and soy sauce and toss to combine thoroughly. Add salt to taste. Remove from heat and serve at once.
Serves 2–4

SIZZLING RICE WITH SWEET & SOUR SEAFOOD
China

8 oz (250 g) short grain rice
1 lb (500 g) small raw shelled, deveined shrimp (prawns) or scallops
½ teaspoon salt
1 egg white
1 tablespoon cornstarch (cornflour)
1 tablespoon peanut oil
1 red bell pepper (capsicum)
3 or 4 scallions (spring onions)
2 oz (60 g) frozen peas
10 canned water chestnuts
½ teaspoon finely grated fresh ginger
½ teaspoon crushed garlic
2¾ cups (22 fl oz, 700 ml) peanut oil for deep frying

Sizzling rice with sweet and sour seafood (recipe this page).

Sauce:
4 tablespoons tomato ketchup
3 tablespoons white vinegar
1 tablespoon light soy sauce
1 tablespoon Chinese wine or dry sherry
4 tablespoons sugar
1 tablespoon cornstarch (cornflour)

Put rice into a large saucepan about 10 in (25 cm) diameter, add 12 fl oz (375 ml) water and bring to a boil. Boil uncovered until there is no visible liquid when pan is tilted and the surface of the rice looks dimpled; do not stir the rice at all. Turn the heat very low, cover the saucepan and cook for a further 15 minutes. Remove from heat and cool.

Lift the rice out of the saucepan with a spatula. Place it on an oiled baking tray and press it with the heel of your hand to flatten it. Put in a preheated oven at 325° F (160° C, gas mark 3) for 30 minutes or until dry and the edge feels crisp when touched. Remove from oven, cool, then break it into pieces roughly 2 in (5 cm) square.

Rinse shrimp, dry them thoroughly, and place in a bowl. Sprinkle with salt, add the egg white, and mix through. Sprinkle cornstarch and oil over, and mix again. Chill for 30 minutes at least.

Dice bell pepper, cut scallions into short lengths, thaw peas, and slice water chestnuts. All this may be done hours ahead.

Prepare the sauce. Put the tomato ketchup, vinegar, soy sauce, wine, and sugar into a saucepan; add 6 fl oz (180 ml) water, and stir over heat to dissolve sugar. Blend cornstarch with 3 tablespoons of cold water, add it to the sauce and stir until mixture boils and thickens. Keep warm.

Heat a wok, add 2 3/4 cups peanut oil and when hot, add shrimp, stirring gently, until they turn pink. Drain at once, pouring through a wire strainer into a heatproof bowl. This oil can be used later for frying the rice cakes.

Return the wok to the heat, add 3 tablespoons of oil, and when hot, add the pepper and stir-fry for 1 minute. Add scallions, ginger, and garlic and fry for 10 seconds or until fragrant. Add peas and water chestnuts. Stir all the vegetables into the warm sauce.

Wipe out the wok, return to heat and once more heat the peanut oil for deep frying. When oil is very hot, fry rice cakes until crisp and golden. Drain and place in a serving bowl.

Reheat the sauce to boiling, add shrimp, and pour into a heated bowl. Quickly take both bowls to the table and pour hot sauce over the hot rice cakes so they sizzle and steam. Serve at once into individual bowls, so that the rice cakes will still be crisp when eaten.

The rice cakes may be made a day or two ahead and stored in an airtight container, then fried just before serving.
Serves 6 with other dishes

❧⚬❧

SOFT FRIED NOODLES
China

Proceed as for boiled noodles (page 258). When noodles are well drained, spread them on a large baking tray lined with kitchen paper and allow them to dry in the air for at least 30 minutes. A little peanut oil may be sprinkled over them to prevent sticking.

Heat 2 tablespoons each of peanut oil and sesame oil in a wok or frying pan and when very hot add a handful of noodles. When golden on one side, turn and fry other side. Repeat with remaining noodles. It may be necessary to add more oil to the pan if a large quantity of noodles is being fried, but make sure the fresh oil is very hot before adding noodles.

Serve with beef, pork, poultry, or vegetable dishes, or combine with stir-fried ingredients for Chow Mein.

❧⚬❧

SPICED RICE & LAMB
Sultanpuri Pilau ◆ India (Uttar Pradesh)

1½ cups (10½ oz, 320 g) long grain rice
1½ lb (750 g) lamb forequarter chops
4 cups (1¾ pts, 1 L) water
1 small onion, chopped
2 cardamom pods, lightly bruised
2 bay leaves
small piece cinnamon stick
2½ teaspoons salt
½ cup (4 fl oz, 125 ml) milk
1 tablespoon ghee
2 tablespoons oil
1 large onion, finely sliced
1 tablespoon finely shredded fresh ginger
2 teaspoons finely sliced garlic
½ teaspoon black cumin seeds
2 fresh red chilies, seeded and sliced
⅛ teaspoon saffron strands or pinch powdered saffron
pinch red coloring powder

Wash rice well and leave to drain. Put lamb into a large saucepan with water, chopped onion, cardamom pods, bay leaves, cinnamon stick, and salt. Bring to a boil, then skim surface, cover and simmer gently for at least 1 hour until meat is tender. Remove meat from pan and leave until cool enough to handle. Measure stock. If more than 2 1/2 cups (20 fl oz, 600 ml) continue cooking with the lid off pan until it is reduced to this amount. Add milk to make 3 cups (24 fl oz, 750 ml). Cut meat into cubes, discarding bones and fat.

Heat ghee and oil in a large, heavy saucepan and fry the finely sliced onion until soft. Add ginger and garlic and continue frying and stirring frequently until they are golden. Remove to a plate. Add meat to pan and fry, stirring, until meat is browned, remove with slotted spoon and set aside with the fried onion mixture. Fry the black cumin seeds and the chilies separately for 1 minute and set aside. Put half the washed and drained rice into the saucepan and spread with the meat and onion mixture, then cover with remaining rice. Sprinkle the black cumin seeds and chilies over rice. Reserve 1 tablespoon of milk and stock and gently pour the stock over the rice. Bring to a boil, then turn heat very low, cover tightly and allow to cook for 20 minutes.

Meanwhile, heat the reserved stock and dissolve the saffron in it. If saffron strands are used, pound them first in mortar and pestle. If powdered saffron is used, put it straight into the hot stock. Add a pinch of red coloring to turn it a bright orange-red. When the rice has cooked for 20 minutes, pour the saffron liquid over the top. It will not make many grains yellow, but this is the way it should be. Replace the lid and leave for a further

5 minutes. Before serving, gently fork the yellow grains through the rice. Serve hot.

Serves 4

STEAMED PEARL BALLS
China

1 cup (7 oz, 220 g) short grain rice
8 dried Chinese mushrooms
8 oz (250 g) ground (minced) lean topside
8 oz (250 g) ground (minced) pork
4 scallions (spring onions), finely chopped
1 teaspoon finely grated fresh ginger
½ teaspoon crushed garlic
1 teaspoon salt
¼ teaspoon ground black pepper
1 tablespoon light soy sauce
1 egg, beaten
¼ cup finely chopped water chestnuts

Soak rice covered in cold water for at least 2 hours, then drain well, spread on kitchen paper and leave to dry while preparing meatballs. Soak mushrooms in hot water for 30 minutes. Squeeze out excess water, discard stems and chop caps finely. Put in a large bowl with all the remaining ingredients and mix very well with the hands. Shape into balls about 1 in (2.5 cm) in diameter, rolling them between your palms. Roll each ball separately in the rice with enough pressure to make the rice stick and coat the ball.

Oil a steamer rack and put the balls on it, leaving space between so the rice can swell as it steams. Fill wok with water up to 1 in (2.5 cm) below rack, bring water to a boil and steam the pearl balls, covered, for 40 minutes. If necessary add more boiling water to wok.

The rice will swell and the balls will be covered with pearly grains when done.

Serves 4–6

STEAMED RICE
Basic Asian

500 g (1 lb) long grain rice
4 cups (32 fl oz, 1 L) water
2½ teaspoons salt, optional

Use a saucepan with a well-fitting lid. If using a stainless steel pan of the type where the lid forms a seal, reduce water by 1/4 cup (2 fl oz, 60 ml).

Spiced rice and lamb or sultanpuri pilau, from India (recipe opposite).

Put rice, water, and salt into pan and bring to a boil. As soon as it comes to a boil turn heat very low, cover tightly and allow to cook for 20 minutes. The liquid should be completely absorbed and the rice cooked perfectly. Uncover and allow steam to escape for a few minutes, then fluff rice with a fork and serve up using a metal spoon, for a wooden spoon would crush the grains.

Short Grain Rice: If cooking short grain rice, remember that the absorption rate is not as great as that of long grain rice. For 1 lb (500 g) rice, allow 2 1/2 cups (20 fl oz, 600 ml) water for a very firm result, or 3 cups (24 fl oz, 750 ml) water for rice that is slightly softer but with each grain separate and not mushy.

Unpolished or Natural Rice: Rice that has not had its outer layer of bran removed is more nutritious as it is rich in Vitamin B. It does, however, take longer to cook. Use the same measurement as for long grain rice, or if a more tender result is preferred, add an extra 1/2 cup (4 fl oz, 125 ml) water. Cook in the same way, on very low heat, for 40 to 45 minutes.

Note: A most important point when cooking rice is that the lid should not be lifted during cooking time, for steam is lost and can affect the cooking time and the final result. Also, rice is never stirred during cooking. If rice needs washing, allow to drain in colander before starting to cook, or the measurement of water will not be accurate. Some cooks prefer to bring the water to a boil and then add the rice, but I find that either way the results are perfect as long as the measurements of rice and water are accurate and the rules for gentle steaming in a tightly covered pan are observed.

Serves 6

STEAMED RICE
India

2½ cups (20 oz, 600 ml) long grain rice
2 teaspoons ghee
4 cups (32 fl oz, 1 L) hot water
2½ teaspoons salt, optional

Wash rice well if necessary. Drain in colander for 30 minutes. Heat ghee in a heavy-based saucepan with a well-fitting lid. Add rice and fry, stirring for about 2 minutes. Add hot water and salt, stir and bring quickly to the boil. Turn heat very low, cover tightly and cook, without lifting lid or stirring, for 20 to 25 minutes. Uncover to allow steam to escape for a minute or two, then lightly fluff up rice with fork, taking care not to mash the grains, which will be firm and separate and perfectly cooked. Dish up using a slotted metal spoon rather than a wooden spoon, which will crush the grains. Serve with curries or other spiced dishes.
Serves 6

⋘⋙

STEAMED RICE CUPS WITH MIXED MEATS
China

8 dried Chinese mushrooms
1 tablespoon dark soy sauce
2 teaspoons sugar
4 teaspoons sesame oil
2 lap cheong (Chinese sausages)
8 oz (225 g) cooked chicken or barbecued pork
1 lb (450 g) glutinous rice or short grain rice
3 tablespoons light soy sauce
1 tablespoon peanut oil
½ teaspoon crushed garlic
½ teaspoon finely grated fresh ginger
½ cup (4 fl oz, 125 ml) Master Sauce (see Note below)
1 tablespoon cornstarch (cornflour)

Soak mushrooms in hot water for 30 minutes. Discard mushroom stems and slice the caps. Put 3/4 cup (6 fl oz, 180 ml) of the mushroom soaking liquid into a small saucepan, add the sliced mushrooms, the dark soy sauce, sugar, and 2 teaspoons of the sesame oil. Simmer, covered, for 10 minutes.

Put the lap cheong in a colander, and steam for 10 minutes; when cool enough to handle, cut into thin diagonal slices. Dice the chicken or pork.

Put rice in a saucepan with 4 cups (1 3/4 pts, 1 L) of water. Add the light soy sauce and the remaining 2 teaspoons of

sesame oil. Quickly bring to a boil, turn heat very low, cover saucepan and cook for 20 minutes.

In a wok, heat the peanut oil and fry the garlic and ginger until golden. Add the Master Sauce and mushroom liquid, bring to a boil, and thicken with cornstarch mixed with a little cold water. Add mushrooms, lap cheong, and diced chicken or pork. Heat through. Remove from heat and stir into the rice.

Using rice bowls or small cups, fill with the rice mixture, press in firmly, then turn out and serve. If prepared beforehand, steam the rice mixture in cups until heated through.

Note: You can make a substitute for Master Sauce by combining 1/4 cup (2 fl oz, 60 ml) of dark soy, 1/4 cup of dry sherry, 1 teaspoon of sugar, and 1 teaspoon of sesame oil.
Serves 8–12

⋘⋙

STIR-FRIED CHICKEN WITH RICE VERMICELLI
Singapore

8 oz (250 g) rice vermicelli (meehoon)
1 lb (500 g) skinned and boned chicken breasts
4 tablespoons peanut oil
1 cup cubed raw potato
2 medium onions, finely sliced
2 teaspoons finely chopped garlic
2 tablespoons light soy sauce
½ cup (4 fl oz, 125 ml) water
¼ teaspoon ground black pepper
3 teaspoons sugar
1 tablespoon chili sauce
salt to taste

Put the rice vermicelli in a large bowl, pour warm water over and leave to soak for 5 minutes, then drain in a colander and set aside. Cut chicken into bite-size pieces. Heat wok, add oil and when oil starts to smoke, add the cubed potato and stir-fry over high heat for 2 minutes, reduce heat to medium and continue frying until cubes are golden. Remove with slotted spoon and set aside.

Add onions and garlic and fry 2 minutes, stirring, on medium low heat, then add chicken, stir-fry for 5 minutes or until chicken is cooked. Add the drained rice vermicelli and half the soy sauce and water mixed together. Toss and stir until water is absorbed, then add remaining soy sauce and water. Add pepper, sugar, chili sauce, and continue stirring until liquid is almost all absorbed. Stir in potatoes, adjust seasoning, and heat through. Serve immediately.
Serves 4

Steamed pearl balls (page 251).

STIR-FRIED FRESH NOODLES
Singapore

1 lb (500 g) hokkien mee (fresh wheat noodles)
4 rashers bacon
8 oz (250 g) lean steak
8 oz (250 g) small shell deveined shrimp (prawns)
3 tablespoons oil
3 teaspoons chili bean sauce
1 teaspoon finely chopped garlic
1 teaspoon finely chopped fresh ginger
2 cups shredded white Chinese (Napa) cabbage
4 scallions (spring onions), cut into 2 in (5 cm) lengths
¾ cup (6 fl oz, 180 ml) hot water
2 tablespoons light soy sauce

Put hokkien mee in colander and steam over boiling water for 5 minutes. Meanwhile, remove rind and cut bacon into fine strips. Cut steak into paper-thin slices and then into shreds. Heat wok, add oil and when hot fry bacon for 1 minute. Add beef, shrimp, chili bean sauce, garlic, and ginger and stir-fry until beef browns. Add cabbage and scallions and stir-fry 1 minute, then add hokkien mee, hot water, and soy sauce.

Cover and simmer on very low heat for 5 to 8 minutes, uncovering and turning over hokkien mee every few minutes so they do not stick on bottom of wok. When they have absorbed all liquid and are soft (but not mushy) the dish is ready. Serve hot.

Note: Hokkien noodles are thick, yellow wheat noodles sold fresh in Chinese produce stores, usually in 1 lb (500 g) bags.
Serves 4–6

❧❀❧

STIR-FRIED NOODLES, HOKKIEN-STYLE
China

1 lb (500 g) Hokkien mee (fresh wheat noodles)
2 pairs lap cheong (Chinese sausages) or 7 oz (220 g)
    cooked pork
8 oz (250 g) small shelled, deveined shrimp (prawns), raw
    or cooked
8 oz (250 g) fresh squid, optional
8 oz (250 g) fresh bean sprouts
5 tablespoons peanut oil
2 teaspoons finely chopped garlic
3 tablespoons dark soy sauce
3 tablespoons Chinese white vinegar
3 tablespoons sweet chili sauce
3 tablespoons stock or water
salt and pepper to taste

4 eggs, beaten
2 tablespoons chopped koo chye (Chinese garlic chives) or
    green part of scallions (spring onions)

Garnish:
3 tablespoons chopped tender celery leaves
2 fresh red chilies, seeded and sliced

Pour boiling water over the hokkien mee to cover, leave for 1 minute, then drain well in a colander.

Steam the lap cheong over simmering water for 5 minutes or until soft. Allow to cool, then cut into slices. If using pork, cut into small dice.

Rinse shrimp, clean and slice the squid. Rinse the bean sprouts and pinch off the straggly tails.

Heat a wok, add 4 tablespoons oil and swirl to coat. Fry the garlic over low heat until golden. Stir-fry the bean sprouts for a few seconds. Add meat and seafood, and stir-fry until they change color (about 1 minute). Add hokkien mee, and fry until heated through.

Add soy sauce, vinegar, chili sauce, and stock or water mixed together; cook, tossing, until the liquid has evaporated. Then remove to a dish.

Rinse the wok, heat it again and when hot, add the remaining 1 tablespoon of oil. Pour in the beaten eggs seasoned with salt and pepper; fry quickly, stirring, until firm. Turn off the heat, chop the egg into small pieces with the edge of a wok chan. Return the fried noodle mixture to the wok and toss together. Finally, scatter the koo chye or scallions over and serve, garnished with the chilies and celery leaves.
Serves 4

❧❀❧

STIR-FRIED RICE NOODLES
Char Kway Teow ◆ Malaysia

2 lb (1 kg) kway teow (fresh rice noodles)
8 oz (250 g) chicken breast, boned
8 oz (250 g) small shelled raw, deveined shrimp (prawns)
4 oz (125 g) barbecued pork
2 lap cheong (Chinese sausages)
1 cup fresh bean sprouts
4 tablespoons shortening (lard) or oil
1 teaspoon finely chopped garlic
2 medium onions, sliced
4 fresh red chilies, seeded and chopped
2 tablespoons dark soy sauce
1 tablespoon light soy sauce
1 tablespoon oyster sauce
3 eggs, beaten

salt and pepper to taste

Garnish:
5 scallions (spring onions), chopped

Cut kway teow into 1/4 in (6 mm) strips. Put into a large bowl, cover with hot water and soak until strips separate easily, then drain in colander. Cut chicken breast into bite-size pieces. Rinse shrimp. Cut barbecued pork into thin slices. Steam lap cheong and cut into very thin slices. Pinch straggly "tails" off bean sprouts.

Heat 2 tablespoons of the shortening in a wok and fry the garlic, onions, and chilies over medium heat, stirring, until they are soft. Add chicken, shrimp, pork, and lap cheong and stir-fry for 2 to 3 minutes or until cooked. Add bean sprouts and toss once or twice, then remove mixture from wok. Heat remaining shortening, and when very hot add the kway teow and stir-fry until heated through. Add all the seasonings and toss well to mix. Push kway teow to sides of wok, pour beaten egg into the middle and stir constantly until it is set. Mix egg with kway teow and return fried mixture to wok, toss to mix well and serve hot, garnished with scallions.

Note: Fresh rice noodles are sold at Chinese produce stores as "sa hor fun" and some are already cut in strips.
Serves 6

Stir-fried noodles, Hokkien-style (recipe opposite).

⬤⬤⬤

SUSHI RICE WITH VINEGAR AND SUGAR
Japan

2½ cups short or medium grain white rice
2½ cups cold water
5 cm (2 in) piece kombu (dried kelp), optional

Dressing:
4 tablespoons rice vinegar or mild white vinegar
3 tablespoons sugar
2½ teaspoons salt
2 tablespoons mirin or dry sherry

Wash rice several times in cold water and allow to drain for 30 minutes, then put into a saucepan with measured water. If dried kelp is used, wash it well in cold water and add it to the pan. Bring to a boil quickly, cover pan, turn heat very low and steam for fifteen minutes without lifting lid. Remove from heat and let it stand, still covered, for a further 10 minutes. Discard kelp and turn rice into a large bowl. Have ready the dressing ingredients, mixed together until sugar dissolves completely. Pour over the rice. Mix gently but thoroughly and cool quickly to room temperature.

TEMPURA DOMBURI
Tendon ◆ Japan

hot cooked rice
12 pieces cooked tempura (page 92), including shrimp
(prawns) or fish
oil for frying

Sauce:
¼ cup (2 fl oz, 60 ml) mirin or dry sherry
¼ cup (2 fl oz, 60 ml) Japanese soy sauce
¾ cup (6 fl oz, 180 ml) dashi (page 6)

While rice is cooking, heat oil and re-fry tempura very briefly. Drain on absorbent paper. Make sauce and cool to room temperature. To serve, put rice in individual bowls, top with 3 pieces tempura each and serve with sauce, which is spooned over to taste. Serve hot.

Sauce: Heat mirin in small saucepan and ignite it with a match. Shake pan gently, away from heat, until the flame dies out. Stir in the dashi and soy sauce. Cool and pour over rice.

Note: This is the way Japanese housewives use up leftover tempura ingredients. Often, though, pieces of fried fish are substituted for tempura.
Serves 4

THAI FRIED RICE
Thailand

4 cups (1½ lb, 750 g) cold cooked rice
3 tablespoons peanut oil
2 medium onions, finely chopped
1 large pork chop, finely diced
8 oz (250 g) raw shrimp (prawns), shelled and deveined
6 oz (185 g) crab meat
3 eggs, beaten
salt and pepper to taste
2 tablespoons fish sauce
1 tablespoon chili sauce, optional
2 tablespoons tomato paste
1 cup (4 oz, 125 g) chopped scallions (spring onions)
3 tablespoons chopped cilantro (fresh coriander leaves)

Cook rice, spread out and allow to cool. Heat oil in a wok or large frying pan and fry the onions on medium low heat, stirring constantly, until soft and translucent. Increase heat to high. Add pork and fry for 3 minutes. Add shrimps and crab meat and fry for a further 3 minutes or until cooked.

Season beaten eggs well with salt and pepper and pour into middle of wok. Stir until just beginning to set, then add rice and stir well. Continue tossing and stirring until rice is heated through. Sprinkle fish sauce over and mix well, then add chili sauce and tomato paste and toss thoroughly so the rice has a reddish color. Remove from heat, stir the scallions through, and transfer to serving platter. Sprinkle with chopped cilantro and serve.
Serves 4

VEGETARIAN FRIED RICE I
China

2 cups (14 oz, 440 g) short grain rice
2½ cups (20 fl oz, 600 ml) water
2 oz (60 g) dried Chinese mushrooms
2 leeks
4 stalks celery
8 oz (250 g) green (string) beans
4 oz (125 g) bean sprouts, optional
1 cup coarsely grated carrots
1 cup sliced bamboo shoot, optional
3 tablespoons peanut oil
1 tablespoon sesame oil
1 teaspoon fresh ginger, finely grated
2 cloves garlic, finely grated
1 cup chopped scallions (spring onions)
½ cup (4 fl oz, 125 ml) mushroom liquid

2 tablespoons soy sauce
salt to taste

Cook rice then spread on a lightly oiled baking tray to cool; chill overnight if possible. With the fingers, separate grains and spread out rice so grains dry. Refrigerate.

Soak mushrooms in hot water for 30 minutes, then squeeze out as much liquid as possible and reserve. With a sharp knife cut off and discard stems, and cut mushroom caps into thin slices. Wash leeks very well in cold water, making sure all grit is washed away, then cut into thin slices. Use the white portion and only 2–3 in (5–7 cm) of the green leaves. String celery and green beans and cut into very thin diagonal slices. Wash and drain bean sprouts and pick off any brown tails.

Heat peanut oil and sesame oil in a large wok or very large frying pan, add ginger and garlic and fry, stirring well, for 30 seconds. Add mushrooms, leeks, celery, beans, and carrots and stir-fry over high heat for 3 minutes. Add bean sprouts and bamboo shoot and fry 1 minute longer. Add rice, toss and fry over high heat until heated through. Add scallions. Mix mushroom liquid and soy sauce together, and sprinkle evenly over the rice. Continue stirring to mix well together and season to taste with salt. Serve hot.
Serves 6

VEGETARIAN FRIED RICE II
China

1½ lb (750 g) cooked rice, chilled (10 oz, 315 g raw rice)
2 squares pressed bean curd
2 eggs, lightly beaten
salt and pepper, to taste
5 tablespoons peanut oil
3 scallions (spring onions), finely chopped
1 teaspoon finely chopped garlic
1 teaspoon finely grated fresh ginger
1 tablespoon dark soy sauce
8 oz (250 g) diced mixed vegetables
1 teaspoon sesame oil
4 tablespoons cilantro (fresh coriander leaves), coarsely chopped

For a more elaborate non-vegetarian version, add diced cooked pork or chicken steamed and sliced lap cheong, cooked and shelled prawns, chopped ham or bacon. Fry before combining with the vegetables and rice. The bean curd may be omitted.

Cook rice, then spread on a lightly oiled baking tray to cool; chill overnight if possible. Dice the bean curd. Lightly beat the eggs, with salt and pepper to taste.

Heat wok, add 1 tablespoon of peanut oil; swirl. Pour in the

Thai fried rice (recipe opposite).

egg mixture, and stir until firm. Cut egg into small pieces with a wok chan then remove from the wok and set aside.

Heat the remaining 4 tablespoons of oil and when hot, add the scallions, garlic, and ginger. Fry, stirring, for a few seconds until they smell fragrant. Add bean curd and stir-fry for 1 minute. Add vegetables and stir-fry for a further 1 to 2 minutes until the vegetables are tender but still crisp.

Add rice; stir and toss to heat through. Sprinkle the soy sauce and sesame oil over, and add the cilantro and cooked egg. Toss to mix, and serve immediately.

Note: Use a mixture of colorful and crisp vegetables in season, diced or finely sliced green (string) beans, carrots, celery, zucchini (courgettes), cabbage, broccoli, cooked or frozen peas. Always include scallions (spring onions) with their green tops for flavor.

Serves 4–6

VEGETARIAN SOUP NOODLES
China

8 dried Chinese mushrooms
3 tablespoons dried wood fungus (cloud ears)
1 square pressed bean curd
3 tablespoons light soy sauce
2 teaspoons sesame oil
1 teaspoon sugar
2 small carrots
12 green (string) beans
4 oz (125 g) snow peas (mangetout)
8 leaves Chinese (Napa) cabbage
8 oz (250 g) broccoli
12 oz (375 g) fine egg noodles
3 tablespoons peanut oil
12 scallions (spring onions), chopped
2 teaspoons finely chopped garlic
4 tablespoons cornstarch (cornflour)
3 eggs, beaten

Seasonings:
3 tablespoons light soy sauce
4 tablespoons Chinese wine or dry sherry
2 teaspoons sesame oil
1 teaspoon salt
¼ teaspoon ground white pepper

Soak the dried mushrooms in hot water for 30 minutes. Discard mushroom stems, and cut the caps into fine strips; reserve 2 1/2 pts (1.5 L) of the soaking water (if necessary, make up the quantity with fresh water). Soak the wood fungus in cold water for

10 minutes, then cut into small pieces, trimming off any gritty portions.

Cut the bean curd into small dice or strips. Combine the light soy sauce, sesame oil, and sugar, and toss the bean curd in this mixture.

Wash the carrots and cut wedge-shaped sections out of them, lengthwise, then slice across to give flower-shapes. String and slice the beans very thinly. String the snow peas. Cut leaf ribs of cabbage into bite-size pieces, and finely shred the leaves: keep leaf ribs separate from the shredded leaves. Slice broccoli stems and divide head into florets.

Cook the noodles as described below, drain and divide among six soup bowls.

Heat a wok, add the peanut oil and when hot, fry the chopped scallions and garlic for a few seconds, stirring, but do not let them darken. Add the mushrooms, the leaf ribs of cabbage and the broccoli stems and fry for 1 minute longer. Add mushroom soaking water, and the seasoning ingredients; bring to a boil and simmer, covered, for 5 minutes. Add carrots and beans, and cook for a further 3 minutes. Add snow peas, wood fungus, shredded cabbage leaves, and broccoli florets and cook 1 minute longer.

Dissolve the cornstarch in 4 tablespoons of cold water, and stir into the soup until it boils and thickens. Drizzle in the beaten egg and stir gently so that it sets in fine shreds. Add the bean curd and heat through. Ladle the soup mixture over the noodles and serve hot.

Serves 6

WHEAT NOODLES
China

Noodles made from wheat flour and eggs are the most popular. Generally sold in 1 lb (500 g) packets, each packet consists of seven or eight bundles. Allow one bundle per person. Unlike rice noodles and bean starch noodles, wheat noodles are always boiled before frying.

Boiled noodles: It is important that the bundles of noodles are soaked in hot water for about 10 minutes before dropping them into boiling water — it makes cooking them so much easier. As the bundles soften, the strands separate and the noodles cook evenly. If they were dropped straight into boiling water the outside would cook while some strands would stick together in tough clumps. If the noodles are loose packed, the soaking is not necessary.

Bring to a boil a large saucepan of lightly salted water with 1 tablespoon of peanut oil added to prevent boiling over. Drain the soaked noodles in a colander and add to the fast-boiling water. When the water returns to a boil, cook fine noodles for 2 to 3 minutes, wide noodles for 4 to 5 minutes. Test frequently

Vegetarian soup noodles (recipe opposite).

and do not overcook. They should be al dente.

Run cold water into the pan, drain immediately in a large colander, and run cold water through the noodles to rinse away excess starch and stop the cooking process. Drain thoroughly.

Soft fried noodles: Sprinkle the well-drained noodles with 1 tablespoon of peanut oil and 2 teaspoons of sesame oil, toss well. Spread out on a large baking tray and allow to dry in the air for about 1 hour.

Heat a wok or large, heavy frying pan, and when very hot, add 4 tablespoons of peanut oil. When oil is very hot, coil the noodles into the pan to make a round or oval cake. Reduce the heat to medium, and fry, shaking the pan but not stirring, until the base is golden. Turn the noodles over and fry the other side. If it is necessary to add a little more oil, drizzle the oil down the sides of the wok and allow it to become hot before it reaches the noodles. Cook for a further 5 minutes or until golden, then transfer to serving dish.

Soft fried noodles are ideal for serving as a base with any stir-fried and well-sauced foods, either singly or in combination.

Fresh wheat noodles: You can buy fresh wheat noodles in Chinese stores. They need only the briefest cooking in boiling water before they are used in soups or soft fried. If preferred, they may be steamed over boiling water. Allow 10 minutes steaming time.

Some varieties of wheat noodles — for example, the thick yellow Hokkien noodles — are already cooked and need only to have boiling water poured over them in a colander.

YELLOW RICE
Kaha Bath ◆ Sri Lanka

1 lb (500 g) long grain rice
4 tablespoons ghee
2 medium onions, finely sliced
6 cloves
20 black peppercorns
12 cardamom pods, bruised
1½ teaspoons ground turmeric
3½ teaspoons salt
12 curry leaves
1 stem lemon grass, optional
4 pieces daun pandan or pandanus leaf, optional
about 4 cups (32 fl oz) thin coconut cream

Wash rice and drain thoroughly. Heat ghee in a large saucepan, add onion and fry until it begins to turn golden brown. Add cloves, peppercorns, cardamom pods, turmeric, salt, curry leaves, lemon grass, and pandan leaf. Add rice and fry, stirring constantly, for 2 to 3 minutes, until rice is well coated with ghee and turmeric. Add coconut cream and bring to a boil. Reduce heat, cover and cook for 20 to 25 minutes without lifting lid.

When rice is cooked, the spices will have come to the top. Remove spices and leaves used for flavoring and fluff up the rice lightly with a fork. Serve hot, with curries and accompaniments.
Serves 6

Wheat noodles (opposite) and combination chow mein (page 227).

Vegetables

ASPARAGUS IN OYSTER SAUCE
China

2 bundles fresh asparagus
1 tablespoon peanut oil
1 tablespoon oyster sauce

Wash asparagus spears, slice off and discard any tough ends. Bring plenty of water to a boil in a wok. Add the oil and drop in the asparagus. Return water to a boil and cook for 10 to 15 minutes, or until asparagus spears are tender but still crisp.

Lift asparagus out of the water onto a board and cut the spears into 2 in (5 cm) lengths. Arrange on a serving dish.

Discard the asparagus cooking water. Put 4 tablespoons of cold water in the wok, stir in oyster sauce and bring to a boil. Pour over the asparagus and serve immediately.

Serves 4

BAMBOO SHOOTS, SNOW PEAS & CUCUMBER
China

1 cup sliced winter bamboo shoots
4 oz (125 g) snow peas (mangetout)
1 cucumber
1 tablespoon peanut oil
1 teaspoon sesame oil
¼ teaspoon crushed garlic
¼ teaspoon finely grated fresh ginger
1 teaspoon light soy sauce
salt to taste

Slice the bamboo shoots thinly. Remove stems and strings from snow peas. Peel and cut cucumber into thin slices.

Heat peanut oil in a wok, add sesame oil, garlic, and ginger and stir once, then add bamboo shoots and snow peas. Stir-fry for 1 minute over high heat. Add cucumber slices and cook 2 minutes longer. Add soy sauce and salt. Serve at once.

Note: Winter bamboo shoots, or green bamboo shoots, are smaller, whiter and more tender than the usual variety. If not available substitute the larger kind.

Serves 2–4

BEAN SAYUR
Sayur Buncis ◆ Indonesia

2 tablespoons peanut oil
1 onion, finely chopped
1 teaspoon finely chopped garlic
2 fresh red chilies, seeded and chopped
1 teaspoon dried shrimp paste
1 teaspoon finely grated lemon rind
2 teaspoons ground coriander
1 teaspoon ground cumin
½ teaspoon laos powder
1 teaspoon salt
2 tablespoons tamarind liquid or lemon juice
1 daun salam or 3 curry leaves
3 cups chicken stock
1 lb (500 g) fresh green beans, sliced
1 cooked chicken breast, skinned, boned and diced
1½ cups (12 fl oz, 375 ml) thin coconut cream

Heat oil, fry onion, garlic, chilies, and dried shrimp paste for 5 minutes over medium heat, stirring and crushing shrimp paste with back of spoon. Add lemon rind and ground spices, fry 1 minute. Add salt, tamarind liquid, daun salam or curry leaves, stock, and beans. Bring to a boil, simmer for 8 minutes. Add chicken and coconut cream. Simmer 5 minutes and serve.

Note: Rice vermicelli can be added to this sayur when it is the main dish. Soak 125 g (4 oz) of rice vermicelli in very hot water for 10 minutes, and drain well. Add to sayur and cook for further 2 minutes.

Serves 6

BEAN SPROUT SALAD
Kong Namul ◆ Korea

1 lb (500 g) fresh bean sprouts (mung or soy)
1 tablespoon sesame oil
1 tablespoon salad oil
1 tablespoon crushed, toasted sesame seeds
3 tablespoons light soy sauce
1 clove garlic, crushed
2 scallions (spring onions), very finely chopped
1 teaspoon honey or sugar
dash of chili powder or cayenne

Bean sayur, an Indonesian dish (recipe opposite).

Wash bean sprouts. Bring a pan of lightly salted water to a boil, drop in the bean sprouts and return to a boil. Boil for 1 minute if using mung beans, longer for soy beans. The sprouts should be just tender, never overcooked. Drain at once and cool under cold water. Drain well. Combine all other ingredients for the dressing and toss with bean sprouts. Chill before serving.
Serves 6

BELL PEPPERS WITH PORK & SHRIMP
China

8 oz (250 g) raw shelled, deveined shrimp (prawns)
8 oz (250 g) ground (minced) pork
1 teaspoon salt
2 scallions (spring onions)
1 tablespoon cornstarch (cornflour)
3 medium-size red or green bell peppers (capsicums)
1 teaspoon crushed garlic
1 tablespoon dark soy sauce
1 tablespoon Chinese wine or dry sherry
1 tablespoon min sze jeung (bean sauce)
2 teaspoons sugar
5 tablespoons oil
1 oz (30 g) lean ham, cut into matchstick strips

Mince shrimp finely. Combine with the pork, salt, finely chopped scallions, and 2 teaspoons of cornstarch.

Cut peppers lengthwise into quarters; discard seeds and membranes, and wash well. Cut each quarter pepper across into half. Mound the ground mixture evenly on the pepper pieces.

Blend the remaining 1 teaspoon of cornstarch with 1 table-spoon of water. In a small bowl, combine the garlic, soy sauce, wine, min sze jeung, and sugar; mix in 6 tablespoons of water.

Heat half the oil in a wok and fry half of the pepper pieces, meat side down. When the filling is brown, turn over and cook for a further 2 minutes. Remove to a plate. Add remaining oil to the wok and cook the remaining peppers. Remove.

Pour the garlic mixture into the wok, stir until boiling, then thicken with the blended cornstarch. Return peppers and heat through. Scatter matchstick strips of ham over the top, and serve.

Note: If peppers are large, cut into 12 instead of 8 making bite-size pieces.
Serves 6

BITTER MELON SALAD
Amargoso Salad ◆ The Philippines

1 tender bitter melon, thinly sliced
8 oz (250 g) cooked shelled, deveined shrimp (prawns)
2 firm red tomatoes, peeled and diced
2 hard-cooked (boiled) eggs, chopped

Dressing:
3 tablespoons vinegar
½ teaspoon salt
2 teaspoons sugar
¼ teaspoon ground black pepper

Drop bitter melon into boiling water, bring back to a boil for 1 minute, then drain immediately. If shrimp are large, cut into small pieces. Put all salad ingredients into a bowl. Stir dressing ingredients together, pour over salad and toss to mix. Cover and chill.
Serves 4

BITTER MELON WITH SHRIMP
Ampalaya ◆ The Philippines

1 lb (500 g) bitter melons
8 oz (250 g) shrimp (prawns)
8 oz (250 g) pork
shortening (lard) or oil for frying
2 medium onions, chopped
5 cloves garlic, chopped
2 lb (1 kg) ripe tomatoes, peeled and chopped
½ cup (4 fl oz, 125 ml) vinegar
salt and pepper to taste

Cut the bitter melons in halves lengthwise. Scoop out seeds and discard. Cut green portion crosswise into thin slices. Boil shrimp, shell and devein them, reserving stock. Cut pork into thin slices. Heat fat and fry onion and garlic until golden brown. Add pork and fry, then add tomatoes. Cook until tomatoes are reduced to a pulp, then add shrimp and 1 cup (8 fl oz, 250 ml) of reserved stock. Stir until mixture returns to a boil, add vinegar and simmer for a few minutes, add bitter melon. Cook until tender. Season to taste and serve with rice.

Note: Bitter melons (bitter gourds) can be bought at Chinese vegetable stores.
Serves 6

Asparagus in oyster sauce (page 260).

Bell peppers (capsicums) with pork and shrimp (recipe opposite).

BRAISED BITTER MELON
China

3 medium-size bitter melons
12 oz (375 g) ground (minced) pork, or raw shrimp
  (prawns)
2 tablespoons finely chopped scallions (spring onions)
1 teaspoon finely grated fresh ginger
½ teaspoon crushed garlic
½ teaspoon salt
1 egg, beaten
1 tablespoon cornstarch (cornflour)
1 tablespoon canned salted black beans
1 teaspoon finely chopped garlic
5 tablespoons peanut oil
1 tablespoon sesame oil

Sauce:
½ cup (4 fl oz, 125 ml) stock or water
1 tablespoon light soy sauce
1 teaspoon sugar

Cut each bitter melon crosswise into 1 1/2 in (4 cm) slices, discarding stem end and pointed tip. With a sharp knife, remove and discard the spongy middle and seeds, leaving tubular sections.

Mix pork or shrimp with ginger, crushed garlic, salt, 2 tablespoons of the beaten egg, and 2 teaspoons of the cornstarch, combining thoroughly. Fill the sections of melon with this mixture, mounding the filling slightly on one side.

Rinse the black beans in a strainer under cold water, drain well, and mash the beans with a fork or chop finely. Mix with the finely chopped garlic. In a separate bowl, mix the sauce ingredients together.

Heat a wok, add the peanut oil and swirl to coat. Put melon pieces into the wok and fry on medium heat just until filling starts to brown. This can be done in batches. Lift out on a slotted spoon and set aside on a plate.

Pour off all but 1 tablespoon of oil, add the black beans mixture and fry, stirring, for 1 minute. Add the sauce ingredients mixed together and bring to a boil. Return slices of melon to the wok with the rounded side upwards. Cover the wok and simmer on low heat for 15 to 20 minutes.

Remove melon pieces to a serving plate. Mix the remaining cornstarch with 1 tablespoon of cold water, add it to sauce in the wok and stir until it thickens. Drizzle in the remaining beaten egg, stirring as it sets. Turn off heat and stir in sesame oil. Pour over the melon and serve with rice.
Serves 4–6

BRAISED BROCCOLI STEMS
China

stems from a large bunch of broccoli
3 tablespoons peanut oil
½ teaspoon grated fresh ginger
1 tablespoon oyster sauce
1 tablespoon light soy sauce
1 teaspoon sugar
½ teaspoon sesame oil
cooking liquid from blanching the broccoli
2 teaspoons cornstarch (cornflour)

Peel broccoli stems, cut into bite-size lengths, and cut any thick stems in half. Bring lightly salted water to a boil in a saucepan, drop in the stems and return to a boil, then cook for 2 minutes or until bright green and just tender. (If using broccoli florets as well, add them after removing the stems and give them no more than 1 minute's boiling.) Drain in a colander, but save 1/2 cup (4 fl oz, 125 ml) of the liquid.

Heat peanut oil in a wok and stir-fry broccoli and ginger for 1 minute. Add oyster sauce, soy sauce, sugar, sesame oil, and cooking liquid, and let it boil up. Mix the cornstarch with 1 tablespoon of cold water and stir into the liquid until it thickens slightly. Toss broccoli pieces in the sauce and serve at once.
Serves 4

BRAISED CAULIFLOWER
China

2 cups cauliflower sprigs
2 tablespoons peanut oil
½ teaspoon finely grated fresh ginger
1 tablespoon light soy sauce
¼ cup (2 fl oz, 60 ml) water
1 teaspoon sesame oil
1 scallion (spring onion), finely sliced

Use only the tender florets of the cauliflower, wash and drain well.

Heat wok, add peanut oil and swirl around, then add ginger and cauliflower and toss over high heat for 30 seconds. Add soy sauce and water mixed together, cover and cook on high heat for 3 minutes — cauliflower should be tender but still slightly firm and crisp. Stir until liquid has almost evaporated, remove from heat, sprinkle sesame oil over, add scallion and toss. Serve hot.
Serves 2–4

BRAISED CHINESE CABBAGE
China

1 lb (500 g) Chinese (Napa) cabbage (wongah bak),
  trimmed
4 tablespoons peanut oil
½ teaspoon crushed garlic
½ teaspoon finely grated fresh ginger
½ cup (4 fl oz, 125 ml) stock
1 tablespoon oyster sauce or light soy sauce
2 teaspoons cornstarch (cornflour)
1 teaspoon sesame oil

Trim the cabbage, discarding tough leaf portions, and cut into bite-size pieces. Heat peanut oil, and fry the garlic and ginger for a few seconds, then add cabbage and stir-fry for 1 minute. Add stock and sauce, cover and cook for 3 to 4 minutes, just until tender but still crisp. Stir in the cornstarch, first mixed with 1 tablespoon cold water. Sprinkle with sesame oil, toss well and serve.
Serves 4

BRAISED CHINESE MUSHROOMS & BEAN CURD
China

8 dried Chinese mushrooms
8 oz (250 g) fried or pressed bean curd
3 tablespoons peanut oil
2 scallions (spring onions), cut into 2 in (5 cm) lengths
¾ cup (6 fl oz, 175 ml) stock
1 tablespoon dark soy sauce
1 tablespoon oyster sauce
½ teaspoon sugar
1 teaspoon cornstarch (cornflour)
1 teaspoon sesame oil

Soak the mushrooms in water for 30 minutes. Drain, discard mushroom stems and cut caps in half.

Split squares of the fried bean curd into two, and then cut each square diagonally in half. If using pressed bean curd, cut in the same way and then deep fry in hot oil until golden brown. Drain.

Heat a wok, add peanut oil and swirl to coat. When hot, add scallions and mushrooms and stir on medium high heat for about 30 seconds. Add stock, soy sauce, oyster sauce, sugar, and simmer, covered for 20 minutes. Add bean curd slices. Bring to a boil, cover wok and simmer for 5 minutes.

Blend the cornstarch with 1 tablespoon of water and stir it into the sauce until it boils and thickens. Add sesame oil, toss

Braised bitter melon (page 263).

Braised broccoli stems (recipe opposite).

mixture lightly, and serve.

Note: Tofu (soft white bean curd), available in packets, can be used for this dish but take care to avoid mashing it. Cook scallions and mushrooms, add liquids and seasonings, then simmer and thicken as described. At that stage, open the tofu, slide tofu onto a plate and drain off liquid. Cut into squares and carefully slide it into the sauce over a low heat. Do not stir, but spoon some of the sauce over to heat it through. Slide the mixture out of the wok onto a serving dish.
Serves 4

BROCCOLI, BEAN SPROUTS & WATER CHESTNUTS
China

1 lb (500 g) fresh broccoli
8 oz (250 g) fresh bean sprouts
8 water chestnuts, fresh or canned

Dressing:
1 tablespoon sesame oil
2 tablespoons peanut oil
3 tablespoons light soy sauce
1 teaspoon sugar, optional

Separate broccoli into small sprigs, trimming off all but the most tender stems. Bring a small pan of lightly salted water to a boil, drop in broccoli, return to a boil and boil for 1 minute. Drain, then rinse under running cold water to stop cooking and set the color. Wash bean sprouts in cold water and drain in colander. Slice the canned water chestnuts, or peel and slice fresh ones. Toss well together with combined dressing ingredients.
Serves 6

CHILI-FRIED CAULIFLOWER
Sambal Goreng Kembang ✦ Malaysia

3 tablespoons peanut oil
4 fresh red chilies, finely chopped or 2 teaspoons sambal ulek (page 23)
1 large onion, finely chopped
2 cloves garlic, finely chopped
1 teaspoon blacan (dried shrimp paste)
1 teaspoon salt
1 lb (500 g) cauliflower, sliced
2 tablespoons hot water

Heat oil in wok or frying pan and fry the chilies, onion, and garlic over low heat, stirring frequently, until onion is soft and golden. Add blacan and crush with back of spoon. Fry for a minute longer. Add salt, then add the cauliflower and toss and stir constantly until cauliflower is thoroughly mixed with the fried chili and onion mixture. Sprinkle with hot water, cover and cook for 10 minutes. Serve hot.
Serves 6

CHINESE SALAD
Jahp Sik Choy ◆ China

1 large can winter bamboo shoots
1 lb (500 g) fresh bean sprouts
½ a white bok choy (chard)
1 can lychees, optional
2 tablespoons lightly toasted sesame seeds

Dressing:
½ teaspoon finely grated fresh ginger
1 clove garlic, crushed
1½ teaspoons salt
1 tablespoon light soy sauce
2 tablespoons Chinese wine or dry sherry
4 tablespoons sweet Chinese vinegar or other mild vinegar
½ cup (4 fl oz, 125 ml) peanut oil
2 tablespoons sesame oil

Drain bamboo shoots and cut crosswise into thin oval slices. Winter bamboo shoots are smaller, whiter and much more tender than ordinary bamboo shoots. If they are not available use the larger variety but after slicing into bite-size strips, bring to a boil in lightly salted water, simmer for 8 minutes, then drain and cool.

Wash bean sprouts thoroughly, removing any skins and pinching off straggly brown tails. Drain well. Wash and finely shred bok choy. If using lychees for a touch of sweetness in the salad, drain well.

Put shredded bok choy in a bowl and arrange other vegetables on top in concentric circles. Pile lychees in the middle. Sprinkle with sesame seeds, cover with plastic wrap (film) and chill until serving time, then pour dressing over, toss and serve right away.

Dressing: In a screw-top jar put ginger, garlic crushed with salt, soy, wine, and vinegar and shake well. Add both kinds of oil and shake again. Just before using shake the jar very well.
Serves 4–6

CLOUD EARS IN HOI SIN SAUCE
Chu Hau Jeung Mun Wan Yee ◆ China

½ cup dried wan yee (wood fungus, cloud ears)
2 teaspoons hoi sin sauce
2 tablespoons light soy sauce
1 small clove garlic
2 teaspoons peanut oil
1 teaspoon sesame oil
¼ cup (2 fl oz, 60 ml) water
1 teaspoon cornstarch (cornflour)
1 tablespoon cold water

Wash wan yee and soak in hot water in a large bowl for 1 hour. Fungus will swell to many times its original size. Rinse and cut off any gritty parts, then cut large pieces into bite-size bits. Mix hoi sin sauce and soy sauce. Crush garlic. Heat both oils and fry garlic over low heat for half a minute. Add sauces and water, wood fungus, and stir until heated through and boiling. Thicken liquid with cornstarch mixed with cold water and serve immediately with rice or noodles.
Serves 4

COOKED VEGETABLES WITH COCONUT
Urap ◆ Indonesia

8 oz (250 g) fresh green (string) beans
4 carrots
8 oz (250 g) bean sprouts
½ small cabbage
1 canned bamboo shoot
1 cup (3 oz, 90 g) fresh grated or unsweetened desiccated coconut
2 tablespoons hot milk or water (if using desiccated coconut)
1 small onion, finely chopped
½ teaspoon sambal ulek (page 23) or chili powder
1 teaspoon salt
2 tablespoons lemon juice
½ teaspoon trasi (dried shrimp paste)

Prepare beans, carrots, bean sprouts, and cabbage as for gado-gado (page 284). Cut bamboo shoot into strips the same size as the beans. Put the coconut into a bowl (if using desiccated coconut, sprinkle hot milk or water over and mix with the fingertips to moisten evenly). Add onion, sambal or chili powder, salt, lemon juice, and trasi which has been wrapped in

Braised Chinese mushrooms and bean curd (page 264).

foil and broiled (grilled) for 5 minutes, or heated in a dry frying pan. Mix thoroughly together. Sprinkle coconut mixture over vegetables, reserving some to garnish the dish when served. Put vegetables in a steamer and steam for 5 to 8 minutes. Turn onto serving dish and sprinkle with reserved coconut. Use as an accompaniment to a meal, or as a salad by itself.
Serves 4–6

⋖⋗∞⋖⋗

CUCUMBER SALAD
Oyi Namul ◆ **Korea**

2 large green cucumbers
3 teaspoons coarse salt
1 cup (8 fl oz, 250 ml) water
2 tablespoons mild vinegar
1 teaspoon sugar
¼ teaspoon cayenne
1 clove garlic, finely chopped
1 scallion (spring onion), finely chopped
3 teaspoons toasted, crushed sesame seeds

Peel cucumbers thinly and cut crosswise into thin slices. Put in a bowl, sprinkle with salt and add water. Soak for 15 minutes, then drain off all liquid. Combine other ingredients, pour over cucumbers, mix well and serve chilled.
Serves 6

⋖⋗∞⋖⋗

DRY POTATO CURRY
Sukhe Alu ◆ **India (Punjab)**

1 lb (500 g) peeled potatoes
1½ tablespoons ghee or oil
1 teaspoon panch phora (page 12)
1 medium onion, finely chopped
*2 tablespoons chopped fresh mint or cilantro
    (fresh coriander leaves)*
1 teaspoon ground turmeric
1½ teaspoons salt
½ teaspoon chili powder, optional
¼ cup (2 fl oz, 60 ml) hot water
1 teaspoon garam masala
1 tablespoon lemon juice

Cut potatoes into quarters or, if very large, into cubes. In a heavy saucepan with lid, heat ghee or oil and add the panch phora. When mustard seeds in the panch phora begin to pop add the onion and fry, stirring, until soft. Add chopped herbs, turmeric, salt, and chili powder (if used). Add potatoes, stir well, sprinkle with hot water and cover pan tightly. Cook over very low heat for 20 minutes, shaking pan occasionally to prevent potatoes sticking. Sprinkle with garam masala and lemon juice, replace lid and cook for a further 10 minutes or until potatoes are tender. Serve with chapatis, parathas, or rice.
Serves 4–6

EGGPLANT PETJAL

Pecal Terung ◆ Indonesia

2 large firm eggplants (aubergines)
1½ tablespoons peanut oil
5 candlenuts or macadamia nuts
1 teaspoon trasi (dried shrimp paste)
½ teaspoon laos powder
½ teaspoon sambal ulek (page 23)
1 tablespoon tamarind liquid
1 tablespoon dark soy sauce
1 teaspoon palm sugar or dark brown sugar
½ cup (4 fl oz, 125 ml) thick coconut cream

Peel the eggplant and cut into cubes. Drop into lightly salted boiling water or cook over steam until tender. Drain well. Heat oil in a wok or small frying pan and fry the candlenuts or macadamia nuts and trasi over low heat, stirring constantly and crushing the trasi into the oil. Add laos, sambal ulek, tamarind liquid, soy sauce, sugar, and coconut cream. Simmer gently, pour over eggplant before serving.
Serves 6

EGGPLANT WITH YOGURT

Baigan Dahi ◆ India & Pakistan

2 medium eggplants (aubergines)
3 tablespoons ghee or oil
2 medium onions, finely chopped
3 cloves garlic, finely chopped
2 teaspoons finely grated fresh ginger
2 teaspoons ground coriander
1 teaspoon ground cumin
½ teaspoon ground turmeric
½ teaspoon chili powder

1½ teaspoons salt, or to taste
½ teaspoon garam masala, optional
sugar, optional
1 cup (6½ oz, 200 g) yogurt

Put eggplants under a preheated broiler (grill), about 6 in (15 cm) from heat and broil until skins are blackened and eggplants soft throughout. Cool, then peel. Mash flesh of eggplants roughly, or chop into small pieces.

In a medium saucepan heat ghee or oil and fry onions, garlic, and ginger until onion is soft and golden. Add coriander, cumin, turmeric, chili powder and fry, stirring, for another minute. Stir in salt and add the mashed or chopped eggplant. Stir and cook for a few minutes, then sprinkle with garam masala, cover and cook for 5 minutes longer. Taste and add more salt if necessary, and, if desired, a little sugar — about 2 teaspoons. Mash the yogurt smoothly and mix into the eggplant before serving. Serve with rice and curries and other accompaniments.
Serves 6

FRESH PEANUT CURRY

India

250 g (½ lb) shelled raw peanuts
½ cup (1½ oz) desiccated coconut
2 teaspoons finely chopped garlic
1 tablespoon ground coriander
1½ teaspoon ground turmeric
½ teaspoon ground chili powder
3 tablespoons oil
2 medium onions, finely sliced
1 tomato, peeled and chopped
1 teaspoon sugar, or to taste
1½ teaspoons salt
hot water
½ teaspoon garam masala

Garnish:
2 tablespoons chopped cilantro (fresh coriander leaves)

Soak peanuts in water for 2 hours, then boil for 20 minutes. Drain and set aside. Place coconut, garlic, coriander, turmeric, and chili powder in container of electric blender with enough water to allow blades to move freely. Blend to a paste on high speed, remove contents and set aside.

Heat oil and fry onions till soft and golden. Add tomato and the blended mixture and cook, stirring, until it smells fragrant and the oil comes to the surface.

Add nuts, sugar, salt, and 1 cup hot water. Bring to a boil, cover and simmer for 15 minutes or until peanuts are cooked. Sprinkle with garam masala and garnish with chopped cilantro (coriander leaves). Serve with hot rice and accompaniments.

Serves 2–4

⟨⟨⟩⟩

FRIED BITTER MELON & EGGPLANT

Karela Baigan Bhaji ✦ India (Punjab)

1 large or 2 small karela (bitter melons)
1 medium or 2 small eggplants (aubergines)
3 medium onions, chopped
½ teaspoon panch phora (page 12)
2 fresh red or green chilies, seeded and sliced
4 tablespoons oil
2 teaspoons finely grated fresh ginger
½ teaspoon ground turmeric
approximately ¼ cup (4 fl oz, 125 ml) hot water
1 teaspoon salt

Halve the karela lengthwise and if seeds are large and mature remove and discard them. If the karela are tender, the seeds may be left in. Slice thickly lengthwise, then cut into 2 in (5 cm) lengths. Wash but do not peel eggplants and cut into small cubes.

Heat oil in a heavy saucepan and add the panch phora. Fry for 1 minute, then add onions and chilies. Fry, stirring occasionally, until onions are golden. Add ginger and turmeric, then fry the karela for 3 minutes, stirring. Add eggplant and salt. Stir well, adding about 1/4 cup hot water or just enough to cover base of pan. Cover and cook on low heat about 20 minutes or until the vegetables are cooked through. Stir occasionally, being careful not to mash the pieces of karela and eggplant. When vegetables are tender, if there is much liquid left in pan cook uncovered so that most of the liquid evaporates. Serve with rice or chapatis.

Note: Fresh bitter gourds or karela as they are called in India are sold in Chinese greengrocers as 'bitter melon'. Buy these whenever possible but if canned ones are used add them only during the last few minutes of cooking.

Serves 4–6

⟨⟨⟩⟩

FRIED VEGETABLES, BURMESE STYLE

Akyaw ✦ Burma

2 teaspoons sesame or corn oil
1 or 2 onions, finely sliced lengthwise
2 cloves garlic, sliced lengthwise
salt and pepper
ngan pya ye (fish sauce), optional

Heat oil until a haze rises, add onions and garlic and reduce heat immediately. Add 3 to 4 cups washed and prepared vegetables. Stir-fry until vegetables are tender but still crisp to the bite. Add salt and pepper to taste and a sprinkling of ngan pya ye if desired. Do not prepare vegetables this way until just before serving, for if left to stand they will go limp.

Vegetables are prepared for stir-fry in the following ways:
Okra (ladies' fingers): top and tail, slice thinly
Eggplant (aubergine): slice thinly or dice small
Marrow, squash: peel, seed and cut into strips
Zucchini (courgettes): cut in thin slices
Giant white radish: cut in strips
Bitter melon: slice thinly, sprinkle with salt, then rinse
Green (string) beans, butter beans, French (runner) beans or long (snake) beans: cut in bite-size lengths
Snow peas (mangetout): remove strings and leave whole
Carrots: scrape and slice very thinly
Cucumbers: halve lengthwise, seed and slice thickly
Cabbage: shred lengthwise
Spinach: tear into pieces
Bean sprouts: use whole, pinch off tails if necessary
Bamboo shoot: fresh bamboo shoot must first be boiled until tender, then sliced or cut in matchstick pieces
Celery: slice diagonally
Onions: slice lengthwise
Scallions (spring onions): cut into bite-size lengths.

⟨⟨⟩⟩

GARLIC CURRY
Lasan Kari ◆ India (Madras)

8 oz (250 g) garlic
8–10 small onions, preferably red (salad) onions
8 large fresh mild chilies
2 tablespoons coconut oil (or other vegetable oil)
1 teaspoon fenugreek seeds
1 teaspoon chili powder
½ teaspoon ground turmeric
1½ cups (12 fl oz, 375 ml) thin coconut cream
½ teaspoon salt, or to taste
2 teaspoons tamarind pulp or ½ teaspoon instant tamarind
¼ cup (2 fl oz, 60 ml) hot water

Choose garlic with as large individual cloves as you can find. Peel the cloves but leave them whole. Peel the onions. Cut stalks from the chilies but leave them intact, with the seeds inside.

Heat oil in a heavy saucepan and fry the garlic, onions, and chilies over gentle heat, not letting them brown too much. Remove from pan. Add fenugreek seeds to the oil in pan and stir over low heat just until they are golden. Add the chili powder and turmeric, fry for a few seconds, then add the coconut cream, salt, and stir while bringing slowly to simmering point. Return the garlic, onions, and chilies and allow to simmer, uncovered, until garlic cloves are soft, about 30 minutes depending on size. Meanwhile dissolve tamarind in hot water, strain into curry for last 10 minutes of cooking. Serve with hot white rice.

Note: If the amount of garlic sounds terrifying, tone down the content by substituting small new potatoes, halved or quartered, for some of the garlic.
Serves 4

✧✦✧

GREEN MANGO OR APPLE SALAD
Yam Ma Muang ◆ Thailand

3 green mangoes or 3 green cooking apples
1 teaspoon salt
1 tablespoon peanut oil
4 cloves garlic, thinly sliced
6 scallions (spring onions), sliced
8 oz (250 g) pork filet, shredded
1 tablespoon dried shrimp (prawn) powder
1 tablespoon fish sauce
2 tablespoons roasted peanuts, crushed
1 teaspoon palm sugar or dark brown sugar
pepper to taste
finely chopped red chilies, optional

Peel and thinly slice mangoes, put into a large bowl and sprinkle with salt. Heat oil and fry garlic and scallions separately and set aside. In the same pan quickly fry the pork until cooked, add the shrimp powder, fish sauce, peanuts, and sugar. Remove from heat. Just before serving mix everything together, add pepper to taste and sprinkle finely chopped red chilies over the top if desired.
Serves 6

✧✦✧

HEAVENLY BRAISED VEGETABLES
China

12 dried Chinese mushrooms
3 tablespoons dried wood fungus (cloud ears)
8 oz (250 g) can bamboo shoot
14 oz (440 g) can young corn cobs
2 tablespoons peanut oil
2 tablespoons soy sauce
1 teaspoon sugar
2 cups (16 fl oz, 500 ml) mushroom liquid
1 tablespoon sesame oil

Soak mushrooms in 3 cups (24 fl oz, 750 ml) hot water for 30 minutes. Squeeze out excess moisture, remove and discard stems. Reserve mushroom liquid. Soak fungus in water for 10 minutes, rinse and drain, then cut each piece in two. Slice bamboo shoots thinly. Drain corn.

Heat peanut oil in a wok and fry mushrooms until brown, about 5 minutes on high heat, stirring all the time. Add remaining ingredients, except wood fungus. Add mushroom liquid, cover and simmer over low heat for 25 to 30 minutes. Add wood fungus and heat briefly. Sprinkle sesame oil over and toss to mix through.
Serves 4–6

✧✦✧

HONEY GLAZED MUSHROOMS
China

1 lb (500 g) fresh young mushrooms
1 tablespoon peanut oil
1 tablespoon honey
2 tablespoons soy sauce

Wipe mushrooms clean and trim stalks level with caps. Heat oil in wok and swirl so that oil coats inside of wok. Add mushrooms and stir-fry for 1 minute over medium high heat. Add honey and soy sauce, turn heat low, cover and cook for about 3 minutes. Uncover and cook until liquid thickens, turning mushrooms in the honey and soy mixture to coat them. Serve hot or cold as an accompaniment or as a side dish with barbecued meats.
Serves 4

⋘⋙

LEEKS FRIED WITH CHILI
Leeks Mirisata ◆ Sri Lanka

4 medium-size leeks
¼ cup (2 fl oz, 60 ml) oil
½ teaspoon ground turmeric
1 teaspoon chili powder, or to taste
2 tablespoons pounded Maldive fish or dried shrimp
   (prawns)
1 teaspoon salt

Wash leeks very well, taking care to remove all sand and grit. Discard any tough or withered leaves but use the green portions as well. With a sharp knife slice very thinly. When slicing the leaves make a tight bundle and hold firmly.

Heat oil in a large saucepan and add the leeks. Fry, stirring, for 5 minutes, then add remaining ingredients and stir well. Cover and cook over low heat for 30 minutes, stirring occasionally. The leeks will reduce considerably in volume. Uncover and cook until liquid evaporates and leeks have an oily appearance. Serve as an accompaniment to a rice meal.
Serves 6

⋘⋙

LONG BEANS &
TOMATO CURRY
Burma

250 g (8 oz) long beans, chopped 3.75 cm (1½ in)
2 tablespoons peanut oil
6 curry leaves
1 medium onion, finely sliced
1 teaspoon dried shrimp paste
½ teaspoon salt
½ teaspoon ground black pepper
1 teaspoon chili powder
1 large tomato, finely chopped
2 teaspoons finely chopped garlic
½ cup hot water
1 teaspoon sesame oil

Heat oil in a saucepan, add curry leaves then add onion and stir till soft and golden. Add dried shrimp paste, salt, pepper, chili, tomato, and garlic. Stir well for 2 minutes, add water, lower heat, cover and simmer till oil comes to the surface.

Raise heat and stir in the beans for 1 minute. Cover and simmer till cooked, crunchy but not mushy. Add sesame oil, stir and serve with rice and accompaniments.
Serves 2–3

⋘⋙

MIXED VEGETABLES,
SINDHI STYLE
Sabzi Bhaji ◆ India

2 large carrots
2 large potatoes
2 medium onions
2 fresh red or green chilies
1 tablespoon ground coriander
1 ½ teaspoons ground turmeric
2 tablespoons ghee
2 tablespoons oil
1½ teaspoons finely grated fresh ginger
½ cup chopped cilantro (fresh coriander leaves)
2 firm ripe tomatoes, peeled and diced
1 cup (6½ oz, 200 g) yogurt
1½ teaspoons salt
lemon wedges or lemon juice to taste

Peel carrots and potatoes and cut both in julienne strips. Finely chop onions and seed and finely slice chilies. Combine all in a bowl, sprinkle coriander and turmeric over and toss well. Leave for half an hour.

In a large saucepan heat the ghee and oil and fry the ginger, stirring, until golden. Add the mixed vegetables and fry for a few minutes. Stir in half the cilantro, tomatoes, yogurt, and salt. Cover and cook for 10 to 15 minutes or until vegetables are tender. Serve hot with the remaining cilantro sprinkled over and accompanied by wedges of lemon or, if preferred, add lemon juice to taste.

Serves 4

MIXED VEGETABLES WITH COCONUT
Aviyal ◆ India (Kerala)

About 6 cups mixed vegetables cut into julienne strips —
carrots, French (runner) beans, zucchini (courgettes),
pumpkin (squash), bell peppers (capsicum), eggplant
(aubergine), chayote (choko), cucumber, etc.
½ cup fresh green peas
½ cup freshly grated coconut or 3 tablespoons unsweetened
desiccated coconut
1 cup (8 fl oz, 250 ml) water
1 teaspoon cumin seeds
1 teaspoon chopped garlic
2 fresh green chilies, seeded
½ cup (3½ oz, 100 g) thick coconut cream
1½ teaspoons salt
6 curry leaves
2 teaspoons coconut oil

In a saucepan bring to a boil enough lightly salted water to cover one kind of vegetable. Boil each vegetable separately, just long enough to make it tender but not soft and mushy. Take out vegetables on slotted spoon and put them in a bowl. Use the same water for all the vegetables, adding a little water at a time as it boils away, but keeping the quantity small. Save the cooking liquid.

In a blender put the coconut, water, cumin seeds, garlic, and chilies. Blend on high speed until the coconut is very finely ground. Put this into the saucepan with the vegetable stock, add the coconut cream, salt, and curry leaves and bring to a boil. Add the vegetables, simmer uncovered for 5 minutes. Stir in coconut oil and serve hot with rice.

Serves 6–8

MUSHROOM CURRY
Dhingri Kari ◆ India & Pakistan

1 lb (500 g) mushrooms
2 leeks or 4 scallions (spring onions)
2 tablespoons ghee or oil
2 cloves garlic, crushed
½ teaspoon finely grated fresh ginger
6 curry leaves
2 teaspoons curry powder
1 teaspoon salt
½ teaspoon garam masala
½ cup (3½ oz, 100 g) thick coconut cream
2 teaspoons lemon juice

Wipe mushrooms clean and cut stems into slices, caps into quarters. Slice leeks or scallions finely. Heat ghee and fry garlic, ginger, curry leaves, and leeks until soft but not brown. Add curry powder, salt, and mushrooms and continue to stir over low heat until mushrooms are soft. Cover and cook on low heat 8 to 10 minutes, then sprinkle with garam masala, add coconut cream and cook uncovered, stirring constantly, just until heated through. Remove from heat and stir in lemon juice. Serve with white rice or vegetable pilau.

Note: Choose large, open mushrooms, because they have the strongest flavor.

Serves 4

MUSHROOMS FRIED WITH CHICKEN
Hmo Kyaw Kyet ◆ Burma

1 lb (500 g) fresh mushrooms
1 lb (500 g) chicken meat
3 tablespoons oil
1 large onion, finely sliced
3 cloves garlic, finely chopped
1 tablespoon light soy sauce
salt to taste

Wipe mushrooms with damp kitchen paper. Do not wash. If large, cut in halves or quarters. Slice chicken meat into narrow strips. Heat oil in wok and fry onion and garlic until golden brown. Add chicken and stir-fry for 2 minutes, on high heat, then cover and cook for 3 minutes on medium heat. Add soy sauce and salt to taste, then the mushrooms. Cover and simmer for 3 to 4 minutes, then raise heat and cook uncovered until most of the liquid has evaporated. Serve hot with rice.

Serves 6

NEPALESE PEA & POTATO CURRY
Nepal

3 tablespoons ghee and oil mixture
1 large onion, finely sliced
½ teaspoon ground black pepper
3 green chilies, chopped
2 teaspoons finely chopped garlic
1 teaspoon finely chopped fresh ginger
½ teaspoon ground turmeric
1 teaspoon salt, or to taste
1 lb (500 g) potatoes, peeled and cubed
2 cups fresh green peas
2 large tomatoes, chopped
2 teaspoons ground coriander
1 teaspoon toasted ground cumin
1 cup (12 fl oz, 250 ml) hot water

Garnish:
2 tablespoons fresh cilantro (coriander leaves), chopped

Heat ghee and oil mixture in a saucepan and fry onion till soft and golden. Stir in pepper, chilies, garlic, ginger, turmeric, and salt. Continue cooking for 2 or 3 minutes then add potatoes and stir till light brown all over.

Add remaining ingredients and hot water, stir well, cover and simmer till vegetables are tender and the oil shows on the surface. Garnish with chopped cilantro (coriander leaves) and serve with chapatis or rice, and accompaniments.
Serves 4

❖

OKRA FRIED IN BATTER
Bhendi Pakorha ◆ India (Punjab)

8 oz (250 g) small, tender okra (ladies' fingers)
1 teaspoon oil
2 teaspoons ground coriander
2 teaspoons ground rice
¼ teaspoon ground turmeric
1 teaspoon finely grated fresh ginger
2 fresh green chilies, seeded and finely chopped
1 teaspoon salt
squeeze of lemon juice to taste

Batter:
½ cup besan (chickpea flour)
½ cup self-raising flour
approximately ¾ cup (6 fl oz, 180 ml) water

½ teaspoon garam masala
½ teaspoon chili powder
1 teaspoon crushed garlic
1 teaspoon salt
oil for deep frying

Wash okra, wipe dry with kitchen paper and make a slit on one side of each pod. Heat the oil and fry the coriander, ground rice, turmeric, ginger, and chilies, stirring constantly, until the spices are golden brown. Remove from heat, mix in the salt and a squeeze of lemon juice to taste. Put a little of this mixture in the slit made in each okra pod.

Mix the besan and self-raising flours smoothly with the water to make a fairly liquid dipping batter. Stir in the garam masala, chili powder, garlic, and salt. Heat enough oil to deep fry the okra. Dip each one into the batter and drop into the hot oil. Fry over medium high heat until golden brown. Drain on absorbent paper and serve as an accompaniment to rice and curries.
Serves 4

❖

PAPAYA SALAD
The Philippines

1 medium, firm papaya (pawpaw)
1 small ripe pineapple, peeled and diced
2 scallions (spring onions), finely sliced
1 cooking apple, peeled and diced
½ cup thinly sliced celery
½ cup (4 oz, 125 g) salad dressing or mayonnaise
salt and pepper to taste

Peel papaya, cut in half and scoop out seeds. Cut flesh into dice. Combine with all the other ingredients, cover and chill before serving.
Serves 6

❖

PICKLED CHINESE CABBAGE
Kim Chi ◆ Korea

1 large white Chinese (Napa) cabbage
common salt (not iodised)
cayenne
6 scallions (spring onions), finely chopped
6 cloves garlic, finely chopped
3 fresh red chilies, finely chopped
3 teaspoons finely chopped fresh ginger
2 cups dashi stock (page 6)
2 teaspoons light soy sauce

Cut base off cabbage, then slice lengthwise into 6 segments. Dry in the sun for half a day, cut each segment in half crosswise, then put into an unglazed earthenware pot alternately with good handfuls of salt and a sprinkling of cayenne, making several layers. Cover with a wooden lid just small enough to fit inside the pot so that it rests directly on the cabbage. Weight it down with a heavy stone and leave for a week, then rinse the cabbage thoroughly under cold running water. Squeeze out as much moisture as possible. Slice into 1 in (2.5 cm) sections or chop more finely if preferred and put into the rinsed-out jar, this time layering with the onions, garlic, chilies, and ginger. Fill pot with the dashi stock mixed with the soy sauce. Cover with wax (greaseproof) paper, put lid back on top and refrigerate. After 4 or 5 days the kim chi is ready for eating. Serve with hot white rice and a dash of soy sauce.

Note: In cold weather kim chi does not require refrigeration, but in warm weather, store in refrigerator for up to 3 weeks.

❖❖❖

PICKLED MUSTARD CABBAGE
China

8 oz (250 g) sugar
3 cups (24 fl oz, 750 ml) water
1 tablespoon salt
⅔ cup (5 fl oz, 170 ml) cider vinegar
1 bunch 1 lb (500 g) gai choy (Chinese mustard cabbage)
4 slices of fresh ginger

Put the sugar, water, salt, and vinegar into a saucepan and stir over heat until sugar dissolves. Bring to a boil and simmer for 5 minutes. Leave to cool completely.

Using only the stem and leaf ribs of the well-washed gai choy, cut into chunks 1 in (2.5 cm) long. After trimming there should be 8 oz (250 g). The leaves can be shredded and used in soup or other dishes.

Bring a large saucepan of water to a boil and blanch the gai choy chunks for 1 minute. Drain, and cool under running cold water.

Rinse out a large glass jar with hot water, put in the gai choy and ginger. Top up with the spiced vinegar mixture, cover and refrigerate for 3 to 4 days before using.

This crisp pickled vegetable makes a refreshing snack, and the flavor is enhanced when eaten with a little sesame oil.

❖❖❖

PICKLED VEGETABLES
China

1 small white turnip
½ cucumber
½ carrot
10 slices fresh ginger
1 red chili, diced
1 red bell pepper (capsicum), diced
4 teaspoons salt
5 tablespoons sugar
5 tablespoons cider vinegar

Cut the turnip, cucumber, and carrot into bite-size pieces. Add the ginger slices, red chili, bell pepper, and salt. Mix well, and leave to stand for 6 hours.

Lightly rinse the vegetables, drain, then return them to a bowl. Add sugar and vinegar, mix well and allow to stand for 6 hours in the refrigerator.

Note: The ingredients may be diced, shredded or diagonally cross-cut into big or little pieces according to your preference, and the soaking time should be adjusted accordingly.

❖❖❖

PINEAPPLE COCONUT CURRY
Pacari ◆ Indonesia

1 small pineapple, not too ripe
1 tablespoon oil
1 small onion, finely chopped
1 clove garlic, finely chopped
small stick cinnamon
3 whole cloves
3 cardamom pods, bruised
3 teaspoons ground coriander
1½ teaspoons ground cumin
½ teaspoon chili powder, or 1 fresh chili, seeded and sliced
1 teaspoon salt
1 cup (6½ oz, 200 g) thick coconut cream
1 teaspoon palm sugar or dark brown sugar

Peel pineapple with a sharp knife and remove the eyes. Cut in quarters lengthwise and remove the hard core. Cut each quarter in two lengthwise, then into thick slices crosswise. Heat oil in a saucepan and fry onion, garlic, and whole spices over medium heat, stirring frequently, until onion is soft. Add coriander, cumin, chili, and salt and stir for a few minutes until spices are browned. Add pineapple and stir well to coat with the spice mixture. Add coconut cream and sugar and bring to simmering point, stirring constantly. Do not cover pan. Simmer

Pickled vegetables from China (recipe opposite).

for 3 or 4 minutes, or until pineapple is just tender. Fruit should not be too soft.
Serves 6

⋊⋈⋉

PUMPKIN & COCONUT CURRY
Burma

1 lb (500 g) pumpkin, peeled and cubed
1 large onion, finely sliced
2 teaspoons finely chopped garlic
1 teaspoon turmeric
1 teaspoon chili powder

1 teaspoon salt
½ teaspoon ground black pepper
1 teaspoon dried shrimp paste
2 tablespoons creamed coconut or ½ cup thick coconut cream
1½ cups (12 fl oz, 375 ml) hot water
2 fresh green chilies, sliced

Place all ingredients, except pumpkin, into a saucepan and bring to a boil. Lower heat and simmer for 5 minutes. Then add pumpkin, cover and simmer until tender. Serve with boiled rice and accompaniments.
Serves 2–4

SALT FISH & EGGPLANT CURRY
Karavadu Vambotu Curry ◆ Sri Lanka

8 oz (250 g) dried salted fish
2 medium eggplants (aubergines), about 1 lb (500 g)
1 teaspoon ground turmeric
1 teaspoon salt
12 large fresh sweet chilies
oil for frying
10 cloves garlic, peeled and left whole
1 large onion, finely sliced
3 cups thin coconut cream
3 tablespoons Ceylon curry powder (page 8)
small stick cinnamon
walnut size piece of tamarind pulp
¼ cup malt vinegar
½ teaspoon salt, or to taste
1–2 teaspoons sugar

Wash the dried fish, drain, then cut into 2 in (5 cm) pieces. Slice eggplants thickly, rub each slice with turmeric and salt and set aside for 30 minutes. Wash chilies, slit and remove seeds. Drain liquid given off from eggplant slices and dry on kitchen paper.

Heat about 1/4 cup oil in a frying pan and fry separately the dried fish, chilies, garlic, onion, and eggplant, removing each to a dish as fried. It may be necessary to replenish the oil as it is used up, for the eggplants absorb quite a lot.

Put the coconut cream into a saucepan with the ground and whole spices, tamarind dissolved in vinegar, and salt. Stir until it comes to a boil, add fried ingredients and keep stirring frequently as the mixture cooks, uncovered. When it is thick, add sugar and stir to dissolve before serving.
Serves 6

SAVORY FRIED BEANS
Same ka Bhaji ◆ India (Karnataka)

1 lb (500 g) green (string) beans or long (snake) beans
1 tablespoon oil or ghee
½ teaspoon black mustard seeds
1 medium onion, finely chopped
½ teaspoon finely grated fresh ginger
1 teaspoon ground turmeric
1 teaspoon garam masala
1 fresh red or green chili, seeded and chopped
½ cup (4 fl oz, 125 ml) thin coconut cream
1½ teaspoons salt or to taste

Top and tail beans, remove strings and cut into 2 in (5 cm) lengths. Heat oil or ghee in a saucepan and fry the black

mustard seeds until they pop. Add onion and ginger and fry, stirring, until onion is soft and golden. Add turmeric, garam masala, chili, and beans, and fry for 2 or 3 minutes. Add coconut cream and salt and cook uncovered, stirring now and then, until beans are just tender.
Serves 4–6

SAVORY POTATOES & PEAS
Alu Mattar Bhaji ◆ India (Uttar Pradesh)

2 tablespoons ghee or oil
2 medium onions, finely chopped
1 teaspoon finely grated fresh ginger
1 teaspoon black mustard seeds
½ teaspoon black cumin seeds
½ teaspoon ground turmeric
½ teaspoon chili powder
1½ teaspoons salt
1 lb (500 g) peeled, diced potatoes
8 oz (250 g) fresh green, shelled peas or 1 cup frozen peas
¾ cup (6 fl oz, 180 ml) hot water

Heat ghee or oil in a heavy saucepan and fry the onions and ginger, mustard, and cumin seeds. When onions are soft and golden add the ground turmeric, chili powder, and salt. Toss potatoes and peas in this mixture for 5 minutes, then add hot water, cover tightly and cook on low heat for 30 minutes.
Serves 4

SHREDDED CABBAGE
Gova Mallung ◆ Sri Lanka

8 oz (250 g) cabbage
1 medium onion, finely chopped
2 fresh green chilies, seeded and chopped
¼ teaspoon ground turmeric
¼ teaspoon ground black pepper
½ teaspoon ground black mustard
1 teaspoon salt
2 teaspoons pounded Maldive fish powder, optional
½ cup unsweetened desiccated or freshly grated coconut

Shred cabbage very finely. Wash well, drain and put into a large saucepan with water clinging to the cabbage. Add all other ingredients except the coconut. Cover and cook gently until cabbage is tender but not overcooked, stirring from time to time. Uncover and add coconut. Stir well, and when any liquid in the pan has been absorbed by the coconut, the mallung is ready.
Serves 6

SHREDDED GREEN LEAVES WITH COCONUT
Mallung ◆ Sri Lanka

2 cups finely shredded green leaves
1 medium onion, finely chopped
2 green chilies, seeded and chopped, optional
½ teaspoon ground turmeric
2 teaspoons pounded Maldive fish or dried shrimp (prawn)
    powder
2 tablespoons lemon juice
1 teaspoon salt
2–3 tablespoons freshly grated or unsweetened desiccated
    coconut

Put leaves into a saucepan with all the ingredients except coconut. If there is not much water clinging to leaves after washing, add a sprinkling of water. Stir well, cover and cook over medium heat, about 6 minutes. Uncover, add coconut and toss over low heat until coconut absorbs all the liquid. Remove from heat. Serve hot or cold as an accompaniment to rice.

Note: A mallung is best described as a very tasty, dry accompaniment eaten with rice. One or two different mallungs are served with every meal.

The leaves of many common plants are used, one of the most popular being "gotukolle", a type of cress. Common curly parsley is a good substitute.
Serves 6

⟨⟩∞⟨⟩

SICHUAN-STYLE EGGPLANT
China

2 eggplants (aubergines) about 1 lb (500 g) each, or 2 lb
    (1 kg) smaller eggplants
1⅔ cups (15 fl oz, 475 ml) peanut oil
1 teaspoon finely grated ginger
1 teaspoon finely chopped garlic

Sauce:
5 tablespoons dark soy sauce
4 teaspoons vinegar
4 teaspoons Chinese wine or dry sherry
2 tablespoons sugar
1 teaspoon sesame oil
1 teaspoon chili oil, optional
1–2 teaspoons sweet chili sauce

Sichuan-style eggplant (recipe above).

Slice off and discard the stalk end of the eggplants, but do not peel them. Cut in half lengthwise, then into wedges lengthwise, each about 1 in (2.5 cm) thick. Cut the wedges into 2 in (5 cm) lengths.

Heat the peanut oil in a wok or frying pan, and on high heat fry half the pieces of eggplant at a time, turning so that they are evenly browned. Cook until a dark golden brown, then lift out with a slotted spoon and drain on absorbent kitchen paper. When all have been fried, set aside to cool. The oil that remains may be strained and used again.

Combine sauce ingredients and stir until sugar dissolves.

Pour off all but 1 tablespoon of oil from the pan. Heat, add ginger and garlic and stir quickly over medium heat until they turn golden.

Add the sauce mixture, bring to a boil, then return the eggplant and cook over high heat, turning the pieces over until most of the sauce is absorbed. Transfer to a serving dish (don't leave eggplant in the wok or a metallic taste will develop) and serve warm or cold.

Serves 6

SPICED STEAMED CAULIFLOWER

Dum Gobi ◆ India (Uttar Pradesh)

1 small cauliflower
2 tablespoons butter or ghee
salt and pepper to taste
¼ cup finely chopped cashews
2 teaspoons chironji nuts or sunflower seeds
½ teaspoon garam masala

Steam the cauliflower until half cooked. Put into an oven dish, spread with half the butter or ghee and season with salt and pepper. Cover and bake in a moderate oven 350°F (180°C, Gas Mark 4), until tender, then remove lid and brown under broiler (grill). In remaining butter or ghee lightly fry the cashews until golden, add chironji or sunflower seeds and fry a little longer. Mix in the garam masala and sprinkle over the cauliflower. Serve hot.

Serves 4

SPICY CABBAGE IN COCONUT CREAM

Sayur Kol ◆ Indonesia

1 lb (500 g) cabbage
2 onions, chopped
2 cloves garlic
2 fresh red chilies, seeded and chopped, or 1 teaspoon chili powder
1 teaspoon trasi (dried shrimp paste)
1 daun salam or 3 curry leaves
2 tablespoons peanut oil
2 strips lemon rind
1½ cups (10½ fl oz, 300 ml) thick coconut cream
1 teaspoon salt
3 tablespoons tamarind liquid

Wash and coarsely shred the cabbage. Put chopped onions, garlic, and chilies into container of electric blender and blend to a purée. Or grate onions and garlic, and chop chilies finely or substitute chili powder. Wrap the trasi in a piece of foil and cook under broiler (grill) for 5 minutes, turning halfway through. In a wok or large saucepan fry the leaves in hot oil for 1 minute, turn in the blended mixture and trasi and fry, stirring, until the mixture darkens. Stir constantly or mixture might catch to base of pan. Add lemon rind, coconut cream, and salt, stir well while bringing to simmering point. Add cabbage and simmer, uncovered, for a few minutes until the cabbage is cooked but still crisp. Stir in tamarind liquid and serve.

SPICY DICED VEGETABLES

Cho Chori ◆ India (Bengal)

3 medium carrots
2 medium potatoes
12 tender green (string) beans
2 firm ripe tomatoes
2 tablespoons mustard oil or other vegetable oil
2 teaspoons black mustard seeds
2 dried red chilies, optional
2 onions, finely chopped
1 teaspoon finely chopped garlic
1 teaspoon finely chopped fresh ginger
1 teaspoon ground coriander
1 teaspoon ground cumin
½ teaspoon chili powder, optional
1 teaspoon salt
2–3 tablespoons water
½ teaspoon garam masala, optional

Peel and dice the carrots and potatoes. Top and tail the beans and cut them into short lengths, the same size as the diced vegetables. Peel and dice the tomatoes.

Heat oil in a saucepan and fry the mustard seeds and chilies until the seeds pop. Add onions, garlic, and ginger and fry, stirring, until golden. Add coriander, cumin, and chili powder (if used) and fry for a few seconds, then add vegetables and salt and toss until coated with the spices and oil. Add water, cover and cook 15 minutes or until vegetables are tender, stirring gently every 5 minutes and adding a little extra water if necessary. Sprinkle with garam masala, if used, towards end of cooking. Serve with rice or chapatis.

Serves 4

⟨≋⟩

SPICY FRIED POTATOES
Alu Bhaji ◆ India

1 lb (500 g) potatoes
3 tablespoons oil
1 teaspoon black mustard seeds
½ teaspoon ground turmeric
1 large onion, finely sliced
1 or 2 fresh green chilies, seeded and sliced
1½ teaspoons salt
¼ cup (2 fl oz, 60 ml) hot water
1 tablespoon lemon juice

Boil potatoes in their skins until just tender. Peel and dice. Heat the oil in a saucepan and fry the mustard seeds until they pop. Add the turmeric, sliced onion, and chilies and fry until onions are soft and golden. Add the salt and water, bring to a boil, add potatoes, cover and cook until liquid is absorbed. Remove from heat. Sprinkle with lemon juice and stir well.

Serves 4

⟨≋⟩

SPICY FRIED CAULIFLOWER
Gobi Bhaji ◆ India (Punjab)

½ small cauliflower
1 green bell pepper (capsicum)
2 fresh red or green chilies
2 tablespoons oil
½ teaspoon black cumin seeds
½ teaspoon black mustard seeds
½ teaspoon cumin seeds
1 teaspoon green masala paste (page 10) or
  ½ teaspoon grated fresh ginger and
  ½ teaspoon crushed garlic
1 teaspoon salt
1 tablespoon water

Break cauliflower into florets, seed the bell pepper and cut into strips, seed and slice the chilies.

Heat oil in saucepan and fry the seeds, stirring, until the mustard seeds pop. Add ginger and garlic, salt, and the vegetables and stir and toss to mix thoroughly with the spice mixture.

Add water and immediately put the lid on the pan to trap the steam. Cook covered over medium heat, shaking pan occasionally, for about 8 minutes or until cauliflower is tender but still crisp. Serve with rice or chapatis.

Serves 4

⟨≋⟩

SPINACH WITH FRESH CHEESE
Palak Panir ◆ India (Punjab)

8 oz (250 g) fresh spinach leaves (without stems) or other
  greens
1 tablespoon dried fenugreek leaves, optional
8 oz (250 g) panir (Indian cottage cheese) or ricotta
oil for deep frying
1 tablespoon ghee
½ teaspoon ground turmeric
1½ cups (12 fl oz, 375 ml) hot water
¼ teaspoon black cumin seeds
small pinch asafoetida, optional
1 tablespoon ground coriander
½ teaspoon chili powder
½ teaspoon finely grated fresh ginger
1 teaspoon salt
½ teaspoon sugar
1 cup (6½ oz, 200 g) yogurt

Put the well-washed spinach leaves into a pan with the water still clinging to them, add the fenugreek leaves (if used), cover and steam until spinach is soft. Drain well and chop finely.

Cut the panir into cubes and spread on absorbent paper for a few minutes so that surface moisture is absorbed. In a small, deep frying pan heat enough oil to deep fry the cubes of panir. Add a tablespoon of ghee. When oil is very hot, fry a handful of panir cubes at a time. Have ready the turmeric stirred into 1 cup (8 fl oz, 250 ml) of hot water and when the panir is pale golden lift out on a slotted spoon and drop the cubes into the turmeric water. Repeat until all the panir is fried, leave in the water for about 5 minutes, then drain.

Heat about 2 tablespoons of the oil in a saucepan and add the black cumin seeds, asafoetida, coriander, chili powder, and ginger. Stir and fry briefly, taking care not to burn the spices. Add the spinach and salt and stir for a minute or two, then add about 1/2 cup (4 fl oz, 125 ml) hot water and the sugar. Simmer for 5 minutes. Stir the yogurt until smooth, add to the spinach and stir well. Add cubes of panir and simmer for 10 minutes longer. Serve hot with rice or chapatis.
Serves 4–5

SPINACH WITH POTATOES
Palak Alu ◆ India (Maharashtra Parsi)

1 lb (500 g) scrubbed, new potatoes
1 bunch spinach
2 tablespoons ghee or oil
1 teaspoon black mustard seeds
1 teaspoon cumin seeds
½ teaspoon ground turmeric
½ teaspoon ground coriander
½ teaspoon ground cumin
2 fresh green chilies, slit and seeds removed
1 teaspoon salt or to taste
approximately ½ cup (4 fl oz, 125 ml) water
½ teaspoon grated nutmeg

Cut potatoes into small cubes. Wash spinach in several changes of water. Discard tough stems and put into a large saucepan with just the water clinging to the leaves. Cover and steam for 10 minutes or until tender, then chop roughly. Do not discard any liquid in pan.

In a large frying pan heat the ghee or oil and fry mustard and cumin seeds until mustard seeds pop. Cover pan or they will fly all over the stove. Add turmeric, coriander, cumin, and the chilies. Add potatoes, stir and fry for a few minutes, then add salt and the water, cover and cook for 10 minutes. Add spinach, stir, cover and cook for 5 or 10 minutes longer. Sprinkle nutmeg over and serve with rice or chapatis.
Serves 4

STEAMED MUSHROOMS WITH PORK FILLING
Jing Yeung Buck Gwoo ◆ China

8 oz (250 g) fresh button mushrooms (champignon)
8 oz (250 g) lean ground (minced) pork
6 water chestnuts, finely chopped
1 tablespoon cornstarch (cornflour)
1 tablespoon light soy sauce
¾ teaspoon salt
½ teaspoon finely grated fresh ginger
½ teaspoon sugar
sesame oil
cilantro (fresh coriander leaves) to garnish

Choose mushrooms of an even size, about 1 1/2 in (4 cm) in diameter. Wipe mushrooms with damp kitchen paper. Do not peel. Remove stems carefully with a little twist, leaving caps intact. Reserve stems for another use.

Put pork, water chestnuts, cornstarch, and all seasoning ingredients into a bowl and mix thoroughly. Put a teaspoonful of the mixture into each mushroom cap, mounding it very slightly and firming the filling into the cap. Put in a heatproof dish lightly coated with sesame oil, cover dish tightly with foil, and steam mushrooms for 25 to 30 minutes. Allow to cool slightly and serve, garnished with a few sprigs of cilantro if desired.

If mushrooms are being served as appetizers, save liquid in plate for adding to soups or sauces. If they are part of a meal, thicken liquid slightly by bringing to a boil in a small saucepan (adding more stock or water if necessary) and thickening slightly with cornstarch mixed smoothly with cold water. Pour over mushrooms on serving dish and serve with white rice.
Makes about 24

STEAMED POTATOES
Alu Dum ◆ India (Kashmir)

1 lb (500 g) small, scrubbed new potatoes
1 small onion, roughly chopped
1 teaspoon chopped garlic
1 teaspoon chopped fresh ginger
1 tablespoon lemon juice
1 tablespoon water
1 teaspoon salt
1 tablespoon ghee or oil
1 small cinnamon stick
3 cardamom pods, bruised
2 whole cloves

1 bay leaf, crumbled
½ teaspoon ground turmeric

Garnish:
½ teaspoon cumin seed
½ cup (3½ oz, 100 g) yogurt
½ teaspoon garam masala
2 tablespoons chopped cilantro (fresh coriander leaves) or
  2 fresh chilies, seeded and sliced

Put potatoes into a saucepan with just enough water to almost cover, bring to a boil and boil for 5 minutes with lid on pan. Drain immediately and with a fine skewer prick the potatoes lightly all over.

Put onion, garlic, ginger, lemon juice, 1 tablespoon water, and salt in electric blender and blend to a purée. If blender is not available chop onion finely, crush garlic, and finely grate the peeled ginger. Heat ghee or oil in saucepan and fry the cinnamon, cardamom, cloves, and bay leaf for 2 minutes. Add the turmeric and stir, then add the blended mixture and fry, stirring, until the mixture smells cooked. Rinse out blender container with about 2 tablespoons extra water, add to pan with the potatoes and stir well. Cover pan tightly, turn heat very low and allow to steam for 15 minutes or until potatoes are cooked.

Roast cumin seeds in a dry pan, stirring constantly until dark brown. Combine yogurt with garam masala, roasted cumin seed roughly crushed or pounded, and a pinch of salt. Serve potatoes with yogurt mixture spooned over and sprinkled with cilantro or fresh chilies.
Serves 4

⋈

STIR-FRIED LONG BEANS & GROUND PORK
China

1 lb (500 g) long (runner) beans
4 tablespoons peanut oil
1 tablespoon finely grated fresh ginger
8 oz (250 g) ground (minced) pork
4 tablespoons roughly chopped scallions (spring onions)

Sauce:
½ cup (4 fl oz, 125 ml) chicken stock
1 tablespoon light soy sauce
2 teaspoons oyster sauce
1 teaspoon cornstarch (cornflour)

Top and tail beans, wash and pat dry on kitchen paper. Cut into 2 in (5 cm) lengths and set aside.

Mix the sauce ingredients except for cornstarch; set aside. Separately, mix the cornstarch with 1 tablespoon of cold water; set this aside as well.

Heat a wok, add 3 tablespoons of the oil and swirl to coat. Fry 1 teaspoon of the ginger for 10 seconds, then add the beans and stir-fry for 1 minute. Remove to a plate.

Return the wok to the heat, add the remaining tablespoon of oil and when hot, add the remaining 2 teaspoons of ginger, fry for a few seconds, then add the pork and stir-fry on high heat until it browns. Keep tossing, and press against the hot wok with back of frying spoon so that it is all well cooked. Add sauce ingredients and beans, stir, cover, and cook for 3 minutes. Uncover, add scallions and toss over high heat. Stir in the cornstarch paste until the sauce thickens. Serve immediately.
Serves 4–6

⋈

Stir-fried long beans and ground pork (recipe this page).

STIR-FRIED LETTUCE
China

1 firm lettuce
2–3 tablespoons peanut oil
½ teaspoon crushed garlic
¼ teaspoon finely grated fresh ginger
¼ teaspoon salt
1 teaspoon sugar
2 teaspoons light soy sauce
few drops of sesame oil

Wash lettuce, drain and dry well. Cut into halves lengthwise, cut each half twice lengthwise and twice crosswise to give chunky, bite-size pieces.

Heat a wok, add peanut oil and swirl to coat. Add garlic, and ginger and stir-fry for 10 seconds, then add lettuce and stir-fry on high heat for 30 to 40 seconds. Turn off heat, add salt, sugar, soy sauce, and sesame oil and toss to distribute the seasonings. The lettuce should retain its crisp texture. Serve at once, by itself or as a bed for other dishes.
Serves 4–6

STIR-FRIED SALAD SPROUTS
China

8 oz (250 g) bean or lentil sprouts or alfalfa
1 large carrot
2 scallions (spring onions)
stalks of choy sum (Chinese greens), optional
1 tablespoon peanut oil
½ teaspoon finely chopped garlic
1 tablespoon light soy sauce
1 tablespoon oyster sauce
few drops of sesame oil

Rinse the salad sprouts in a large bowl of cold water. Drain well in a colander. Pinch off straggly tails of the bean sprouts.

Cut the carrot into long diagonal slices no more than 1/4 in (6 mm) thick; then stack three or four slices together and cut into matchstick strips. Either blanch the carrot strips in boiling water for 1 minute, or cover with plastic wrap and microwave for 30 seconds.

Cut the lower half of the scallions into bite-size lengths; roughly chop the green leaves (keep the two separate). If using choy sum, cut into bite-size lengths.

Heat a wok and when hot, pour in the peanut oil, allow to heat then swirl so that wok is coated with oil. Throw in the garlic and scallion leaves, and stir-fry for 30 seconds. Add choy sum,

and stir-fry for 1 minute. Add the well-drained sprouts, white portion of scallions, and carrot, and stir-fry for 1 minute. Then add soy sauce and oyster sauce, and mix well. Turn off the heat, sprinkle the sesame oil over, toss to mix, and serve at once.

Note: If desired, you can add bean curd (cut into strips or dice) with the sprouts.
Serves 4

STUFFED EGGPLANT
Rellenong Talong ◆ The Philippines

2 medium eggplants (aubergines)
1 tablespoon oil
3 cloves garlic, finely chopped
1 medium onion, finely chopped
8 oz (250 g) ground (minced) pork
1 large ripe tomato, chopped
1 teaspoon salt
¾ teaspoon ground black pepper
1 cup soft fresh breadcrumbs
1 egg, beaten
dry breadcrumbs for coating
oil for frying

Cut eggplants in halves lengthwise, parboil in lightly salted water, but do not let them become too soft. Remove from water and drain, cut side downwards. Scoop out some pulp, leaving a firm shell.

Heat oil and fry garlic and onion until golden, add pork and fry until all pinkness disappears. Add tomato, salt, and pepper and cook for 15 minutes. Add chopped eggplant pulp and continue cooking until mixture is not too moist. Remove from heat, mix in soft breadcrumbs, taste and add more seasoning if necessary. Divide mixture among eggplant halves and fill them, then brush tops with beaten egg and coat with breadcrumbs. Heat oil for shallow frying and fry eggplants first on one side, then on the other, until golden. Serve hot.
Serves 4

THAI-STYLE CUCUMBER SALAD

Yam Tang Kwa ◆ Thailand

2 green cucumbers
1 small onion
2 tablespoons dried shrimp (prawn) powder
1 or 2 fresh red chilies, seeded and chopped
2 tablespoons fish sauce
lemon juice to taste

Peel, seed, and coarsely grate the cucumbers. Peel and grate the onion. Mix all ingredients together and serve.

VEGETABLE CURRY

Sayur Masak Lemak ◆ Malaysia

1 onion, finely sliced
1 clove garlic, finely chopped
2 fresh red or green chilies, seeded and sliced
½ teaspoon blacan (dried shrimp paste)
½ teaspoon ground turmeric
1 cup (8 fl oz, 250 ml) thin coconut cream
1 large potato, peeled and diced
3 cups coarsely shredded cabbage
1 teaspoon salt
1 cup (8 fl oz, 250 ml) thick coconut cream
lemon juice to taste

Put onion, garlic, chilies, blacan, turmeric, and thin coconut cream into a saucepan and bring to simmering point. Add potato and cook for 10 minutes or until potato is half cooked. Add cabbage and salt, cook for 3 minutes, then add the thick coconut cream and stir gently until cabbage is cooked. Remove from heat and add lemon juice to taste.
Serves 6 as an accompaniment

VEGETABLE PICKLE

Acar Kuning ◆ Malaysia

1 cup carrot sticks
1 cup green (string) beans
10 fresh red and green chilies
1 green cucumber
2 tablespoons peanut oil
2 cloves garlic, finely grated

2 teaspoons finely grated fresh ginger
3 candlenuts or brazil kernels, grated
1 teaspoon ground turmeric
½ cup (4 fl oz, 125 ml) white vinegar
½ cup (4 fl oz, 125 ml) water
2 teaspoons sugar
1 teaspoon salt
1 cup cauliflower sprigs

Cut carrots into julienne strips. Cut beans into pieces of the same length, then slice each piece in two lengthwise. If beans are very young and slender you will not need to slice them. Leave the chilies whole, but remove stems. Peel cucumber and cut in half lengthwise, remove seeds and slice into pieces the same size as the carrots and beans.

Heat oil in a saucepan and fry garlic and ginger on low heat for 1 minute, add grated nuts and turmeric and fry for a few seconds longer. Add vinegar, water, sugar, and salt and bring to a boil. Add carrots, beans, chilies, and cauliflower sprigs, return to a boil and boil for 3 minutes. Add cucumber and boil for 1 minute longer.

Turn into an earthenware or glass bowl and allow to cool. Use immediately or bottle and store in refrigerator for a week or two.

VEGETABLES IN COCONUT GRAVY

Sayur Lodeh ◆ Indonesia

1–1½ lb (500–750 g) fresh vegetables
2 tablespoons peanut oil
1 onion, finely chopped
2 cloves garlic, crushed
1 teaspoon sambal ulek (page 23), or 1 fresh red chili, seeded and chopped
1 teaspoon trasi (dried shrimp paste)
1 stalk lemon grass, or 2 strips lemon rind, or ½ teaspoon sereh powder
1 large ripe tomato, peeled, seeded and chopped
2 cups (16 fl oz, 500 ml) vegetable, chicken or beef stock
1½ cups (12 fl oz, 375 ml) thin coconut cream
3 teaspoons peanut sauce or peanut butter
2 teaspoons salt, or to taste

Slice vegetables into small pieces: cauliflower or broccoli should be broken or cut into florets; beans sliced very thinly; cabbage shredded coarsely and the shreds cut across once or twice — if they are too long it makes the dish awkward to eat; zucchini or pumpkin can be sliced thinly or diced; winter bamboo shoots, much more tender than the ordinary variety, are cut into short strips, or can be halved and sliced for a half-moon shape.

Heat oil in a medium saucepan and fry the onion until soft and starting to turn golden, then add garlic, sambal, and trasi and fry over low heat for 2 minutes, crushing the trasi with the back of the spoon and stirring the mixture. Add lemon grass and tomato, stir and cook to a pulp.

Add stock and coconut cream and bring to simmering point with lid off. Add vegetables according to the time they take to cook. They should be tender but still crisp. In the selection suggested you would add the beans, simmer for 4 minutes, then add the cauliflower and broccoli, simmer for a further 3 minutes, then add the cabbage, zucchini, pumpkin, and bamboo shoots and cook for 3 minutes longer. Stir in the peanut sauce and add salt to taste. A squeeze of lemon juice may be added if a sharper taste is preferred.

Note: Any vegetables in season can be used. French (runner) beans, cabbage, cauliflower, broccoli, zucchini (courgettes), pumpkin, and winter bamboo shoots are an excellent combination.
Serves 6

VEGETABLES WITH PEANUT SAUCE
Gado-Gado ◆ Indonesia

3 large potatoes, boiled
8 oz (250 g) fresh bean sprouts
1 lb (500 g) green (string) beans
3 carrots
½ small cabbage
1 green cucumber
small bunch watercress
3 hard-cooked (boiled) eggs
peanut sauce (page 16)

Peel potatoes and cut in slices. Wash bean sprouts, pinching off any brown tails. Pour boiling water over bean sprouts, then rinse under cold water. Drain. String beans and cut in diagonal slices or bite-size lengths and cook in lightly salted boiling water until just tender. Beans should still be crisp to bite. Scrub carrots and cut into thin strips, cook until tender. Drain. Slice cabbage, discarding tough middle stem. Blanch in boiling salted water for a minute or two, until tender but not limp. Drain and refresh under cold water. Score skin of cucumber with a fork and cut into very thin slices. Wash watercress and break into sprigs, discarding tough stalks. Chill until crisp.

Put watercress on a large dish and arrange the various vegetables in separate sections on top. Surround with slices of cucumber and put wedges of hard-cooked egg in middle. Serve cold, accompanied by peanut sauce, which is spooned over individual servings.
Serves 6–8

WATERCRESS IN SWEET GRAVY
Gulai Manis Kangkung ◆ Indonesia

1 lb (500 g) kangkung or substitute
4 tablespoons dehydrated shrimp (prawn)
1½ cups (12 fl oz, 375 ml) thin coconut cream
1 large onion, finely chopped
1 small clove garlic, crushed
1 teaspoon salt
1 teaspoon finely grated fresh ginger
1 fresh red chili, seeded and sliced
2 tablespoons palm sugar or dark brown sugar
½ teaspoon laos powder

Thoroughly wash greens in several changes of cold water and drain. Slice coarsely. Pour 1/2 cup (4 fl oz, 125 ml) hot water over shrimp and soak 5 minutes. If using the brownish dried shrimp instead of the white dehydrated shrimp, they will need longer soaking, about 25 minutes. Put coconut cream and all other ingredients into a large saucepan and bring to a boil, uncovered. Add soaked shrimp, the water in which they soaked, and the green vegetable. Cover and simmer on low heat for 20 minutes or until tender. Serve hot with rice and other dishes.
Note: Kangkung is a very nutritious dark green leaf used in Asian countries. Substitute watercress, spinach or chicory.
Serves 6

WHITE RADISH SALAD
Mu Saingchai ◆ Korea

2 giant white radishes
1 or 2 crisp cooking apples
juice of half lemon
3 scallions (spring onions)

Dressing:
3 tablespoons light soy sauce
1 tablespoon salad oil
2 teaspoons sesame oil
3 tablespoons mild vinegar
3 teaspoons sugar
1 teaspoon salt
1 tablespoon toasted, crushed sesame seeds
1 fresh hot red chili, seeded and finely chopped

Peel radishes and cut into matchstick strips. Peel apples and cut into similar strips, and soak in cold water with a good squeeze of lemon juice to prevent discoloration. Slice the scallions very finely, including white and green portions.

*Vegetable pickle, or **acar** kuning from Malaysia (page 283).*

Combine all remaining ingredients and toss with the radish, well-drained apple, and scallion. Cover and chill before serving.
Serves 4

YELLOW PUMPKIN CURRY
Vatakka ◆ Sri Lanka

1 lb (500 g) pumpkin (squash)
1 small onion, finely chopped
1 teaspoon finely chopped garlic
3 fresh green chilies, seeded and chopped
8–10 curry leaves
½ teaspoon fenugreek seeds
½ teaspoon ground turmeric
2 teaspoons pounded Maldive fish or dried shrimp (prawns)
1½ cups (12 fl oz, 375 ml) thin coconut cream
1 teaspoon salt
½ cup (4 fl oz) thick coconut cream
1 teaspoon black mustard seeds

Peel pumpkin and cut into large chunks. Put into a pan with all the ingredients except the thick coconut cream and mustard seeds. Bring slowly to simmering point and cook gently, uncovered, until pumpkin is almost tender.

Meanwhile, grind the mustard seeds in mortar and pestle and mix with the thick coconut cream. Add to the simmering pot and cook for 5 minutes longer on a very gentle heat.
Serves 6

YOUNG CORN COBS & SNOW PEAS WITH CUCUMBER
Jun Ju Shun Ho Lan Dau Chang Gwa ◆ China

14 oz (440 g) can young corn cobs
8 oz (250 g) snow peas (mangetout)
1 cucumber
1 tablespoon peanut oil
1 teaspoon sesame oil
¼ teaspoon crushed garlic
¼ teaspoon finely grated fresh ginger
salt to taste

Drain liquid from can of corn. Remove stems and strings from snow peas. Peel and cut cucumber into thin slices. Heat peanut oil in a wok, add sesame oil, garlic, and ginger and stir once, then add corn and snow peas. Stir-fry for 1 minute over high heat. Add cucumber slices and cook 2 minutes longer. Serve at once.
Serves 4

ZUCCHINI OR MARROW PURÉE
Gooda Bartha ◆ India & Pakistan

1 lb (500 g) zucchini (courgettes) or marrow
1 tablespoon ghee or oil
1 teaspoon cumin seeds
½ teaspoon black mustard seeds
2 fresh green chilies, seeded and sliced
1 medium onion, finely chopped
½ teaspoon salt
½ teaspoon chili powder, optional

Peel and roughly chop zucchini or marrow, discarding seeds. Put in a saucepan with water to almost cover, cook until soft, then drain well and mash. Heat ghee in a saucepan and fry the cumin and mustard seeds until mustard seeds start to crackle. Add chilies and onion and cook until onion is soft. Add zucchini, salt, and chili powder and cook uncovered for 5 minutes or until liquid evaporates. Serve warm or at room temperature.
Serves 4

Young corn cobs and snow peas with cucumber (recipe opposite).

Breads, Cakes, Desserts & Drinks

AGAR-AGAR JELLO
Singapore

6 cups (48 fl oz, 1.5 L) water
4 teaspoons agar-agar powder
1 cup (8 oz, 250 g) sugar
few drops red food coloring
3 or 4 drops rose extract (essence)
½ teaspoon vanilla extract (essence)
few drops green food coloring
3 or 4 drops almond extract (essence)

Pour water into a saucepan, sprinkle the agar-agar powder over the surface and bring slowly to a boil. Boil until agar dissolves, 5 to 10 minutes. Add sugar and stir over heat until it dissolves. Remove from heat, pour 2 cups of the jello (jelly) into a bowl, turn pink with red coloring and flavor with rose extract. Pour into a glass bowl rinsed with cold water. Keep remaining jello warm in a pan of hot water. Refrigerate pink jello.

As soon as the first layer sets (this takes only a few minutes) pour 2 cups more agar mixture into the bowl and add the vanilla. Pour gently over the first layer and chill. Repeat with remaining jello colored a pale green and flavored with almond extract. Chill until serving time and serve from the bowl.
Serves 6

ALMOND BEAN CURD
Hung Yun Dau Fu ◆ China

4 cups (32 fl oz, 1 L) water
4 teaspoons powdered agar-agar or 1 cup soaked and
  drained agar-agar strands
1 can sweetened condensed milk
2 teaspoons almond extract (essence)

Put water into a saucepan, sprinkle agar-agar over and bring to a boil. Boil and stir until agar-agar is dissolved. Powdered agar takes only a couple of minutes to dissolve, strands take longer. Add condensed milk and almond extract and stir well. Pour into a large shallow glass dish or a large cake tin. Allow to cool and set, then chill. Cut into cubes or diamond shapes and serve by itself or with canned fruits or melon balls.
Serves 6–8

ALMOND BISCUITS
Singapore

4 oz (125 g) shortening (lard)
½ cup (3½ oz, 100 g) superfine (caster) sugar
1 teaspoon almond extract (essence)
few drops yellow food coloring, optional
1½ cups (6 oz, 185 g) all-purpose (plain) flour
8 blanched almonds
1 egg yolk
1 tablespoon water

Soften shortening to room temperature and beat together with sugar until soft and creamy. Add almond extract and, if desired, a little yellow coloring. Add the unsifted flour gradually, stirring well to combine. After adding the last of the flour, work the mixture with your hand, but it should still be of a crumbly consistency.

Take level tablespoons of the dough and shape into flat round cakes about 2 in (5 cm) in diameter. Edges of cakes will have little cracks in them. Put on a well-greased baking tray. Put almonds in a small pan with a little cold water, bring to a boil. Drain. Split almonds in two. Press half an almond in the middle of each biscuit. Beat egg yolk with water and brush tops of biscuits.

Bake in a slow oven (300°F, 150°C, Gas Mark 2) for 30 minutes or until pale golden. Cool slightly on tray, then carefully lift onto wire rack, using a spatula. When cold, store airtight.
Makes approximately 16

ALMOND MILK DRINK
Thandai ◆ India (Punjab)

20 almonds
5 peppercorns
2 teaspoons chaar magaz or sunflower seeds
1½ cups (12 fl oz, 375 ml) water
1 cup (8 fl oz, 250 ml) milk
sugar to taste
rose water or extract (essence) to flavor

Blanch the almonds and put into electric blender with peppercorns, seeds, and half the water. Blend at high speed until finely ground and strain into a jug through a fine clean muslin bag. Return the ground mixture left in the cloth to the blender with remaining water, blend again and once more extract the

These small brandied cakes, called capuchinos, originate in the Philippines (page 310).

liquid. (The finely ground almond residue may be refrigerated or frozen and used for thickening curries.) Mix milk with the almond liquid, add sugar to taste and rose water or extract. Add crushed ice, or keep refrigerated until served. A pretty touch is to float a few small rose petals on top of the drink.

Serves 2

❖

BANANA CAKE WITH CASHEWS

Chuoi Nuong ◆ Vietnam

3 eggs
1 cup (8 oz, 250 g) sugar
¾ cup (6 fl oz, 200 ml) thickened cream
1½ cups (6 oz, 185 g) all-purpose (plain) flour
2 lb (1 kg) fully ripe bananas
1 cup (5 oz, 150 g) coarsely chopped fresh cashews
1 cup (3 oz, 90 g) grated fresh coconut (do not substitute
*   desiccated)*

Beat eggs and sugar together with electric mixer until thick and pale. Add cream and beat for a few seconds longer, just to mix. Sift flour, add to bowl with cashews and coconut and stir with spoon.

Peel bananas and smash with the flat side of a chopper, but do not mash. Add to batter and stir gently only until combined. Grease or line with baking paper a large rectangular pan, 9 in x 11 in (23 cm x 30 cm). Spoon mixture into pan, levelling it with a spatula. Bake in a preheated moderate oven, 350°F (180° C), for 50–60 minutes or until top is golden brown. Serve warm or cold. This is a very solid, pudding-like but flavorsome cake.

Makes 24 squares

❖

BANANAS COOKED IN COCONUT CREAM

Kuay Namuan ◆ Cambodia & Laos

6–8 large ripe bananas
2 cups (13 oz, 400 g) thick coconut cream
2 tablespoons sugar

Peel and cut each banana into 3 or 4 pieces. Simmer coconut cream and sugar until thick and creamy. Add bananas and cook gently until bananas are soft but not mushy. Serve warm.

Serves 6

BANANA SNACKS

Ngapyaw Kyaw ◆ Burma

Long green bananas, short yellow bananas, three-cornered bananas, large red bananas, small sour bananas, sweet and butter-smooth bananas – they all grow in Burma and are available all year round. Sweet, delicately flavored varieties are eaten as they are, but others are the starting point for all sorts of sweet snacks. They can be sliced, rolled in flour and fried; boiled in coconut cream; mashed with egg and a little all-purpose (plain) flour to make a thick batter and shallow fried. These snacks are often served with a syrup made from palm sugar.

❖

BLACK BEAN STEAMED BUNS

China

2½ cups (10 oz, 315 g) all-purpose (plain) flour
1¾ teaspoons double-acting baking powder (3½ teaspoons
*   baking powder)*
3 tablespoons superfine (caster) sugar
2 tablespoons softened shortening (lard)
about ½ cup (4 fl oz, 125 ml) lukewarm water
½ teaspoon white vinegar
½ teaspoon salt
1 can dow saah (sweet bean paste)
squares waxed (greaseproof) paper
1 tablespoon sesame oil

Dough for steamed buns: Sift flour and baking powder into a bowl, stir in sugar and rub in shortening with fingertips until evenly distributed. Add water, vinegar, and salt mixed together, and knead to a fairly soft dough. Shape into a smooth ball, cover and rest dough for 30 minutes.

Divide dough into 8 equal portions and roll each into a circle about 3 in (8 cm) in diameter. Put a teaspoon of dow saah in the middle of each circle, gather sides together, folding and pleating to make a neat join. Twist dough to seal. Put each bun, join downwards, on a square of waxed paper lightly brushed with sesame oil. Put in bamboo steamer, cover and steam for 20 minutes. Serve warm. Buns can be refrigerated overnight and reheated by steaming for 3 minutes before serving.

Note: If using a metal steamer, put a clean tea cloth across steaming tray before covering with lid to prevent condensation dropping on top of buns.

❖

BUTTERMILK OR YOGURT DRINK
Lassi ◆ North India

2 cups (16 fl oz, 500 ml) cultured buttermilk
2 cups (16 fl oz, 500 ml) iced water
* or*
1 cup (6 ½ oz, 200 g) yogurt
3 cups (24 fl oz, 750 ml) iced water
salt and pepper to taste
pinch of cumin, toasted and ground, optional

Mix equal parts of cultured buttermilk and iced water, or beat yogurt until smooth and gradually stir in iced water. Season with salt, pepper, and a pinch of toasted, ground cumin. Alternatively, sweeten lightly with sugar. Serve with ice.

To make another popular yogurt drink, beat 2 tablespoons yogurt with 2 teaspoons of sugar in a tall glass, with iced soda or lemonade added. It will froth and look like a milk shake and even children who do not like yogurt will find it acceptable.

Makes 4 servings

❖❖❖

CARAMEL CUSTARD
Leche Flan ◆ The Philippines

½ cup (4 oz, 125 g) sugar
¼ cup (2 fl oz, 60 ml) water
3 large eggs
2 egg yolks
½ cup (3 ½ oz, 100 g) superfine (caster) sugar
2 ½ cups (20 fl oz, 600 ml) hot milk
2 teaspoons vanilla extract (essence)

Put sugar and water into a small saucepan and heat without stirring until a deep golden brown. Remove from heat and pour at once into a 6 cup heatproof ring tin. Rotate tin to coat base and sides with caramel.

In a large bowl beat the whole eggs and egg yolks until foamy. Gradually add the sugar, beating until thick and light. Heat milk and add very gradually, beating constantly. Stir in vanilla, then strain custard into the caramel-lined tin. Put tin into a baking dish and pour boiling water around to come halfway up the tin. Bake in a slow oven 300°F (150°C, Gas Mark 2) for 35 to 45 minutes or until a knife inserted in middle of custard comes out clean. Remove from oven and cool. When cold, cover and chill in refrigerator overnight at least, preferably for two days. Run a knife around edge, invert a chilled serving plate over the tin, then grasping both together turn them over so that the custard slips onto the serving plate. Serve chilled.

Serves 6–8

CHAPATIS
India

3 cups (12 oz, 375 g) fine wholewheat (wholemeal) flour
* or roti flour*
1–1½ teaspoons salt, or to taste
1 tablespoon ghee or oil, optional
1 cup (8 fl oz, 250 ml) lukewarm water

Put flour in mixing bowl, reserving about 1/2 cup (2 oz, 60 g) for rolling chapatis. Mix salt through the flour in the bowl, then rub in ghee or oil, if used. Add water all at once and mix to a firm but not stiff dough. Knead dough for at least 10 minutes (the more it is kneaded, the lighter the bread will be). Form dough into a ball, cover with clear plastic wrap (film) and stand for 1 hour or longer. (If left overnight the chapatis will be very light and tender.)

Shape dough into balls about the size of a large walnut. Roll out each one on a lightly floured board (using reserved flour) to a circular shape as thin as a French crêpe. After rolling out chapatis, heat a griddle plate or heavy-based frying pan until very hot, and cook the chapatis, starting with those that were rolled first (the resting between rolling and cooking seems to make for lighter chapatis). Put chapati on griddle and leave for about 1 minute. Turn and cook other side a further minute, pressing lightly around the edges of the chapati with a folded tea cloth (towel) or an egg slice. This encourages bubbles to form and makes the chapatis light. As each one is cooked, wrap in a clean tea cloth until all are ready. Serve immediately with butter, dry curries, or vegetable dishes.

Note: In India, the chapatis are cooked on the tawa or griddle and are held for a moment or two right over the fire. This makes them puff up like balloons. You can do this over a gas flame, holding them with kitchen tongs.

Yield 20–24

❖❖❖

CHICKPEA FLOUR BREAD
Besan Roti ◆ India (Uttar Pradesh)

2 cups (8 oz, 150 g) roti flour or atta (fine wholewheat, wholemeal) flour
1 cup (5 oz, 155 g) besan (chickpea) flour
2 teaspoons salt
½ teaspoon ground black pepper
1 tablespoon ghee or oil
2 fresh green chilies, seeded and finely chopped or 3 tablespoons finely chopped bell pepper (capsicum)
3 tablespoons finely chopped cilantro (fresh coriander leaves)
3 tablespoons finely chopped scallions (spring onions)
3 tablespoons finely chopped English spinach
¼ teaspoon crushed ajowan seeds
1 cup (8 fl oz, 250 ml) water
ghee or oil for shallow frying

Sift both kinds of flour together with salt and pepper into a bowl. Rub in ghee or oil and mix the other dry ingredients through. Add water and mix to a dough, kneading firmly until smooth and elastic. Cover with plastic wrap (film) and set aside for 1 hour or longer.

Take balls of the dough and roll out on lightly floured board to the size of a large saucer, and a thickness of about 1/10 in (2.5 mm). Heat a griddle or heavy frying pan liberally greased with ghee, and fry roti, turning and spreading with more ghee, until golden brown.
Makes about 15

⊰⊱⋙⊰⊱

COCONUT CAKE
Bolo De Coco ◆ Sri Lanka

3 cups (9 oz, 270 g) unsweetened desiccated coconut
3 cups (24 fl oz, 750 ml) water
4 eggs, separated
2 cups (16 oz, 500 g) white sugar
2 cups (12 oz, 375 g) rice flour
1 cup (4 oz, 125 g) self-raising flour
1 teaspoon double-acting baking powder (2 teaspoons baking powder)
½ teaspoon ground cardamom
¼ teaspoon ground cloves
¼ teaspoon ground cinnamon
1 tablespoon rose water or ½ teaspoon rose extract (essence)
4 oz (125 g) raw cashew nuts or blanched almonds, finely chopped
extra ¼ cup (2 oz, 60 g) sugar

Preheat oven to moderately slow (325°F, 160°C, Gas Mark 3). Line a deep 10 in (25 cm) square cake tin with buttered waxed (greaseproof) paper, or use two loaf pans.

Put 1 1/2 cups (4 1/2 oz, 150 g) desiccated coconut and 1 1/2 cups (12 fl oz, 375 ml) water into container of electric blender and blend on high speed until coconut is finely ground, about 1 minute. Empty blender container, repeat with remaining coconut and water.

In large bowl of electric mixer, beat yolks of eggs and 2 tablespoons of the coconut mixture with the sugar until light and creamy. Add remaining coconut and beat well. Sift the flour with baking powder and ground spices and stir into the mixture with the rose water or extract and nuts. Beat egg whites until stiff peaks form, add extra sugar and beat again until thick and glossy. Fold into coconut mixture. Pour into prepared tin and bake in oven for 1 1/4 to 1 1/2 hours or until risen and golden brown on top. A fine skewer inserted in middle of cake should come out clean. Half cool cake in tin, then lift out and cool completely on a wire rack. Cut into squares to serve.
Makes 10 in (1 x 25 cm) square cake or two loaves

⊰⊱⋙⊰⊱

CREAMED ALMONDS
Badam Kheer ◆ India (Uttar Pradesh)

4 cups (32 fl oz, 1 L) milk
1 cup (8 fl oz, 250 ml) light (single) cream
1 tablespoon ghee
1 cup almonds
6 tablespoons sugar
⅛ teaspoon saffron strands
2 tablespoons boiling water
¼ teaspoon ground cardamom

Garnish:
flaked almonds, optional
edible silver leaf, optional

Put milk, cream, and ghee into a saucepan and bring to a boil, stirring constantly. When it starts to boil turn the heat very low and simmer for 15 minutes, stirring occasionally. Meanwhile, in a small pan blanch almonds for 2 or 3 minutes, then drain and plunge into cold water.

Slip off the skins and slice the almonds very thinly, using a vegetable peeler. If they are soft from being blanched this is easier to do. Alternatively, grind the almonds in an electric blender. Add almonds and sugar to the milk and cook, stirring. Pound saffron strands in a mortar and pestle, dissolve in the boiling water and add. Continue cooking until it is the

Creamed rice and bananas (page 294), with pappadams (page 24) and puris (page 305).

consistency of custard. Remove from the heat, stir in cardamom, and pour into a dessert dish. Cover and chill before serving. Garnish with a few extra flaked almonds and silver leaf, if desired.

Serves 4–5

❦

CREAMED RICE & BANANAS

Panchamrit ✦ India (Karnataka)

1 cup powva or phoa (flaked rice)
3 cups (24 fl oz, 750 ml) milk
3 tablespoons sugar
¼ teaspoon ground cardamom
2 tablespoons ghee
3 soft ripe bananas

Wash and drain the powva. Bring milk to a boil with the sugar, add the drained rice and cook until it is slightly thick and creamy. Add the cardamom and ghee and the bananas cut in thin slices. Cook, stirring, for a few minutes longer, then leave to cool. It should have the consistency of thin custard. Usually served as part of a vegetarian meal in the central and southern parts of India.

Serves 6

❦

CREAMY VERMICELLI PUDDING

Seviyan Kheer ✦ Punjab, India

5 cups (2 pts, 1.5 L) milk
½ cup broken vermicelli
6 tablespoons sugar
2 tablespoons golden raisins (sultanas)
¼ cup blanched, slivered almonds
2 drops kewra extract (essence)
1 tablespoon chopped pistachios

Bring milk to a boil, stirring constantly. Add the vermicelli and continue to cook until vermicelli is soft. Add the sugar, golden raisins, and almonds. Stir over medium heat until the mixture is like a thick custard. Remove from heat, add the kewra extract and spoon into dessert dish or individual bowls. Decorate with pistachios. Serve warm or chilled.

Note: Kewra extract, is available at specialized Indian produce stores.

Serves 4

CRISP FARINA SHORTBREAD

Nan Khatai ✦ India

4 oz (125 g) ghee
½ cup (4 oz, 125 g) sugar
1 cup (5 ½ oz, 170 g) fine farina (semolina)
¼ cup (1 oz, 30 g) all-purpose (plain) flour
1 teaspoon ground cardamom

Cream ghee and sugar together until light. Add the sieved farina, flour, and cardamom, mix well. Allow mixture to stand for 30 minutes.

Take a level tablespoon of the mixture, roll into a ball, then flatten slightly and place on an ungreased baking tray. Repeat process with remaining mixture, leaving a little space between biscuits.

Bake in a slow oven until biscuits are pale golden, approximately 30 minutes. Cool on a wire cooling tray. Store in an air-tight container.

Makes approximately 24

❦

CRISP FRIED BATTER SPIRALS

Jalebi ✦ India (Gujarat)

Batter:
2 cups (8 oz, 250 g) all-purpose (plain) flour
½ cup (3 oz, 90 g) ground rice or rice flour
¼ oz (7 g) fresh compressed yeast or scant teaspoon dried
  yeast
½ cup (4 fl oz, 125 ml) lukewarm water
¼ teaspoon saffron strands
2 tablespoons boiling water
1 tablespoon yogurt
oil for deep frying

Syrup:
3 cups (24 oz, 750 g) sugar
3 cups (24 fl oz, 750 ml) water
1 tablespoon light corn (golden) syrup or pinch cream of
  tartar
rose extract (essence) to flavor
1½ teaspoons liquid orange food color

Sift the flour and ground rice into a large bowl. Sprinkle yeast on the lukewarm water in a small bowl, leave to soften for 5 minutes and stir to dissolve. Pound saffron strands in mortar and pestle, dissolve in boiling water.

Pour dissolved yeast and saffron water into a measuring jug. Add lukewarm water to make up to 2 1/4 cups (18 fl oz, 560 ml).

Stirring with a wooden spoon, add the liquid to the flour and beat well until batter is very smooth. Add yogurt and beat again. Leave to rest for 1 hour. Batter will start to become frothy. Beat vigorously once more before starting to fry jalebi. (While batter is resting make the syrup and leave it until just warm.)

Heat oil in a deep frying pan and when hot pour in the batter using a small funnel, or in a cloth icing bag with a small opening. Make circles or figures of eight or a series of loops. Fry, turning once, until crisp and golden on both sides. Lift out on a slotted spoon, let the oil drain for a few seconds, then drop the hot jalebi into the syrup and soak it for a minute or two. Lift out of the syrup using another slotted spoon and put on a plate to drain.

Transfer jalebi to a clean plate and serve as soon as possible after making because their crispness diminishes after some time.

Syrup: Heat sugar and water over low heat, stirring until sugar dissolves. Raise heat and boil hard for 8 minutes. Syrup should be just thick enough to spin a thread. Remove from heat, allow to cool until lukewarm, add rose extract and orange food coloring.

Makes about 24

✧∞✧

CUMIN & TAMARIND DRINK
Zeera Pani ◆ India (Uttar Pradesh)

½ cup dried tamarind pulp
2 cups (16 fl oz, 500 ml) hot water
3 teaspoons finely grated fresh ginger
2 teaspoons ground cumin
pinch chili powder, optional
½ teaspoon garam masala
3 teaspoons sugar, or to taste
salt to taste
iced water and crushed ice

Garnish:
mint sprigs and lemon slices

Soak tamarind pulp in the hot water and leave for 2 hours. Squeeze to dissolve the pulp and separate the seeds and fibers. Strain through a fine nylon sieve. Add remaining ingredients, stir well, then strain again through a very fine sieve or cheesecloth. Chill. At serving time dilute to taste with iced water, add crushed ice and garnish with mint and sliced lemon.

Serves 3–4

✧∞✧

DEEP FRIED DATE WONTON
China

8 oz (250 g) stoned dates
2 oz (60 g) walnuts or almonds
1 teaspoon finely grated orange rind
1 tablespoon orange juice
8 oz (250 g) wonton pastry squares (page 315)
peanut oil for deep frying
confectioner's (icing) sugar for dusting

Chop dates and nuts finely. Combine dates, nuts, grated rind, and just enough juice to make the mixture hold together. Form into small cylinders which will fit on the pastry squares diagonally, leaving enough pastry to twist at each end like a cracker.

Place the date rolls on the pastry, take one corner and tuck it under, then roll up to enclose the filling. Twist the ends, putting a finger in the pastry to give it a Christmas cracker shape.

When all the wonton are wrapped, heat about 3 1/2 cups (28 fl oz, 875 ml) peanut oil in a wok and fry a few at a time, turning them, until they are golden brown all over. Lift out with a wire spoon and drain on absorbent paper placed on a wire rack. When cool, sprinkle lightly with sugar. Store in an airtight container, — they will keep for a week.

Note: If preferred, use canned lotus nut paste or sweet bean paste for the filling.

Makes about 50

✧∞✧

DUTCH CHRISTMAS CAKE
Breudher ◆ Sri Lanka

10 oz (315 g) unsalted butter
10 oz (315 g) superfine (caster) sugar
5 eggs
2 teaspoons vanilla extract (essence)
8 oz (250 g) golden raisins (sultanas)

Basic dough:
½ cup (4 fl oz, 125 ml) milk
3 teaspoons sugar
2 teaspoons salt
3 oz (90 g) butter
1½ cups (12 fl oz, 375 ml) warm water
1 oz (30 g) compressed yeast or 1 packet active dry yeast
5½–6 cups (22 oz, 700 g) unsifted all-purpose (plain)
*   flour*
1 tablespoon gluten flour

Cream butter and sugar until light and creamy. Add dough in small pieces, beating well, until all the dough has been incorporated. An electric mixer is essential unless you have a strong beating arm. Add the eggs, one at a time, beating well after each. Stir in vanilla and golden raisins. Divide dough between two well-buttered 10-cup tube pans and leave in a warm place, protected from draughts, for 30 minutes or until almost double in bulk. Bake in a moderate oven for 30 to 35 minutes or until well risen and golden brown on top. If top starts to brown too soon, cover with foil or paper and cook until a thin skewer comes out clean. Cool in pan for 10 minutes, then turn out onto a wire rack and cool completely before cutting. Serve spread with unsalted butter and sprinkled with superfine sugar, or if preferred, with thin slices of Dutch edam cheese.

Basic dough: Scald milk, stir in sugar, salt, and butter and cool to lukewarm. Measure warm water into a large warm bowl. Sprinkle yeast over water, stir until dissolved. Add lukewarm milk mixture and 3 cups (12 oz, 375 g) of the flour sifted with the gluten. Beat with a wooden spoon until smooth. Add enough extra flour to make a soft dough. Turn onto a lightly floured board, knead until smooth and elastic, about 10 minutes. Shape into a smooth ball. Put in a greased bowl, turn dough to grease top. Cover with a cloth and allow to prove in a warm place, free from draughts, until doubled in bulk, about 1 hour.

Makes 2 large cakes

❖

FARINA PUDDING
Sanwin Makin ◆ Burma

1 cup (5 ½ oz, 170 g) medium fine farina (semolina)
3 cups (19 ½ oz, 600 g) thick coconut cream
1 cup (8 oz, 250 g) sugar
4 oz (125 g) ghee or butter
pinch of salt
¼ teaspoon ground cardamom
3 eggs, separated
2–3 tablespoons sesame seeds

Put the farina in a large, heavy saucepan and gradually stir in the coconut cream, keeping the mixture free from lumps. Add sugar, and over medium heat bring to a boil, stirring all the time. When the mixture boils and thickens add a small amount of ghee or butter at a time and continue cooking until mixture becomes very thick and leaves the sides of the pan. Add salt and ground cardamom and mix well.

Beat in the egg yolks, one at a time, then stiffly beat the egg whites and fold in. Turn the mixture into a buttered 9 in (22 cm) cake pan or heatproof dish and smooth the top. Toast the sesame seeds in a dry pan over medium heat, stirring constantly, until they are golden. Sprinkle liberally over farina mixture.

Bake in a moderately slow oven for 45 minutes to 1 hour or until well risen and golden brown. Cool in the dish, then cut into large diamond-shaped pieces. Serve as a sweet snack or as dessert.

❖

FORTUNE COOKIES
China

2 egg whites
3 oz (90 g) superfine (caster) sugar
1 oz (30 g) cornstarch (cornflour)
1 oz (30 g) all-purpose (plain) flour
½ teaspoon vanilla extract (essence)
1 teaspoon peanut oil
*Have the "fortunes" typed on short strips of paper, ready to
  enclose*

Preheat the oven to 350°F (180°C, Gas Mark 4). Prepare baking trays by brushing with oil and dusting with cornstarch; tap off excess cornstarch. Mark two circles about 3 1/2 in (9 cm) across, using a bowl or mug.

Lightly beat the egg whites just until frothy. Add and mix in the sugar. Stir in sifted cornstarch and flour. Add the vanilla extract, and peanut oil. Stir to combine. Place 2 teaspoons of the mixture on each circle and spread evenly with a knife.

Bake in the oven for about 8 minutes or until evenly golden. Immediately remove the cookies, one at a time. Place a "fortune" on the cookie, press the edges together and bend the folded side of the cookie over the edge of a bowl to give it a twist. Immediately fold other cookie. If it has firmed, return it to the oven to soften. If the cookies are too hot for you to handle, use a cloth or oven mitts. Allow to cool on wire racks, and store in an airtight container.

Makes 12–14

❖

From Sri Lanka: top, traditional Christmas cake (page 314); middle, Dutch Christmas cake (page 295), bottom, love cake (page 301).

FRIED SWEET POTATO BALLS
Pilus ♦ Indonesia

1 lb (500 g) sweet potatoes
1 tablespoon palm sugar or dark brown sugar
1–2 tablespoons ground rice
oil for frying

Peel sweet potatoes, dropping them into cold water immediately to prevent discoloring. Cut into even-size pieces and boil until tender but not mushy. Drain well, dry off in the pan and mash until free of lumps. Mix in the sugar and enough ground rice to make the mixture firm enough to shape. Roll into small balls, the size of a large marble. Deep fry in hot oil over medium heat until deep golden brown all over. Serve plain or with sugar syrup as in Sago Pudding (page 307) and fresh grated coconut.

FRIED WHOLEWHEAT BREAD
Bhatura ♦ India (Punjab)

¾ cup (5 oz, 155 g) yogurt
2 teaspoons sugar
½ teaspoon baking (bicarbonate of) soda
1 cup (4 oz, 125 g) all-purpose (plain) flour
2 ½ cups (10 oz, 315 g) atta (fine wholewheat, wholemeal) flour
2 teaspoons salt
1 tablespoon ghee or butter
½ cup (4 fl oz, 125 ml) lukewarm water
oil for deep frying

Mix yogurt, sugar, baking soda, and all-purpose flour in a bowl, cover with cheesecloth (muslin) and leave overnight in a warm place to allow natural fermentation to take place. Sift the atta flour and salt into a bowl, rub in the ghee or butter. Add the fermented mixture and lukewarm water. Mix to a dough, adding as much extra all-purpose flour as necessary. Knead hard for 10 minutes. Cover and leave in a warm place for about 2 or 3 hours. Divide into 12–14 portions.

Roll out each one thinly on a floured board to the size of a saucer. Fry one at a time in hot, deep oil, spooning oil on top. Bhatara will puff and become golden when they are done. Remove with slotted spoon and drain on absorbent paper. Serve warm.
Makes 12–14

GOLDEN BEAN CAKES
Khanom Bualoi ♦ Thailand

8 oz (250 g) mung dhal (hulled and split mung beans)
1 cup (8 oz, 250 g) white sugar
½ cup (4 fl oz, 125 ml) water
superfine (caster) sugar

Put mung dhal into a saucepan with sufficient water to come just to the level of the beans and bring to a boil. Cook until beans are very soft (about 1 hour). Drain thoroughly and while beans are still hot, mash to a smooth paste.

Put sugar and water in a heavy-based saucepan and stir over medium heat until sugar dissolves. Add bean paste and cook, stirring occasionally at the start and more frequently as mixture thickens. When the bean mixture is thick and starts to come away from side of pan, it is ready. Allow to cool until it can be handled, and make small balls of the paste. Roll in superfine sugar and leave to dry. Put in small paper cases.
Makes 36

GUAVA JELLY
The Philippines

4 lb (2 kg) slightly under-ripe guavas
4 green cooking apples
sugar
lemon juice

Wash fruit and cut into quarters. Put into a large saucepan with just enough cold water to cover. Cook, uncovered, until fruit is soft and loses its color, at least 1 hour. Strain through 2 or 3 layers of cheesecloth (muslin). Do not squeeze or jelly will not be sparkling and clear. Wet the cloth and wring it out before pouring fruit into it, or a lot of juice will be absorbed by the cloth.

Measure the strained juice and cook no more than 4 or 5 cups (32–40 fl oz, 1–1.25 L) at a time. Allow 3/4 cup (6 oz, 185 g) sugar to each cup of juice. Bring juice to a boil, add warmed sugar and about 2 tablespoons strained lemon juice and stir until sugar dissolves. Now cook jello without stirring, skimming off any froth that rises to the top, until jello will set. To test, take a spoonful of the liquid, cool slightly and pour back into pan from the side of the spoon. When it no longer runs off in a steady stream but thickens and 'sheets' as it falls, it is ready. To store, pour jelly into sterile jars and cover with a thin layer of melted paraffin.

Classic mandarin pancakes (page 301), and fortune cookies you can make for yourself (recipe page 296).

ICED COCONUT CREAM WITH SAGO
Moh–Let–Saung ◆ Burma

1 cup sago
4 cups (32 fl oz, 1 L) water
¾ cup chopped palm (or brown) sugar
ice cubes
4 cups (32 fl oz, 1 L) thin coconut cream

Wash and soak sago for approximately 1 hour, drain and put in a large saucepan with 3 cups (24 fl oz, 750 ml) of the water. Bring to a boil and simmer over a moderate heat until sago grains are clear. Cool and chill.

Put palm sugar in a small saucepan with remaining water and heat gently until the cakes of sugar dissolve. Cool and strain the syrup.

For each serving, put approximately 4 tablespoons of chilled sago into a tall glass, add 3 tablespoons syrup (or more according to taste) and mix well. Add 2–3 ice cubes and fill up with coconut cream. Stir and serve immediately.

ICED JELLO DRINK
Kyauk Kyaw ◆ Burma

syrup made from palm sugar (or dark brown sugar) or slab
　　sugar sold in Chinese stores
rose concentrate
iced water
crushed ice
1 can grass jello (jelly)

Make a syrup from the sugar and water, and when cool flavor
lightly with rose concentrate. Chop grass jello into thin slivers.
Put a tablespoon of jello into each glass. Add a couple of
spoons of the syrup, then fill up with iced water and crushed
ice. Stir well and serve. Another version of this uses thin
coconut cream instead of water, and is also delicious and
cooling on a hot day.

　Note: Chopped agar-agar jello can be used in place of
canned grass jello, which is a black jello made from seaweed
and available at Chinese grocery stores.

INDIAN FARINA PUDDING
Soojee Halwa ◆ India

¾ cup sugar
1¼ cups water
¼ cup milk
good pinch powdered Spanish Saffron
4 oz (125 g) ghee
¾ cup fine farina (semolina)
2 tablespoons sultanas
2 tablespoons slivered almonds
1 teaspoon ground cardamom
extra slivered almonds to decorate

Put sugar, water, milk and saffron into a saucepan and bring to
a boil, stirring to dissolve sugar. Set aside. In a large saucepan
melt the ghee, add farina and fry over low heat, stirring
constantly, until mixture is golden. Add the syrup, sultanas,
almonds, and cardamom and cook over medium heat, stirring
with a wooden spoon, until mixture thickens and leaves sides
of pan. Pour into buttered dish and when it is cold cut into
diamond shapes and decorate with almonds.

　This halwa can be served warm or cold, with or without
cream, as a dessert. A popular way of serving it in India is with
puris (page 305) and , surprising though it may seem to many
Westerners, at the beginning of the meal instead of at the end.

KASHMIRI TEA
Qahwah ◆ India (Kashmir)

4 cups (32 fl oz, 1 L) boiling water
1 teaspoon Kashmiri green tea
4 cardamom pods, bruised
1 small piece cinnamon stick
pinch of saffron strands
2 tablespoons finely flaked almonds
sugar or honey to taste

Prepare a samovar with coals in its central tube, or warm a
teapot by letting it stand for a minute or two with boiling water
in it. Rinse out, put in the tea and spices and pour the boiling
water over. Allow to steep for 5 minutes.

　In each little bowl put a teaspoonful of almonds. Pour the
tea over the almonds, sweeten to taste and drink hot.

LOVE CAKE (1)
Sri Lanka

7 eggs, separated
1 lb (500 g) superfine (caster) sugar
8 oz (250 g) farina (semolina)
12 oz (375 g) raw cashews, finely chopped
2 tablespoons rose water
2 tablespoons honey
½ teaspoon finely grated lemon rind
½ teaspoon ground mace or nutmeg
½ teaspoon ground cardamom
½ teaspoon almond extract (essence), optional

A very popular cake in Sri Lanka, though no one knows why it
is called by this name.

　Grease and line an 8 in (20 cm) square tin with 2 thicknesses of
waxed (greaseproof) paper. Brush inner paper with melted butter.

　Beat the egg yolks and sugar until light and creamy. Stir in the
farina, cashews, rose water, honey, lemon rind, spices, and almond
extract. Beat egg whites until they hold firm peaks and fold into
the mixture, turn into prepared tin and bake in moderately slow
oven (300ºF, 150ºC, Gas Mark 2) until cake is evenly golden brown
on top and feels firm to the touch, about 1 hour. If cake starts to
brown too quickly, cover top with paper or foil.

　When cooked the middle of the cake should still be slightly
moist so the skewer test is not recommended.

　Remove from oven and leave in the tin to get quite cold
before cutting. Do not attempt to turn out this cake. Cut into
small squares and lift each one separately onto serving plate.

LOVE CAKE (2)
Sri Lanka

4 oz (125 g) butter
8 oz (250 g) farina (semolina)
10 egg yolks
1 lb (500 g) superfine (caster) sugar
6 oz (185 g) raw cashew nuts, finely chopped
2 tablespoons each rose water and honey
¼ teaspoon each grated nutmeg, lemon rind, and cinnamon

Soften butter and mix with farina. Beat egg yolks and sugar until thick and creamy. Add farina and butter mixture and beat until well mixed. Add chopped nuts, rose water, honey, nutmeg, lemon rind, and cinnamon and mix well together. Pour mixture into a flat cake tin lined with greased paper and bake in a moderately slow oven (300°F, 150°C, Gas Mark 2) until top is nicely browned and cake cooked through.

⊰≫∞≪⊱

LYCHEES AND ORANGES
China

4 oranges
18 oz (560 g) can lychees
1 cup (8 oz, 250 g) white sugar
2 cups (16 fl oz, 500 ml) water

Peel oranges, removing all the white pith. With a sharp knife cut into segments, discarding all the dividing membrane. Put orange segments into a serving bowl and combine with canned lychees and their syrup. Chill well before serving. If using fresh lychees you will need 1 lb (500 g) of lychees. Peel lychees and put into a bowl.

Make a light sugar syrup by combining sugar and water. Dissolve over low heat, boil for 5 minutes, then cool completely before pouring onto the fruit and chilling in the refrigerator.
Serves 4–6

⊰≫∞≪⊱

MANDARIN PANCAKES
China

8 oz (250 g) all-purpose (plain) flour
¾ cup (6 fl oz, 180 ml) boiling water
4 teaspoons sesame oil

Measure the unsifted flour into a bowl. Bring water to a boil and pour at once onto the flour, stirring with chopsticks or the handle of a wooden spoon for a few minutes. As soon as it is cool enough to handle, knead for 10 minutes until the mixture is a soft, smooth dough. Put the dough on a board and cover with a bowl, then let it stand for at least 30 minutes.

Roll the dough into a cylindrical shape and cut it into ten slices of equal size. Keep covered with plastic wrap (film) to prevent drying out.

Take one dough slice at a time and cut into two equal pieces. Form each to a smooth ball, then roll out on a lightly floured board to a circle about 3 in (8 cm) in diameter. Brush one circle lightly with sesame oil, taking it right to the edge of the circle. Put the second circle on top of the first one and roll again, both circles together this time, until the pancakes are 6–7 in (15–18 cm) across. They must be very thin. Cover each pancake with plastic as it is made.

When they are all rolled out, heat a heavy frying pan or griddle and cook the pancakes one at a time on the ungreased surface. Cook over low heat until pancake develops small bubbles. Turn it frequently so that it cooks on both sides. A few golden spots will appear.

Remove from pan and gently pull the two circles apart. The sesame oil they were brushed with makes this quite easy. Pile the cooked pancakes on a plate, and cover tightly or they will dry out. Pancakes should be soft and pliable, not brittle.

To reheat, arrange the pancakes in a steamer lined with a clean tea cloth, cover and put over simmering water for 1 to 2 minutes. To serve, fold each pancake into quarters.

Note: These pancakes are traditionally served with Peking Duck, but are also used to enclose a variety of fillings such as shredded pork or chicken. The filling is seasoned with a dab of a rich sauce, then rolled up and eaten.
Serves 4–5

⊰≫∞≪⊱

MANGO ICE CREAM
The Philippines

2 cups (16 fl oz, 500 ml) milk
2 eggs
½ cup (3 ½ oz, 100 g) superfine (caster) sugar
1½–2 cups mango pulp, fresh or canned
1 teaspoon unflavored gelatin
2 tablespoons water
1 cup (8 fl oz, 250 ml) light (single) cream

Turn freezer to its coldest setting. Put milk in a saucepan and bring slowly to a boil. Meanwhile separate eggs and beat the yolks with half the sugar in a bowl until thick and light. Pour a little of the hot milk onto the yolks, stirring constantly, then return yolk mixture to saucepan and cook over hot water or on very low heat. Stir all the time and do not allow to reach simmering point or the custard will curdle. As soon as it is thick enough to lightly coat back of spoon, remove from heat and keep stirring until it cools somewhat. Pour into freezer tray and freeze until mushy.

Sprinkle gelatin over cold water in a cup and stand the cup in a small saucepan of water. Bring water to a boil so gelatin dissolves. Stir this into the mango pulp. Whip the cream until it holds soft peaks. Do not overbeat or ice cream will have a buttery texture. Beat egg whites until soft peaks form, add remaining sugar and beat until soft and glossy.

Scrape half-frozen custard into a bowl and beat with rotary beater until it is smooth, but do not let it melt. Chilling bowl and beater helps in hot weather. Fold in the mango pulp, egg whites, and whipped cream and return to freezer trays. Freeze until firm.
Serves 6

⟨≷⟩∞⟨≷⟩

MANY-LAYERED SPICE CAKE
Spekkoek Kueh Lapis ◆ Indonesia

10 egg yolks
1½ cups (10 ½ oz, 333 g) superfine (caster) sugar
8 oz (250 g) butter
2 teaspoons vanilla extract (essence)
8 egg whites
1½ cups (6 oz, 185 g) all-purpose (plain) flour, sifted
1 teaspoon ground cinnamon
1 teaspoon ground nutmeg
1 teaspoon ground cardamom
½ teaspoon ground cloves
extra melted butter, optional

In electric mixer whisk the egg yolks with 1/2 cup (3 1/2 oz, 100 g) sugar until thick and light. Cream butter with 3/4 cup (5 1/2 oz, 170 g) sugar and the vanilla extract until light and smooth. In a clean, dry bowl whisk the egg whites until stiff, add the remaining 1/4 cup (2 oz, 60 g) sugar and whisk again until glossy.

Thoroughly mix egg yolk and butter mixtures. Fold in the flour, then the egg whites. Divide mixture into two almost equal portions and mix the ground spices into the slightly larger portion.

Preheat oven to moderately slow (325°F 160°C, Gas Mark 3). Generously butter an 8 in (20 cm) springform cake tin with softened butter and line the base with buttered waxed (greaseproof) paper. Dust with flour and tip out excess.

Put about 1/3 cup (3 fl oz, 90 ml) of spice batter into tin (it makes it easier to use a ladle of this capacity).

Spread the batter thinly with a spatula, then tap the tin very firmly on the bench top to help the batter spread thinly and evenly. Bake in the middle of the oven until firm, about 10 minutes. Meanwhile, preheat broiler (grill) and place the tin under for 30 to 40 seconds, about 6 in (15 cm) from heat, until top is evenly browned. Watch carefully so it does not burn, but it should be a really dark coffee color.

Now spread the same amount of plain batter over the spicy layer. Return to oven and cook 10 minutes, then broil as before. Continue until all the batter has been used, putting spice and plain layers alternately and spreading the batter as thin as possible. The layers should be hardly thicker than a wafer biscuit.

If you like a really buttery cake, lightly brush the extra melted butter over each layer after it has been broiled and before the next layer of batter is spread over.

When the last layer has been baked, insert a skewer in the middle. It should emerge slightly buttery, but not with uncooked batter clinging to it. Bake for a few minutes longer if necessary. Cool on a wire rack, remove the side of the springform and cut the cake in thin, small slices to serve.

Note: This recipe is for a light-textured cake but if you prefer a sweeter, moist cake with a puddingy texture use only 1/2 cup (2 oz, 60 g) flour and four egg whites instead of eight.
Makes 1 x 8 in (20 cm) round or square cake

⟨≷⟩∞⟨≷⟩

Fresh fruit is the perfect finish to a Chinese meal. Here is the simple but opulent oriental fruit basket (page 304).

ORIENTAL FRUIT BASKET
Doong Fong Sik Gow Lahm ◆ China

Take a medium-size watermelon and cut off the top third. With a melon-baller scoop out melon flesh, discarding seeds. Combine melon balls with any of the following: canned lychees, longans, loquats, mandarin segments. Mix with some of the syrup from the cans. Cover and chill at least 3 hours. If desired, a few canned or bottled chow chow preserves can be added. Before serving, arrange fruits in the watermelon shell and spoon some of the syrup over.

Note: Chow chow preserves can be bought at chinese stores.

❖❖❖

PANCAKES WITH COCONUT FILLING
Alebele ◆ India (Goa)

2 eggs
½ cup (4 fl oz, 125 ml) milk
½ cup (4 fl oz, 125 ml) water
pinch salt
1 tablespoon melted butter
1 cup (4 oz, 125 g) all-purpose (plain) flour, sifted
butter or ghee for frying
raw cashews, roughly chopped, optional

Filling:
1 coconut, freshly grated
4 oz (125 g) jaggery or brown sugar

In a large bowl, beat the eggs lightly until combined but not frothy. Add milk, water, salt, and melted butter and mix, then add all the flour and beat with a wooden spoon or rotary beater until smooth. Leave batter for 1 hour at least before cooking.

Grease a heavy pancake pan with butter or ghee, using only just enough to give a thin film. Pour in a small ladle of the batter and swirl the pan to coat the base thinly. Cook over medium heat until golden brown on the underside. Turn pancake over and cook other side for a few seconds. Turn onto a plate. Cook all the batter in this way, then fill each pancake with 2 tablespoons of the coconut filling and roll up. If liked, sprinkle with roughly chopped raw cashews.

Filling: Combine coconut with the jaggery which has been finely scraped with a knife or on a grater, or broken into pieces and pounded with mortar and pestle.

Note: Some versions of the filling include a little lemon juice, a few sultanas, a pinch of crushed anise, or a little grated fresh ginger, but I prefer the delicate coconut flavor on its own.
Serves 4

❖❖❖

PARATHA
(FLAKY WHOLEWHEAT BREAD)
India

1½ cups (6 oz, 185 g) fine wholewheat (wholemeal) flour
1½ cups (6 oz, 185 g) all purpose (plain white) flour or
*   roti flour*
1½ teaspoons salt
6–8 tablespoons ghee
1 cup (8 fl oz, 250 ml) water
extra ghee for cooking

Sieve wholewheat flour, all purpose flour and salt into a mixing bowl and rub in 1 tablespoon of the ghee. Add water, mix and knead dough as for chapatis. Cover dough with clear plastic and set aside for 1 hour.

Divide dough into 12–14 equal portions and roll each into a smooth ball. Melt ghee over a low heat and cool slightly. Roll each ball of dough on a lightly floured board into a very thin circular shape. Pour about 2 teaspoons of the melted ghee into the middle of each and spread lightly with the hand.

With a knife, make a cut from the middle of each circle to the outer edge. Starting at the cut edge, roll the dough closely into a cone shape. Pick it up, press the apex of the cone and the base towards each other and flatten slightly. You will now have a small, roughly circular lump of dough again. Lightly flour the board again and roll out the dough very gently, taking care not to press too hard so that the air does not escape at the edges. The parathas should be as round as possible, but not as thinly rolled as the first time — about the size of a breakfast plate.

Cook on a hot griddle liberally greased with extra ghee, turning parathas and spreading with more ghee, until they are golden brown. Serve hot with curries or grilled kebabs, sambals, and fresh mint chutney (page 21).

Note: The wholewheat and all purpose or roti flour can be replaced by 3 cups (12 oz, 375 g) all purpose flour.
Makes: 12–14

❖❖❖

A Goanese dessert, pancakes with coconut filling (recipe opposite). To make the cocktail pictured, add a touch of lime juice to the juice in a fresh coconut. In Goa I have tried it with feni – a locally produced liquor that has a kick like a mule!

POTATO HALVA
Alla Aluwa ◆ Sri Lanka

1½ cups (12 oz, 375 g) sugar
1½ cups (12 fl oz, 375 ml) milk
14 oz (440 g) can sweetened condensed milk
4 oz (125 g) ghee or butter
1 cup prepared instant mashed potato
1 cup (4 oz, 125 g) finely chopped cashew nuts, optional
2 tablespoons rose water
1 teaspoon ground cardamom

Put sugar, milk, condensed milk, and ghee into a large, heavy saucepan. Cook, stirring continuously, until mixture reaches soft ball stage or 240°F (116°C) on a candy thermometer. Remove from heat, add potato, and nuts if used. Return to heat and cook until mixture reaches soft ball stage again. Remove from heat, add rose water and cardamom and mix well.

Pour into a greased shallow dish. Press lightly with a piece of greased aluminum foil to smooth and flatten the surface. Allow to set, then cut into diamond shapes.

PURI
(DEEP-FRIED WHOLEWHEAT BREAD)
India

Proceed as for chapatis (page 291). When all the dough is rolled out heat approximately 1 in (2.5 cm) of oil in a deep frying pan. When a faint haze rises from the oil, fry puris one at a time, over a moderate heat. Spoon hot oil continually over the cooking puri until it puffs and swells. Turn over and fry other side in the same way. When both sides are pale golden brown, drain on absorbent paper. Serve immediately with curries.

Note: Puri is pronounced "poo-ree".

RICE FRITTERS
Bombones De Arroz ◆ The Philippines

2 cups (12 oz, 375 g) cooked rice
2 large eggs, beaten until frothy
½ cup (4 oz, 125 g) sugar
½ teaspoon vanilla
½ teaspoon grated nutmeg
6 tablespoons all-purpose (plain) flour
1½ teaspoons double-acting baking powder (3 teaspoons baking powder)
oil for deep frying
confectioner's (icing) sugar for sprinkling

In a large bowl mix rice, eggs, sugar, vanilla, and nutmeg. Mix flour and baking powder together and stir into rice mixture until thoroughly combined. Heat oil in a deep frying pan and when moderately hot drop spoons of mixture into the oil and fry on medium heat until golden brown and nicely puffed, turning to brown all over. Lift out with slotted spoon and drain on absorbent paper. Sprinkle with sugar and serve warm.
Makes about 24

ROSE-FLAVORED COLD DRINK
Sharbat Gulab ◆ North India

3 cups (24 oz, 750 g) white sugar
2 cups (16 fl oz, 500 ml) water
20 drops rose extract (essence)
1 teaspoon liquid red food coloring
1 teaspoon tulsi seeds
iced water and crushed ice for serving

Put sugar and water in a saucepan and cook over gentle heat until sugar dissolves. Cool. Add rose extract and red coloring. Rose syrup should be a strong color, for it will be mixed with a large proportion of water.

Soak the tulsi seeds in a cup (8 fl oz, 250 ml) cold water. After a few minutes they will develop a jello (jelly)-like coating. (The seeds can be kept soaking in the refrigerator for a week. They are supposed to have a very cooling effect, and are used in almost every type of sherbet drink.)

At serving time put 2 tablespoons of syrup in each glass and fill up with iced water and crushed ice. Syrup can be increased or decreased according to taste. Add a spoonful of soaked tulsi seeds, stir in and serve.

ROSE-FLAVORED MILK SHERBET
Falooda ◆ India

agar-agar jello (jelly), diced
rose syrup as in Sharbat Gulab (this page)
ice cold milk as required, about 1 cup (8 fl oz, 250 ml) for each serving
crushed ice
2 teaspoons soaked tulsi seeds, optional

Jello:
3 cups (24 fl oz, 750 ml) water
4 teaspoons agar-agar powder or 1 cup soaked agar-agar strands
6 tablespoons sugar
12 drops rose extract (essence)
1 teaspoon liquid red food coloring
1 teaspoon liquid green food coloring

Put about 2 tablespoons each of diced jello and rose syrup into each tall glass, fill up with ice-cold milk and crushed ice. If liked, some soaked tulsi seeds can be floated on top.

Jello: Measure water into a saucepan and sprinkle agar-agar powder over. If agar-agar strands are used, soak at least 2 hours in cold water, then drain and measure 1 cup loosely packed. Bring to a boil and simmer gently, stirring, until agar-agar dissolves. Powder takes about 10 minutes and the strands take longer, about 25 to 30 minutes. Add sugar and dissolve, remove from heat, cool slightly and add rose extract. Divide mixture between two large shallow dishes and tint one red and the other green. Leave to set. When quite cold and firm, cut with a sharp knife first into fine strips, then across into small dice.

ROSE-FLAVORED SWEETMEATS IN SYRUP
Gulab Jamun ◆ India (Bengal)

8 tablespoons full-cream milk powder
3 tablespoons self-raising flour
¼ teaspoon baking (bicarbonate of) soda
¼ teaspoon ground cardamom
1 tablespoon soft butter or ghee
approximately 3 tablespoons water
ghee or oil for deep frying

ROTI
Sri Lanka

2 cups (12 oz, 375 g) roti flour, rice flour or (8 oz, 250 g)
self-raising flour
½ cup (1½ oz, 45 g) unsweetened desiccated coconut
1 teaspoon salt
scant 1 cup (8 fl oz, 250 ml) water
ghee or oil for cooking

Mix flour, coconut, and salt in a mixing bowl. Add enough water to form a soft dough. Knead dough until it forms a ball and does not stick to sides of the bowl. Rest dough for about 30 minutes.

Shape dough into balls, approximately the size of a golf ball. Pat each one out to a circle the size of a saucer. Cook on a hot griddle or in a heavy frying pan very lightly greased with ghee or oil. Serve hot.

Serves 6–8

Indian breads: from the top, cooked chapatis (page 291), puris (page 305), and parathas (page 304) in the making.

SAGO PUDDING
Gula Melaka ◆ **Malaysia**

8–10 cups (64–80 fl oz, 2–2.5 L) water
1 small stick cinnamon, optional
2 cups sago
2 tablespoons thin coconut cream
pinch of salt

For serving:
8 oz (250 g) gula melaka (palm sugar) or substitute
½ cup (4 fl oz, 125 ml) water
2 strips pandan leaves, fresh or dried
1¼ cups (10 fl oz, 300 ml) thin coconut cream
pinch salt

Syrup:
2 cups (16 oz, 500 g) white sugar
4 cups (32 fl oz, 1 L) water
5 cardamom pods, bruised
2 tablespoons rose water or few drops rose extract (essence)

Sift milk powder, flour, baking soda, and ground cardamom into a large bowl. Rub in butter or ghee, then add enough water to give a firm but pliable dough which can be shaped into balls the size of large marbles, or into small sausage shapes.

Heat ghee or oil flavored with a little ghee and fry the shapes over low heat until they slowly turn golden brown. Lift out on slotted spoon and drain on absorbent paper.

Syrup: Before frying the gulab jamuns, make the syrup by combining sugar, water, cardamom pods and heating until sugar is dissolved. Put the fried gulab jamun into the warm syrup and when they have cooled a little, add rose water. Leave for at least 4 hours, or overnight. The gulab jamun will swell and become soft and spongy. Serve at room temperature or chilled. They look like small brown sausages but taste superb.

Makes about 18 (6 serves)

In a large saucepan bring the water to a fast boil, with the cinnamon stick if used. Slowly dribble the sago into the water and let it boil for 5 to 7 minutes. Turn off heat, cover the pan with a well-fitting lid and leave for 10 minutes. The sago will finish cooking in the stored heat and the grains will be clear. Run cold water into the pan, stir, then drain in a sieve, shaking the sieve so the water runs off. Discard the cinnamon.

Turn the sago into a bowl, stir in the 2 tablespoons of coconut cream and pinch of salt. This quantity of cream is just enough to give it a pearly white appearance instead of that unattractive grey look. Divide between individual dessert dishes, or pour into one large ring tin. Chill until set.

Take out of tin and serve chilled, with gula melaka syrup and coconut cream. Stir in a good pinch of salt, into the coconut cream as this accentuates the flavor. A little syrup may be poured around the shape when it is turned out on the serving dish, but it is more usual to serve the syrup and coconut cream in small jugs or bowls with spoons so each person may help themselves.

Gula melaka syrup: Chop the gula melaka into small pieces or shave with a sharp knife. Put into a small saucepan with the water and pandan leaves and heat gently until the sugar is melted. Strain through a fine sieve to remove any small impurities. Cool and chill.

Either extract coconut cream from grated fresh coconut or use a good brand of canned coconut cream. Canned coconut cream may need diluting with a little water if very thick. Coconut cream should be freshly made and served at room temperature, as chilling will solidify the fat content.

Note: Palm sugar is sometimes sold as "coconut preserves" in a solid cylinder of concentrated sweetness derived from the sap of coconut or other varieties of palm. If you find it difficult to buy, substitute an equivalent amount of black or brown sugar. For each cup of sugar add 1/2 cup (2 1/2 oz, 75 g) maple syrup.
Serves 6–8

⋄⟨⟩⋄

SEAWEED JELLO
Kyauk Kyaw ◆ Burma

¼ oz (7 g) agar-agar strands or 4 teaspoons agar-agar powder
4 cups (32 fl oz, 1 L) thin coconut cream
½ cup (4 oz, 125 g) sugar
few drops rose water

This jello (jelly) is made from transparent strands of refined seaweed agar-agar that look like crinkled strips of cellophane. This is sold in Chinese stores as refined agar-agar. Agar-agar powder is sold in packets at Chinese stores and pharmacies. The name of the recipe is pronounced 'chow chaw'.

Soak the strands of agar-agar in cold water overnight or at least 1 hour. Drain and measure. There should be 1 1/2 cups, loosely packed. Put the strands and coconut cream into a saucepan and stir constantly while bringing to a boil. Add sugar and keep stirring and simmering for 15 to 20 minutes, or until all the strands are completely dissolved. If using agar-agar powder, sprinkle on top of the milk and bring to a boil, then simmer and stir for 10 minutes. Add rose water to taste, pour into a dish rinsed out with cold water, and allow to set. Cut into squares. This is a very firm jello (jelly) and can be picked up with the fingers.
Makes about 18 pieces

SESAME BALLS
China

4 oz (125 g) stoned dates
3 tablespoons sesame paste
12 oz (375 g) sweet potatoes
5 oz (155 g) flour
5 tablespoons brown sugar
1 egg white
5 oz (155 g) sesame seeds
peanut oil for deep frying

Put dates into a small saucepan with water to cover. Bring to a boil and boil for 1 minute. Drain, then mash to a paste. Blend in the sesame paste.

Peel sweet potatoes and cut into chunks. Put into a saucepan with water to cover, bring to a boil and simmer for 20 to 30 minutes until potato is tender. Drain well, then mash and force through a sieve.

Sift 4 oz (125 g) of the flour into a bowl, add sweet potato and mix with a fork. The mixture will be lumpy at this stage.

Heat the sugar with 1 tablespoon of water until boiling, stirring to dissolve the sugar. Add this hot syrup to the flour and potato mixture. Form it into a dough, adding a little more flour if necessary. Knead lightly on a floured surface for 1 minute.

Divide the dough evenly into 20 portions and roll each portion into a ball. Flatten the ball with the palm of your hand. Place a teaspoon of the date-sesame mixture in the middle. Shape into a ball, completely enclosing the paste. Repeat with the remaining dough and filling.

Place the balls in an oiled steaming basket and steam over gently boiling water for 10 minutes.

Dip the balls in lightly beaten egg white and then roll them in sesame seeds.

Heat a wok, add oil for deep frying. When hot, fry the sesame balls until golden. Drain and serve warm or cold.
Makes 20

⋄⟨⟩⋄

This attractive Burmese dessert is a seaweed jello called kyauk kyaw (recipe opposite).

SESAME SEED AND PALM SUGAR BALLS
Thala Guli ◆ Sri Lanka

2 cups sesame seeds
1 lb (500 g) palm sugar or substitute
generous pinch of salt

In a mortar and pestle pound the sesame, a little at a time, until the seeds are crushed and oily. As each batch is done, turn it into a bowl. Grate the palm sugar and add to the sesame with the salt. Mix well with hands. The heat of the hands and vigorous kneading slightly melts the palm sugar, and after a while the mixture will hold togerher. Make balls the size of a large marble. These are wrapped in rectangular pieces of wax or greaseproof paper fringed at the ends. The paper is twisted on either side of the thala guli so each one looks like a miniature Christmas cracker. Serve at the end of a curry meal, or as a between-meal treat.

⋘∞⋙

SILVER FUNGUS IN SWEET SOUP
China

3 tablespoons silver fungus
2 cups water
¾ cup rock sugar or white sugar
1 can longans or lychees
12 ice cubes

Wash silver fungus and soak in hot water until it swells and softens, about 10 minutes. Drain and put into a saucepan with sugar. Bring to a boil, stirring until sugar dissolves. Cover and simmer 10 minutes. Cool and chill. Before serving, combine with fruits and syrup in a pretty serving bowl and add the ice cubes. Serve in bowls with porcelain spoons. Alternatively, serve warm or at room temperature and omit the ice cubes.

Note: Silver fungus is a Chinese delicacy prized for its crunchy texture and pretty appearance. It is usually available in dried form from Chinese specialty stores.
Serves 6

⋘∞⋙

SMALL BRANDIED CAKES
Capuchinos ◆ The Philippines

¼ cup (2 fl oz, 60 ml) melted butter
½ cup (2 oz, 60 g) all-purpose (plain) flour
¼ teaspoon double-acting baking powder (½ teaspoon
  baking powder)
pinch salt
2 large eggs
½ cup (4 oz, 125 g) sugar
1 tablespoon brandy

Syrup:
½ cup (4 oz, 125 g) sugar
½ cup (4 fl oz, 125 ml) water
1 tablespoon brandy

Make syrup and set aside to cool. Preheat oven to hot (400°F, 200°C, Gas Mark 6). Grease muffin tins. Melt butter and allow it to cool. Sift flour, baking powder, and salt together.

Beat eggs with rotary beater until frothy, add sugar gradually and continue beating until thick and light. Mix in melted butter and brandy, then fold in the dry ingredients.

Half fill muffin tins with batter and bake in a hot oven for 10 to 12 minutes or until cakesä are golden brown. Remove from tins, dip briefly into syrup for no more than a second and put on a cake cooler to dry.

Syrup: Put sugar and water into a small saucepan and dissolve sugar over low heat. Boil hard for 2 minutes, then allow to cool and stir in brandy.
Makes 12

⋘∞⋙

STEAMED COCONUT CREAM PUDDING
Khanom Talai ◆ Thailand

1¼ cups (8 oz, 250 g) thick coconut cream
2½ tablespoons rice flour
pinch salt
4 tablespoons palm sugar or dark brown sugar

Stand coconut cream for 30 minutes so that the richest part rises to the surface. Spoon off 1/2 cup (3 1/2 oz, 100 g) of this rich cream, and add it gradually to 1 tablespoon of the rice flour, mixing until smooth.

In remaining coconut cream dissolve the palm sugar and add salt. In another bowl combine the remaining 1 1/2 tablespoons rice flour with the milk, adding liquid gradually and stirring until smooth.

This brilliantly unusual sweet dish from Thailand is created by steaming custard in a pumpkin shell (page 312).

Strain this through a fine sieve. Pour the sweetened mixture into small cups — sake or Chinese wine cups are an ideal size — two thirds filling them. Set the cups carefully in a steamer and steam for 15 minutes or until set. With a spoon pour the white mixture over to almost fill the cups, cover and steam for a further 20 to 25 minutes. Serve at room temperature.
Makes 10 tiny cupfuls

❖❖❖

STEAMED CUSTARD IN PUMPKIN SHELL
Sankhaya ◆ Thailand

3 eggs
½ cup (3 oz, 90 g) palm sugar or dark brown sugar
¾ cup (5 oz, 155 g) thick coconut cream
few drops rose water
1 medium-size pumpkin or squash

Beat eggs slightly, add sugar. Mix with coconut cream and stir until sugar dissolves, then add the rose water.

Wash the pumpkin well, and if it is a large round one cut a hole in the top and remove all seeds and spongy tissue, scraping well with a spoon to leave the pumpkin smooth. If it is a long straight pumpkin or squash, cut off the top and then cut a round hole into the middle to remove seeds and spongy tissue, leaving a shell of pumpkin about 1 in (2.5 cm) thick.

Strain the custard and pour into the pumpkin to come just to the top. Put the pumpkin in a dish that just fits it and put the dish and pumpkin in a steamer. Steam for 1 hour or until a knife inserted in the middle of the custard comes out clean. Cool, chill and serve cut into slices so that there is a portion of custard surrounded by pumpkin. Run a knife around the edge of each slice and remove skin. Serve with sweetened coconut cream to pour over if desired.

Note: This custard may also be steamed in young coconuts, husks removed and the shell cut straight across the top. This quantity fills a medium butternut pumpkin. For a large pumpkin, double the quantities.
Serves 4–6

❖❖❖

SWEET BREAD ROLLS
Ensaimada ◆ The Philippines

1 oz (30 g) compressed yeast
¼ cup (2 fl oz, 60 ml) lukewarm water
3 teaspoons sugar
4 cups (16 oz, 500 g) all-purpose (plain) flour
6 oz (185 g) butter or margarine
½ cup (3 ½ oz, 100 g) superfine (caster) sugar
6 egg yolks
½ cup (4 fl oz, 125 ml) milk
extra ½ cup (4 oz, 125 ml) melted butter
4 oz (125 g) finely grated sharp (mature) cheese, preferably Dutch Edam
2–3 tablespoons extra superfine (caster) sugar

In a small bowl crumble yeast into warm water. Stir in 3 teaspoons sugar until dissolved. Sprinkle with a spoonful of flour and set aside in a warm place.

Beat butter or margarine until soft, add superfine sugar and continue beating until light. Add egg yolks one at a time, beating well after each. Stir in flour and milk alternately, through the yeast mixture. Beat well until smooth. (Depending on absorbency of flour, which varies, it may be necessary to add a tablespoon or two more of flour. The dough should be soft but not so soft that it sticks to the sides of the bowl.) Form dough into a ball and leave on a floured board for 10 minutes. Wash bowl in hot water, dry well, grease lightly and put dough back in the bowl. Cover with a cloth and leave in a warm place until double volume, about 1 hour.

Divide dough into 2 equal portions and roll each on a lightly floured board to a rectangle 18 x 15 in (45 cm x 38 cm). Brush with some of the melted butter and sprinkle with the grated cheese. Cut rectangle into 3 equal strips lengthwise and roll up each strip like a jelly (Swiss) roll, starting at the long end. Cut each long roll into 3 pieces, so you have 9 pieces in all.

Roll each piece with hands on the board until as thin as a pencil, then shape into snail-like coils or twists. Put on a greased baking sheet, leaving spaces in between, cover with a dry cloth and leave in a warm place 30 to 40 minutes or until dough once more almost doubles in bulk.

Preheat oven to moderate, and bake 10 to 15 minutes or until golden brown. Remove from oven and while hot brush with melted butter and sprinkle with superfine sugar. Serve ensaimadas warm or at room temperature.
Makes 18

❖❖❖

SWEET COCONUT BUNS
China

4 oz (125 g) slab sugar
¼ cup (2 fl oz, 60 ml) water
1 cup (3 oz, 90 g) unsweetened desiccated coconut
dough for steamed buns (see Black Bean Steamed Buns, page 291)
1 tablespoon sesame oil for brushing

Put slab sugar and water into a small saucepan and heat gently until sugar is dissolved in the water, then stir in coconut and cool. Shape and steam buns as described for Black Bean Steamed Buns (page 291), using a teaspoonful of the coconut mixture for filling.

Note: Slab sugar is a pale brown sugar in tablet form available from Chinese stores.

Makes 8

TEETHING CAKE
Moh Loung Ye Baw ◆ Burma

1 cup (4 oz, 125 g) all-purpose (plain) white flour
1 cup (6 oz, 185 g) rice flour
pinch salt
½ teaspoon baking (bicarbonate of) soda
1 tablespoon light sesame or corn oil
⅔ cup (5 fl oz, 170 ml) water
1 cup fresh grated coconut
½ cup grated palm sugar or brown sugar
4 cups (32 fl oz, 1 L) thin coconut cream for simmering
1 tablespoon or more sugar

This is the famous cake that is prepared and sent around to neighbours and friends, or fed to the poor, in celebration of a baby's first tooth. They are little dumplings cooked in coconut cream.

Sift the flours, salt, and baking soda into a bowl. Mix thoroughly, and rub in the oil. Add enough water to make a firm paste, knead well to a smooth dough. Mix together the grated coconut and palm sugar. Take little lumps of dough, roll into balls, then flatten to a circle and put a very little of the coconut and palm sugar mixture on each. Close up and roll into a ball again.

Boil the coconut cream and sugar in a large saucepan and when boiling fast, drop in the balls. They will sink at first but rise slowly to the top as they cook. Stir gently in case some stick to the bottom. When cooked the balls will float on the surface. Simmer for at least 10 minutes after they start to float. Serve hot or cold with a little of the liquid.

TOFFEE APPLES
Singapore

3 medium-size cooking apples
1 egg
⅔ cup (5 fl oz, 170 ml) cold water
1 cup (4 oz, 125 g) all-purpose (plain) flour
peanut oil for deep frying

Glaze:
1½ cups (12 oz, 375 g) sugar
½ cup (4 fl oz, 125 ml) cold water
2 teaspoons black sesame seeds

Quarter the apples, peel and core the pieces, then cut each quarter into 2 thick slices, 3 if the apples are large. Set aside. Beat the egg in a medium-size bowl, add the water and beat again until combined, then tip in all the flour at once and beat vigorously with rotary beater until batter is smooth. Do not overbeat. Let batter stand while preparing glaze. As sugar cooks, start to heat oil for deep frying. Try to have oil for frying and sugar glaze ready at the same time. If oil is not put over too high a heat this should not be difficult.

When a haze begins to rise from the surface of the oil drop pieces of apple into the batter, turn to coat them completely, then take one piece at a time with chopsticks, a fondue fork, or fingers and drop into the oil. Do not cook too many at one time. Deep fry until the batter is golden, then lift out with a slotted spoon and put immediately into the saucepan containing the glaze. Turn pieces of apple in the glaze to coat the entire surface, then lift out and drop into a bowl of cold water and ice cubes. The glaze will harden and become brittle almost at once. Lift them out quickly and put on a lightly oiled serving plate. Serve as soon as possible. If left to stand too long the glaze will melt and the batter become leathery.

Glaze: Put sugar and water into a small saucepan and place over medium high heat. Do not stir at all. This is important. If you do, the sugar will crystallize and the glaze will not be clear. Let sugar mixture bubble until it starts to turn faintly golden around the edges of the pan. Stir in sesame seeds and turn heat as low as it will go. Or remove pan from heat, replacing it from time to time if sugar begins to harden before all the apples have been dipped.

Makes 24 pieces

TOFFEE YAMS WITH BLACK SESAME SEEDS
China

1 lb (500 g) sweet potatoes
1 egg
1 cup (4 oz, 125 g) all-purpose (plain) flour
peanut oil for deep frying

Glaze:
1 teaspoon peanut oil
12 oz (375 g) sugar
4 teaspoons black sesame seeds

Peel sweet potatoes and cut into diagonal slices. Drop into a large saucepan of boiling water for 5 minutes. Drain and cool.

Beat the egg in a medium-size bowl, add 2/3 cup (5 fl oz, 170 ml) cold water, and beat again until combined. Then tip in all the flour at once and beat vigorously until the batter is smooth. Allow batter to stand while preparing the glaze.

Glaze: Over a medium heat, heat oil in a saucepan, add sugar and 1/2 cup (4 fl oz, 125 ml) cold water. Do not stir at all. If you do, the sugar will crystallize and the glaze will not be clear. Let the sugar mixture bubble until it starts to turn golden around the edge of the pan. Then stir in the sesame seeds and turn the heat as low as it will go. Or remove the saucepan from heat, replacing it from time to time if sugar begins to harden before the sweet potatoes have been dipped.

As the sugar cooks, start to heat the oil for deep frying. Try to have the oil hot and the sugar glaze ready (that is, deep golden) at the same time. If the oil is put over a moderate heat, this should not be difficult.

When a haze begins to rise from the surface of the oil, drop pieces of sweet potato into the batter, turn to coat them completely, then take one piece at a time with chopsticks, a fondue fork, or fingers and drop it into the oil. Deep fry until the batter is golden, then lift out with a slotted spoon and put straight into the saucepan containing the glaze. Do two or three pieces at a time, turn them so that the glaze coats their entire surface, then lift out onto an oiled plate.

Serve immediately, together with a bowl containing cold water and ice cubes. Each person takes a piece of glazed yam and drops it into the bowl. The glaze will harden and become brittle almost at once. Lift out quickly and eat. If left to stand too long, the glaze will melt and the batter will become leathery.

Note: You can also use apple or firm ripe bananas, peeled and cut into chunks but not pre-cooked.
Serves 6

TRADITIONAL CHRISTMAS CAKE
Sri Lanka

8 oz (250 g) seedless raisins
12 oz (375 g) golden raisins (sultanas)
8 oz (250 g) mixed glace fruit
8 oz (250 g) preserved ginger
2 small cans chow chow preserves or 1 lb (500 g) melon and ginger jam
4 oz (125 g) mixed peel
8 oz (250 g) glace cherries
8 oz (250 g) raw cashews or blanched almonds
¼ cup (2 fl oz, 60 ml) brandy
12 oz (375 g) butter
1 lb (500 g) superfine (caster) sugar
12 egg yolks
2 teaspoons grated lemon rind
1½ teaspoons ground cardamom
1 teaspoon ground cinnamon
1 teaspoon grated nutmeg
¾ teaspoon ground cloves
2 tablespoons vanilla extract (essence)
1 tablespoon almond extract (essence)
2 teaspoons rose extract (essence)
1 tablespoon honey
8 oz (250 g) fine farina (semolina)
6 egg whites

Almond paste:
8 oz (250 g) ground almonds
1 lb (500 g) pure confectioner's (icing) sugar, sifted
1 small egg, beaten
1 tablespoon brandy
1 tablespoon sherry
½ teaspoon almond extract (essence), optional
beaten egg white

Line a 10 in (25 cm) round or square cake tin with three thicknesses each of newspaper and brown paper, then two layers of waxed (greaseproof) paper liberally brushed with melted butter.

Chop raisins and sultanas. Cut glace fruit into small pieces (use a mixture of pineapple, apricot and quince — avoid figs). Drain syrup from preserved ginger and chow chow preserves and chop finely. Chop mixed peel. Cut cherries in halves. Chop nuts very finely or put through a nut mill. Combine fruits and nuts in large bowl, sprinkle with brandy, cover and leave while mixing cake. This can be done the day before, allowing the fruit more time to soak in the brandy.

Cream butter and sugar until light. Add yolks of eggs one at a time, beating well after each addition. Add grated rind, spices, flavorings, and honey and mix well. Add farina and beat until well combined, then mix in fruit. Use biggest bowl or pan you have and mix in fruit with both hands (it's much easier than a spoon and professional pastry cooks do it this way). When fruit is thoroughly mixed in, whip egg whites until stiff and fold through mixture.

Turn into prepared cake tin and bake in slow oven 250°F, (130°C, Gas Mark 1) for 2 1/4 to 2 1/2 hours, covering cake with paper after first hour to prevent over-browning. The result will be very rich and moist. If you prefer a darker and drier result, bake for 4 1/2 to 5 hours. It will not be dry, but certainly firmer.

Cool completely, preferably overnight, then remove paper and wrap cake in foil. A tablespoon or two of brandy may be sprinkled over cake after it is cold.

Mix ground almonds and confectioner's sugar in a large bowl, add egg mixed with brandy, sherry, and almond extract, then knead until it holds together. If too moist knead in a little extra sifted sugar. Roll out half the almond paste on pastry board dusted with sugar and cut to fit top of cake. Brush cake with beaten egg white, place almond paste on top and press lightly with rolling pin. Roll remaining almond paste into a strip and fit around side of cake. In Sri Lanka it is traditional for the cake to be cut into pieces and each piece individually wrapped. You can use foil and colored cellophane. This cake will keep in an airtight tin for a year or longer.

Note: Chow chow preserves can be purchased at Chinese stores or specialty food stores. The nearest equivalent is melon and ginger jam.

⋘⋙

VISHNU IN THE SEA OF MILK
Narayana Bantom Sindhu ◆ Thailand

2 tablespoons mung (soy) bean flour
2 cups (16 fl oz, 500 ml) water
rose water to taste
green food coloring
4 cups (32 fl oz, 1 L) thin coconut cream
4 tablespoons white sugar
crushed ice

Blend together bean flour and water and stir over low heat until it boils, thickens and becomes clear. Remove from heat, stir in 2 or 3 teaspoons rose water (available from chemists) or a few drops of rose concentrate to give it a faint but definite flavor. Tint it a delicate shade of green. Push through a colander into a bowl of cold water. Leave until firm, drain and chill. Dissolve sugar in the coconut cream, add a little rose flavoring and chill separately. At serving time put a large spoon of the bean flour mixture into a tall glass, fill with coconut cream and crushed ice. *Serves 6–8*

⋘⋙

WONTON WRAPPERS
China

8 oz (250 g) flour
½ teaspoon salt
1 egg
extra flour
cornstarch (cornflour)

Sift the flour and salt into a large bowl. Make a well in the middle.

Beat the egg lightly with 4 fl oz (125 ml) water, and pour it into the well in the flour. Mixing from the middle with a fork, gradually work in the flour. Knead into a ball, then turn it out onto a well-floured surface and knead the dough for 5 or 6 minutes until smooth. Cover with a damp cloth and leave to rest for 30 minutes.

Cut the dough into four portions, and roll each portion out on a well-floured surface. Using a ruler, cut dough into 3 in (8 cm) squares. Stack in piles, dusting liberally with cornstarch to prevent sticking. Wrap the piles in plastic and store in the refrigerator.

Note: Wonton wrappers are readily available at Chinese stores if you don't feel like making your own.
Makes 40–50 wrappers

⋘⋙

Index